The
Spirit and the
Flesh

Sexual Diversity in American Indian Culture

Walter L. Williams

Beacon Press / Boston

Beacon Press
25 Beacon Street
Boston, Massachusetts 02108

Beacon Press books
are published under the auspices of
the Unitarian Universalist Association of Congregations.

95 94 93 92 91 90   8 7 6 5 4

Text design by Dennis Anderson

Grateful acknowledgment is made for permission to reprint the following:
the lines from "Winkte" from *Only as Far as Brooklyn* by Maurice Kenny
(Good Gay Poets, 1979), by permission of the author; the lines from
"Beloved Women" from *Skins and Bones* by Paula Gunn Allen (*Conditions
Magazine,* Spring 1982), by permission of the author.

Library of Congress Cataloging-in-Publication Data
Williams, Walter L., 1948–
   The spirit and the flesh.
   Bibliography: p.
   Includes index.
   1. Indians of North America—Sexual behavior.
2. Homosexuality, Male—North America.   3. Sex role—
North America.   I. Title.   II. Title: Sexual diversity in American Indian
culture.
E98.S48W55 1986   306.7'66'08997   86-47505
ISBN 0-8070-4602-7
      0-8070-4611-6 (pbk.)

The Spirit and the Flesh

To my friends

Joe Carrier, Harry Hay, Jonathan Katz, Jim Kepner, Dorr Legg, and Gregory Sprague, whose pioneering research helped make this book possible,

and to

the traditionalist Indian people who generously took me into their homes, and who gave me a deeper appreciation of the magic of life

To my friends

Joe Carrier, Harry Hay, Jonathan Katz, Jim Kepner, Dorr Legg, and Gregory Sprague, whose pioneering research helped make this book possible,

and to

the traditionalist Indian people who generously took me into their homes, and who gave me a deeper appreciation of the magic of life

Contents

Acknowledgments

This book could not have been written without the willingness of American Indian people who talked with me about their traditions and their contemporary lives. Several of my main berdache informants, who are intensely private persons, do not wish to have their names printed, so I have changed their names in the citations. I wish to thank them from the bottom of my heart. They took me into their homes, shared their most intimate feelings, and imparted to me not only a joy of the wonders of life but a deeper appreciation for the spiritual essence that surrounds us all. In no other academic study have I ever become so deeply involved in or been so personally affected by what I learned.

Other Indian people, who can be named, who have been especially helpful in teaching me about berdachism in their own or related tribes include Paula Gunn Allen (Laguna Pueblo), Don Anderson (Pomo), Jerry Baldy (Hupa), Florentine Bluethunder (Lakota), Tony Brown (Cherokee-Creek), Randy Burns (Paiute), C. B. Clark (Creek), Tony Dedam (Micmac), Calvin Fast Wolf (Lakota), Donald Fixico (Creek-Sac and Fox), Twila Giegle (Lakota-Chippewa), Charlotte Heth (Cherokee), Jennie Joe (Navajo), Gary Johnson (Crow), Calvin Jumping Bull (Lakota), Maurice Kenny (Mohawk), Ronnie Loud Hawk (Lakota), Robert Lynch (Haliwa-Saponi), Beatrice Medicine (Lakota), Joe Medicine Crow (Crow), Elva One Feather (Lakota), Ellie Rides A Horse (Crow), Victor Robinson (Omaha), Phyllis Rogers (Navajo-Lumbee), Tommy Rubideaux (Lakota), Myron Standing Bear (Lakota), Robert Stead (Lakota), Lenore Stiffarm (Gros Ventre), Pat Thunder Hawk (Lakota), Joe Tiona (Lakota), William Tohee (Otoe), Richard White

(Omaha), Michael White Bear Claws (Lakota), William Willard (Cherokee), Terry Wilson (Osage), Al White Eyes (Omaha-Lakota), Thomas Yellowtail (Crow), and James Young (Lakota).

Besides Indian people themselves, my other major informants for this multitribal study have included anthropologists and historians who have lived as members of reservation communities, and who are intimately familiar with the particular tribe of their study. Some of the Indian people listed above are also anthropologists and historians, but other non-Indian researchers who have given me considerable knowledge include Beverly Chiñas, Henry Dobyns, Fadwa El Guindi, Raymond Fogelson, Wes Fortney, Richard Grant, Liz Grobsmith, Robert Grumet, Richard Herrell, Herbert Hoover, Luis Kemnitzer, Nancy Lurie, Harvey Markowitz, Alexander Moore, Triloki Pandey, Omer Stewart, Clark Taylor, and Joan Wiebel-Orlando.

Along with those to whom the book is dedicated—Joe Carrier, Harry Hay, Jonathan Katz, Jim Kepner, Dorr Legg, and Gregory Sprague—Sue-Ellen Jacobs has been incredibly supportive during every stage of this project. Others who have also provided important sources and insights include Dennis Altman, Don Amador, Allen Berube, Evelyn Blackwood, Paul Bohannan, Vern Bullough, B. R. Burg, Martin Duberman, Wayne Dynes, Stephen Foster, James Foshee, Judy Grahn, Ramon Gutierrez, William T. Hagan, Paul Hardman, Laud Humphreys, Valerie Kirkgaard, Lyle Koehler, Margaret Lanacz, Kenneth Lincoln, Indiana Matters, John Money, Kenneth Morrison, James O'Donnell, Theda Perdue, Hoang Phan, Harold Poor, Kieran Prather, William Reeve, Will Roscoe, Charles Silverstein, James Steakley, James Weinrich, Peter Wood, John Woodall, and Wayne Wooden. Several of those mentioned above have provided detailed and valuable critiques of earlier versions of the manuscript. It has been only with the completion of this book that I have become fully aware of how much my approach has been influenced by my colleagues in the USC Program for the Study of Women and Men in Society, especially Gloria Orenstein and Lois Banner.

The major part of the library research on which this book is based was done at the University of Southern California (especially in the Human Relations Area Files), the American Indian Studies Center at the University of California, Los Angeles, the Newberry Library Center for the History of the American Indian, the University of South Dakota, the University of Cincinnati, ONE Institute of Homophile Studies, and the International Gay and Lesbian Archives. In all of those places, the librarians were extremely helpful.

For assistance in translations of documents, Michael Lombardi, Cynthia Saunders, Ann Twinam, and Raymundo Concha deserve my thanks. For illustrations, besides the archives and galleries where the materials are located, I wish to acknowledge the help of Will Roscoe, Joseph Agonito, and Gay American Indians. Friends who generously volunteered to type parts of the manuscript are David Pierce, David Spencer, and my sister June Williams Arthurs.

For financial support while conducting this study, I am deeply indebted to the University of Cincinnati faculty research fund, the Taft Fund Foundation, the Woodrow Wilson Foundation, and the UCLA American Indian Studies Center.

As always, my parents expressed their love in uncounted ways. For the affection and personal support that made my life richer during the years while the book was in preparation, I wish to express my love and friendship always for Steve Saunders, Larz Ulvaeus, Johnny Louie, Michael Puente-Piña, and Joey Chávez.

Los Angeles, 1985   *Walter L. Williams*

Introduction

Because it is such a powerful force in the world today, the Western Judeo-Christian tradition is often accepted as the arbiter of "natural" behavior of humans. If Europeans and their descendant nations of North America accept something as normal, then anything different is seen as abnormal. Such a view ignores the great diversity of human existence.

This is the case for the study of gender. How many genders are there? To a modern Anglo-American, nothing might seem more definite than the answer that there are two: men and women. But not all societies around the world agree with Western culture's view that all humans are either women or men. The commonly accepted notion of "the opposite sex," based on anatomy, is itself an artifact of our society's rigid sex roles.

Among many cultures, there have existed different alternatives to "man" or "woman." An alternative role in many American Indian societies is referred to by anthropologists as *berdache*. This book will take an anthropological and historical approach to understand this topic. The role varied from one Native American culture to another, which is a reflection of the vast diversity of aboriginal New World societies. Small bands of hunter-gatherers existed in some areas, with advanced civilizations of farming peoples in other areas. With hundreds of different languages, economies, religions, and social patterns existing in North America alone, every generalization about a cultural tradition must acknowledge many exceptions.

This diversity is true for the berdache tradition as well, and must be kept in mind. My statements should be read as being specific to a particular culture, with generalizations being treated as loose patterns that might not apply to peoples even in nearby areas. Defining the character of the berdache tradition is the subject of Part I of the book.

Briefly, a berdache can be defined as a morphological male who does not fill a society's standard man's role, who has a nonmasculine character. This type of person is often stereotyped as effeminate, but a more accurate characterization is androgyny. Such a person has a clearly recognized and accepted social status, often based on a secure place in the tribal mythology. Berdaches have special ceremonial roles in many Native American religions, and important economic roles in their families. They will do at least some women's work, and mix together much of the behavior, dress, and social roles of women and men. Berdaches gain social prestige by their spiritual, intellectual, or craftwork/artistic contributions, and by their reputation for hard work and generosity. They serve a mediating function between women and men, precisely because their character is seen as distinct from either sex. They are not seen as men, yet they are not seen as women either. They occupy an alternative gender role that is a mixture of diverse elements.

In their erotic behavior berdaches also generally (but not always) take a nonmasculine role, either being asexual or becoming the passive partner in sex with men. In some cultures the berdache might become a wife to a man. This male-male sexual behavior became the focus of an attack on berdaches as "sodomites" by the Europeans who, early on, came into contact with them. From the first Spanish conquistadors to the Western frontiersmen and the Christian missionaries and government officials, Western culture has had a considerable impact on the berdache tradition. In the last two decades, the most recent impact on the tradition is the adaptation of a modern Western gay identity. This historical perspective is the subject of Part II of the book.

To Western eyes berdachism is a complex and puzzling phenomenon, mixing and redefining the very concepts of what is considered male and female. In a culture with only two recognized genders, such individuals are gender nonconformist, abnormal, deviant. But to American Indians, the institution of another gender role means that berdaches are not deviant—indeed, they do conform to the requirements of a custom in which their culture tells them they fit. Berdachism is a way for society to recognize and assimilate some atypical individuals without imposing a change on them or stigmatizing them as deviant. This cultural institution confirms their legitimacy for what they are.

Societies often bestow power upon that which does not neatly fit into the usual. Since no cultural system can explain everything, a common way that many cultures deal with these inconsistencies is to imbue them with negative power, as taboo, pollution, witchcraft, or sin. That which is not understood is seen as a threat. But an alternative method of dealing with such things, or people, is to take them out of the realm of threat and to sanctify them.[1] The berdaches' role as mediator is thus not just between women and men, but also between the physical and the spiritual. American Indian cultures have taken what Western culture calls negative, and made it a positive; they have successfully utilized the different skills and insights of a class of people that Western culture has stigmatized and whose spiritual powers have been wasted.

Many Native Americans also understood that gender roles have to do with more than just biological sex. The standard Western view that one's sex is always a certainty, and that one's gender identity and sex role always conform to one's morphological sex is a view that dies hard. Western thought is typified by such dichotomies of groups perceived to be mutually exclusive: male and female, black and white, right and wrong, good and evil. Clearly, the world is not so simple; such clear divisions are not always realistic. Most American Indian worldviews generally are much more accepting of the ambiguities of life. Acceptance of gender variation in the berdache tradition is typical of many native cultures' approach to life in general.

Overall, these are generalizations based on those Native American societies that had an accepted role for berdaches. Not all cultures recognized such a respected status. Berdachism in aboriginal North America was most established among tribes in four areas: first, the Prairie and western Great Lakes, the northern and central Great Plains, and the lower Mississippi Valley; second, Florida and the Caribbean; third, the Southwest, the

Great Basin, and California; and fourth, scattered areas of the Northwest, western Canada, and Alaska. For some reason it is not noticeable in eastern North America, with the exception of its southern rim.

In a recent tabulation of the distribution of berdachism north of Mexico, Charles Callender and Lee Kochems could not determine a correlation between the presence of berdachism and the type of social organization in a particular culture. None of the other anthropologists' commentaries accompanying their essay provided a satisfactory explanation as to why berdachism existed in one culture but not in another.[2] Why did the Pimas look down on berdaches while most of their neighbors in the Southwest respected it? Why did Apaches hold negative attitudes toward berdaches (if we can trust the ethnographic reports that say they did), in contrast to their Athapaskan cousins the Navajos, who practically deified berdaches? Supposedly the Iroquois and their relatives the Cherokees did not have a berdache status, yet Raymond Fogelson has discovered a document in which Cherokees told a white traveler about 1825, "There were among them formerly, men who assumed the dress and performed all the duties of women and who lived their whole life in this manner."[3] If such memories were accurate, then berdachism may have existed but it disappeared quite early among eastern Indians. All the evidence is not in. If other ethnohistorians can discover new documentary references in archives, they can add to our knowledge of the practice.

The published reports and documents that are known have been examined and reexamined; what is now needed is more fieldwork to see if further answers can be found. I have interviewed Indians who were raised in a berdache role, and are treated as such by their communities, among groups that the printed sources suggest have no berdache status. Other recent fieldworkers also report finding berdaches where they were not thought to be.[4] We cannot assume that berdaches were completely absent from any Native American culture, and we need to question statements that suggest its nonexistence.

While I am hopeful that further field studies will be done on this question, this book focuses on those societies which, at least aboriginally, provided berdaches a respected status. My purpose is to examine how a culture can accommodate gender variation and sexual variation beyond man/woman opposites, without being threatened by it. Societies that do not provide a respected role for the berdache, if we were to trust the documents on them, are not within this book's subject matter. It remains for other ethnographers to investigate tribes other than the ones mentioned in this book, to add to or revise the story.

Early ethnographers sometimes interviewed berdaches, but did so within a single tribe, and almost always as a peripheral topic to their general tribal ethnography. With only a few exceptions, most of the writings of the nineteenth and early twentieth centuries devoted only a few sentences or paragraphs to berdachism. Those ethnographers did not have a cross-cultural interest or expertise in sexuality or in gender variation. In an essay published in 1940, anthropologist Alfred Kroeber referred to the berdache tradition, saying that "the time is ready for a synthetic work on this subject."[5] Kroeber's essay was the first significant attempt to generalize about the tradition across tribal boundaries, followed by Henry Angelino and Charles Shedd, who in 1955 wrote a brief article in the *American Anthropologist*.[6] No other multitribal study was published until thirteen years later, when Sue-Ellen Jacobs wrote an essay reviewing the previously published literature.[7] Such has been the scarcity of writings on berdachism.

In 1976 historian Jonathan Katz reprinted numerous documents referring to berdaches, which greatly facilitated research on the topic.[8] These documents, many of which were located by researcher Stephen W. Foster, stimulated my and others' interest in berdaches. None of my anthropology teachers had ever mentioned the subject, and I had seen only a few brief citations on it. Though I had been teaching American Indian studies for several years before reading this book, I had no idea that so much documentation on it existed. Inspired by this work, a few anthropologists began to publish essays on the topic.[9] Yet despite their value in adding to a theoretical understanding of the berdache tradition, all of these essays published since 1940 have been based solely on the previously published anthropological sources. None of these post-1940 authors has had intensive fieldwork experience with berdaches. Because of this, and be-

cause of the limitations of the original sources that these theoretical analyses share, the berdaches themselves have been presented only abstractly, rather than as real people. They are seen
from a detached, nonpersonalized perspective. We know little
about their viewpoints and their feelings about themselves and
their place in their community.

Dissatisfied with this deficiency in the literature, in 1980 I
began doing research on the berdache tradition while on a fellowship at the UCLA American Indian Studies Center. I soon
discovered the resources, nearby in Los Angeles, of the ONE
Institute of Homophile Studies and of the International Gay and
Lesbian Archives. The directors of these libraries, Dorr Legg
and Jim Kepner, introduced me to Harry Hay, who had lived
for years among Southwestern Indians. Hay put me in touch
with Sue-Ellen Jacobs, and they led me to question the conventional wisdom among anthropologists that the berdache tradition had disappeared. I decided that this was a subject in which
modern fieldwork needed to be undertaken. In 1982 I began the
effort to locate a living berdache. The effort was much easier
than I had thought it would be. The first reservation I visited in
my trip westward from Chicago, in June 1982, was the Omaha.
Shortly after my arrival, I was introduced to an elderly person
who fulfills this role. From his family I made other contacts on
a Lakota reservation, where I stayed with another berdache.
This person put me in touch with berdaches on two other
nearby reservations. I spent the major part of the summer on
one of these reservations, living as part of the household of a
traditional Lakota berdache I will refer to as Terry Calling
Eagle. I participated with him in his ceremonial roles, and
learned from him the Lakota religion. I also visited with other
Lakota berdaches and traditional people. After leaving the Lakotas, toward the end of the summer I visited the Crow and
Northern Cheyenne reservations in Montana, where I did more
fieldwork and interviewing.

Emboldened by the success of this fieldtrip, I next decided to
go to an entirely different area, in Yucatán, Mexico. There also
I found a berdache tradition among contemporary Maya people.
I spent the month of January 1983 in various Maya villages,
interviewing berdaches and their relatives. Though my spe-

cialty is American Indian studies for the area north of Mexico, and I make no claim to full coverage of Latin America, I am including the information I found. My fieldwork in Yucatán was undertaken primarily as a comparative study, and should be seen as such.[10] Since that time I have also conducted more interviews with Indian people of various tribes of the Southwest, Great Basin, and California.

My usual approach with traditionalist Indians was to get to know them and let them feel comfortable with me before attempting an interview. If at all possible, I had another Indian introduce me to them. My interviewing strategy was to begin by telling them that I was trying to learn more about some of the old Indian traditions that were very different from white ways. I would mention the concept of the "Contrary," in which a person did things backward, as an example. I said the tradition that I was most interested in existed in many tribes and was referred to by early white explorers as berdache. Usually they did not know that word, so next I would tell them the name for berdache in their own language. It was crucial to use the native word before going any further. I told them that I had read what white people had written on this, but that I wanted the traditionalist knowledge so that my book would be more accurate.

When interviewing people, I tried not to sound pushy or disrespectful of the traditions, and I purposefully did not mention anything about the tradition or make any references to sexuality or gender variation. I wanted to hear their own definitions, and their own emphasis in explaining it. A major goal of this study is to allow Indian people to speak for themselves. There has been much too much theorizing without listening to what Native Americans themselves have to say. In an attempt to provide an additional body of empirical knowledge on which future writers may theorize, I have quoted liberally from the words of Indian people. The idea is to present the flavor of their attitudes as much as possible.

Although sophisticated literature has appeared on sexual and gender variance, prior to this book there was no major study that combined the historical documentation, anthropological literature, and direct fieldwork with American Indian berdaches of a number of different tribes. Why is it that, nearly half a century after Kroeber said "the time is ready," his call for a synthesis was not fulfilled?

Part of the explanation reflects the limits of traditional historical and anthropological disciplines in dealing with questions of gender and sexuality. The greatest offenders have been historians. Until the last decade or so, historians paid precious little attention to any aspect of the internal history of Native American societies. Indians were seen as savages, foils for the great advance of Western civilization. They were of little interest to historians, other than in their role as adversaries of the frontiersmen. Similarly, on the question of sex, North American historians' writings at least until recently treated sex as an unmentionable topic. Even in our own time, historians of sexuality run up against the notion that sex in history is somehow less important in understanding the past than, for example, men's proclivity to kill each other in wars.

An American Indian custom like the berdache institution, with its overtones of sexual variance, was usually known about but was seen as something that was better ignored. Even in 1980, when I presented my first paper on the berdache tradition at a history conference, I was scolded by a leading historian. He had earlier complimented me on my publications in American Indian studies, and had written supportive letters of recommendation for me. He bluntly told me that if I pursued this topic I would threaten my scholarly reputation. Later, when I asked him to write another letter of recommendation, he refused with a homophobic comment. Academia has many ways to discourage certain research.

These kinds of restrictions have been much more forcefully applied to other academics. As a consequence, much of the historical research on berdachism has been done by researchers outside of universities. Jonathan Katz, a historian not employed in academia, has published work that provides a perfect example of the contributions that nonacademic researchers have made in this field.

Even where historians have pursued research on berdachism, they often run up against the inhibitions of informants. With relatively little material about berdachism finding its way into print, researchers working on this topic must depend heavily on interviews. Interviewing has its own set of problems. In the early 1950s, for example, when Edith McLeod, a local historian, decided to collect information on a Klamath berdache named White Cindy, she followed the Indian custom of using the feminine pronoun. McLeod reported, "Old timers of Klamath Falls, Oregon, remember her well, as do I, for I well remember that as a child I always crossed the street when I saw her coming, being afraid of her from stories that I had heard." When McLeod contacted local whites for information for a story, they refused, saying, "I know considerable about her—but it is not exactly printable." Even a close friend of McLeod's, who had done extensive work with the Klamath Indians, said simply, "Yes, I know quite a bit about her—but I can't tell you."[11]

What was it about berdachism that made it such a taboo subject? A history of the word *bardache* gives us a clue. It is not a term from an Indian language, but was used by European explorers in North America. The word originally came from the Persian *bardaj*, and via the Arabs spread to the Italian language as *bardasso* and to Spanish as *bardaxa* or *bardaje* by the beginning of the sixteenth century. About the same time the word appeared in French as *bardache*.

Thorough research by linguist Claude Courouve has turned up a common meaning in these various languages. The 1680 edition of *Dictionnaire français*, for example, gives this definition: "a young man who is shamefully abused (Caesar was the *bardache* of Nicomedes)." The 1718 edition of P. J. LeRoux's *Dictionnaire comique* defines it more explicitly: "A young man or boy who serves another's succubus, permitting sodomy to be committed on him. These abominations are so common in France that women have rightly complained of them, and I could even name several individuals who keep *bardaches,* generally beautiful boys, as others keep [female] courtesans." This dictionary offers as a synonym for bardache the term *ganimede,* after the boy who was the lover of Zeus in Greek mythology.[12]

The dictionaries, however, make it clear that both *bardache* and *ganimede* refer to the passive homosexual partner. The French word *bougre* was used for the active male partner, akin to the English words *bugger* and *bougie man. Sodomy* was the other most commonly used term, but it was used to describe specific sexual acts, usually but not always anal intercourse. Sodomy could describe sexual acts between man and woman as well as between man and man. In the sixteenth to eighteenth centuries, as evidenced by European songs, poems, plays, and literature, the terms *bardache* and *bougre* were the most commonly used to denote male homosexuality. The words clearly distinguished the active and passive roles. For example, in a satirical text, *Deliberations du Conseil general des bougres et des bardaches,* published in France in 1790, the author wrote "the *bardaches* dropped their trousers, and the *bougres,* becoming erect as satyrs, took advantage of them."[13]

When French explorers came to the New World, they used the term with which they were most familiar in describing aboriginal Americans. The term *bardache* had a clear homosexual implication in its European usage. But the Indians had another practice that puzzled the Europeans: the adoption of female dress by these males. Some of the Europeans incorrectly assumed that such individuals must be hermaphrodites, with both female and male genitalia. Joseph François Lafitau, a Jesuit missionary in French Canada from 1711 to 1717, knew of berdaches among the Illinois, the Sioux, and the natives of Louisiana and Florida. He reported: "The view of these men dressed as women surprised the Europeans who first encountered them in America. . . . They were convinced that these were people in whom the two sexes were confounded." Lafitau pointed out that the berdaches were not hermaphrodites, but were anatomically normal males.[14]

Nevertheless, there has continued to be confusion on this matter, with whites using the term *hermaphrodite* as a synonym for *berdache.* When anthropologists began doing fieldwork among American Indians in the late nineteenth century, inexplicably changing the spelling from *a* to *e* in *berdache,* even they sometimes incorrectly referred to berdaches as hermaphrodites. Interestingly, when I have asked modern Indian people about the practice, by asking them to define their languages' terms for berdache, some have explained it by using the English word *hermaphrodite.* When I asked them if this meant that the individual had the sexual parts of both sexes, they said no. I can only construe that this is the word that they had heard whites use for berdaches.

Still another matter on which writers have confused the issue has to do with Indian women who take a nonfeminine role. The term *berdache* clearly was always used to apply to males until the twentieth century, when confusion arose because some anthropologists began talking about "female berdaches." Beyond the fact that the word originated as a term for a passive male homosexual, this is an improper usage as far as Indians are concerned. With a few possible exceptions, Native Americans conceptualize females who take on a hunter-warrior role separately from male berdaches. Female gender variation was recognized in a number of cultures, but it had a separate and distinct status of its own. Therefore, this study uses the term *berdache* solely for male (or, in rare cases, hermaphroditically ambiguous) individuals who take on a social role that is more or less feminine.

Recognizing that the female status needs a word of its own as a generic term comparable to berdache, I use the word *amazon*. For historical reasons explained in Chapter 11, I feel that this is the best English word to use. The chapter on amazons depends heavily on the ideas of Evelyn Blackwood, Paula Gunn Allen, and Beverly Chiñas. While my interpretation is closest to that of Paula Gunn Allen, herself an Indian and a professor of Native American studies, I realize that I as a male cannot address this topic as deeply as I have done with the berdache. Feeling strongly that fieldwork is at the base of such a study, and knowing as I do that much knowledge is only revealed by such persons to another of the same sex and orientation, I feel that the story of these amazons deserves its own study. What I have done is to present material that seems important to me, with the hope that this may be used by women researchers to aid their own fieldwork on American Indian women's roles.

Most of the writing that has been done about American Indians in the past century has been done by anthropologists. Given the masses of detail that anthropologists have churned out about Native American cultures, what is surprising is that no more has been written about the berdache tradition than there has been. Part of the reason for anthropologists' avoidance of this topic is that few of them have felt genuinely comfortable in writing about sexual variance. Indeed, it sometimes seems that the first generations of anthropologists who associated on a personal level with berdaches (most of those who come to mind are women: Matilda Coxe Stevenson, Elsie Clews Parsons, Ruth Underhill, Margaret Mead, Ruth Landes), were an iconoclastic bunch who would dispassionately describe whatever they saw. They seemed more likely to be sympathetic than more recent scholars. On more than one occasion I have interviewed anthropologists who have written ethnographies of specific tribes, but whose books do not mention berdaches. When I specifically ask them about it, they often will admit to knowing about it. When I have asked them why this information was not included in their book, some have seemed rather proud to say, "Such things don't interest me."

Such an attitude is all too common among contemporary anthropologists. Despite their claims of objectivity, most anthropologists have been raised in Western cultural traditions which include those same taboos about sex that have inhibited historians. With Western aversions to the discussion of homosexuality, and the assumption—contrary to all the scientific data—that this behavior is relatively rare, many have avoided discussion of the topic. Anthropologist Kenneth Read has analyzed this avoidance, pointing out that many anthropologists evidently feel personally uncomfortable with the topic. Besides, they "could find no justification for homosexual behavior. It was far easier, for example, to excuse infanticide (a custom also abhorrent by Western standards) since it could be shown to have a rational basis in some demographic situations: it 'produced' something. But homosexual behavior did not 'produce' anything." [15]

Same-sex behavior, Read points out, is far more widely distributed throughout the world than would be assumed from reading that compendium of ethnographic knowledge, the Human Relations Area Files. He even suggests that popular international "gay guides," which list almost every nation in the world, often contain more accurate information than ethnographic reports. Since ethnographers have conducted research in many of these same places without reporting anything, Read concludes that they were misled, were more or less blind, were morally queasy, or for other reasons refrained from reporting what they knew.

In 1975 the Executive Board of the American Anthropological Association even voted "not to endorse anthropological research on homosexuality across national borders." Though that resolution was later repealed after protests from gay anthropologists, such an incredible effort at censorship, Read concludes, "is indicative of the persistence of Western attitudes toward homosexual behavior as a sensitive subject which, though it is probably as prevalent as witchcraft, is morally distasteful." [16] As a consequence, even when they do talk about it many anthropologists have simply not asked the right questions, and have been content to abandon the topic after a brief statement in imprecise language. [17]

Critical statements about the anthropological approach to sexuality have regularly appeared over the past decade in the newsletter of the Anthropological Research Group on Homosexuality. No doubt what I have written will offend some anthropologists who are defensive about their colleagues. This book will offend others as well, but those people I am most concerned about offending are Native Americans. Some American Indians—those who have accepted the Christian propaganda on sexuality, or those who are ashamed of their past customs—will no doubt wish that this topic be suppressed. But other Indians, who do respect the traditions, sometimes feel that information about their aboriginal cultures which whites find obnoxious should not be publicized. Some traditionalists feel antagonistic to outside researchers, having been exploited in the past. A Cheyenne elder told me, "I am not much interested in talking about our traditions to non-Cheyenne researchers. We want to keep our history within the Cheyenne people." [18] Such an approach is one of the ways that Indians have managed to keep their traditions hidden and protected. This argument has legitimacy.

The view that certain topics are best not discussed beyond the Indian community has in fact led me to hesitate about publishing some of the information I have learned. The berdache institution involves sacred matters for many tribes. I have followed the wishes of traditionalists, and used their guidance with respect to people's privacy and by approaching the topic in a respectful manner. With regard to some ceremonial aspects, I have not included certain statements that were told to me in confidence and that, if related here, might violate Indians' sense of holiness.

But I have obviously decided to go ahead with publication, with the feeling that the importance of this topic outweighs such issues of privacy. It is important for non-Indians in our pluralistic society to learn how other cultures deal with gender variation. Even more important is the situation of Indian youth. On many reservations today the status of the berdache has declined, and younger individuals who would formerly have taken a respected position in their tribe are currently stigmatized and lost in a society that is no longer independent of colonial control. It is crucial for young Indian people to be able to have this knowledge about their past traditions. That is why traditionalists have explained these things to me, and that is why I feel a sense of responsibility to convey their message.

Rather than becoming secretive and defensive about their cultural past, Indian people need to consider the anguish that their defensiveness causes for young people who are struggling to understand themselves in a racist and homophobic society. By redeveloping and adapting the old traditions like those of the berdache, Indian people today can be committed to the preservation of their heritage and the establishment of a new sense of pride.

Part I

The Character of the Berdache

1 Of Religions and Dreams: The Spiritual Basis of the Berdache Tradition

When the French Jesuit missionary Joseph François Lafitau wrote his book on American Indians in 1724, he condemned berdaches for acting like women. Yet he admitted that this was not the Native American view. "They believe they are honored," he wrote uncomprehendingly. Lafitau pointed out that among the Indians of the western Great Lakes, Louisiana, and Florida, the berdaches "never marry, they participate in all religious ceremonies, and this profession of an extraordinary life causes them to be regarded as people of a higher order, and above the common man."[1] On his first voyage to America, the French explorer Jacques Marquette reported that among the Illinois and neighboring tribes, the berdaches were prominently present at all of the solemn ceremonies of the sacred Calumet pipe: "They are summoned to the Councils, and nothing can be decided without their advice. Finally, through their profession of leading an Extraordinary life, they pass for Manitous—That is to say, for Spirits—or persons of consequence."[2]

How is it that berdaches had such a prominent role in Native American ceremonialism? The French missionaries, coming from the Western Christian tradition with its condemnation of gender variations, could not even comprehend the relationship between berdachism and religion. Yet, it is the spiritual question that is, for most tribes, at the heart of the berdache tradition. Without understanding that, it is impossible to understand anything else about this aboriginal institution.

AMERICAN INDIAN RELIGIONS

Native American religions offered an explanation for human diversity by their creation stories. In some tribal religions, the Great Spiritual Being is conceived as neither male nor female but as a combination of both. Among the Kamia of the Southwest, for example, the bearer of plant seeds and the introducer of Kamia culture was a man-woman spirit named Warharmi.[3] A key episode of the Zuni creation story involves a battle between the kachina spirits of the agricultural Zunis and the enemy hunter spirits. Every four years an elaborate ceremony commemorates this myth. In the story a kachina spirit called *ko'lhamana* was captured by the enemy spirits and transformed in the process. This transformed spirit became a mediator between the two sides, using his peacemaking skills to merge the differing lifestyles of hunters and farmers. In the ceremony, a dramatic reenactment of the myth, the part of the transformed *ko'lhamana* spirit, is performed by a berdache.[4] The Zuni word for berdache is *lhamana,* denoting its closeness to the spiritual mediator who brought hunting and farming together.[5] The moral of this story is that the berdache was created by the deities for a special purpose, and that this creation led to the improvement of society. The continual reenactment of this story provides a justification for the Zuni berdache in each generation.

In contrast to this, the lack of spiritual justification in a creation myth could denote a lack of tolerance for gender variation. The Pimas, unlike most of their Southwestern neighbors, did not respect a berdache status. *Wi-kovat,* their derogatory word, means "like a girl," but it does not signify a recognized social role. Pima mythology reflects this lack of acceptance, in a folk tale that explains male androgyny as due to Papago witchcraft. Knowing that the Papagos respected berdaches, the Pimas blamed such an occurrence on an alien influence.[6] While the Pimas' condemnatory attitude is unusual, it does point out the importance of spiritual explanations for the acceptance of gender variance in a culture.

Other Native American creation stories stand in sharp contrast to the Pima explanation. A good example is the account of the Navajos, which presents women and men as equals. The Navajo origin tale is told as a story of five worlds. The first people were First Man and First Woman, who were created equally and at the same time. The first two worlds that they lived in were bleak and unhappy, so they escaped to the third world. In the third world lived two twins, Turquoise Boy and White Shell Girl, who were the first berdaches. In the Navajo language the word for berdache is *nadle,* which means "changing one" or "one who is transformed." It is applied to hermaphrodites—those who are born with the genitals of both male and female—and also to "those who pretend to be *nadle,*" who take on a social role that is distinct from either men or women.[7]

In the third world, First Man and First Woman began farming, with the help of the changing twins. One of the twins noticed some clay and, holding it in the palm of his/her hand, shaped it into the first pottery bowl. Then he/she formed a plate, a water dipper, and a pipe. The second twin observed some reeds and began to weave them, making the first basket. Together they shaped axes and grinding stones from rocks, and hoes from bone. All these new inventions made the people very happy.[8]

The message of this story is that humans are dependent for many good things on the inventiveness of *nadle.* Such individuals were present from the earliest eras of human existence, and their presence was never questioned. They were part of the natural order of the universe, with a special contribution to make.

Later on in the Navajo creation story, White Shell Girl entered the moon and became the Moon Bearer. Turquoise Boy, however, remained with the people. When First Man realized that Turquoise Boy could do all manner of women's work as well as women, all the men left the women and crossed a big river. The men hunted and planted crops. Turquoise Boy ground the corn, cooked the food, and weaved cloth for the men. Four years passed with the women and men separated, and the men were happy with the *nadle.* Later, however, the women wanted to learn how to grind corn from the *nadle,* and both the men and the women had decided that it was not good to continue living separately. So the women crossed the river and the people were reunited.[9]

They continued living happily in the third world, until one day a great flood began. The people ran to the highest mountaintop, but the water kept rising and they all feared they would be drowned. But just in time, the ever-inventive Turquoise Boy found a large reed. They climbed upward inside the tall hollow reed, and came out at the top into the fourth world. From there, White Shell Girl brought another reed, and they climbed again to the fifth world, which is the present world of the Navajos.[10]

These stories suggest that the very survival of humanity is dependent on the inventiveness of berdaches. With such a mythological belief system, it is no wonder that the Navajos held *nadle* in high regard. The concept of the *nadle* is well formulated in the creation story. As children were educated by these stories, and all Navajos believed in them, the high status accorded to gender variation was passed down from generation to generation. Such stories also provided instructions for *nadle* themselves to live by. A spiritual explanation guaranteed a special place for a person who was considered different but not deviant.

For American Indians, the important explanations of the world are spiritual ones. In their view, there is a deeper reality than the here-and-now. The real essence of wisdom occurs when one finally gives up trying to explain events in terms of "logic" and "reality." Many confusing aspects of existence can better be explained by actions of a multiplicity of spirits. Instead of a concept of a single god, there is an awareness of "that which we do not understand." In Lakota religion, for example, the term *Wakan Tanka* is often translated as "god." But a more proper translation, according to the medicine people who taught me, is "The Great Mystery."[11]

While rationality can explain much, there are limits to human capabilities of understanding. The English language is structured to account for cause and effect. For example, English speakers say, "It is raining," with the implication that there is a cause "it" that leads to rain. Many Indian languages, on the other hand, merely note what is most accurately translated as "raining" as an observable fact. Such an approach brings a freedom to stop worrying about causes of things, and merely to relax and accept that our human insights can go only so far. By not taking ourselves too seriously, or overinflating human importance, we can get beyond the logical world.

The emphasis of American Indian religions, then, is on the spiritual nature of all things. To understand the physical world, one must appreciate the underlying spiritual essence. Then one can begin to see that the physical is only a faint shadow, a partial reflection, of a supernatural and extrarational world. By the Indian view, everything that exists is spiritual. Every object—plants, rocks, water, air, the moon, animals, humans, the earth itself—has a spirit. The spirit of one thing (including a human) is not superior to the spirit of any other. Such a view promotes a sophisticated ecological awareness of the place that humans have in the larger environment. The function of religion is not to try to condemn or to change what exists, but to accept the realities of the world and to appreciate their contributions to life. Everything that exists has a purpose.[12]

One of the basic tenets of American Indian religion is the notion that everything in the universe is related. Nevertheless, things that exist are often seen as having a counterpart: sky and earth, plant and animal, water and fire. In all of these polarities, there exist mediators. The role of the mediator is to hold the polarities together, to keep the world from disintegrating. Polarities exist within human society also. The most important category within Indian society is gender. The notions of Woman and Man underlie much of social interaction and are comparable to the other major polarities. Women, with their nurturant qualities, are associated with the earth, while men are associated with the sky. Women gatherers and farmers deal with plants (of the earth), while men hunters deal with animals.

The mediator between the polarities of woman and man, in the American Indian religious explanation, is a being that combines the elements of both genders. This might be a combination in a physical sense, as in the case of hermaphrodites. Many Native American religions accept this phenomenon in the same way that they accept other variations from the norm. But more important is their acceptance of the idea that gender can be combined in ways other than physical hermaphroditism. The physical aspects of a thing or a person, after all, are not nearly as important as its spirit. American Indians use the concept of a person's *spirit* in the way that other Americans use the concept of a person's *character*. Consequently, physical hermaphroditism is not necessary for the idea of gender mixing. A person's character, their spiritual essence, is the crucial thing.

THE BERDACHE'S SPIRIT

Individuals who are physically normal might have the spirit of the other sex, might range somewhere between the two sexes, or might have a spirit that is distinct from either women or men. Whatever category they fall into, they are seen as being different from men. They are accepted spiritually as "Not Man." Whichever option is chosen, Indian religions offer spiritual explanations. Among the Arapahos of the Plains, berdaches are called *haxu'xan* and are seen to be that way as a result of a supernatural gift from birds or animals. Arapaho mythology recounts the story of Nih'a'ca, the first *haxu'xan*. He pretended to be a woman and married the mountain lion, a symbol for masculinity. The myth, as recorded by ethnographer Alfred Kroeber about 1900, recounted that "These people had the natural desire to become women, and as they grew up gradually became women. They gave up the desires of men. They were married to men. They had miraculous power and could do supernatural things. For instance, it was one of them that first made an intoxicant from rainwater."[13] Besides the theme of inventiveness, similar to the Navajo creation story, the berdache role is seen as a product of a "natural desire." Berdaches "gradually became women," which underscores the notion of woman as a social category rather than as a fixed biological entity. Physical biological sex is less important in gender classification than a person's desire—one's spirit.

The myths contain no prescriptions for trying to change berdaches who are acting out their desires of the heart. Like many other cultures' myths, the Zuni origin myths simply sanction the idea that gender can be transformed independently of biological sex.[14] Indeed, myths warn of dire consequences when interference with such a transformation is attempted. Prince Alexander Maximilian of the German state of Wied, traveling in the northern Plains in the 1830s, heard a myth about a warrior who once tried to force a berdache to avoid women's clothing. The berdache resisted, and the warrior shot him with an arrow. Immediately the berdache disappeared, and the warrior saw only a pile of stones with his arrow in them. Since then, the story concluded, no intelligent person would try to coerce a berdache.[15] Making the point even more directly, a Mandan myth told of an Indian who tried to force *mihdacke* (berdaches) to give up their distinctive dress and status, which led the spirits to punish many people with death. After that, no Mandans interfered with berdaches.[16]

With this kind of attitude, reinforced by myth and history, the aboriginal view accepts human diversity. The creation story of the Mohave of the Colorado River Valley speaks of a time when people were not sexually differentiated. From this perspective, it is easy to accept that certain individuals might combine elements of masculinity and femininity.[17] A respected Mohave elder, speaking in the 1930s, stated this viewpoint simply: "From the very beginning of the world it was meant that there should be [berdaches], just as it was instituted that there should be shamans. They were intended for that purpose."[18]

This elder also explained that a child's tendencies to become a berdache are apparent early, by about age nine to twelve, before the child reaches puberty: "That is the time when young persons become initiated into the functions of their sex. . . . None but young people will become berdaches as a rule."[19] Many tribes have a public ceremony that acknowledges the acceptance of berdache status. A Mohave shaman related the ceremony for his tribe: "When the child was about ten years old his relatives would begin discussing his strange ways. Some of them disliked it, but the more intelligent began envisaging an initiation ceremony." The relatives prepare for the ceremony without letting the boy know of it. It is meant to take him by surprise, to be both an initiation and a test of his true inclinations. People from various settlements are invited to attend. The family wants the community to see it and become accustomed to accepting the boy as an *alyha*.

On the day of the ceremony, the shaman explained, the boy

is led into a circle: "If the boy showed a willingness to remain standing in the circle, exposed to the public eye, it was almost certain that he would go through with the ceremony. The singer, hidden behind the crowd, began singing the songs. As soon as the sound reached the boy he began to dance as women do." If the boy is unwilling to assume *alyha* status, he would refuse to dance. But if his character—his spirit—is *alyha,* "the song goes right to his heart and he will dance with much intensity. He cannot help it. After the fourth song he is proclaimed." After the ceremony, the boy is carefully bathed and receives a woman's skirt. He is then led back to the dance ground, dressed as an *alyha,* and announces his new feminine name to the crowd. After that he would resent being called by his old male name.[20]

Among the Yuman tribes of the Southwest, the transformation is marked by a social gathering, in which the berdache prepares a meal for the friends of the family.[21] Ethnographer Ruth Underhill, doing fieldwork among the Papago Indians in the early 1930s, wrote that berdaches were common among the Papago Indians, and were usually publicly acknowledged in childhood. She recounted that a boy's parents would test him if they noticed that he preferred female pursuits. The regular pattern, mentioned by many of Underhill's Papago informants, was to build a small brush enclosure. Inside the enclosure they placed a man's bow and arrows, and also a woman's basket. At the appointed time the boy was brought to the enclosure as the adults watched from outside. The boy was told to go inside the circle of brush. Once he was inside, the adults "set fire to the enclosure. They watched what he took with him as he ran out and if it was the basketry materials, they reconciled themselves to his being a berdache."[22]

What is important to recognize in all of these practices is that the assumption of a berdache role was not forced on the boy by others. While adults might have their suspicions, it was only when the child made the proper move that he was considered a berdache. By doing woman's dancing, preparing a meal, or taking the woman's basket he was making an important symbolic gesture. Indian children were not stupid, and they knew the implications of these ceremonies beforehand. A boy in the enclosure could have left without taking anything, or could have taken both the man's and the woman's tools. With the community standing by watching, he was well aware that his choice would mark his assumption of berdache status. Rather than being seen as an involuntary test of his reflexes, this ceremony may be interpreted as a definite statement by the child to take on the berdache role.

Indians do not see the assumption of berdache status, however, as a free will choice on the part of the boy. People felt that the boy was acting out his basic character. The Lakota shaman Lame Deer explained:

They were not like other men, but the Great Spirit made them *winktes* and we accepted them as such. . . . We think that if a woman has two little ones growing inside her, if she is going to have twins, sometimes instead of giving birth to two babies they have formed up in her womb into just one, into a half-man/half-woman kind of being. . . . To us a man is what nature, or his dreams, make him. We accept him for what he wants to be. That's up to him.[23]

While most of the sources indicate that once a person becomes a berdache it is a lifelong status, directions from the spirits determine everything. In at least one documented case, concerning a nineteenth-century Klamath berdache named Lele'ks, he later had a supernatural experience that led him to leave the berdache role. At that time Lele'ks began dressing and acting like a man, then married women, and eventually became one of the most famous Klamath chiefs.[24] What is important is that both in assuming berdache status and in leaving it, supernatural dictate is the determining factor.

DREAMS AND VISIONS

Many tribes see the berdache role as signifying an individual's proclivities as a dreamer and a visionary. Among the Papagos, for example, these qualities are accepted as a compelling gift from the supernatural world.[25] The Yumas also believe it is connected to dreaming. They see berdachism as a result of a child's dreams at the time of puberty. A dream about a particular mountain that is associated with transformation, or of the arrowweed, which they believe to be capable of changing its sex, symbolizes berdachism. By Yuma belief, a person who has a particularly acute capability for dreaming has the potential for transforming his mind. According to a Yuma elder in the 1920s, speaking about an *elxá,* "his mind was changed from male to female."[26]

A Yaqui berdache, born in northern Mexico in 1950, gained a reputation as a dreamer by the time he was nine years old. He has extremely vivid dreams, in which he takes on identities of other people or creatures. This dreaming ability is valued by his traditionalist family, who see it as a reflection of his spirituality. By the time he was twelve his position as a dreamer was formalized in the ceremony that awarded him his adult name. The translation of his name is First Star Before Light or Morning Star. It signifies the bringing of illumination. He is the precursor of light, the way to get to the light, a guide through the darkness of ignorance. He does not provide the light itself (which is one's own realization of one's spiritual nature), but he helps others find the light that is individual to their own selves. He dreams for others, spiritually healing and sorting out a person's confusion.[27]

Some Indian groups in northern California have a ceremony similar to the Papagos', in which the boy is placed in a brush enclosure that is set on fire, and then the people watch to see if he runs out with the man's tools or the woman's. Stephen Powers, a journalist who visited California Indians in 1871–72 and wrote a series of articles on them, reported this brushfire ceremony on the Round Valley reservation. He met a Yuki *i-wa-musp* ("man-woman"), and learned that the Pomo word for man-woman was *dass.* Powers pursued the topic in his interviews with the residents on the reservation.

When questioned about it the Indians always seek to laugh the matter away; but when pressed for an explanation they generally reply that they do it because they wish to do it; or else with that mystifying circumlocution peculiar to the Indian, they answer with a long rigmarole . . .[that] the spirit moves them to do it, or, as an Indian would say, that he feels a burning in his heart which tells him to do it.[28]

The "long rigmarole" that Powers was so impatient to understand captures his informants' viewpoint exactly. In providing the Indians' words, Powers unwittingly furnished the Yuki explanation, in line with their view that people's character traits were directed by spiritual forces. These forces caused "a burning in his heart" which led an individual to become a man-woman.

The wide distribution of berdachism may indicate its antiquity. The Yuki explanation for berdachism seems to have prevailed among California Indians. Yokuts explained that their berdaches, *tongochim* or *tunosim,* were not delegated to their status, but entered it "in response to an irresistible call of their natures."[29] Other California tribes simply stated that berdaches were "made that way" from birth, "were born that way," or "acted upon a dream."[30]

Among the northern Plains and related Great Lakes tribes, the idea of supernatural dictate through dreaming—the vision quest—had its highest development. The goal of the vision quest is to try to get beyond the rational world by sensory deprivation and fasting. By depriving one's body of nourishment, the brain could escape from logical thought and connect with the higher reality of the supernatural. The person doing the quest simply sits and waits for a vision. But a vision might not come easily; the person might have to wait for days.

The best way that I can describe the process is to refer to my own vision quest, which I experienced when I was living on a Lakota reservation in 1982. After a long series of prayers and blessings, the shaman who had prepared me for the ceremony took me out to an isolated area where a sweat lodge had been set up for my quest. As I walked to the spot, I worried that I might not be able to stand it. Would I be overcome by hunger? Could I tolerate the thirst? What would I do if I had to go to the toilet? The shaman told me not to worry, that a whole group of holy people would be praying and singing for me while I was on my quest.

He had me remove my clothes, symbolizing my disconnection from the material world, and crawl into the sweat lodge. Before he left me I asked him, "What do I think about?" He said, "Do not think. Just pray for spiritual guidance." After a prayer he closed the flap tightly and I was left in total darkness. I still do not understand what happened to me during my vision quest, but during the day and a half that I was out there, I never once felt hungry or thirsty or the need to go to the toilet. What happened was an intensely personal experience that I cannot and do not wish to explain, a process of being that cannot be described in rational terms.

When the shaman came to get me at the end of my time, I actually resented having to end it. He did not need to ask if my vision quest were successful. He knew that it was even before seeing me, he explained, because he saw an eagle circling over me while I underwent the quest. He helped interpret the signs I had seen, then after more prayers and singing he led me back to the others. I felt relieved, cleansed, joyful, and serene. I had been through an experience that will be a part of my memories always.

If a vision quest could have such an effect on a person not even raised in Indian society, imagine its impact on a boy who from his earliest years had been waiting for the day when he could seek his vision. Gaining his spiritual power from his first vision, it would tell him what role to take in adult life. The vision might instruct him that he is going to be a great hunter, a craftsman, a warrior, or a shaman. Or it might tell him that he will be a berdache. Among the Lakotas, or Sioux, there are several symbols for various types of visions. A person becomes *wakan* (a sacred person) if she or he dreams of a bear, a wolf, thunder, a buffalo, a white buffalo calf, or Double Woman. Each dream results in a different gift, whether it is the power to cure illness or wounds, a promise of good hunting, or the exalted role of a *heyoka* (doing things backward).

A white buffalo calf is believed to be a berdache. If a person has a dream of the sacred Double Woman, this means that she or he will have the power to seduce men. Males who have a vision of Double Woman are presented with female tools. Taking such tools means that the male will become a berdache. The Lakota word *winkte* is composed of *win*, "woman," and *kte*, "would become."[31] A contemporary Lakota berdache explains, "To become a *winkte*, you have a medicine man put you up on the hill, to search for your vision. You can become a *winkte* if you truly are by nature. You see a vision of the White Buffalo Calf Pipe. Sometimes it varies. A vision is like a scene in a movie."[32] Another way to become a *winkte* is to have a vision given by a *winkte* from the past.[33]

In other Plains tribes, berdache visions are often associated with a moon spirit, like Double Woman, whose changes symbolize transformation. In the Omaha language, the word for berdache is *mexoga* (also spelled *mixu-ga* or *mingu-ga*), meaning "instructed by the moon." James O. Dorsey, one of the first ethnographers to do fieldwork on the Plains in the 1880s, described a berdache vision quest in detail. He reported that *mexoga* is considered sacred, because the Moon Being takes a special interest in him. When an Omaha boy sees the Moon Being on his vision quest, the spirit holds in one hand a man's bow and arrow and in the other a woman's pack strap. "When the youth tried to grasp the bow and arrows the Moon Being crossed his hands very quickly, and if the youth was not very careful he seized the pack strap instead of the bow and arrows, thereby fixing his lot in later life. In such a case he could not help acting the woman, speaking, dressing, and working just as Indian women used to do."[34] This type of vision, conferring high status because of instruction from the Moon spirit, was also reported by ethnographers who did fieldwork among the Winnebagos, Lakotas, Assiniboine, Pawnees, Mandans, and Hidatsas.[35]

By interpreting the result of the vision as being the work of a spirit, the vision quest frees the person from feeling responsible for his transformation. The person might even claim that the change was done against his will and without his control. Such a claim does not suggest a negative attitude about berdache status, because it is common for people to claim reluctance to fulfill their spiritual duty no matter what vision appears to them. Becoming any kind of sacred person involves taking on various social responsibilities and burdens.[36]

Hidatsa men expressed this reluctance. They believed that when a man looked at a coil of sweetgrass, the female spirit could "cause his mind to weaken so that he would have no relief until he 'changed his sex.' Often a man would tell of his experiences, how everywhere he looked he would see the coiled sweetgrass and how hard he was trying to keep from changing over." Of those who became berdaches, the other Indians would say that since he had been "claimed by a Holy Woman," nothing could be done about it. Such persons might be pitied because of the spiritual responsibilities they held, but they were treated as mysterious and holy, and were respected as benevolent people who assisted others in time of starvation.[37]

A story was told among the Lakotas in the 1880s of a boy who tried to resist following his vision from Double Woman. But according to Lakota informants "few men succeed in this effort after having taken the strap in the dream." Having rebelled against the instructions given him by the Moon Being, he committed suicide.[38] The moral of that story is that one should not resist spiritual guidance, because it will lead only to grief. In another case, an Omaha young man told of being addressed by a spirit as "daughter," whereupon he discovered that he was unconsciously using feminine styles of speech. He tried to use male speech patterns, but could not. As a result of this vision, when he returned to his people he resolved himself to dress as a woman.[39] Such stories function to justify personal peculiarities as due to a fate over which the individual has no control.

Despite the usual pattern in Indian societies of using ridicule to enforce conformity, receiving instructions from a vision inhibits others from trying to change the berdache. Ritual explanation provides a way out. It also excuses the community from worrying about the cause of that person's difference, or the feeling that it is society's duty to try to change him.[40] Native American religions, above all else, encourage a basic respect for nature. If nature makes a person different, many Indians conclude, a mere human should not undertake to counter this spiritual dictate. Someone who is "unusual" can be accommodated without being stigmatized as "abnormal." Berdachism is thus not alien or threatening; it is a reflection of spirituality.

2   *Sacred People: Berdache Mystical Power and Ceremonial Roles*

By understanding the spiritual basis of the berdache tradition, it is easier to comprehend reports written by unaware whites who observed the reverence with which other Indians treated the berdaches. At the beginning of the nineteenth century, for instance, explorer Peter Grant wrote about his time among the Ojibwas of the western Great Lakes:

They have the greatest faith in dreams, by which they imagine that the Deity informs them of future events, [and] enjoins them certain penances. . . . I have known several instances of some of their men who, by virtue of some extraordinary dream, had been affected to such a degree as to abandon every custom characteristic of their sex and adopt the dress and manners of the women. They are never ridiculed or despised by the men on account of their new costumes, but are, on the contrary, respected as saints or beings in some degree inspired.[1]

Such feelings were very widespread among the aboriginal peoples of the New World. Even in Peru, the Spanish explorer Cieza de León reported that among the Indians of Puerto Viejo:

In each important temple or house of worship they have a man or two, or more, depending on the idol, who go dressed in women's attire from the time they are children, and speak like them, and in manner, dress, and everything else imitate women. With these, almost like a rite and ceremony, on feast and holy days, they have carnal, foul intercourse, especially the chiefs and headmen. I know this because I have punished two. . . . The devil held such sway in this land that, not satisfied with making them fall into so great sin, he made them believe that this vice was a kind of holiness and religion.[2]

The Europeans were not only aghast, but amazed and dumbfounded as to why berdaches were considered sacred.

The holiness of the berdache has to do with Indian views that everything that exists is a reflection of the spiritual. If a person is different from the average individual, this means that the spirits must have taken particular care in creating this person. If the spirits take such care, by this reasoning, such an individual must be especially close to the spirits. Thus, among the Lakotas a *winkte* is described as *wakan,* a term that means very sacred or holy and is incorporated in the name for the Greatest Holiness, *Wakan Tanka.*[3]

In a religion like the Lakotas', berdaches are seen as magical holders of unique ritual instructions. Since they are guided by a spirit, they are not bound by normal rules of conduct. This unusualness is an indication of their sacredness. According to Alfred Bowers, who did fieldwork on the Hidatsa reservation in the 1930s, "Berdaches comprised the most active ceremonial class in the village. Their roles in ceremonies were many and exceeded those of the most distinguished tribal ceremonial leaders. There was an atmosphere of mystery about them."[4] This mystery is what makes it so difficult to get traditional Indian people to talk about berdachism. According to a Cheyenne informant, "Like the military societies, it is kind of secret, and people don't talk about it much because they want to retain the secrecy and the magic of it."[5] Nevertheless, several anthropologists have managed to publish interesting information on berdaches. One of the earliest was Matilda Coxe Stevenson, who did fieldwork with the Zunis in the 1880s and 1890s. She became close friends with a *lhamana* named We'wha, who like many other berdaches had a reputation for high intelligence. We'wha was especially conspicuous in ceremonials and well versed in religious matters, often taking a leading part in dramatizations of Zuni myths.[6] We'wha was also known as the smartest person in the pueblo. Stevenson, using the feminine pronoun form, observed about this berdache that "Owing to her bright mind and excellent memory, she was called upon . . . when a long prayer had to be repeated or a grace was to be offered over a feast. In fact she was the chief personage on many occasions" (see illustration).[7]

These remarks on dramatization and performance are interesting in that they suggest parallels with other cultures. There seems to be a tendency for effeminate males in widely separated societies, from Indonesia to the modern United States, to gravitate to the acting profession. At a young age, these boys are unusually adept at role playing and stage presentation, often before they could possibly be familiar with the reputation of the theater as a social haven for effeminate males. Some scientists have suggested that this cross-cultural tendency indicates an inborn character trait for effeminacy among a set proportion of males, which will appear in any given population.[8]

SHAMANISM

In American Indian cultures, the occupation in which acting ability is most developed is the office of the shaman. Since so much of the shaman's work centers on ceremonial mystery and magic, theatrical qualities are of great use in the shaman's performances. But the shaman is much more than an actor. His or her role consists of duties that Western society accomplishes with priests, therapists, and medical doctors. This is why shamans are sometimes referred to as "medicine men." Shamanism is not a hereditary office, but is open to any man or woman who is effective. Despite the fact that tribal peoples are generally egalitarian, the shaman has a special status.

Shamans gain their high status on the basis of how well they can relate to the spirit world. Certain individuals are seen as having this skill, just as other individuals might be better at hunting, at gathering, or at making things. Everyone has his or her own contribution to make. To survive, tribal societies have to emphasize group solidarity rather than competition. So, instead of an individual gaining status by "getting ahead" of others, the tribal person who receives the most status is the one who does the most to benefit others. By putting the group's welfare before her or his personal welfare, the shaman receives the respect of others.

Among tribal peoples the shaman is the primary person responsible for the group's welfare. Since the aboriginal view suggests that everything that happens is due to the spirit world, the way to keep bad things from happening is to pay attention to spiritual concerns. Health and success can be gained by knowing the proper ceremonies to placate the spirits. As with any population, a major disaster for people in small-scale societies is bad health. According to their view that sickness is caused by a violation of the spiritual harmony of the universe, the shaman is the person to whom one turns. If a person is sick, it might be that someone violated this harmony. They might have offended a spirit by forgetting to offer prayers, or they might have shown jealousy, possessiveness, or greed. These were some of the greatest crimes of aboriginal America.

Curing is closely connected to religion. But American Indian shamans do not ignore the physical aspects of disease. They are quite skillful in setting broken bones and using medicinal herbs for healing. In fact, many substances that pharmacists use today originally derived from plants that were first utilized by Indian shamans. But beyond this, shamans understand that a basic aspect of healing involves more than techniques for repairing bodies. They realize that a more important function of health is healing the mind.[9]

I can illustrate this by giving an account of a healing ceremony that I attended on a South Dakota reservation in 1982. The ceremony, led by a traditional shaman, was called in the Lakota language *Yuwipi*.[10] It was held to help an elderly Lakota woman. Those of us who were participating entered a room that had been carefully prepared. All the windows were covered so no light could get in. After the sick woman was helped into a chair, the shaman started elaborately stringing his sacred objects around the room. As he did so, another person started playing a drum and everyone began singing. When the shaman was finished preparing this shrine, he directed me to turn off the light. After the room was plunged into complete darkness, the shaman began a prayer. Next he began to sing a trancelike song that went on a long time. Then everyone sang. After that, the shaman began a long prayer in Lakota. Then there was more drumming and singing, then more prayers, then more singing. When the last prayer was over, there was silence. Next we heard the hoot of an owl in the room, and felt the breeze as the owl's wings flapped near our faces.

By this time the ceremony was so intense and powerful that I felt as if I had left the rational world. I had never been so moved by a religious event. At the end, when the lights came on again, no one in the room had dry eyes. It was impossible not to be affected by the supportive feeling being demonstrated by the shaman and the others, all done for the woman's health. Though no medicinal treatment had been administered to the frail elder, she seemed greatly helped and comforted by this outpouring of concern.

By working for hours beside the sick person, in intricate and exact procedures, the shaman's effort and concern is obvious. A shaman understands that the body's healing process is facilitated by the ill person's belief that someone cares and is working hard for her or his health. Empathy with suffering, in and of itself, is a powerful psychic healing motivator; an important part of health *is* spiritual. That is, if a person's spirit is improved, they will more likely reach wellness. The shaman thus helps a person get well, physically and spiritually.

Shamans are not necessarily berdaches, but because of their spiritual connection, berdaches in many cultures are often considered to be powerful shamans. Among the Navajos, *nadle* shamans are considered particularly excellent as chanters. They have special chants for curing illness and insanity, and for aiding childbirth.[11] The same talents are ascribed to *winktes* among the Lakotas. They also have good powers for love medicine, which are related to their medicine for childbirth.[12] Some have more than others, but every *winkte* has at least some sacred powers to doctor illnesses. "*Winktes* made miraculous cures when they gave medicine."[13] Cheyenne war parties almost always had a skilled berdache curer along to care for the wounded.[14] An elderly Cheyenne man remembers his grandfather telling about how he got shot in the leg, and a berdache shaman put the leg together and it never hurt after that.[15]

The Mohaves believed that female shamans were spiritually stronger than male ones, but that berdache shamans were stronger than either women or men. This was true as well (at least before 1940) with the Klamath, the Yurok, and many California Indian groups.[16] Since they were involved with the sick, California Indian berdaches also oversaw funeral rites. This role was also true of the Timucua berdaches sketched by Le Moyne (see illustration). Among the Yokuts, they alone prepared bodies for burial and conducted the singing and dancing rites at funerals.[17] Even today on a Lakota reservation, when someone dies, a *winkte* is the first person the relatives run to for help in preparing the funeral and the wake. *Winktes* will often do the cooking at the wake.[18]

SACRED ROLES

Many times, however, berdaches are not shamans, but are the special people from whom shamans request advice. A Lakota reveals, "*Winktes* can be medicine men, but [are] usually not because they already have the power. They are *wakan*."[19] Even when they are not shamans, berdaches often (but not in every culture) have important ceremonial roles. Navajo *nadle* are often responsible for preparation and cooking of sacred food at large ceremonial gatherings.[20] A *winkte* is asked to prepare the food whenever someone wants to do a thanksgiving ceremony.[21]

Among the Plains tribes, early ethnographic reports stated that it was a berdache who was responsible for blessing the tree used for the Sun Dance ceremony, the chief religious rite of Plains culture.[22] While I had read of this practice, I would not have predicted that I would experience it for myself. A month after my arrival on a Lakota reservation, the shaman who directed my learning was preparing a Sun Dance. When it came time to cut down a tree for the Sun Dance pole, he gave the axe to the *winkte* Terry Calling Eagle. Once the tree was felled, the people carried it to the middle of the dance grounds. Brightly colored pieces of cloth were tied to the upper branches. When the pole was fully prepared, emotions peaked as it was brought into place to be set up. The participants placed the lower end of the trunk next to a hole dug for the purpose. Then all action came to a stop. The shaman turned to Terry, who began to recite a prayer in Lakota. He was praying just as I had read in documents from the nineteenth century. But these are traditionalist people who have not received their ideas about their culture from an anthropology book. Their behavior represents an unbroken cultural tradition passed down through the generations. The berdache's role is set by tradition as much as the rest of the ceremony. It was no accident that Terry had been asked to bless the Sun Dance pole; this was the proper way of assuring a successful ritual. After he completed his prayer, the hands of the participants seemed to barely touch the pole, yet it shot up into the sky erect. Terry pushed dirt into the hole in which the tree trunk now stood so majestically. It was a beautiful sight, as everyone stood transfixed by the gently waving cloths on the branches above our heads. This part of the ceremony completed, there was a silent retreat before the dance itself would begin.

In a number of ceremonial instances, the role of the berdache was integrated into the procedure. There was a place for the special contributions of the berdache in the society generally, as represented ritually by his special role in the ceremonies. People would try to gain the spiritual assistance of a berdache in all sorts of matters, from the grandness of the Sun Dance to the mundaneness of minor ritual behavior. Among the Potawatomi, women normally groomed the men's hair before they left on a hunt. But if a berdache did this, then it would provide a special spiritual advantage and protection for the hunter.[23]

Among the Lakotas, a berdache can offer a boy a sacred *winkte* name. Having such a name provides spiritual protection for the male child and helps to insure good health and a long life. The boy's father goes to the winkte and flirts with him sexually. If he favors the father, the berdache will decide on a secret name, which is invariably erotic.[24] A *winkte* can do no more than four naming ceremonies per year. The *winkte* begins to prepare himself for a naming ceremony by fasting and undertaking a vision quest, to gain some insight into the child's future. The *winkte* must sacrifice to be fully sincere, and will work with the boy and his family for the entire year, making spiritual preparations and offering close guidance to the boy. After the ceremony is over, it is the *winkte*'s responsibility to help look after that child for life. He makes a medicine bag for the child to carry with him always. Inside are some sacred objects that are closely associated with the *winkte*.[25]

This ceremony ties together the berdache with a boy, and this association continues in a way that is not unlike the institution of the godparent. The Lakota shaman Lame Deer remarked: "The secret name a *winkte* gave to a child was believed to be especially powerful and effective. . . . to bring its bearer luck and long life. In the old days it was worth a fine horse—at the least. The *winkte* told me that these names are very sexy, even funny, very outspoken names. You don't let a stranger know them; he would kid you about it. Having a *winkte* name could make a man famous. Sitting Bull, Black Elk, even Crazy Horse had secret *winkte* names."[26]

This power for ensuring luck and long life extended to the berdache himself. They were always believed to live longer than average men.[27] If they were not warriors, they obviously had a better chance of living longer, but even when they were confronted with a threat they were able to survive. The idea of luck and power for berdaches is a common theme in many tribal legends. In a Hidatsa oral history recorded in the 1930s, concerning a famous nineteenth-century warrior named Four Bears, one story recounted how Four Bears once made the mistake of attacking an Assiniboine Sioux berdache: "But the berdache was brave, saying 'You can't kill me for I am holy. I will strike coups on you with my digging stick.'" Then the berdache chanted a magical song and began to chase the warriors. They were afraid of the special power of the berdache so they ran. But Four Bears shot an arrow at the berdache, and though it hit the berdache it did not penetrate the skin. They realized that the berdache had great supernatural powers. Since Four Bears had been successful in other ventures up to that point and did not want to spoil his luck, he canceled his entire raiding party. As the story was told, the Indians concluded, "Four Bears used good judgment, for it was hard to kill a berdache since they were holy."[28] What is interesting in this story as it had been passed down for a century is the message that people should not bother berdaches. The fact that a culture hero like Four Bears learned this lesson, and could admit his mistake, was a clear example for others to follow. Such stories functioned as educational parables to teach people respect for berdaches.

RESPECT, FEAR, AND RIDICULE

By this time the skeptical reader may be suspecting that only the positive side of berdachism is being told. Surely attitudes could not be that supportive. Indeed, some aboriginal American cultures did not recognize berdaches as a respected status (for example, the Iroquois, Apaches, Pimas, and Comanches), and in others there existed a range of attitudes. Even in the societies that have been the focus of this study, there are periodic references to berdaches which seem to denote some negativism. Most of these derogatory statements are a result of the influence of white people and their Christian religion. Some anthropologists have been less than clear about recognizing these acculturative influences, and instead have blithely attributed derogatory statements to a supposed aboriginal heritage. Also, some anthropologists themselves have shown prejudicial attitudes toward the berdache.

Nevertheless, when all of these influences are accounted for, there still are some statements in the literature where Indians ridicule or joke about berdaches. To an outsider, this implies a lack of respect for the berdache. Unfortunately, when ethnographers have noted these statements, they rarely make it clear who is doing the talking and what their relationship is to the berdache. One of the most explicit statements of public taunting of a berdache was recorded by Ruth Landes among the Santees. The *winkta* was subjected to persistent teasing. Yet Landes makes it clear that this teasing was done by his cousins. In many Indian societies, there are certain relatives who have a joking relationship with one another. Joking relatives are properly maligned in public; indeed they expect it and might think something is wrong in its absence.[29]

When I was living on the Eastern Cherokee reservation in 1973–74, after a few months a man my age to whom I became closest began a joking relationship with me. The joking insults between us sometimes flew nonstop, and went to unrelenting and merciless levels. To an outsider it might seem as if we were intense rivals. At times it even became too much for me, and I had to back off, but when that happened he was puzzled at my reactions. We were very close friends, and the taunting was simply a mark of our close friendship and of his accepting me into his family. Anyone who has lived with Indian people knows that once you are accepted into the group, joking and kidding abound. It is part of the glue that holds the society together.

Joking relationships often involve sexual themes, so with a berdache it is obvious that the taunting would focus on homosexuality. In a perceptive essay David Greenberg has concluded that much of this "ridicule" noted by white observers was in fact nothing more than joking relationships between relatives. There is no reason to believe, Greenberg suggests, that this taunting denoted a rejection of homosexuality, or that berdaches would have been teased any less if their sexual partners were women instead of men.[30]

Moreover, Greenberg notes, the ridicule may have been more directed at the berdache's prestige than at his sexuality or character differences. Persons of respect and prestige are more subject to ridicule than anyone else. While this gossipy aspect of Indian society can be frustrating to someone who takes the initiative, it does function to preserve a basic egalitarianism by taking potentially pretentious persons and reminding them that they had better not overestimate their self-importance. It is one among many mechanisms that Indians use to inhibit social stratification.[31]

It is in this context that I later understood one of my earliest fieldwork experiences on the northern Plains. When I first began doing research on the Omaha reservation I interviewed two Omaha men in their twenties, and I asked them to define *mexoga.* They laughed and said it was "like a faggot." Their joking manner at first led me to believe that they were typical homophobes. But after seeing that I was approaching the topic in a serious manner, they went on to say: "Indians accept it, and don't condemn it like white people do. I don't care what reservation you go to, you always find at least one among every group of Indians."[32] It soon became obvious that these men simply accepted it as part of life, nothing to get upset about. In fact, they later took me to meet a *mexoga,* and they treated him in a most respectful manner. Another Omaha man refers to a *mexoga,* saying "People leave him alone and don't tease him. He is an oddball, but that is his right. We respect a man for what he is."[33]

While there might be joking or ridicule, it never went beyond that. The literature does not show instances where a berdache was physically attacked because of his differences. As Terry Calling Eagle states, "*Winktes* are not hurt, because if someone did something bad happens to them."[34] Again, it is the spiritual element that protects the berdache.

This spirituality can also provoke fear, and that in itself leads to ambivalent feelings about berdaches in some tribes. An early twentieth-century Klamath berdache shaman named White Cindy, referred to by tribesmen as "she," outrivaled the chief in power. Indians told of their fear of her shamanistic power, as when she willed that a certain tree be struck by lightning, and it was struck. Many Indians were afraid of her, because when angry at someone she threatened to bring a curse on them. Yet, the Klamaths respected her, and she was not scorned but was generally well liked.[35]

Since berdaches were seen as possessed of unique ritual instructions secured directly from the spirit world, their conduct was often mysterious. Among the Hidatsas, berdaches surrounded themselves with many individual rules of conduct for people in contact with them. As with outstanding shamans surrounded by similar kinds of rules, people tended to fear and respect the berdaches, and this fear made for a nervousness that was sometimes alleviated by joking about it. People's ambivalent reactions were thus a reflection of the unique and special mysterious supernatural powers of the berdache.[36] Fear and respect is even more a theme in Lakota culture. A Lakota shaman sums up the ambivalence by saying, "Winktes were both joked about and respected at the same time."[37]

DOUBLE VISION AND PROPHESY

The berdache receives respect partly as a result of being a mediator. Somewhere between the status of women and men, berdaches not only mediate between the sexes but between the psychic and the physical—between the spirit and the flesh. Since they mix the characteristics of both men and women, they possess the vision of both. They have double vision, with the ability to see more clearly than a single gender perspective can provide. This is why they are often referred to as "seer," one whose eyes can see beyond the blinders that restrict the average person. Viewing things from outside the usual perspective, they are able to achieve a creative and objective viewpoint that is seldom available to ordinary people. By the Indian view, someone who is different offers advantages to society precisely because she or he is freed from the restrictions of the usual. It is a different window from which to view the world.[38]

With this different perspective, this double vision, berdaches see themselves as unique. Jerry Baldy, a Hupa, expresses this idea about his childhood: "I knew I was different, being so attracted to men and being effeminate, but there was something else different about me beyond all that. I always wanted to explore the unknown."[39] Likewise, Michael One Feather, a Lakota *winkte,* specifies his differentness in growing up: "I always knew I had a different concept from what everybody else had. Of things, of life; how I saw things. Most people didn't see the way I saw. What I would call a way of looking at things. My ideas were always spectacular—overshooting, you know, and over-achieving. I always had to do something more, to do it my way, based on my different view."[40]

Since they have such vision, many cultures hold that berdaches can also see into the future. As a consequence, they are respected as prophets. Winnebago berdaches were noted for their ability to foretell future events.[41] A Lakota berdache explains that a shaman helped to interpret his dreams: "He respected me, and said I could foretell the future. Since then I have often predicted things that would happen. For example, one time I had a feeling that a specific relative would die, and then later I found out that that relative did die suddenly with no warning right at the time I was having my vision. People realize that I am a seer."[42]

In 1971 the Sioux shaman Lame Deer interviewed a berdache: "He told me that a *winkte* has a gift of prophesy and that he himself could predict the weather. . . . He told a woman she would live to be eighty years old, and she gave him a fine pair of moccasins for that. He told me that if nature puts a burden on a man by making him different, it also gives him a power."[43]

It is this power, based on the spiritual origins of berdachism and in the context of ceremonial leadership, in which the respected status of the berdache is rooted. Proceeding from the view that a person's different character is a reflection of her or his closeness to the spiritual, berdaches are often associated with shamanism and sacredness. Such spiritual abilities mean that berdaches may take on specific ceremonial tasks that are recognized as specifically their own. Whether in blessing ceremonies, providing lucky names, offering spiritual protection, or predicting the future, berdaches are both respected and feared for their qualities of strength and power. They utilize their strength to be of special benefit to others, in particular to their own family.

3 Family Matters: The Economic and Social Position of the Berdache

A French explorer in the upper Mississippi Valley in the 1680s described berdaches as male Indians who are "Batchelours to their dying day, and never appear either at hunting or in warlike expeditions, as being either lunatick or sickly: But at the same time they are as much esteem'd as the bravest and hailest men in the country."[1] How is it that berdaches could be so highly esteemed without fulfilling a man's role? How could they fit into the family structure while remaining bachelors? Why might they be seen as "lunatick or sickly" and still be respected?

While the spiritual explanation of berdachism provides an important justification for acceptability, a supportive family structure allows berdaches to be raised as proud and productive members of society. American Indian societies are kin-based, so most of a berdache's personal interactions take place with relatives. The extended family and the clan serve many of the functions that governmental institutions provide in a society that is state-based. Because of the way berdaches are raised and the economic role they fulfill, many kinship systems provide a secure place for them.

The major factor affecting the role of the berdache within the family is the notion that the berdache is taking the role because of spiritual guidance. According to a Lakota traditionalist, it is because of directions from a spirit that "*Winktes* had to assume the role, because if they did not, something bad would happen to them or their family or their tribe."[2] This belief effectively restrained parents from trying to change a child who was showing berdachelike behavior.

On the other hand, a family might try to encourage one of their youngsters to take on a berdache role. In some cultures

44

berdaches are known to be from specific prominent clans. A few societies supposedly restricted berdache status to such clans.[3] More commonly, berdaches may come from any family, but it is sometimes said that a certain family will have a tradition of having several berdaches in their family line.[4] A Lakota berdache remembers that when he was about twenty years old his grandparents told him that one male in every generation of the family was a *winkte,* so they accepted it on those terms. The elders told him stories about several *winktes* in his family history who were chosen to do ceremonials in association with a shaman.[5] A family might have a special reputation for having gifted children, one of whom might be a berdache. For example, a famous Omaha *mexoga* had a brother who was a shaman. People told me about both of them: "That whole family was classified." When I asked what they meant, they explained that the family was prominent in the tribe and had special respected roles.[6] Having a berdache for a child is similar to having a shaman in the family; both are sacred.

ASSIGNED GENDER IN CHILDHOOD

It is unclear to what extent parents choose to raise a boy as a berdache. In some cases there does appear to be parental direction. Among the Aleut and Kodiak Islanders in southern Alaska, for example, a Russian explorer in 1812 described berdaches, called *shopan* or *achnucek,* as respected shamans: "A Koniag who has an Achnucek instead of a wife is regarded as lucky. A father or a mother design a son for an Achnucek from his infancy, if he seems to them to resemble a girl."[7] Kodiak parents would select their most handsome and promising boy to raise as feminine. His hair was styled like a woman's, he was dressed in women's clothing, and any facial hair was carefully plucked out. At the age of ten to fifteen years, he would be married to a wealthy man. The husband regarded his boy-wife as a major social accomplishment, and the boy's family benefited from association with their new wealthy in-law. Since the boy was treated with great respect, this practice seemed to provide a no-lose situation for easy social mobility among Aleut and Kodiak families. It is thus not surprising that early observers reported the pride of the parents in having such a son, and the frequent appearance of berdaches.[8]

Likewise, a Spanish explorer among the Lache Indians of Colombia, South America, reported:

It was a law among them that if a woman bore five consecutive male children, without giving birth to a female, they could make a female of one of the sons when he reached the age of twelve—that is to say, they could rear him as a woman and teach him the habits of a woman, bringing him up in that wise. In their bodily form and manners they appeared so perfectly to be women that no one who beheld them could distinguish them from the others, and these were known as *cusmos* and they performed womanly tasks with the strength of men, as a result of which, when they had attained the proper age, they were given in wedlock as women. And indeed the Laches preferred them to true women, whereby it follows that the abomination of sodomy was freely permitted.[9]

In California, Spanish priests writing in the 1820s implied that a similar practice existed among the Luiseño and Gabrielino Indians. One wrote that the chiefs greatly valued berdaches as auxiliary wives. While still young, berdaches "were selected and instructed as they increased in years in all the duties of the women—in their mode of dress, of walking, and dancing; so that in almost every particular, they resembled females."[10]

What is interesting in these references is the implication for gender flexibility. But we should not let these sources imply that berdache status would be imposed on any young boy against his will. Indian children generally have wide latitude to live where they are comfortable, and in a manner that is compatible with their inclinations. I have observed instances, in several tribes, where a child decides to live in a different household. Their wishes are respected, and no one tries to coerce them. Children are allowed to live where and how they wish.

If children feel manipulated, in a direction other than the one they are inclined to take, they refuse to cooperate. Refusal is interpreted as a reflection of the child's "spirit." The more likely pattern with the youngsters is that such boys as are "chosen" by families to be raised as berdaches would already have evidenced an inclination for nonmasculine behavior. A Tewa boy nicknamed Missy was allowed to develop in this role beginning when he was nine years old. Yet, even before then, according to older people in his pueblo, "There had never been any doubt in anyone's mind, who remembered him at six years old, as to where he would be heading." He had by that age begun to act nonmasculinely, and his mother let him wear his sister's dresses when he asked for them.[11]

In a reference that may denote a similar practice, a pueblo berdache now in his sixties remembers that when he was six years old his family told him that he would become a "substitute woman," and that they were not going to raise him as an ordinary man but as someone special. They stated this simply and as a matter of fact, based on their observations of his character. The boy accepted it in the same spirit. He feels special, as an especially chosen one. He values his specialness, and is happy in his secure position in the Pueblo traditional community.[12]

AVERSION TO MASCULINITY

The variation of the family origins of berdachism is evidenced by a Lakota man's statement: "*Winktes* come from families where they are raised with lots of sisters and no brothers. They come from different ways—it could be how they are brought up."[13] Perhaps, it has been suggested, berdachism is related to cultural expectations of masculinity. Some anthropologists see berdaches as boys who in childhood have a strong aversion to the ultramasculine male role. Many Indian societies, especially those of the nineteenth-century Plains, placed extreme pressure on males to achieve individual prestige through warfare. Boys had to be prepared for the warrior role from early childhood, to learn toughness and physical endurance. They were expected to take life-threatening chances. The mechanism in Plains culture for conditioning boys to face pain and death was through extremely rough team games. Even young boys were prepared for warfare through the "Fire-throwing Game," in which boys struck each other with burning sticks. A variation on the game involved throwing at each other mud balls with live coals in the middle. The object for another such game, called "Swingkicking," was kicking those on the other team in the face until they bled.[14]

It was not only on the Plains that extreme demands were placed on boys to compete in brutal games of physical competition. By the time they reached their late teens boys were participating in both the hunt and the fight. Mohave males, for example, were expected to be exceptionally warlike and to participate in raids. Cowards were despised. Mohave men, like men in many tribes, prized bravery above most other virtues. Yet despite these values, no demands for demonstrations of bravery were placed on berdaches. *Alyha* were known as "rather peaceful persons" and were respected as such. While bravery was valued, power obtained in a dream was even more highly prized. The Mohave explanation was spiritual; berdaches, after all, had received their instructions from a vision.

Taking a Western perspective, ethnographer George Devereux considered the possibility that such aggressive masculinity pressures might have had something to do with the inclination of a "faint-hearted boy" to opt out of the system by becoming a berdache.[15] The problem with this interpretation is that it is not sufficient in itself. It might have prompted some boys in warlike cultures of the Plains, but if this interpretation is correct, why do we not find berdaches in all warlike tribes? Among tribes that value some of the most aggressive male roles, like the Comanche or the Iroquois, references to berdaches are notably absent. And, more important, why does a berdache tradition exist in native cultures that are not warlike? There is no simple correlation between aggressive male roles and berdachism.[16]

Another problem is that this explanation lends itself to a theory of causation by "overmothering." Using Freudian terminology, Donald Forgey concluded that "Overmothering produced a child neurotically anxious about his own masculinity. . . . A 'mama's boy'—when finally confronted with the period in which he is expected to adopt the ultramasculine, aggressively individualistic and often dangerous role of the adult male—might instead identify with the principal source of his childhood dependency and protection—his mother." Forgey's view that berdachism is a "flight from masculinity," and his use of terms like "neurotically anxious" are merely Freudian value judgments.[17] Berdaches seem anything but neurotic, and their peaceful inclinations would be honored in many gentler cultures. Furthermore, a boy's relation with his mother has been shown not to be the determining factor in gender variance in Anglo-American society. The basic propositions of the thesis have been rejected by most psychologists.[18]

INBORN CHARACTER AND CHILDHOOD ACTIVITIES

Rather than being seen as due to outside causes like overmothering or a "flight" from masculinity, the main emphasis of American Indian explanations is that berdachism is a reflection of the child's individual character. This recognition of an inborn character is at the heart of the Indian spiritual explanation. For example, among the Navajos, a people who place great value on individual freedom, becoming a *nadle* is considered to be solely a reflection of the basic nature of the individual child. Parents would not try to impose such a role on a child, without the child's initiative.[19]

The Zapotec Indians of Oaxaca, Mexico, would never consider that the berdache has chosen to live as he does, because the idea that someone could freely choose her or his character is as ludicrous to the Zapotecs as the idea that someone could freely choose eye color. They defend the right of *ira' muxe* to their different gender and sexual roles simply because "God made them that way." Both characteristics are accepted as integral to the character of berdaches.[20] It is this emphasis on a person's character, or "spirit," that is one of the most important elements of berdachism.

Indians claim that such a future role is easily observed by families. A Lakota traditionalist says, "It is obvious from infancy that one is a *winkte*. He is a beautiful boy, and the sound of his voice is effeminate. It is inborn. The mother realizes this soon, and allows the boy to do feminine things (how to prepare meat and other foods). They all end up being homosexual."[21] Tewa Indians claim that a *kwih-doh* child's nature of doing things in his own special way nearly always begins to show by about age three to five. Only after then will such a child be singled out as special.[22] A Hupa berdache recalls, "I was real feminine as a child, from as early as I can remember. Noticing how I liked to do cooking and cleaning, my grandmother said I would grow up as a woman. Within the family, Indians believe you can be whatever you choose."[23]

Descriptions by anthropologists of preberdache children support this viewpoint. Margaret Mead, writing about a boy who later became a berdache, said that even as a small boy he showed "marked feminine physical traits."[24] In the 1910s Elsie Clews Parsons knew three adult berdaches at Zuni, but also a six-year-old boy whom she felt was likely to become a berdache. She wrote about him, "His features are unusually fine and delicate. . . . Whenever I saw him playing about he was with a girl."[25]

Among the Crows in the 1850s Edwin Denig remarked about the numerous "berdeches" who, as young children, "cannot be brought to join in any of the work or play of the boys, but on the contrary associate entirely with the girls. . . . When arrived at the age of 12 or 14, and his habits are formed, the parents clothe him in a girl's dress."[26] Half a century later, S. C. Simms met a Crow berdache who was "almost gigantic in stature, but was decidedly effeminate in voice and manner. I was told that, when very young, these persons manifested a decided preference for things pertaining to female duties." Even if parents tried to invite such children to take a standard male role, they invariably resisted.[27] It was more a matter of the family adjusting to the child than vice versa.

The consistency of reports from various culture areas over the centuries is amazing. Even as early as 1702, a French explorer who lived for four years among the Illinois Indians noted that berdaches were known "from their childhood, when they are seen frequently picking up the spade, the spindle, the axe [women's tools], but making no use of the bow and arrows, as all the other small boys do."[28] Among groups like the Papagos, who designed a brushfire test for a berdache, it was only after a family noticed that "a boy liked female pursuits" that he was put through the test.[29] A modern Indian of the Southwest in the

1970s indicated that throughout his life he had "no interest in being a male, in taking over aspects of male roles, or in daydreaming of pleasurably masculine experiences." He remembered that he preferred playing with girls and in games played only by girls. While schoolteachers had forced him to participate in boys' games, he did this unwillingly. He was interested in girls' roles from his earliest memories.[30] Faced with masculinizing pressures, it is not surprising that some boys who were nonmasculine in their disposition would avoid rough and brutal play, and might instead seek the gentler play of girls. It is this characteristic that is most commonly noted about the childhood of berdaches.

While the published literature does not suggest it, my own interviewing turned up a pattern that is more individual and unique than strictly feminine. A Lakota *winkte* remembers his childhood, being raised by his grandparents on the reservation, as unlike other children's:

I was different. I never played with the boys. I played with the girls a little, or off in my own little world. There were other things I had to do besides play. I did drawings and things. I hung around my grandparents a lot. My grandfather taught me the traditions, and my grandmother taught me how to sew and cook. I was the only child there and they basically responded to my interests. I loved things like beadwork. I was mostly involved in doing artistic things. It isolated me from the other kids, so I took a liking to it. I did all the isolating things. You do beadwork and you're not bothered with other kids.[31]

Likewise, a Hupa berdache remembers, "I was always into something else, things that were never expected of me. I did what I wanted to do, and I liked that."[32]

This pattern of uniqueness was also observed by the family of a Yaqui berdache, who characterized him as having always been more androgynous than feminine. This is a distinction that white observers, used to thinking in either-or opposites, are likely to miss. By the time he was eight or nine years old he manifested extreme noncompetitiveness and lived with a cooperative approach to life. He had an unusual proclivity for dreams. His family certainly recognized that he was not typical, but rather than look down on him they valued and understood his uniqueness. According to his cousin, who was raised with the berdache, the boy lived as if he had some higher understanding of life.

He is a very wise old young man. He can draw out of people their feelings. One time we kids got down on him for not being typically masculine, but my Great Aunt, who is the clan matriarch, came down on us *real* strongly. She said it was part of his character and we should respect him. After that, we protected him when he was around *mestizos* [those of mixed indigenous and European heritage]. They were typically machismo, but we did not let anyone trouble him. I have really learned to value him. His being my cousin made me question the homophobia in society, similar to my great aunt's leadership with questioning women's roles.[33]

This tendency for a family to feel protective toward a berdache member has also been observed among the Hopi. In 1978 Richard Grant, an ethnographer, met a fifteen-year-old Hopi boy whom he described as quite androgynous. He wrote that in the boy's family "everyone manifests a special kind of protective attitude toward him." Four years later, at a ceremonial dance, Grant began to chat casually with the young man after not having seen him for a while. At that point, Grant wrote in his fieldnotes, other Hopis "sort of moved in around him and I had a distinct impression of threat coming from them. It was very clear that they were strongly committed to protecting him. So I backed off. . . . I was able to continue observing, and I noted that his companions continuously formed a protective ring around him while he, in his turn, was quite flagrant in his behavior (what we would call a real 'queen')."[34]

Grant described the young man's speech patterns as part of this flagrancy, saying "He consistently uses 'female talk' forms in his speech. This is especially obvious in the frequent tongue smack (a kind of click formed by the middle of the tongue against the soft palate). Also, his inflection pattern is definitely female speech."[35] This use of women's speech patterns is often mentioned in the sources. In many Native American languages, female and male styles of speech are distinct, in some cases being practically different dialects. Elsie Clews Parsons saw this at

Zuni, where she noticed that a boy was using "the expressions of a girl, their exclamations and turns of speech."[36]

This female speaking style also carried over into singing events, a popular Indian form of entertainment. A nineteenth-century observer at a Navajo night singing reported that the *nadles* sang in falsetto.[37] Hupas today still have such singing roles for berdaches.[38] Even though the Cherokees did not have a recognized berdache status, I remember quite clearly how popular a male falsetto singer was at a 1973 traditional Cherokee songfest on the North Carolina reservation. He was from Oklahoma, quite openly effeminate, and without a doubt the star of the singing. While his sexuality was never mentioned, Indians of all ages were fawning over him the way elderly women do for Liberace or youth in the United States have done over androgynous rock stars like Little Richard, Michael Jackson, and Boy George.[39] Even today on the Crow reservation a *badé* will go for "Forty Nines" singings, in which the young people get together after ceremonies to sing love songs. He takes a leading role in these singings, and always stands with the women and sings a woman's role. People appreciate his singing, so he is always invited.[40]

Western psychiatrists seem most interested in finding a "cause" that will supposedly explain why a boy becomes effeminate. The motivating factor in much of this research seems to be to find a way to prevent such behavior. American Indians, in contrast, seem most interested in the social position of the berdache. Whether taking an active role in encouraging a child to become a berdache, or accepting it as a reflection of an innate spiritual character, Indian parents have no motive to discourage such a child. Seeing such gender variation as an acknowledged reality, they provide a recognized social alternative and simply admit that this is the way their son will be.

Families take a role in accepting a child as a berdache even today. One Lakota *winkte* now in his twenties remembers that when he was about twelve years old, "My mother explained *winkte* to me, and asked me if I was going to be that way. By then I had decided I was the way I was, so she never tried to change me since then."[41] Another says, "*Winktes* have to be born that way. People know that a person will become a *winkte* very early in his life. About age twelve, parents will take him to a ceremony to communicate with past *winktes* who had power, to verify if it is just a phase or a permanent thing for his lifetime. If the proper vision takes place, and communication with a past *winkte* is established, then everyone accepts him as a *winkte*."[42]

BERDACHES AS FAMILY MEMBERS, TEACHERS, AND PARENTS

The family of a berdache is more interested in accepting the contribution the child can offer to the family than in finding a supposed cause. Not being stigmatized and alienated, a berdache can offer positive advantages to a family. I stayed with an elderly berdache on the Omaha reservation, in his scrupulously clean house. Even though he lives by himself, he often has members of his extended family over for dinner. They bring their children, who appreciate the care and attention he shows to them. He has provided a home for most of his teenage nephews when their parents' house has gotten too crowded, and he has assisted various relatives financially with school expenses and helped them get established in a new job.

Jerry Baldy, a berdache on the Hupa reservation, says, "You live your life around your family. My aunt says, 'I'm counting on you.' What she means is that someone like me has a special responsibility to help care for the elders."[43] Likewise, a Navajo woman whose uncle was a well respected *nadle* healer says:

They are seen as very compassionate people, who care for their family a lot and help people. That's why they are healers. *Nadles* are also seen as being great with children, real Pied Pipers. Children love *nadles,* so parents are pleased if a *nadle* takes an interest in their child. One that I know is now a principal of a school on the reservation. . . . *Nadle* are not seen as an abstract group, like 'gay people,' but as a specific person, like 'my relative so-and-so.' People who help their family a lot are considered valuable members of the community."[44]

Thus it is in the context of individual family relations that much of the high status of berdaches must be evaluated. When family members know that one of their relatives is this type of person, and when they have positive cultural reinforcements that account for such individuals, then barriers are not placed inside the family. Without interference from outside religious groups claiming that there is something wrong with parents who raise such a child, unprejudiced family love can exert itself.

Berdaches are recognized as having a special talent in educating children. Part of this recognition is due to the berdache's reputation for high intelligence. A Kwakiutl chief in the 1930s said that a berdache he knew was the wisest man in the community: "All the stories from the beginning of the world he knows, and he makes songs."[45] Upon visiting the Yuki and Pomo reservation at Round Valley, California, in 1871–72, Stephen Powers met a Yuki *i-wa-musp* ("man-woman") and a Pomo *dass:* "They are set apart as a kind of order of priests or teachers. . . . [They] devote themselves to the instruction of the young by the narration of legends and moral tales . . . spending the whole time in rehearsing the tribal history in a sing-song monotone to all who choose to listen."[46]

Berdaches in the twentieth century have continued to be reputed as effective teachers of the young. In the 1930s ethnographer Ruth Landes met a Potawatomi young man who was a teacher in the primary school on the Kansas reservation. He was admired by the other Indians because "he loved to care for the children, to advise their parents, and to scrub the schoolhouse till it shone."[47] Landes's description could be used word for word to describe a *winkte* I met in 1982. He is recognized as the best teacher in the elementary school on his reservation. A very spiritual person, active in traditional Lakota religion, his great interest is his teaching. He loves children, and seems more animated when discussing his students than any other topic. He wants to have his own children someday. That will undoubtedly be possible through adoption.

A berdache can easily take a parental role, since adoption of children is commonly accepted in most American Indian societies. Adoption may involve orphaned children or children from overcrowded families. The ease with which children above their fifth year move from one household to another, often to distant kin and on their own initiative, is remarkable.

When children were captured in warfare they were almost always adopted as a family member by someone related to their captor. It was very seldom that children would be left to starve if their parents were killed. Believing that the essence of a person is the spiritual character rather than the physical body, Indian shamans of many tribes commonly invoked a ceremony that incorporated the spirit of a departed relative into the body of the captured child. By this means adopted individuals were accepted into the family as a full-fledged member, without any stigma that they were alien or not "really" a member of the family. This ease of adoption is also extended to non-Indians, which is why so many white captive children on the frontier became socialized as Indians and refused to return to white society if later recaptured.[48] In this context it was quite common for berdaches to adopt older children and adolescents, either as orphans or as captives.[49]

Even today berdaches are known to be very good with children. Terry Calling Eagle, a Lakota berdache, states, "I love children, and I used to worry that I would be alone without children. The Spirit said he would provide some. Later, some kids of drunks who did not care for them were brought to me by neighbors. The kids began spending more and more time here, so finally the parents asked me to adopt them."[50] After those children were raised, Terry was asked to adopt others. In all, he has raised seven orphan children, one of whom was living with him when I was there. This boy, a typical masculine seventeen-year-old, interacts comfortably with his *winkte* parent. After having been physically abused as a young child by alcoholic parents, he feels grateful for the stable, supportive atmosphere in his adoptive home. The two of them live in a close extended family household, along with Terry's mother, sister, and nephew. A male cousin also lives with them off and on, when he does not have an off-reservation job, and his grandmother's sister stays there part of the time. During the summer I was living there, various other relatives were coming and going in a rather bewildering pattern of changing residence. In this Lakota family at least, people seem almost as nomadic as they were in their days on horseback. In the midst of all this hubbub, however, Terry and his mother are the central persons of the household, looked up to by all.

Thus, an individual who in Western culture would be considered a misfit, an embarrassment to his family who would likely be thrown out of the household, is instead made central to the family. Since other relatives do not feel threatened, family disunity and conflict are avoided. The berdache is not expected to suppress his tendency for feminine behavior. Neither does he internalize a low self-image. He thus avoids the tendency of those considered deviant in Western culture to engage in self-destructive behavior. Berdaches who value their traditions do not tend to be alcoholic or suicidal, even in tribes where such problems are common. They are too valued by their families. In Native American lifestyles, seldom is anything thrown away unused—including people.[51] A Crow traditionalist says, "We don't waste people, the way white society does. Every person has their gift."[52]

ECONOMIC POSITION OF THE BERDACHE

Instead of being discarded, the unique energies of the berdache are put into productive labor, work of benefit to the family. As already noted, it is an interest in female pursuits that often indicates a developing berdache. For example, among the Yurok the first sign of a *wergern* proclivity is when a boy begins to show interest in weaving baskets and grinding acorn meal, as women do.[53] Or a boy might, as among the Maricopa and Yuma, enjoy playing with women's tools.[54] In most aboriginal Indian economies, there were two divisions of work roles. Men hunted and participated in warfare; while women did most of the work near the village. If a boy did not go out on the hunt or the warpath, and stayed near home, about the only thing to do besides craftswork was women's work. Boys who had from childhood stayed around the house and preferred women's work were expected to make a work decision by puberty.

Matilda Coxe Stevenson reported about the Zuni in 1901: "If they are to continue woman's work they must adopt woman's dress; and though the women of the family joke the fellow they are inclined to look upon him with favor, since it means that he will remain a member of the household and do almost double the work of a woman." Sometimes the men grumbled about the boy assuming berdache status, but this had more to do with the fact that they were losing a male from the men's work group, than with disrespect of the berdache role. Among the women's work group, female family members would take time off from their work, due to menstruation, pregnancy, or nursing of a baby. But the berdache "is ever ready for service, and is expected to perform the hardest labors of the female department." They were known as the finest potters and weavers in the pueblo. Stevenson noted that the Zuni *lhamana* named We'wha "most willingly took the harder work from others of the family. She would not permit idleness; all had to labor or receive an upbraiding from We'wha, and nothing was more dreaded than a scolding from her."[55]

Berdaches were known among the Winnebagos as doing women's tasks "better than any normal woman could perform them."[56] This has also been stated by informants from groups as diverse as the Hopi, Lakota, Mohave, Assiniboine, and Crow.[57] They were almost universally known to be hard workers, doing good beadwork, pottery, weaving, saddlemaking, and tanning, and being good providers for their family. Pete Dog Soldier, an elderly Lakota *winkte* who died in the 1960s, is remembered by other Indians as able to do "anything and everything better than a woman: cooking, crocheting, everything women do. He was neat and *very* clean."[58] In 1903 the Crow *badé* were reported as being famous for having the largest and best-decorated tipis, being the best cooks and sewers in the tribe, and being highly regarded "for their many charitable acts."[59] Berdaches among the Guajiro Indians of Venezuela are noted for the quality of their weaving.[60]

While they help the women in their work, berdaches also provide women company. Since the boy has already been in the girls' play group, he is socialized to feminine concerns and can offer psychological closeness. One Papago woman spoke fondly of a "man-woman" named Shining Evening, who "was very pleasant, always laughing and talking, and a good worker. She was so strong! She did not get tired grinding corn. . . . I found the man-woman very convenient."[61] The man-woman was a clever potter and basketmaker, and a tireless gatherer on plant-foraging expeditions. The women of a family appreciated such a productive member of their work group.[62] Among the Zapotecs "Women especially feel close to and trust nonrelated *ira' muxe*. They are often referred to and addressed as 'niña' (little girl) by women and seem to enjoy this form of address."[63]

Despite considerable variation in the institution among different cultures, every tribe with a recognized berdache status has reported the individual doing at least some women's work. Since some cultures do not emphasize berdache spirituality, anthropologists recently have stressed that taking a woman's occupational role is the most important aspect of defining berdachism.[64] Along with a nonmasculine character, this seems to be a universal characteristic of berdachism, and it denotes the important economic role of a berdache within the family.

Part of the berdaches' economic productivity is due to their freedom from child-care responsibilities. Without having an infant to nurse, berdaches could put all their efforts into production. But the high-quality work is also a result of rising to one's level of expectations. With religious or social ideas propounding the view that berdaches will be successful, this is a powerful inspiration for young berdaches to become so. Among the Zapotecs, for example, *ira' muxe* are believed to be the brightest, most gifted children. As a consequence, Zapotec parents value them as the best bet for education, and will keep them in school for a longer time. During her two decades of fieldwork there, Beverly Chiñas has observed that many of the *ira' muxe* do fulfill this image.[65] On the Plains, the spirit of Double Woman was associated with skill in craftwork, so a youth who saw a vision of her would be considered skilled as well.[66] A young woman who saw such a vision would be as highly respected as a berdache. To tell a woman that her craftwork is as good as a berdache's is not sexist but rather the highest compliment—a recognition that she and the berdache have had similar visions.[67]

Exceptional ability itself can be an indicator of supernatural power. The expectation of one contributes to the other. It is not clear as to what extent people value a berdache's crafts because they are physically superior, or because they carry some of the spiritual power of the maker. Likely it is a combination of both, but whatever the reason berdaches have a reputation for outstanding work. Explaining this reputation, a contemporary Lakota *winkte,* says simply, "I feel feminine, and enjoy doing women's things."[68]

Striving for Prestige

But more is involved than enjoyment. Whether helping to heal people through their shamanistic abilities, serving as teachers for the young, working hard for the well-being of their family, showing their generosity, or displaying their talents in superior craftwork, the theme that unites all of these endeavors is a striving for prestige.

As a male child the berdache is subjected to the standard male socialization that emphasizes competition for prestige. He may not demonstrate bravery in warfare or success in the hunt, the usual means for gaining masculine prestige. But instead of feeling defeated, and abandoning the effort for prestige, the berdache merely redirects it into other areas. If he does not wish to count coup (gather honors) as a warrior, he can still gain renown for spiritual, intellectual, and artistic skills. Moreover, the berdache role offers a way to gain notable material prosperity through the production of specialized crafts.[69] Because of the high valuation and prestige of women's craftwork products, a male who engages in such production need not accept a lower status. Berdaches in California might reap prosperous rewards thanks to the particular skills they possess. Tolowa berdache shamans (see plate 13) were the most prestigious curers of illnesses, and Yokuts *tongochim* prepared the dead for burial and were entitled to keep for themselves the property that was placed with the body.[70]

The economic opportunities for berdaches to gain wealth are especially evident for the Navajos. *Nadle,* unlike average men or women, can participate in economic activities that are open to both sexes. The only masculine activities in which they do not participate are warfare and hunting, but they do raise sheep. They direct the farming, supervising the other family members in planting and working the fields. *Nadle* also tan hides and make pottery, baskets, and woven goods. Since crafts production is restricted, and with their reputation as outstanding craft-workers, *nadle* products are always heavily in demand as trade goods. Beyond all this, because they are believed to be lucky in amassing wealth they usually act as the head of their family and have control of the disposal of all the family's property.[71]

With their opportunities for gaining wealth being greater than those of ordinary persons', it is easy to justify the belief that *nadle* ensure prosperity. In 1935 ethnographer W. W. Hill published an interview with a Navajo *nadle* named Kinipai. Before my own research, it was the most recent extensive quotation of a berdache's own words. As such it is a most valuable historical document. We can see the self-confidence and spirit of the berdache, as Kinipai told Hill:

A family that has a *nadle* born into it will be brought riches and success. . . . I have charge of everything that my family owns. I hope that I will be that way until I die. Riches do not just come to you; you have to pray for what you get. . . . My parents always took better care of me. . . . The family, after I grew up, always gave me the choice of whatever they had.[72]

While desire for material wealth cannot be seen as a cause for otherwise masculine boys becoming berdaches, it certainly does make it easier for both the nonmasculine boy and his family to accept his assumption of an alternative status.[73]

DEALING WITH THE UNUSUAL

Beyond the argument that berdachism reflects the standard male drive for prestige, there is a psychological factor involved in the berdache's striving for excellence. Atypical children, soon recognizing their difference from the usual person, easily absorb a negative self-image. As the huge caseload of U.S. psychiatric therapy testifies, severe damage can result from these feelings of deviance or inferiority. The way out of this self-hatred is either to deny any meaningful difference ("I am the same as you except for this one minor difference"), or to construct an appreciation for the gifts of one's uniqueness. Difference is transformed from "deviant" to "exceptional." The difference is emphasized, becoming a basis for respect rather than stigma. American Indian societies are able to utilize the talents of berdaches precisely because they offer prestige rewards beyond what would be available for the average person.

Having the best-decorated tipi or being noted for one's cleanliness and neatness is amazingly similar to the emphasis on personal looks, clothing style, and interior decoration in the contemporary urban gay subculture. Both trends manifest a sense of individual pride in oneself for doing well in a cultural system where one is not typical. The difference is that Anglo-American society and family structure gives only a grudging tolerance to the nonmasculine male, at best, while in American Indian cultures, to use the words of a Lakota, "If a *winkte* is in a family, that family would feel fortunate."[74] As an example of this attitude, Ruth Landes knew a Potawatomi berdache who was the son of highly traditional parents. "His mother, a noted shamaness, set the old-fashioned standard for him; his whole family appreciated him and encouraged him." The berdache was looked upon as "tradition's enshrinement of a unique personality, with admirable gifts."[75]

The position of the berdache in the extended family, and from that base into the community as a whole, varies of course depending on the personality and talent of particular individuals. But for the category as a whole, those cultures that recognize it generally accord it a respected status. This respect is clearly indicated by Matilda Coxe Stevenson, who described the family position of the Zuni *lhamana* named We'wha.

His strong character made his word law among both the men and the women with whom he associated. Though his wrath was dreaded by men as well as by women, he was beloved by all the children, to whom he was ever kind. . . .

He was always referred to by the tribe as "she"—it being their custom to speak of men who don woman's dress as if they were women. . . . She was perhaps the tallest person in Zuni: certainly the strongest, both mentally and physically. . . . She possessed an indomitable will and an insatiable thirst for knowledge. Her likes and dislikes were intense. She would risk anything to serve those she

loved, but toward those who crossed her path she was vindictive.
Though severe she was considered just.

In 1896 We'wha became seriously ill. Stevenson movingly described the reactions of the pueblo. From the moment people
realized that We'wha had heart disease, they remained with her
constantly. "The writer never before observed such attention as
every member of the family showed her." Despite their concern,
a few days later We'wha went into a coma and died.

Darkness and desolation entered the hearts of the mourners. . . .
We'wha's death was regarded as a calamity, and the remains lay in
state for an hour or more, during which time not only members of
the clans to which she was allied, but the rain priests and theurgists
and many others, including children, viewed them. When the blanket was finally closed, a fresh outburst of grief was heard. . . . [It
was] a death which caused universal regret and distress in Zuni.[76]

There are few documents like this one. Because it was written
by a person who had more than just a perfunctory acquaintance
with a berdache, Stevenson's text is all the more important.

Another ethnographer who talked with berdaches in depth
was W. W. Hill, and he also emphasized the extremely favorable
attitudes of families toward berdaches:

The family which counted a transvestite among its members or had a
hermaphrodite child born to them was considered by themselves and
everyone else as very fortunate. The success and wealth of such a
family was believed to be assured. Special care was taken in the rais-
ing of such children and they were afforded favoritism not shown to
other children of the family. As they grew older and assumed the
character of *nadle,* this solicitude and respect increased. . . . This respect verges almost on reverence in many cases.[77]

Hill quotes from several Navajo informants to illustrate these
attitudes:

They know everything. They can do both the work of a man and a
woman. I think when all the *nadle* are gone, that it will be the end of
the Navaho.

If there were no *nadle,* the country would change. They are responsible for all the wealth in the country. If there were no more left,

the horses, sheep, and Navaho would all go. They are leaders just like President Roosevelt. A *nadle* around the hogan will bring good luck and riches. They have charge of all the riches. It does a great deal for the country if you have *nadle* around.

You must respect a *nadle*. They are, somehow, sacred and holy.[78]

Spiritual justification, ceremonial roles, and a secure place in the economic and social life of the extended family combined to give berdaches a firm footing upon which to construct their lives and around which they could build a proud and unique identity.

4　Men, Women, and Others: The Gender Role of the Berdache

On his first voyage down the Mississippi River in the 1670s, the Jesuit Jacques Marquette was mystified by the fact that berdaches were treated with respect by other Indians. He wrote back to France, "I know not through what superstition some Illinois, as well as some Nadouessi, while still young, assume the garb of women, and retain it throughout their lives. There is some mystery in this, For they . . . glory in demeaning themselves to do everything that the women do."[1] Four decades later, another French missionary in French Canada reported that there were "men cowardly enough to live as women. . . . debasing themselves to all of women's occupations."[2] These Frenchmen were alarmed that men would "demean" and "debase" themselves to be like women. In the European view, such persons were giving up their male privilege by lowering themselves to the level of mere women. Why did this not similarly concern the Native Americans? How could berdaches be doing this, and still be regarded as "persons of consequence"?

We have to understand berdache gender status, especially their economic role in the family, as a reflection of the fact that women also were persons of consequence. Exceptions exist, mainly in areas where the majority of the food is supplied by male hunters or fishers, but American Indians offer some of the world's best examples of gender-egalitarian societies. Anthropologists have debated whether male dominance is universal, and while such dominance clearly exists in many parts of the world, most specialists in North American Indian studies emphasize that at least aboriginally many societies operated on a gender-equal basis. Native American women were (and are still, to a great extent) independent and self-reliant personalities, rather than subservient dependents. Traditionally, women had a high level of self-esteem for they knew that their family and band economically depended on them as much as or more than it did on men. They were centrally involved in the society's economy, controlling distribution of the food they grew or gathered.[3]

Since women had high status, there was no shame in a male taking on feminine characteristics. He was not giving up male privilege, or "debasing" himself to become like a woman, simply because the position of women was not inferior. It may be accurate to suggest that the status of berdaches in a society is directly related to the status of women. In societies with low status for women, a male who would want to give up his dominant position would be seen as crazy. But where women have high status, there is no lowering of social role for a male to move in a feminine direction. For example, among the Navajos, women have very high positions of respect, and this is reflected in the virtual deification of the *nadle*. The status and interests of nonmasculine people, whether female or male, are closely related.

Many cultures that recognize berdaches, the Keres Pueblos, for example, believe that masculine qualities are only half of ordinary humanness. But feminine qualities are seen as automatically encompassing the masculine as well as many other characteristics that go beyond the limits of masculinity. Consequently, there is a recognized enhanced status for those males who have the ability to transcend the limits of masculinity.[4] As we will see in chapter 11, women of many cultures have sporadically participated in activities normally associated with men, without leaving their female gender role. But for a male, it is not as easy to be feminine while remaining within the confines of the man's role. If a male wants to incorporate feminine aspects, he has to move beyond masculinity.

An important aspect of gender in American Indian societies is the performance of certain duties: hunting and warfare usually done by men, farming and gathering wild plants usually done by women. Though there might be considerable overlap and flexibility, the specialization of tasks by gender means that women and men are tied together in an interdependent system of reciprocity. A berdache would, especially in an economic sense, take on a role that was similar to that of women, but his prestige in women's work does not mean that he thereby "dominates" females by becoming a "superior woman."[5] After all, the berdache is not a woman. There has been much confusion on this matter because white observers often have not recognized the distinctions between the feminine and the nonmasculine, assuming instead that nonmasculinity automatically means femininity.

DIFFERENT FROM WOMEN

From American Indian perspectives, berdaches are not women, not even socially defined women. We can understand this by realizing that berdaches do certain things which women do not do, and vice versa. There are several aspects of berdachism that differ from the standard roles of women. In the first place, even though berdaches remain around the home and perform women's work, they are not much involved in infant care because they cannot breastfeed. Berdaches may be domestic, but it is economic involvement in home production rather than child care. They reserve their attention for older children and youths, in their capacity as teachers. Even when they adopt children, it is evidently older children. They are different from women, who spend much of their young adult years as nursing mothers of small children.

Berdaches have been noted as being physically different from women. In fact, in a number of instances their robust stature is emphasized. The Zuni We'wha was the tallest person in the pueblo.[6] Crow berdaches were reported as being "of large build" and "almost gigantic in stature," and a similar statement was made about a Potawatomi berdache.[7] A modern investigator had this to say about "a feminized Indian": "To me, his appearance is neuter, not feminine, effeminate, or masculine. He is tall and thin, with long straight black hair. . . . muscular, bony, and strong."[8]

The Spanish explorer Cabeza de Vaca, writing about Florida Indians around 1530, reported similar descriptions of the many berdaches he saw: "They are more corpulent than other men and taller; they bear very heavy burdens." De Vaca also noted that while these "effeminates" dressed like women and did the work of women, they also did hunting like men.[9] Another traveler among the Timucua Indians of Florida, a Frenchman in 1564 named René Goulaine de Laudonniére, wrote that there were many persons, whom he mistakenly called "hermaphrodites," who cared for the sick and infirm and carried heavy loads. Why these two duties were combined is suggested by an artist on the same expedition. Jacques Le Moyne de Morgues drew a sketch of berdaches and noted that they were quite common. "As they are strong," they carried the provisions when a chief went to war. They carried the dead for burial, and transported the sick on their shoulders so as to care for them until they got well. Le Moyne (see illustration) was impressed with their strength as well as their curing abilities.[10] This special role for berdaches was different from the usual role for women.

Sometimes berdaches participated directly in warfare, and were noted for their bravery. One Crow berdache was named Osh-Tisch, which means "Finds Them and Kills Them" (see plate 12). He got this name in 1876, when he turned warrior for that one day. He put on men's clothes and attacked a Lakota party in the Battle of the Rosebud, and was distinguished by his bravery.[11] Among the Osage, a successful warrior had a vision that enjoined him to become a berdache, which he did. But he loved warfare so much that he periodically put on men's clothes and led a raid.[12] While exceptional, this example does show that berdaches did not take on the status merely to avoid fighting. When engaged in raiding, however, they were expected to dress as men.

Another with a reputation for bravery was a Saulteaux (Chippeway) in Manitoba who was called Berdach by the French. In 1801 he was referred to by some Hudson's Bay Company traders as being the best runner among the Saulteaux. Years before, the traders were told, when a group of Lakotas attacked his band, he ordered the others to escape "without minding him, as he feared no danger. He then faced the enemy, and began to let fly his arrows." By doing this several times, Berdach successfully covered the retreat, thus keeping off a whole Lakota war party by himself until everyone else was safe. Berdach's feat of bravery, the traders remarked in their journal, was often recounted by the Indians.[13]

Berdaches would often be taken along on a hunting expedition, but usually not as a hunter. A French explorer in the Missouri Valley wrote in 1805, "If they are taken along, it is only to watch over the horses, to skin or carry the pelts of game that are killed, to carry the meat, cut the wood, light the fire, and, in the absence of women, to satisfy a brutal passion abhorrent to nature."[14] What applied to hunting parties applied to war parties also. A Lakota traditionalist recounts: "Most *winktes* did not go to war, but some did. My grandfather told me stories about how this *winkte* did the cooking, taking care of camp, and curing wounds of the warriors."[15] This also was a position for berdaches that was distinct from what a woman would do.

Especially among the Cheyennes, *he man eh* (berdaches) were closely associated with the warfare complex. When a raiding group was organized, one of them was asked to join. George Grinnell's informants told him: "Large war-parties rarely started without one or two of them. They were good company and fine talkers. When they went with war-parties they were well treated. They watched all that was being done, and in the fighting cared for the wounded."[16] Their presence on war parties was also desired because of their special spiritual powers. While *he man eh* had rejected the usual kind of male power, they had other kinds of power that might lead to good luck on the raid.[17]

When a successful Cheyenne war party returned to the village, the best scalps were given to the *he man eh*. They placed the scalps on poles and led the triumphant war party into the camp. That evening they led the village in the Scalp Dance. This was one of the major ceremonies of the Cheyennes. The entire village lined up in four rows, making a square: drummers and singers on the west, young men on the north, young women on the south, and older people on the east. Grinnell's informants noted, "The halfmen–halfwomen took their places in the middle of this square and were the managers of the dance. No one was allowed in the middle of the square except these persons."[18] Among the Papagos, berdaches played an important role in the dances commemorating the taking of scalps. This may have been a way of insulting the enemy scalps, by having a nonwarrior taunt them.[19]

In most tribes' social dances, women dance in one section and men dance in another. Berdaches usually dance in the women's section. This is true among the Navajos,[20] as well as the Lakotas. One informant told me, "Pete Dog Soldier always danced with the women. He danced at the head of the circle, leading the women."[21] This is also the case among the Creeks and Seminoles. Berdaches in those groups wear turtle-shell leg rattles worn by the women, and lead the female turtle-shell dancers.[22]

In other groups, however, there is variation. Among the Zapotecs, men do not dance at all, except for a rare dance like the *zandunga*. However, *ira' muxe* dance openly with the women and each other. This is considered very improper behavior for men, but is quite natural for *ira' muxe*.[23] In contrast to this, Omaha *mexoga* Pollack Parker (c. 1900–1943) was a member of the warrior society, and thus danced with men. He did not dance with the women.[24] In Zuni the *lhamana* moved back and forth between the male and the female dance lines,[25] perhaps signifying the between-the-sexes status of the berdache.

GO-BETWEENS FOR MEN AND WOMEN

Because of their in-between status, berdaches in many cultures serve as "Go-Betweens" for women and men. If a problem arises, a person will let a third party know this, and it is the social duty of the third party to go tell the other person in the dispute. The third party goes back and forth between the two until they have reached a settlement. Usually the settlement involves some sort of compromise, with perhaps some payment or favor being done. The Go-Between thus has an important negotiation role, similar in technique to a real estate agent in Western business practice. In trying to ensure that each side overcomes any resentment and feels satisfied by the settlement, a skillful Go-Between is a valuable community asset.[26] Because they can move freely between the women's and men's groups, berdaches are a natural Go-Between for disputes between the sexes. Navajo *nadle* are asked by married people to resolve spousal conflicts, and at least among the Omahas such services by *mexoga* are paid for.[27]

A Go-Between also performs services on joyous occasions. The Navajo, Omaha, and other cultures employ berdaches to facilitate budding romances between young women and men. Among the Lakota, the *winkte* is customarily the woman's cousin.[28] This role reached its highest development among the Cheyennes. At the end of the Scalp Dance, the *he man eh* who were directing the dance would match up all the unmarried young men with the young women. Cheyenne informant George Bent said "These halfmen-halfwomen . . . were very popular and especial favorites of young people, whether married or not, for they were noted matchmakers. They were fine love talkers. . . . When a young man wanted to send gifts for a young woman, one of these halfmen-halfwomen was sent to the girl's relatives to do the talking in making the marriage." They were valued in these efforts for their spiritual power as well. Hoebel's informants told him, "Young people like them because they possess the most powerful of all love medicines. A suitor who is able to get their help is fortunate indeed, for no girl can resist the power of their potions. They are especially sought out as intermediaries to lead the gift-laden horses to a girl's household when a marriage proposal is being made."[29]

BERDACHISM AND TRANSVESTISM

We can also see the Go-Between role reflected in the dress of berdaches. In many of the early sources berdaches are referred to as wearing women's clothes, and much of the anthropological writing refers to them as transvestites. This is not an accurate term to use for several reasons. First, there are instances in which men dressing as women were not berdaches. A few Midwestern tribes forced some men who behaved cowardly in battle to wear women's clothing as a mark of disgrace. These instances were not spiritually derived, and were not seen to be a reflection of the basic character of the man. In the Indian view this kind of transvestism had no relationship to berdachism.[30]

Second, if we define transvestism as dressing in the clothes of the opposite sex, then we find (in cases where the dress is explicitly described) that berdaches wore all women's clothing no more often than they wore a mixture of female and male dress. We have already seen that berdaches usually wore male clothes on those occasions when they participated in hunting or warfare, and in other cases they dressed practically depending on the activity in which they were involved. Navajo *nadle* dressed sometimes as men and sometimes as women, depending on their inclination and their marital status.[31]

Variation in clothing marked the berdache from childhood, when boys first began to show signs of femininity. In 1916 Elsie Clews Parsons reported a six-year-old feminine Zuni boy. In response to his femininity, his parents began to treat him differently. "He is still dressed as a male . . . but his shirt is of a considerably longer cut. . . . Around his neck is a bead necklace . . . not altogether commonplace for either little boys or girls. His haircut is the usual all round short cut for boys."[32] By dressing him distinctly, the parents were recognizing his unique personality, distinct from both boys and girls.

Margaret Mead described in detail an Indian youth, probably of the Omaha tribe, just at the time when he was making his berdachism explicit in terms of dress. She referred to the boy as a "congenital invert" who since childhood had showed "marked feminine physical traits." As he reached puberty, she remarked,

he began to specialize in women's occupations and to wear female underclothing, although he still affected the outer costume of a male. He carried in his pockets, however, a variety of rings and bangles such as were worn only by women. At dances in which the sexes danced separately, he would begin the evening dressed as a man and dancing with the men, and then, as if acting under some irresistible compulsion, he would begin to move closer and closer to the women, as he did so putting on one piece of jewelry after another. Finally a shawl would appear, and at the end of the evening he would be dressed as a berdache, a transvestite. The people were just beginning to speak of him as "she."[33]

Even though Mead refers to this boy's dress as making him "a transvestite," it is unclear from the description if he was still wearing men's pants after he put on the shawl. And even if he had completely dressed like a woman for the dance, we do not know if he always dressed that way in daily life.

The degree to which a berdache might dress in female clothing would vary. Some dressed completely as women, all the time. Pierre Liette, a French explorer who lived among the Illinois Indians from 1698 to 1702, wrote that berdaches "are girt with a piece of leather or cloth which envelops them from the belt to the knees, a thing all the women wear. Their hair is allowed to grow and is fastened behind the head. They are tattooed on their cheeks like the women and also on the breast and the arms, and they imitate their accent, which is different from that of the men. They omit nothing that can make them like women."[34] A Crow elder remembers the berdache named Osh-Tisch, who died about 1928, saying: "She dressed as a woman, and associated with women. She would not do men's dances, but stayed with the women."[35] Elsie Clews Parsons described a Zuni *lhamana* named Kasineli in 1916, saying "his dress was in every particular as far as I could see like a woman's."[36] And certainly, anyone who looks at the photographs of We'wha in the 1880s (see plate 10) would be hard pressed to tell much difference between his style of dress and that of a Zuni woman.[37]

On the other hand, there are some subtle differences. One cannot look at the Le Moyne sketches (see illustration) of the Timucuan berdaches without recognizing that they are men. And Cheyenne *he man eh* "usually dressed as old men."[38] Today, one Omaha *mexoga* dresses as a man, but is known by his relatives to wear women's underwear. His nephew, who had observed these undergarments in the wash and in the closet, asked his uncle about it. His uncle replied that he had been directed by a spirit to wear these clothes, and that if he did not wear at least one article of different clothing something bad would happen. Given this spiritual explanation, the nephew of course accepted his uncle's nonmasculine behavior.[39]

While whites would most likely notice a berdache when he was dressing in women's clothing, we cannot always trust their judgment that he was dressing just like a woman. There may have been subtle differences that whites would not recognize.

So even though I will argue that there have been changes over time in berdache patterns of dress, it is also possible that there were mixed styles earlier. As in other aspects of berdachism, there is much cultural and individual variation.

It could also be that a berdache sometimes dressed as a woman, in which case white writers would notice him, and at other times would dress like a man. Among Lakotas, *winktes* dress differently for ceremonials. One says: "Sacred pipe people [traditionalists] would not object if a *winkte* dresses as a woman in ceremonies. They would only see it as the *winkte* getting more spiritual power."[40] In ceremonials, *winktes* dance like women and wear an article or two of women's clothing, but otherwise dress as a man. In daily life, they mostly dress like a man.[41] Pete Dog Soldier, an elderly traditionalist *winkte* who died in the 1960s, is remembered as having worn a woman's breastplate, shawl, and undergarments, but always men's pants.[42]

This pattern of a mixture of both women's and men's clothing was very common. A nineteenth-century Kutenai male who was described as *stammiya,* "acts like a woman," was remembered as wearing "a woman's dress, below the bottom of which his masculine-type leggings were visible. He was described as a large, heavy-set person with a deep voice with which he attempted to imitate a woman's way of speaking." Among the Omahas, a *mexoga* named Richard Parker, who died about 1943, sometimes wore women's blouses and his hair in long braids. But since women's and men's hairstyles and clothing styles were not well known by non-Indians, Omahas feel that an outsider would not have been able to tell he was different.[43]

In preparation for ceremonial dancing, Terry Calling Eagle made a special costume that was purposefully distinct from either men's or women's clothing. An ethnographer observing him said he was dancing with the women and wearing his hair long like a woman, but that he was wearing "men's clothes."[44] Terry's view, that he was dressing differently, was seen by the anthropologist as men's clothing. Whites, trained to look at all clothing as either "women's clothing" or "men's clothing," are not always the best witnesses to observe what Indians may feel is distinct from either. Thus, we get ridiculous statements like this one from W. W. Hill about *nadle:* "Transvestites wear the garb of either sex."[45]

Modern berdaches emphasize that they dress in a way that is distinct from either sex. At my first meeting with Terry Calling Eagle in 1982, the words of Lame Deer came immediately to mind: "I wasn't even sure of whether I was talking to a man or to a woman."[46] Terry wears his hair long and pulled back in a ponytail, but this is a hairstyle that some Lakota men might wear. At the same time, it is the style of women. Similarly, he wears clothing that looks consciously designed to be unisex. His features and his whole bearing suggest androgyny rather than femininity per se.

The other aspect of this distinctiveness is its flamboyance. Zapotec *ira' muxe* "dress is more masculine than feminine but is distinct from either. On occasion some wear cosmetics and such feminine attire as high-heeled pumps, neither of which is used by Zapotec women."[47] If berdaches' dress is more exaggeratedly "feminine" than women's dress, is it really proper to call it feminine? The Klamath berdache named White Cindy was remembered from the 1890s as having "an abnormal love of color" that made her different from Klamath women, "even to the extent of being unusual in a tribe loving bright colors. She would wear a green and white striped skirt, a pink waist, and a hat brightly bedecked with brilliantly colored flowers. Two or three red or orange bandanas often graced her neck."[48] Perhaps flamboyance is too mild a word to use. Likewise, Michael One Feather remembers his feelings growing up on the reservation:

I always dressed differently. I never liked the clothes they [other people] wore. I always created my own clothes. I designed my clothes to be *very* flamboyant. I looked at magazines a lot to design my own clothes. Sometimes in the privacy of my own home I would dress like a girl. I knew that I looked like one. I used to get mistaken for a girl all the time when I was little. That intrigued me because I knew I could always use that as an asset later on in life. I knew that I did not look like the rest of the boys, and I was glad I did not look like them. I dyed my hair and curled it. It was different from either girls or boys—unique, that's what I wanted.[49]

For berdaches, the particular clothing one wears is less important than one's basic character, one's spirit. If we only listen to what Indian people say, we realize that "transvestite" is not an accurate description; the style of dress is less meaningful than the androgynous character. A Kwakiutl chief knew berdaches in his tribe who wore "women's earrings, and all kinds of women's brooches . . . and women's rings," but otherwise dressed like a man. In the chief's words, such a person "played the part of women but didn't dress like that. We call men like that 'Act Like a Woman.' One was a man from Quatsino, and the way he acts when he works is the way women do when they do anything. . . . The way his body acts is like a woman."[50] To put it simply, as Ronnie Loud Hawk says with a quiet assured dignity, "I accept my feminine nature as part of my being."[51] His nature, rather than his style of dress, is crucial to the understanding of berdachism.

BERDACHISM AND HERMAPHRODITISM

There is much controversy among anthropologists about the nature of the gender status of the berdache. Is it crossing from the male to the female ("gender crossing" or transsexual), a mixture of female and male traits, or the establishment of a third, alternative gender? The berdache tradition contains elements of each of these alternatives, which is why the scholarly debate is so lively. Not only are there variations between tribes, but among individuals as well. This is in keeping with American Indian tolerance for individual difference, but it makes for imprecise generalizations.

When asking traditionalist Indian people to define their word for berdache, certain phrases appear over and over. Among the Cheyenne, the most common description for *he man eh,* or *a-he-e ma' ne',* is "halfman-halfwoman." When I asked informants what that explanation meant, they said "a man who acts like and fits in like a woman" and "a man who does not like to do man things."[52] Among Lakotas, *winktes* are consistently described as "sacred people," "halfmen-halfwomen" and "half and half people."[53] If asked for clarification, they may use the word *hermaphrodite,* but their meaning is different from that of whites. If we analyze closely what they are saying, we can gain a more accurate definition of berdachism.

An elderly Lakota shaman typically defined *winkte* as "a half-man-halfwoman; a man who acts like a woman. He does not have breasts or female genitals, but is a hermaphrodite. It is his nature. He was born that way." This comment seems contradictory, in that it implies *winktes* do not have female sexual organs but are hermaphrodites. Because the term means different things to Indians than it does to whites, *hermaphrodite* is not a useful word.

Whites have believed that a person called "halfman-halfwoman" must have the physical attributes of both sexes. This shows the emphasis in the English language on the physical attributes of a person (skin color, sexual organs), and the limitations of English in acknowledging gender role variations. But American Indians see physical body parts as much less important than a person's spirit or character. So when Indians say a berdache is a "hermaphrodite, it is his nature," they are referring to the person's spiritual essence.[54]

Whenever there is clear physical evidence by bodily examination, the report is that berdaches are anatomically male. Stephen Powers, who surveyed California Indians in 1871–72, met a Yuki *i-wa-musp,* whom he had heard was a hermaphrodite. "At my instance the [government] agent exerted his authority and caused this being to be brought to headquarters and submitted to a medical examination. This revealed the fact that he was a human male without malformation." Matilda Coxe Stevenson recalled her mistake upon moving to Zuni, when she initially referred to *lhamana* as hermaphrodites. She was led into this mistake, she wrote, because the Indians would say, "She is a man." A respected Crow medicine man examined the body of Osh-Tisch when he died in 1929, and saw that the berdache had normal male genitalia.[55]

Though there are a few other questionable examples,[56] the Navajo is the main culture in which physical hermaphrodites are classified as *nadle,* along with berdaches. But even Navajos make a linguistic distinction between those born with ambiguous genitalia (the presence of fully developed genitalia of both sexes is extremely rare; more likely cases are males with very small penises, females with very large clitorises, and boys with undescended testicles),[57] and those who have normal genitals but whose behavior is androgynous. Navajos define hermaphrodites as "real *nadle*" and nonhermaphrodites as "those who pretend to be *nadle,*" but both inhabit the same gender category. Navajos are also the only tribe in which the same berdache terminology applies to morphological males and females.[58]

One might speculate that the reason the Navajos emphasize hermaphroditism is that their group's genetic code contains a tendency toward ambiguous genitalia. If families with a hermaphrodite do well financially, they would tend to have more children and thus pass along such a trait through the reproductivity of the sisters and brothers of the hermaphrodite. This hypothesis has not been investigated, but there are other examples of populations elsewhere with such tendencies.[59]

The Navajos, in using the word *nadle* for women, men, and hermaphrodites alike, are clearly an exception in North America.[60] Among most groups, the word *hermaphrodite* is used because it has been commonly used by whites. Used by Indians themselves, the word does not imply genital difference. For example, the traditionalist Omaha chief defines *mexoga* as "different, unusual, halfman-halfwoman. Then we called them hermaphrodites, but today they would be called homosexuals. Sometimes he was a full man, but at other times his other side would come out."[61] The Indian view emphasizes behavioral, not physical, traits. As a consequence, anthropologists since the 1950s have defined berdaches as persons of definite physiological sex, with hermaphrodites being distinguished as a separate group.[62]

Another difference between berdaches and hermaphrodites is that berdachism is not necessarily a permanent condition. Although most berdaches take on the role at puberty, and continue it for life, the exceptions to this rule further frustrate attempts to define berdachism. Since the status is usually seen as permanent, the community accepts it as such: "People take for granted they aren't going to change him, that's his life and they accept him." Still, there are cases where berdaches will change their status, to become like regular men.[63]

Sometimes a man known for his masculinity will change and become a berdache as an adult, like one Lakota man "who was a good bronc rider and a roughneck; after he got wounded in World War II, when he came back he had a vision and became a *winkte*. He was well regarded as a war hero, and also as a *winkte* he had a lot of respect from people. He helped people, liked children, and was well respected."[64] There is one *winkte* today on a Lakota reservation who goes in and out of the *winkte* role.[65] These unusual exceptions point out the strong sense of individualism in the berdache tradition, and the inherent problems in formulating blanket theories about berdaches' gender status.

BERDACHISM AND TRANSSEXUALISM

With so much variation, how do we define the gender role of the berdache? In 1955 Henry Angelino and Charles Shedd tried to provide a workable definition. They clarified once and for all that berdachism is different from · hermaphroditism and transvestism. But they confused things further by defining a berdache as an individual "who assumes the role and status of the opposite sex."[66] They had built on the analysis of Alfred Kroeber, who labeled berdaches "institutionalized women. . . . Born a male he became accepted as a woman socially."[67] This view has led recent theorists like Harriet Whitehead to characterize berdaches as "gender-crossers . . . becoming a member of the opposite sex." The analogy she finds for berdachism in our society is the transsexual, which she defines as a person who assumes "the behavior and public identity of the opposite sex." Whitehead calls the phenomenon "a psychological orientation in its own right, distinct from homosexuality."[68]

It is easy to see why scholars have moved in this direction. Many words that define berdache mention women; for example, the Hidatsa word *miati* translates as "to feel an involuntary inclination to act like a woman."[69] When reading definitions like this one, it is easy to make the assumption that berdachism is "crossing" the gender line from male to female, becoming a transsexual institutionally equivalent to a woman.

However, while berdaches certainly do women's work and

are nonmasculine in character, their social role is not the same as that of women's. In terms of their physical body, lack of involvement with nursing infants, special roles in warfare, participation in dances, status as Go-Betweens for women and men, variable dress, and ability to abandon berdache status, these males need to be seen as something other than the institutional equivalents of females.

The concept of a "transsexual" is a Western one, clearly linked with a medical procedure and based on the notion that there are two "opposite sexes." It is therefore not an apt description of berdaches. Within Western thought, with its numerous dichotomies of paired opposites, there is little tolerance for ambiguities outside of the categories of "women" and "men." As a result, people who are dissatisfied with their gender role will often feel that they have only one alternative, to *trans*fer themselves from one sex to the other. Many transsexuals, as products of our culture, make this transfer completely, by surgical reassignment and hormones. Many lead happier lives, once they do not feel that they are a "female trapped in a male body." But others do not make so happy an adjustment, and may feel no more comfortable as a woman than as a man. Their unhappiness, I would suggest, is the result of a restricted social value, which sees only two opposite possibilities.[70]

The Western notion of two opposite sexes is akin to the idea I grew up hearing in the South: that there were only two races and they were opposites. By this view, all the world is divided into black and white, and the only choice for a "mongrel" is to be assigned to one race or the other, or to try to "pass" for white. It was only when people began to be exposed to the larger reality of the world that they could challenge this notion. It is worth noting that many transsexuals may pass for women because there is no respected alternative to masculinity in this society. Bodily mutilation is a heavy price to pay for the ideology of biological determinism.

American Indian cultures, through the berdache tradition, do provide alternative gender roles. Indians have options not in terms of either/or, opposite categories, but in terms of various degrees along a continuum between masculine and feminine.

A MIXTURE OF FEMALE AND MALE AS AN ALTERNATIVE GENDER ROLE

In the Navajo language, *nadle* means "one who is transformed," and the individual would be addressed by male or female kin terms depending on whether she or he was wearing men's or women's clothing.[71] When W. W. Hill was interviewing the *nadle* in the 1930s, Kinipai preferred to be addressed as "she," but in the course of the interview sometimes referred to herself with male as well as the female terminology.[72] Among the Lakotas, a *winkte* may be referred to as "she" in some instances, as "he" in others, but "he-she" is also commonly used.[73] It is the mixture that is important, with categories less rigid and gender concepts more fluid. Just as berdaches can physically move freely between the women's group and the men's group,[74] so the lack of boundaries marks their gender status as well. They are mixing the attributes of both female and male, and adding alternative aspects that are unique to the berdache status.

Berdaches are seen as a distinct association. Among the nineteenth-century Crows, berdaches did not have a special ceremonial role, but they were respected as a social group. While they spent much of their time with women, they also had their own separate group within the village. They had their own tipis, and set them near each other in camp so that they could be together. They called each other "sister," and saw Osh-Tisch as their leader.[75] In 1889 the Crow reservation physician, A. B. Holder, interviewed a *badé,* who told him of a group of berdaches among the Gros Ventres, Lakotas, Flatheads, Nez Percés, Crows, and Shoshonis, who all associated together beyond their own tribe. Holder concluded, "There seems a species of fellowship among them." This separate status implies a third category, like the Crow translation for *badé:* "not man, not woman."[76]

Some anthropologists have seen this type of evidence as indicating that berdaches occupy a third gender. Beverly Chiñas concludes that among the Zapotecs *ira' muxe* are perceived as innately different: "not as either women or men but as *muxe,* i.e., male-female. I have referred to them as the third sex, which seems to reflect most accurately Zapotec reality." They do both women's and men's work, dress closer to the masculine manner, participate in religious ceremonials as men, but unlike men develop especially close friendships with women.[77]

Ethnographer Sue-Ellen Jacobs also rejects the concept of gender crossing, in favor of the term "third gender." Among the Tewa Pueblos, Jacobs's recent fieldwork has turned up interesting information about a berdache role, pronounced *kwih-doh* in men's speech[78] but spelled *quetho* by Jacobs. No one before Jacobs has published anything on the Tewa berdache, leading anthropologists to assume that such a role did not exist. *Quetho* are designated as a third gender, distinct from women and men. *Quetho* are identified quite young, as having "Special relationships to deities or supernatural forces; a mid-gender or androgynous personality with 'gentle' qualities prevailing; and resistance to full adolescent socialization into traditional men's or women's roles. . . . A *quetho* should be raised 'to be who they are.'" Tewa elders would not assign a male or female sex to *quetho,* and only became exasperated as Jacobs tried to get them to assign individuals on the basis of their genital anatomy.

On this basis she criticizes the definition of berdache offered by Charles Callender and Lee Kochems in 1983, which continues the Angelino and Shedd view that berdaches "assumed the dress, occupations, and behavior of the other sex."[79] By their definition, Jacobs argues, the *quetho* would be excluded from consideration because they did not dress like the opposite sex. Yet, she does see *quetho* as berdachism, and suggests that "We are still asking the wrong questions because in Euroamerican culture we have a difficult time accepting that there can be a genuinely conceptionalized third gender." Jacobs and I both feel that too much emphasis has been placed on style of dress and occupational choice, and not enough on the personality and character of the berdache.[80] I also feel that spirituality and sexuality are more important than recent writers suggest.

In what directions are berdache studies going with regard to gender status? Scholars now seem in agreement that berdachism is not a complete shift from man to woman, but is "a movement toward a somewhat intermediate status."[81] Callender and Kochems have now moved even further away from the "institutionalized woman" view, seeing it as a mixed-gender status that they call "men and not-men."[82] There are some continuing disagreements about berdache sexuality and about the survival of berdachism up to the present, but these are matters of degree rather than of kind. What is needed now is not more armchair theorizing, but more fieldwork in other reservations to get a clearer perspective of Indian peoples' thoughts.

Whether berdaches are seen as a third gender or as a mixture of female and male, with some distinctive elements added, there is perhaps no crucial difference. The Indian languages themselves are in a sense imprecise about this. For example, the Cree word for berdache, *ayekkwew*, can be translated as "neither man nor woman" or "man and woman."[83] If those languages are intentionally vague on this matter, perhaps we should not split hairs. Man-woman, halfman-halfwoman, notman-notwoman—all convey the same idea. In Manitoba in 1801, two Hudson's Bay Company traders were probably most accurate in not categorizing a berdache whom they had met, beyond saying that he was "a curious compound between a man and a woman."[84] The real problem that scholars have been facing is that there is no good label in the English language to communicate a complex concept like berdachism. Perhaps the closest synonym is *androgyne,* which at least incorporates both gendermixing and third gender concepts, as well as implying mystical and sexual ambiguity.

The fact that berdaches are not simply "institutionalized women" or "transsexuals" can be seen most clearly in their rite of passage into the afterlife. After the death of the Zuni *lhamana* We'wha in 1896, Matilda Coxe Stevenson beheld the family preparing We'wha for burial by dressing her in female clothes, but then pulling on a pair of white trousers over the legs, "the first male attire she had worn since she had adopted women's dress years ago." Carried thus for interment in a mixture of female and male clothes, the *lhamana* were always buried on the men's side of the cemetery.[85]

A Plains Cree berdache was named Piecuwiskwew because, according to Cree informants, Piecuw was a man's name and Iskwew was a woman's name—"half and half just like he was."

It was said that Piecuwiskwew died from wearing a dress that had been worn by a menstruating woman. He had been killed by the power of the woman's menstrual blood just as the Cree believed a man would have been. Only if he had been a woman would he not have been harmed. Piecuwiskwew straddled both the separated worlds of women and men. He was both female and male, but he was not entirely either.[86] The Lakota shaman Lame Deer recounted a conversation with a *winkte* who told him that "In the old days *winktes* . . . had a special hill where they were buried. I asked him when he died . . . what he would be in the spirit land, a man or a woman. He told me he would be both."[87]

DIFFERENT FROM BOTH MEN AND WOMEN

Berdaches get a special recognition in native society not because they become social females, but because they take a position between the genders. They serve a mediating function as Go-Between for women and men, in more than just a social sense. Because they are not considered the same as men or as women, their emphasized difference is a way of defining what women are, and what men are. Their androgyny, rather than threatening the gender system, is incorporated into it. Berdaches seem to symbolize the original unity of humans, their differentiation into separate genders, and the potential for reunification as well. Ironically, by violating gender norms, berdachism enhances the society's definition of what is woman and what is man.[88]

A metaphor for the berdache's position is seen in the Cheyenne Scalp Dance. It is no accident that in the dance, the *he man eh* moved in the middle of the square, circulating between the row of women and the row of men. Their position symbolizes their status as halfmen-halfwomen. Each of them had both a woman's name and a man's name, and "even their voices sounded between the voice of a man and that of a woman."[89] There may be feminine things about berdaches, but in the Indian view that does not make them women. Vincent White Cloud says: "*Winktes* talk in woman's dialect, using women's speech patterns. But they are different from both men and women."[90] Ronnie Loud Hawk, a Lakota berdache, explains, "I would be terribly scared to be a man or a woman. . . . *Winktes* are two spirits, man and woman, combined into one spirit."[91]

Terry Calling Eagle reiterates that his character *is* his spirit. That is what ties his whole gender role into a spiritual realm. It is not a case of berdaches assuming the status because of childhood interests versus having a vision, or doing women's work versus being a sacred mediator, or dressing differently versus being sexually involved with men. It is all of these things interacting, as part of their basic androgynous character. One contributes to the other; they are not in opposition or hierarchically related. In taking an *etic* viewpoint, a perspective outside of the culture, most recent theorists on the subject have ignored the *emic* perspective, the Indians' own perceptions. As I have reiterated thus far in this book, we need to listen to the words of the berdaches themselves. Only then do we realize that understanding the spiritual dimension is crucial to understanding the position of the berdache in society. Only after I lived with him for a month did Terry Calling Eagle agree to tell me his personal story. This is what he said:

I have always filled a *winkte* role. I was just born this way, ever since I can remember. When I was eight I saw a vision, of a person with long grey hair and with many ornaments on, standing by my bed. I asked if he was female or male, and he said "both." He said he would walk with me for the rest of my life. His spirit would always be with me. I told my grandfather, who said not to be afraid of spirits, because they have good powers. A year later, the vision appeared again, and told me he would give me great powers. He said his body was man's, but his spirit was woman's. He told me the Great Spirit made people like me to be of help to other people.

I told my grandfather the name of the spirit, and Grandfather said it was a highly respected *winkte* who lived long ago. He explained *winkte* to me and said, "It won't be easy growing up, because you will be different from others. But the spirit will help you, if you pray and do the sweat." The spirit has continued to contact me throughout my life. If I practice the *winkte* role seriously, then people will respect me.[92]

A Lakota traditionalist explains this respect as arising from the vague and undefined gender role that berdaches fill in the social order: "It is easy to pick out a *winkte*. They act and talk like women, but are really half and half. . . . *Winkte* is different, neither man nor woman. It is a third group, different from either men or women. That is why *winkte* is regarded as sacred. Only the Great Spirit, Wakan Tanka, can explain it, so we accept it."[93]

5   The Spirit and the Flesh: Sexual Aspects of the Berdache Tradition

Another important aspect of the berdache tradition involves sexual behavior. Berdaches are recognized partly by their sexual contacts with men. This is one of the first things about them that European explorers noticed. There is an amazing degree of uniformity in the explorers' reports from various areas of the Americas. The Spanish chronicler Oviedo reported about the aboriginal peoples of Middle and South America: "Very common among the Indians in many parts is the nefarious sin against nature. Even in public the Indians who are headmen or principal who sin in this way have youths with whom they use this accursed sin, and those consenting youths as soon as they fall into this guilt wear 'naguas' [skirts] like women."[1] For the Lache Indians of Colombia, Fernandez de Piedrahita, explaining that the men preferred a berdache over a woman, concluded that "the abomination of sodomy was freely permitted."[2]

In North America, Pedro Fages, the Spanish colonial governor in California, wrote about berdaches among the natives there:

I have substantial evidence that those Indian men who, both here and farther inland, are observed in the dress, clothing, and character of women—there being two or three such in each village—pass as sodomites by profession (it being confirmed that all these Indians are much addicted to this abominable vice) and permit the heathen to practice the execrable, unnatural abuse of their bodies. They are called *joyas,* and are held in great esteem.[3]

Many of the European observers were mystified by these practices, saying only that the American Indian tribes "are strangely given to sodomy."[4] One imagines the Indians wondering why the European men were strangely restricted in their sexual behavior to women only. On La Salle's exploration in the upper Mississippi Valley in the 1690s, Henri de Tonti described Illinois men as being sexual toward women "with excess, and boys above women, so that [those boys] become by that horrid vice, very effeminate."[5]

Likewise, a priest with La Salle characterized the Indian men as "lewd, even unnaturally so, having boys dressed as women, destined for infamous purposes." Berdaches, he said, were numerous.[6] The French explorer Pierre Liette, after four years living among the Illinois Indians, concluded in 1702 that "The sin of sodomy prevails more among them than in any other nation." Since the young men were not satisfied in their passions by women alone, Liette wrote, "There are men who are bred for this purpose from their childhood. . . . There are men sufficiently embruted to have dealings with them."[7]

Two decades later, a Jesuit missionary wrote that berdaches among the Indians of the Mississippi Valley "abandon themselves to the most infamous passions." He declared: "Effeminacy and lewdness were carried to the greatest excess in those parts; men were seen to wear the dress of women without a blush, and to debase themselves so as to perform those occupations which are most peculiar to the [female] sex, from whence followed a corruption of morals past all expression; it was pretended that this custom comes from . . . religion. . . . If the custom I speak of had its beginning in the spirit, it has ended in the flesh."[8] Native Americans, of course, saw no opposition between matters of the spirit and of the flesh.

While there is much variation in sexuality across Indian cultures, we can draw certain conclusions. First, berdaches usually participate in sex with men, but homosexual acts are not limited to berdaches. Second, sexuality in many Native American societies is not seen as solely for the purpose of reproduction, and is not restricted by the institution of marriage. It is instead conceived as a gift from the spirit world, to be enjoyed and appreciated. In a society without many cultural proscriptions repressing human sexual variations, there is an attitude of comparative casualness regarding sexuality. What Ruth Underhill wrote about Papago sexual attitudes applies to many groups: "There was considerably less scope for sexual offenses than in modern society and a man, particularly, had a great deal of freedom."[9] Stigmatizing people because of their sexual behavior, or restricting people's choices generally, is not seen as a valid function of society. Personal freedom is too highly regarded for such an approach to exist.

How such a society operates is best seen by looking at traditional Mohave culture as an example. This Colorado River people's aboriginal heritage was explored by ethnographer George Devereux, who lived among them in the 1930s. While Devereux's writings are controversial to some anthropologists, contemporary Mohaves who know their traditions tell me that what he had to say about sexuality is accurate.[10] Devereux concluded that the Mohave have an "easy" culture, providing "a rational, supportive, lenient and flexible upbringing" for children. This easygoing pattern of child rearing does not of course entirely eliminate domestic conflicts or psychological stress, but Devereux found that it does diminish the incidence and severity of mental illness.[11]

The Mohave attitude toward sexuality fits in with this carefree way of life. Devereux noted that "Mohave sex-life is entirely untrammelled by social restraint." The people felt that sexual activity was an enjoyable and humorous sport, a gift from nature to be freely indulged. Without social restrictions, and hearing the incessant sexual talk of adults, Mohave children grew up with an adventuresome attitude toward sex. Young children remained completely naked, and boys did not begin to wear clothing until puberty. Among boys, urinating competitions were a favorite game, as were contests to see who could reach orgasm most quickly by masturbating. Casual same-sex relations from early childhood were frequent, and "there is little or no objection to homosexuality among the Mohave."[12]

Though the ease of sexual experimentation, with both sexes, was enjoyed in a lighthearted way, Devereux wrote, "Even the most casual coitus implied, by definition, also an involvement of the 'soul': body, cohabiting with body and soul with soul. . . . Many children cohabited with each other and even with adults long before puberty; the [nonsexual] latency period was conspicuous by its absence. Children were much loved, brought up permissively, and looked after at once generously and lackadaisically." Children spent their prepubertal years exploring their environment with their age mates, playing, swimming, indulging in sexual play and in sex itself. Because the society placed a high value on kindness to children, the Mohave child learned to like and trust everyone. Children interacted, sexually and otherwise, with a number of people of different ages, and did not restrict themselves to an "overintense and exclusive emotional attachment" to a single person. Devereux wrote, "This explains why the adult Mohave is so highly 'available,' both sexually and for friendship."[13] Sexual patterns tell much about the shape of the society in general. The Mohaves' casual attitude toward sexual variance reflects their general carefree and freedom-loving attitude toward life. In such an atmosphere, same-sex relations can take place in an open manner.

This is especially notable with regard to children, whose sexual play was seen as an important element in growing up and learning adult roles. The adult attitude toward a child's sexual experimentation was more likely to be one of amusement rather than alarm. Most males in many different tribes probably had experience with same-sex behavior beginning in childhood.[14] Richard Grant, an ethnographer among the Hopi Indians in the 1970s, reports that even today informants told him, "Everyone considers homosexual behavior normal during adolescence and nearly all boys form special bonds which include sexual behavior. It is expected that all will 'grow out of it,' however, so that by adulthood marriage and the production of children will occur." But until they reach their twenties, males might participate in this form of homosexuality without social disapproval.[15]

Among the seventeenth-century Mayas, these homosexual relationships among boys and young men were institutionalized. The Franciscan friar Juan de Torquemada, in Guatemala before 1615, wrote of the Mayas telling him a story of a god who came down to earth and taught the males how to have sex with each other: "Convinced therefore that it was not a sin, the custom started among parents of giving a boy to their young son, to have him for a woman and to use him as a woman; from that also began the law that if anyone approached the boy [sexually], they were ordered to pay for it, punishing them with the same penalties as those breaking the condition of a marriage."[16]

This custom of an adolescent having a younger boy as a "wife" negates the idea of homosexuality being "abnormal," simply because it was normal for that culture. The norm was for a boy to be a boy-wife in his youth, then to graduate in the teenage years to being a husband of a younger boy, and then in his twenties to get married to a woman. This custom also shows that the inclination of many if not most males is—in the absence of social taboos—to interact sexually with both males and females during at least part of their lifetime.

Among the Zapotecs of Mexico, homosexual behavior among males is common for all age groups. Since it is so common, the sexual behavior itself is not a means of classifying people. Only the nonmasculine *ira' muxe* are seen as different. A masculine man may have sex with *ira' muxe,* another masculine man, or a boy, and none of this will mark him as deviant. Boys commonly become sexually active with men during early puberty if not earlier.[17] Though they have been having sex with other males, when they are between ages twenty and thirty, masculine men almost always marry women and have children. But gossip suggests that some continue to have sexual experiences with males even after they are married. Such a pattern is not too different from that of married men who are completely heterosexual, since they will often have an illicit relationship with a female.[18]

Similarly, among traditionalist Navajos, persons who are married do not experience much limitation on their sexual and affectional life with other people, of whichever sex. Marriages traditionally are primarily economic arrangements, so they are not expected to fill all of one's sexual desires. The whole emphasis of Navajo culture is to provide all persons independence in making decisions about their own lives.[19]

MAN-MAN HOMOSEXUAL BEHAVIOR

A person did not restrict close bonding to her or his marriage partner. In fact, among both women and men, individuals in American Indian cultures generally were emotionally closer to those of their own gender than to the other. Among men, this commonly took the form of an especially warm friendship between two males. A nineteenth-century army officer who studied Indian customs closely reported on these "brothers by adoption." Speaking of Arapaho male pairs, he stated: "They really seem to 'fall in love' with men; and I have known this affectionate interest to live for years." The union of two men was often publicly recognized in a Friendship Dance that they would do together.[20]

One of these friendships among Lakotas was described by Francis Parkman, who met the two men during his journey on the Oregon Trail in 1846. They were, he wrote, "inseparable; they ate, slept, and hunted together, and shared with one another almost all that they possessed. If there be anything that deserves to be called romantic in the Indian character, it is to be sought for in friendships such as this, which are common among many of the prairie tribes."[21]

This is not to suggest that these special friendships should be equated with homosexuality. The emphasis is on a close emotional bond, which might well be nonsexual in many of these friendships. But for those males who feel erotic attraction for another male, these recognized relationships provide a natural place for homosexual behavior to occur. The sexual behavior would not be publicly mentioned, but as reported among the Yumas during the 1920s, "Casual secret homosexuality among both women and men is well known. The latter is probably more common. This is not considered objectionable."[22]

In the event that a man is known to have been the passive partner in sex with another man, this has no effect on his gender identity. As long as he retains his masculine personality, he will not be considered a berdache.[23] White frontiersmen even reported being sexually approached by Indian warriors; this expression was in public and had no impact on the attitudes of other Indians toward these warriors.[24] After a lifetime of direct study interviewing traditionalist Indians of various tribes, anthropologist Omer Stewart concludes, "My impression is that the American Indians were fairly unconcerned one way or the other regarding homosexual behavior."[25]

Even in cultures without a recognized berdache status, homosexual behavior may occur without stigma. Among both the

Kaskas and the Ingalik, for example, men sometimes engaged in anal intercourse, though avoiding oral-genital sex acts.[26] It is important to point out that same-sex eroticism is not limited to the berdache role. When I was living on reservations in the Dakotas, several masculine Lakota men made sexual advances to me. They clearly wanted to take the active role. I asked each one if this homosexual involvement meant that he was a *winkte*. Each man seemed surprised by my question. They answered in the negative, explaining that *winkte* is defined by androgyny, which they are not. Since they did not consider me to be a *winkte*, they were interacting as one male to another.

Yet it is on the berdache that Indian male-male sexuality is mainly focused. Because traditional cultures assume that androgynous males are homosexual, berdaches become the most visible practitioners of that behavior. For example, in the Lakota language the word for male-male anal intercourse (regardless of the participants) is *winktepi*, showing Lakotas' close association between homosexual behavior and berdachism.[27]

BERDACHE SEXUAL BEHAVIOR AND THE INCEST TABOO

Interestingly, most tribes (but not all) do not see it as proper behavior for two berdaches to have sex with each other. Among Lakotas, while masculine men might have sex with each other in secret, berdaches never do. A Lakota berdache states, "'Homosexuals' are two he-men who live together as a couple. That is not done here; it is an effeminate and a he-man." I asked him if the man having sex with a berdache could be gay-identified, and he explained that whether or not the man was exclusively homosexual does not matter. What matters is that the man must be masculine. It is the character difference, the gender identity, that is important in establishing a relationship.

Because of a sense of sameness, which operates like a family relation, for a berdache to have sex with another berdache is like incest. Asked about sex with another like himself, a Pueblo berdache "regards the idea as laughable." He does not look down on androgynous males, but he thinks of them indulgently as "sisters."[28] The incest taboo operates to restrict sexual relations between males in the same way that it does heterosexually; rather than proscribing all homosexual behavior, this taboo restricts sexual relations to persons outside of one's kin group. Berdaches, with their sense of sisterhood, are in essence a fictive kin group.

All societies are to some degree exogamous; that is, they specify that sexual behavior should occur outside the defined family group. While modern industrial society specifies exogamy only with respect to the nuclear family of parents, children, and siblings, many American Indian societies extend incest rules to a much broader network of kin. By expecting people to marry and form affectional relationships with other people outside the kin-group, additional "in-laws" become allied. The number of "kin," upon whom one can call for help, is increased.

Some of the supposed condemnation of berdaches in the anthropology literature is in reality a statement about this incest taboo. In this context we can understand an instance of a Santee berdache who was exiled from his village. Some anthropologists have cited this text as evidence of negative attitudes toward homosexuality, but it is not that at all. Ruth Landes recorded the story of a *winkta* who had been accepted in his village without condemnation until he attempted to seduce several of the men in his village. The people were so upset by this that they held a formal ceremony, exiling the *winkta* for life. This is a very severe penalty, which to Western eyes seems to be a condemnation of homosexuality.

Yet, in this case the *winkta* moved to a neighboring Santee village, where he was freely accepted and the men were happy to partake of his "hospitality." Why was the reaction of the two villages so different? It is important to note that each village was made up of persons in a single clan. Since clans were exogamous among the Santees, it was forbidden for anyone to have sex with another person in their clan. This exile is not evidence of anti-homosexual feelings, but of the *winkta*'s violation of the incest taboo. The men of his own village were like brothers, and so the *winkta* was treated no differently than a man who attempted sex with his sisters. The people of the other village were of a different clan, and therefore were acceptable marriage partners, so it violated no incest taboo for them to indulge in sex with the *winkta*.[29] Rather than reflecting opposition to homosexuality, this exile demonstrates its acceptance into the sexual system.

Likewise, among the Navajo, marriage rules for a *nadle* are exactly the same as for heterosexual marriage. One cannot marry a person from the same clan as one's father or mother, or from the same clan as any of their parents. To do so would be seen as bringing harm on oneself. In traditional Navajo culture, marriages were often set up as economic arrangements by the two families. In this case, it was common that one might have sexual affairs outside of the marriage. Clan rules of exogamy apply also for casual affairs, for *nadle* as well as heterosexual couplings, but sometimes those rules are ignored in the case of casual sexuality. The point is that *nadle* sexual behavior is integrated as a part of the sexual system, with the same rules applying.[30] It is striking that most anthropologists who have written about berdachism did not ask about the kinship relations of the berdache's partners. David Greenberg suggests that an ethnocentric view of homosexuality as psychotic prevented some of these ethnographers from examining the normative structures of homosexual relationships in a culture that does not stigmatize it.[31]

BERDACHE SEXUAL TECHNIQUES

The association made by the Europeans between androgyny and what they called "sodomy" is also made by American Indians. The difference is that the Indian view does not have the negativism evident in European accounts. What many Native American societies try to do is regulate same-sex relations by focusing them on the berdache rather than outrightly prohibiting them to all males. While casual same-sex behavior might still occur between masculine men, the society puts pressure on individuals (to a greater or lesser extent) to follow the accepted, institutionalized form. When men desire male-male sex, they are encouraged to have it with a berdache. The emphasis in traditional culture is on homosexual behavior that in a social sense is not homosexual; it is most accurately described as *heterogender*. The berdache and his male partner do not occupy the same recognized gender status.

These heterogender roles are clarified by looking at the sexual techniques of berdaches and their partners. But gaining accurate knowledge about specific sexual practices is difficult, given the reticence of many Euroamericans on this matter. Many of the sources go no further than vaguely referring to the "heinous crime against nature," "perverted sin," or "unnatural acts." Early anthropologists, who would have been able to get more uninhibited statements from traditionalist Indians, often were reluctant to ask specifics. Alice Fletcher, for example, writing in the late nineteenth century on the Lakota berdache, referred only briefly to sexual behavior, saying nothing more specific than that *winktes* "become subject to gross actions."[32]

On those rare occasions when ethnographers did gather specific information about sex acts, we find that native languages have special terms for lovemaking between males, and the terms used for berdaches are not the same as those used for man-woman sex. For example, the fact that the Lakotas have a special term for male-male intercourse, *winktepi,* is further evidence that berdaches are not simply institutionalized women.

Fellatio is sometimes among the sexual practices of berdaches. Among the Crow Indians in the 1880s, Dr. A. B. Holder, the reservation physician, knew five *badé*. He found out that they produced "sexual orgasm by taking the male organ of the active party in the[ir] lips. . . . Of all the many varieties of sexual perversion, this, it seems to me, is the most debased that could be conceived of."[33] Whether or not this was the only technique among the Crows is unclear, but a Crow berdache in 1982 told me that performing fellatio is his favored sex practice. Among the Mohaves, fellatio is popular with heterosexual couples as well, so the fact that the *alyha* performs fellatio on his partner does not make him stand out as different.[34]

Sometimes there is an exchange of roles in sexual behavior. A Lakota man heard stories from his grandfather, telling him that when a *winkte* has sex with a man, it was usually the *winkte* performing oral sex on the man or being the insertee in anal sex. But sometimes they would reverse roles, and the man would take the passive position. This would be kept private between them, but it did occur. A Hupa berdache says of his partners, "As far as it was publicly known, he was the man. But in bed there was an exchange of roles. They have to keep an image as masculine, so they always ask me not to tell anybody." A Haliwa-Saponi male who plays the passive role in sex told me that the men of his community come to him wanting to take the active role. But there is a phrase that they use—"Everybody wants to wear an apron sometimes"—which signifies when the man wants to be in the passive position. It has been his experience that practically every macho man with whom he has established a relationship will wish to take the passive role at times, but only after the man trusts the berdache not to reveal this fact.

Still, it is clear that the usual sexual behavior of the berdache is to take the insertee position in anal intercourse. Given this preference, it is even more understandable why two berdaches would not have sex with each other. At the beginning of the century, Alfred Kroeber wrote about a Cheyenne berdache who lived and dressed like a woman but "had the voice and genitals of a man." "She" was known to have sexual intercourse with men "by lying on her back and putting her penis on her stomach, permitting access into her anus."[35]

The most dependable sources on sexual techniques are of course berdaches and their mates. George Devereux interviewed several Mohaves who had had sex with berdaches. The *alyhas'* favored sexual act was anal intercourse performed on them. They had erections during intercourse, but resented it if their partner touched their erect penis. Informants told Devereux that intercourse with an *alyha* is surrounded by an etiquette to which the partner had better conform, or else the man could get into all sorts of trouble. Kuwal, a Mohave man who had had several *alyha* as wives, said that they insisted that their penis be referred to as a cunnus (clitoris). He spoke freely and without embarrassment about their sexual behavior:

You may play with the penis of your wife when it is flaccid. I often did it, saying "Your cunnus is so nice and big and your pubic hair is nice and soft to touch." Then my alyha wife would loll about, giggling happily like this "hhh." She was very much pleased with herself and me. She liked to be told about her cunnus. When *alyha* get an erection, it embarrasses them, because the penis sticks out between the loose fibers of the bark-skirt. They used to have erections when we had intercourse. Then I would put my arm about them and play with the erect penis, even though they hated it. I was careful not to laugh aloud, but I chuckled inwardly. At the pitch of intercourse the *alyha* ejaculate. . . . I never dared touch the penis in erection, except during intercourse. You'd court death otherwise, because they would get violent if you play with their erect penis too much.[36]

With the Mohaves having such a strong desire for humor, they would kid the berdaches about these erections. Devereux quoted a Mohave story: "A certain man passing by the house of an *alyha* said to him in jest, 'How is your penis today?' 'Not penis, cunnus,' replied the *alyha* angrily. 'Well then, how big is your cunnus?' the man replied, using the word 'erection' instead of 'big.' The *alyha* picked up a club and for one or two weeks tried to assault the man whenever he saw him."[37]

Another man who freely reported sex with a berdache was a Kwakiutl chief interviewed in the 1930s. He remembered several berdaches, only one of whom wore women's clothing. The one that he knew best he first met in the 1880s when he was an unmarried young man. Upon seeing him, the berdache said "You, young fellow, I'm going to have you for my sweetheart." Later on, the berdache asked him to come visit her at her house: "When I went there, she caught hold of me, and she throwed me right into her bed. My, she was strong—awful strong! . . . She opened her legs and pulled me in, taking hold of my pecker and putting it in. I didn't work; she done all the work." Having enjoyed the experience, the next time he saw her "I called her to come to my bed and lie with me." But she refused him that time. Nevertheless, they did get back together for sex on later occasions, and he described his attempts to touch the berdache's penis: "While I was laying with her, I feel for her privates, but she just take my hand and squeeze it until I couldn't move my hand." The other men told him she did the same with them.[38]

These statements accord with my own fieldwork. A number of Lakota *winktes* confided to me that the only sexual role they have ever taken is in passive anal intercourse with a man. They have never had sex with a woman, and have never taken an inserter role in sex with a man. They do not generally care much for oral sex, and have no desire to do anything other than have a man enter them anally. They will sometimes have orgasms from the excitement of this act, but even if they do not they told me that they will often feel that they have had "an internal orgasm." Men who have been their sexual partners told me that berdaches do not wish to have their penis touched, or to take the inserter role in anal intercourse even if the masculine partner wants to exchange roles.

Berdache Promiscuity

Boys who later became berdaches often began their sexual experiences before puberty. Feminine-acting boys are sought out for sex by older masculine boys. One androgynous male from a Southwestern reservation remembers that after his seventh birthday older boys expressed their attraction to him and to other boys like himself. He was participating in sex with other males well before puberty, always taking "the feminine role." After puberty he would get erections and ejaculate solely from the pleasure of being anally penetrated.[39] Likewise, a Crow Indian told me that when he was a young student at boarding school, the other Indian boys approached him secretly at night for sex. Though he enjoyed the sex, he did not like the furtive and impersonal nature of these encounters.

Others have more pleasant memories, of an ongoing relationship. A Lakota *winkte* states matter-of-factly that he began to be sexually active when he was eight years old, when he had an affair with a forty-year-old man. "Since he was good to me and for me, it was considered by my family to be okay and my own private business—no one else's." Another recalls that when he was eight years old his uncle, who was in his thirties, would give him body rubs in which he would rub the boy's genitals. "I never knew if it was right or wrong. I was too afraid to know what was happening. They'd call it molestation today, but I don't think it had any bad impact on me in the long run one way or the other. There was no harm done. It intrigued me that I could do this. And then my feelings started to awaken inside of me as I got older and I began sexual intercourse with men."

When the same person was ten, two heterosexual Indian men

picked him up when he was hitchhiking, got him intoxicated, and raped him. Despite this bad experience, he went on to have sex with a number of men: "I was never connected to women, never any sexual attraction at all. . . . I knew I liked the male sex, but I didn't like it to be that intense. I didn't like the rape. But then at age ten I began a whole string of involvements in sex, from ministers to tribal presidents to government officials. Mostly Indian, but white as well. I never was attracted to someone my age." Sometimes he took the initiative in beginning an affair, and other times it was the man. These experiences were just sexual involvements rather than a full-time relationship, since most of the men were married. This pattern continued until he was sixteen, at which time he met a thirty-two-year-old masculine construction worker, and they became lovers for six years.

Upon reaching adulthood, some berdaches would themselves take adolescent boys as lovers. These would be masculine boys and young men who were unmarried, who otherwise did not have a socially accepted sexual outlet. One Shoshone *ma ai'pots* was married to two young men at the same time, sleeping with each on alternate nights, while another *ma ai'pots* (who owned a large herd of horses) always had a group of half a dozen teenage boys who would stay with him.[40] Omer Stewart observed a berdache at Zuni in 1939: "He wore woman's dress and arranged his hair in the style of women, and was known in the community as providing an attractive hangout for young men. . . . The Indian governor of Zuni and other members of the community seemed to accept the berdache without criticism, although there was some joking and laughing about his ability to attract the young men to his home."[41]

Sex with Married Men

Berdaches seem to have had no problem attracting partners, including married men. There were certain times when sex with a berdache was more socially accepted and convenient than sex with a woman. Though some *winktes* were the second or third wife for a warrior, according to my informants those *winktes* who were not married had their own tipi where men would visit during the time that they were not having sex with their wives. This would be when the wives were menstruating, pregnant, nursing an infant, or during religious days when heterosexual contact was taboo.

Among the Lakotas at least, there was some subtle discouragement for a man to marry a *winkte,* and encouragement for a *winkte* to remain single and take multiple men as sexual partners. One elderly informant remembers, "None of the *winkte* I knew were married to men; they lived alone and men would visit them." A Lakota *winkte* told me that he greatly prefers this pattern. He lives with his parents and his men friends visit him: "Married men are the best. . . . I want to lie with all the men. I used to keep a list of how many men I had been with."

Similarly, a Pueblo berdache prefers married men who have at least four or five children as proof of their virility. He always takes the passive role in anal and oral sex. His partners are the men of the pueblo whose wives are absent, ill, or ill-disposed toward them. They come knocking on the door of his large house at night.[42] A Kwakiutl man who had an affair with a berdache said that the one he knew "used to go around with quite a lot of boys." Another one "had a lot of chums among our people around here. Some of them says they used to lie in bed with him." Among each other, the men compared their sexual experiences with berdaches.[43]

Not only do the lovers of berdaches not mind being seen with the berdaches, they may serve as a public following for them. Even today among the Hopi, a twenty-year-old berdache, "a real 'queen,'" was observed by an ethnographer at a recent ceremony: "He was accompanied by four other young men, all of whom were *very* good looking while simultaneously looking rather tough." Other Hopis assumed automatically that they were his sexual partners.[44]

Traditionalist Indian men do not have a reluctance to be seen with an androgynous male, in the way that whites often do. One evening when I was with a berdache in a local bar near the Crow reservation, some Indian men recognized my friend and approached him in a quite friendly manner. One of them put his arm around the berdache, gave him a little squeeze on the thigh, just as one might see a man do toward a woman in a bar.

My friend made no advances; it was the man who made all the moves. The man did this without hesitation or embarrassment in front of his friends.

In traditional times, a Lakota informant told me, higher-class *winktes* had up to twelve regular partners. On his reservation even today, he says, "Straight Indian guys will go sexually with a gay here, in a way that whites don't. A man will go out with *winktes* and with women, but he is not considered to be a *winkte*." Another informant, an attractive androgynous young man, estimates that about half of the "straight men" of his community have approached him for sex. One of these masculine men admitted to me that if he had lived in traditional times, he would have wanted to have a *winkte* as a spouse.

What we can see from this pattern is that berdaches serve as a socially recognized outlet for male sexual release beyond the marriage bond. With berdaches serving this function for both unmarried adolescents and married men, they do not need female prostitution. W. W. Hill concluded that, "No stigma is placed on the irregular sex activities of the *nadle*. . . . Their promiscuity is respected rather than censured." Hill interviewed a *nadle* who told him, without a trace of embarrassment, that she had had relations with more than a hundred Navajo men.[45]

Special Occasions for Sex

Beyond all this, there were certain occasions in the aboriginal male life-style when a berdache was especially convenient for sex, such as on hunting expeditions and in war parties. How the berdache interacted with the men on one of these trips away from home is suggested by what happens among modern groups of Indian men. Ethnographer Harald Broch, living among the Hare Indians of Canada's Northwest Territory in 1973, went with a group of men on a firefighting expedition. There were thirty Hare men in this group, plus a twenty-three-year-old male cook whom Broch calls Sony. In contrast to the shabby blue jeans of the men, Sony wore tight-fitting purple or turquoise bell-bottom trousers and fancy colored silky shirts. He always kept his clothing neat and clean, and his shoulder-length hair thoroughly combed. Broch describes Sony as speaking with "a gentle flowing voice, sometimes interrupted by high pitched thrills of laughter. His speech was usually underlined with well controlled movements of arms, hands and fingers. His speech and behaviour formed a sharp contrast to the much rougher appearance of the rest of the crew."[46]

As soon as the tents were erected in the camp, a "mock fight" started between two of the men: "'Me, I want to sleep with Sony,' one of them shouted. 'No way,' the other cried, 'it's going to be me!' A third guy put his arm around Sony's narrow shoulders: 'Come let's go and sleep.' Sony shook him off laughing." Sony decided who he wanted to sleep with, and the other men acted sullen. At the end of each day, when the men returned from fighting the fire, they would tease any man who had stayed in camp, saying "How is Sony in bed? Tell us?"

His special role was understood and accepted by all the men in the camp. Even though there was another cook present, only Sony held the berdache role. Sony was consistently called "mother" or "auntie" as a term of endearment. Unlike the other cook, "he was always very eager to hear whether they liked his cooking or not. . . . If the response was good, Sony shone like the sun." His behavior was in sharp contrast to nonberdache cooks, who did not mother the men the way Sony did. He was always examining the men to see if they looked healthy, saying to them:

"My dear, you look sick, let me treat you. I think you should stay home tomorrow. I will treat you." And, what is important, he was most persistent. Other people could also propose that a man should stay home to rest for a day, but nobody would repeat such a proposal except Sony. And nobody ever became angry or irritated with him. Instead an arm would be put around him: "Thanks for caring for me, mom."[47]

Though he liked these female kin references, Sony sometimes got upset at the men for their constant teasing about his femininity. At times he would kick or hit someone, whereupon the others would just laugh. Broch pointed out how exceptional this response was: "All that was done was to try to keep him at a distance. Carefully he was pushed away. He is the only Hare Indian man I have ever seen hit another man while sober." The men treated him indulgently because of his many kindnesses to them. He was often seen to stroke their hair, dirty with sweat and ashes, and say, "I think you should wash; you would be much handsomer then."[48]

In the camp, Broch observed, "A homosexual aspect seems to be present all the time, and proposals by others to go to bed with Sony were constantly recurring. In some respects this is not too unique. In other instances a man could be teased by another who said he wanted to make love to him because he was so handsome. But this would just be said once and never repeated over and over again as were the proposals directed to Sony. Also Sony halfway accepted such invitations by letting the suitors embrace him." Having said all this, Broch then concludes that there is no reason to believe that homosexual acts occurred in the camp: "It never went further than mockplay."[49]

I do not trust Broch's conclusion. Despite the value of his essay in reporting the homoerotic interaction of the men that he observed in the camp, I do not think he can accurately conclude that there was no sex going on. He does not specify why he concluded that no sex occurred. What Broch's statement does not account for is that the specific sexual behavior might not have been talked about, as a form of politeness or from a sense of privacy.

Broch surely did not get accurate information from Sony himself. The ethnographer did not sleep in Sony's tent, and when he was gone with the firefighters during the day he did not know what went on with a man who stayed in camp with Sony. Such confident statements of denial by ethnographers are responsible for a distorted image of the sexuality of the berdache. It is almost as if Broch is bending over backwards (no pun intended) to make this denial. Broch seems to feel that because Sony had a "girlfriend" back in town, he was not sexual with the men. Was Sony's relationship with this "girlfriend" sexual, or were they just close friends?

The ethnographer admits that he could not get much data about Sony. When he asked others about him, they were protective and "would only reply that it was well known that Sony was quite feminine. Any further information on that topic was hard to obtain."[50] Furthermore, it is obvious that Broch did not

have Sony's confidence. At one point he reported that he followed the Hare men's practice of addressing Sony as "auntie."
Upon hearing this, the heretofore cheerful berdache "closed his
fists and cried out: 'I am not your aunt and don't forget it.'"[51]
Broch could not figure out why Sony had gotten so mad. Are
we to trust a statement about something as private as sexual
behavior from a reporter who so obviously was not familiar
with the berdache? When Broch concludes from his fieldwork
that the majority of American Indian berdaches were not homosexual, I find his conclusion dubious.

My research leads me to question ethnographers' statements
about the supposed nonhomosexuality of berdaches. All of the
berdaches I have interviewed eventually specified their sexual
activities with men, but only after I had gained their confidence.
Many of the people I interviewed mentioned that they would
not confide in a heterosexual researcher. In an example that is
similar to the Hare firefighting team reported by Broch, I interviewed a Micmac Indian who fulfilled a similar role. As with
the Hare, berdaches have not been previously reported among
the Micmac, yet my informant is so well accepted among his
people that he was twice elected chief of his reservation in the
1970s. He told me that everyone on his reservation realizes that
he is sexual with men, and there is no prejudice. There are others like him who are likewise recognized and accepted.

In the 1960s he followed the common pattern for men on his
reservation by being a migrant laborer in the "high steel" construction industry in Boston and New York City. A group of
four to seven Micmac men would go as a group and work together as a team. He would always do the cooking and take care
of anyone who got sick. They would rent a house or apartment
together, and he would choose which man he wanted to sleep
with him. He never had a man refuse him. In the privacy of his
room, they would sleep in the same bed and would make love
often. Though all of those men considered themselves heterosexual, on these trips they were eager for sexual involvement
with him. He says, "I didn't talk about having sex with any of
the others; they didn't talk about me among themselves. I just
chose which one I wanted to sleep with me, and that was that."
Concerning his favorite partner on these trips over the years, he

says, "I really feel in love with him. He married a woman, but we have sex periodically. We're still the best of friends."

If I had been the typical ethnographer, because of the fact that such private behavior is not talked about, I might have concluded that nothing sexual was occurring among these men. I doubt that I could have gotten the men to admit to their sexual activity with the berdache. The assumption of heterosexuality unless there is explicit evidence to the contrary is very suspect in the literature on berdachism. Even with abundant evidence of affection and caring between the berdache and the men in a group like a raiding party, a firefighting unit, or a construction crew, some observers will still conclude that there is nothing homosexual going on.

In a valuable article published in a gay magazine in 1965, a thirty-five-year-old Mohave described his place in tribal society. The author, who stayed with the berdache on the reservation, wrote, "The Indian boys tease each other about sleeping with him, yet their teasing is somehow not ridicule of him. Among the Indians he is accepted with equanimity. . . . They often talk about making love to him (in a crowd which includes him), yet it is understood that they don't really mean it. Men being men, however, more than a few of them actually do share his bed when they're sure none of the others will catch them at it." Asked about all the sexual teasing, the Mohave replied, "I just go along with it. I'm not crazy about it. But, for the most part, we all get along. They don't mean any harm by it. . . . Some of the boys run around with me. We have a good time. Oh, I don't mean like sex all the time. I mean we have a good time like friends—singing Mohave songs and dancing."[52]

Far from being "mockplay," the sexual teasing universally engaged in serves as a smoke screen that preserves the privacy of the men who do have sexual involvement with a berdache. Because all the men are doing the teasing, it means that the man who is actually erotically attracted to the berdache does not stand out. Maybe all the men are having sex, or maybe not, but because the teasing is open and general, and it is understood that no sexual contact is necessarily implied, this practice allows for same-sex affection without suspicion. Such a custom is in sharp contrast to Western society, where any physical touching between men raises eyebrows, and where the result is a pervasive fear among many men (even exclusively heterosexual men) that others will think they are "a homosexual." The sexual teasing of the Indians allows for everyone to be comfortable. It is a mechanism to keep people from invading others' privacy, and reactions like Harald Broch's prove that such a tactic is effective.

Sex with a berdache is by no means limited to times away from the village. Lakota men were known to visit a *winkte* sexually before embarking on a raid, as it was said to increase their ferocity.[53] There were other specific reasons, besides traveling in a male group, which were offered as justification for sex with a berdache—for example, men who wanted a *winkte* to give their son a sacred name would often engage in sex with the *winkte*.

Among the Papagos, the berdache bestowed obscene nicknames on his favored sexual partners. The men were very proud of these names, and since having one was prestigious, they would publicly boast about them. From fieldwork in the 1930s, Ruth Underhill observed that berdaches might marry a man, but since they generally prospered by themselves they tended to live alone and be visited by different men. Underhill concluded, "No scorn was felt for the berdache. He was respected and liked by the women and his sex life with the men was a community institution."[54] During the Drinking Feast and the Maiden's Dance, the usual proprieties were dispensed with as Papagos engaged in a general sexual orgy. At these "official nights of saturnalia . . . homosexual tendencies were openly acknowledged and sanctioned." Moreover, since all men could participate but only unmarried women could attend, there were considerably more males than females present. In such a context the berdache was likely to be quite sexually active.[55]

Another reference to a ceremonial recognition of the sex life of the berdache was recorded by George Catlin, who spent eight years traveling among Western Indians during the 1830s. Among the Sauk and Fox, Catlin attended a feast to the *I-coo-coo-a*. "For extraordinary privileges which he is known to possess, he is . . . looked upon as *medicine* and sacred, and a feast is given to him annually; and initiatory to it, a dance by those few young men of the tribe who can, as in the sketch (see plate 6), dance forward and publicly make their boast (without the denial of the Berdashe), that . . ." Here Catlin switches to writing (ostensibly) in the Sauk and Fox language. However, linguistic analysis shows the lettering to be meaningless gibberish.[56] Nevertheless, it is clear from the context that Catlin means only those men who had had sexual relations with the berdache could dance. "Such, and such only, are allowed to enter the dance and partake of the feast. . . . It will be seen that the society consists of quite a limited number of 'odd fellows.'"[57]

Catlin concludes his discussion with a condemnatory statement, claiming that the Indians made the berdache "servile and degrading." In imposing his own values on the Sauk and Fox, Catlin missed the significance of the event he had witnessed. While some anthropologists have used Catlin as evidence of the berdache's low status, there are many contradictions in his claim. Simply by virtue of being offered a feast, the berdache was accorded a high status. And the men who voluntarily got up to dance did so because there was a certain status in being the sexual partner of the *I-coo-coo-a*. But an even more important element of this dance is that it offered the berdache an opportunity publicly to humiliate any man who dared to dance. Simply by denying past sexual relations, the berdache could make a man's dance seem an empty boast. This surely served as a powerful weapon whereby the *I-coo-coo-a* could ensure that his partners would not mistreat him. All he had to do was to *deny* having sex with them!

As with the Papago men who would boast of having an obscene name given them by the berdache, the Sauk and Fox Indians had to stay on the good side of the berdache or risk public humiliation. This kind of response from the masculine partners tells us much about the status of berdaches themselves. Sexual behavior with men is thus an important element in the berdache tradition. Homosexual behavior may occur between nonberdache males, but the cultures emphasize the berdache as the usual person a man would go to for male sex. With the role thus institutionalized, the berdache serves the sexual needs of many men without competing against the institution of heterosexual marriage. Men are not required to make a choice between being heterosexual or being homosexual, since they can accommodate both desires. Nevertheless, for that minority of men who do wish to make such a choice, a number of cultures allow them the option of becoming the husband to a berdache.

6　A Normal Man: The Berdache's Husband and the Question of Sexual Variance

In 1542, one of the earliest Spanish explorers in Florida, Cabeza de Vaca, reported on his previous five years among the Timucua Indians: "During the time I was thus among these people I saw a devilish thing, and it is that I saw one man married to another."[1] The sources are extremely unsatisfactory in describing these relationships, but the fact that these relationships exist is noted for several tribes, usually by a brief statement saying that the berdache "lived together with a man, as his wife." This was noted as the socially accepted practice for some berdaches among the Ojibwa, Winnebago, Lakota, and Yuma.[2] It was said that the only male homosexual behavior among the Quinault Indians involved those who had relationships with the *keknat-sa'nxwix* ("part woman male").[3]

In a massive survey of northern California Indian cultures conducted in the 1930s, all but one of the groups who recognized a berdache status also recognized his marriage to a "normal man."[4] Next to doing women's work and acting androgynously, sexual behavior with a man is the most commonly noted characteristic of berdache status. This aspect is even more widespread among berdaches than a special ceremonial role.

An ethnographer of the Omahas wrote in the 1880s: "*Min-gu-ga* [*mexoga*] took other men as their husbands. Frank La Fleche knew one such man, who had had several men as his husbands. . . . [They] are publicly known, and do not appear to be despised or to excite disgust."[5] Among the Southern Maidus, a traditionalist informant in the 1920s explained in a respectful manner about *osa'pu:* "They just grew that way, being half-man and half-woman," and in a similar matter-of-fact way said "he lives with a man. . . . No contempt was shown them."[6] The berdache's sexuality is accepted in the same way as his androgyny; both are seen as reflections of his spirit, his basic nature.

THE ROLE OF MARRIAGE IN NATIVE AMERICAN CULTURES

Marriage between a berdache and a man existed in the context of the general position of marriage in aboriginal American Indian society. Although wide ranges of activities are open for both women and men, there is in most Native American societies a basic division of labor into two halves. This is usually referred to as a "division of labor by sex." By dividing the necessary tasks into "men's work" and "women's work," each person has to learn only half of the jobs available. This is important in small-scale societies that do not have much role specialization. It is, however, more accurate to call this pattern a division of labor by *gender,* because people can take on a gender role that is divergent from their genital sex.

Within a marriage in a gender-divided economy, there can be only two roles: husband and wife. The sex of the person who takes these roles may vary, but the roles generally do not. This is an additional reason that two berdaches would not marry, and two masculine men would not marry. Masculine men might have sex, which is their private business, but marriage is a public matter and an economic concern.

Each person has something to gain by entering a marriage. They gain the expertise of the other in tasks that are different from their own skills. Why should two hunters marry, if neither of them is good at gathering plants? The closest exception to this rule is among the Navajos. When *nadle* marry, they dress like men. A Navajo informant explains, "If they marry men, it is just like two men working together."[7] Yet it must be remembered that *nadle* also do women's work, so such a marriage is still viable. Economically, the husband has both a wife and a husband, which partly explains the reputation these marriages have for economic success.

When people get married, they gain another advantage: the economic security that comes with a wider circle of relatives. Nothing is worse in a kin-based society than to be without kin.

Marriage creates an alliance of families, whereby one has twice as many relatives on which to draw for support. In the context of a subsistence economy, with a division of labor by gender, it makes sense that such an economy would be family centered. Families provide extra productive labor and take care of the aged.

Marriages between men and berdaches fit into this pattern. In such a marriage, the man takes the husband role, and the berdache takes the wife role. Recognizing the fluidity of women's and men's roles and the mixed-gender status of the berdache means that there can be considerable variation from this simply stated dichotomy. The Navajo example just cited illustrates the variation in spousal relationships and the mixed-gender status of *nadle*.

In a marriage between a man and a berdache, the berdache supplies women's work and a network of kin, like any other wife. Lakota chief Crazy Horse, for example, had one or two *winktes* for wives, along with his female wives.[8] A berdache wife offered the same economic advantages of any other polygynous marriage. While it is true that a berdache cannot reproduce, many of the reports of such marriages mention that the husband already had children, either through a previous marriage or by taking a berdache as a second or third wife. But with adoption being so commonly accepted, children may even be gained by the berdache. Thus, the same advantages of heterosexual marriage also accrue to the man who marries a berdache.

The two roles of husband and berdache are not to be confused. After I had been living in the household of a well-known *winkte* on a particular reservation for a while, a medicine man told me in private, "People say ——— is a 'he-she' and you must be his lover." They did not say I was a "he-she," because he was clearly the androgynous one. Personal character and gender role, not sexual behavior per se, distinguish the *winkte* role.

THE HUSBAND OF THE BERDACHE

Sexual behavior of berdaches is often considered a serious reflection of their spiritual natures. But for other people, it can be an object of humor. A Pueblo *kwih-doh,* who has sex only with men, participates in this humor. He is a member of the Clown Society; their job is to provide comic relief during the serious religious ceremonies. His references to homosexual behavior are guaranteed to elicit good-natured giggling—such as during a ceremony when he performed a mock wedding ceremony between two unsuspecting men. His humor is not self-critical or malicious; same-sexuality lies comfortably within the expectations of the culture.[9] The attitude expressed in many Indian societies is that sex in general is funny. It is not considered gross or sinful, so there is not an undercurrent of hostility as there often is in the joking that occurs in Anglo-American society.

In some cultures the husband is treated with the same respect as any other husband, but in others he is not. Some tribes do considerable kidding of the husband of the berdache. While part of this simply arises from a joking attitude toward sex in general, it seems especially directed toward anything that varies from the usual. A Lakota traditionalist told me that the humor is similar to that surrounding a young man who has an elderly woman for a spouse. It is not a matter for social condemnation, but the participants open themselves to humorous barbs simply because their relationship is unusual.

Kidding is often directed more toward the husbands than toward berdaches themselves. According to a Crow berdache, "If a Crow man moved in with me, other men would tease him. They wouldn't tease me, because they all know what I am." The joking toward the husband could also be due to the reputation that berdaches have for being highly productive workers. Since the berdaches are very good providers, a Crow traditionalist pointed out to me, and give many gifts to their boyfriends, the man could get a reputation for being lazy. One of the common taunts that Plains Indians might aim at the husband of the berdache is that he wants a wife who not only keeps house but hunts for him as well.[10]

Why would a man go against all this teasing and marry a berdache anyway? Most of the early ethnographers who interviewed berdaches never asked this question. When I have asked Indians this, I get a mere shrug of the shoulders and a vague statement like "I don't know, he just wants to do it." Mohaves attribute the ability of an *alyha* to attract a man to their shaman-istic powers of love magic. More concretely, they consider *alyha* to be lucky, and their luck extends to their husband. Such beliefs can predispose some men to marry berdaches.[11]

This belief is realistic, in the sense that a husband benefits from the much-publicized prosperity of a berdache household. Among the Hidatsa, for example, berdaches did all the work that women did for their husbands. Yet beyond this, they were noted as being stronger than women, and never burdened with pregnancy or nursing an infant. Hidatsa statements from the 1930s tell of berdaches working harder than the average wife and exceeding the usual productivity of women in many activities.[12] This was the reason given for chiefs and other prominent men among the California Mission Indians wanting to marry *cuit, uluqui,* or *coia*.[13] A *lhamana* that Matilda Coxe Stevenson knew at Zuni was one of the richest persons of the pueblo. In the 1880s he "allied himself to a man" and until the time when Stevenson left the pueblo in 1897 "this couple were living to-gether, and they were two of the hardest workers in the pueblo and among the most prosperous."[14]

Another reason for a man to be attracted to marriage with a berdache has to do with marital stability. In contrast to Western notions of feminine "nest building" and masculine promiscuity, among the Mohaves the stereotypes are reversed. Young wom-en are known for their licentious habits and their disinclination to stick with one man for long. Men, who more likely crave a stable home, will often turn to an older woman or an *alyha*.[15]

Berdaches are not generally courted like virgin females, but are flirted with like older women. Either the man or the *alyha* might initiate this flirtation. Given the high value that Mohaves place on jesting, such a dalliance is often done with humor in mind. According to ethnographer George Devereux, a Mohave man might go through formal courtship with an *alyha* "for the sake of creating a comical situation, a thing paramount in the Mohave pursuit of sexual pleasure. . . . It appealed to his sense of the preposterous. . . . At dances even boys who had no in-tention of marrying an *alyha* played around with them, as though they were flirtatious women. In the end some of them made up their minds to become the husbands of *alyha*. Once they were married the *alyha* made exceptionally industrious wives. . . . The certitude of a well-kept home may have induced many a Mohave to set up house with an *alyha*."[16]

The other reason that berdaches attract husbands is simple sexual attraction. Since the favorite methods of sex for Mohave men are as inserter in anal intercourse and receiving fellatio, these acts can be done by an *alyha* as well as by a woman. For the men, sex with an *alyha* is in fact little different from the kind of sex they have with women. That, combined with an incessant search for new thrills, encourages Mohave men to establish such relationships. Some men become so used to having *alyha* spouses that they show no interest in women. But because many men will marry an *alyha* for at least a short time, *alyha* have no difficulty in obtaining husbands.[17]

Some men develop a sexual preference for berdaches. They may be less attracted to women, or they may in fact enjoy the prosperity of the productive berdache. People seldom make choices for only one reason. Perhaps we should merely accept that, as a Nisenan man said, he was simply "much attached" to his berdache wife.[18] But it is pointless to try to explain away the homosexual element in such a man. Unlike the berdache, he is not androgynous, and he does not identify himself as different from other husbands. We cannot account for his sexuality by psychoanalytic theories of "inversion" or "deviancy." His preference is simply evidence of the potential within many "normal" men for sexual enjoyment with another male.

Sexual preference and gender identity are two independent variables, which the distinction between berdaches and their husbands shows quite clearly. One can be homosexual in behavior without being gender nonconformist, and without having an identity different from other men's. American Indian values recognize these differences, which Western culture confuses by labeling anyone who participates in same-sex relations as "a homosexual." By socially constructing only the berdache as different, with their partners as "normal," Indian cultures avoid categorizing people into two opposed categories based on sexual behavior.

COMPARABLE EXAMPLES IN WESTERN CULTURE

We can even see some ambivalence about sexual orientation in Western culture. It is difficult to make comparisons between Indian and Anglo-American cultures because Anglo thought is restricted by the idea that there are only two genders. Nevertheless, there is some resistance among working-class people to dividing all people into opposite orientations based on the anatomical sex of their partners. In an attempt to gain additional insight into the feelings of the husband of the berdache, I have interviewed non-Indian males who have opted against transsexual surgery, but who prefer to dress and live their daily lives as women. They do not identify as gay, but more as androgynes: "like a woman, but not a woman," as one told me.

Some of them are asexual, but most have boyfriends. Their usual method of meeting men is in daily activities at work, or in heterosexual social settings. The men they meet, who are usually working class, believe the person they are relating to is a woman. The feminine male does not bring up sex, but focuses on social compatibility with the man to see if they get along well as a couple. The feminine male resists sexual involvement before he has had time to get to know the man well. When the man eventually does press for sex, what happens is some variation on the following account, told to me by one of these males. Though he dresses and looks like a woman, he does not identify as transvestite or transsexual, but these are the only terms that he knows. He explains:

When I have been going with a man for several weeks, and we have really gotten to know each other, I show him a notebook of newspaper clippings I have collected over the years on transvestism and transsexualism. They ask me why I'm showing them this, and I calmly tell them that I am sort of like that. Most of them go into total shock; they can't believe that I am really a man. They say things like, ". . . but you're so feminine!" None of these men identify as gay, or even bisexual. They have been attracted to me entirely as to a woman. But after a period of surprise, I would say over nine out of ten do not break it off. They will go ahead and develop a sexual relationship with me, with them taking the usual man's role.

Another person I interviewed had been so nervous about telling the boyfriend about his morphological sex that he said nothing. He was afraid that revealing such information would break up the relationship, so he did not reveal his sex even when the boyfriend proposed marriage. The man's family liked their son's "girlfriend," and the man wanted to wait for sex until marriage, so the feminine male kept procrastinating until the wedding. After a long engagement they were married. The first night of their honeymoon the new wife could put it off no longer and told the husband. This informant reported, "He went into total shock, and left me there alone in the motel room. I didn't know what to do, so I just stayed there. A day later he came back, and told me he had thought about it a lot, and he had decided he loved me and it really didn't make any difference." The couple has remained together, and after sixteen years are still happily married. The sex of the wife is not talked about, nor does the husband's family or friends know of the male sex of the wife. The husband does not identify himself as gay or homosexual, though they have a monogamous relationship. They fit in well with their suburban neighbors.

This ability of men who identify as heterosexual to adapt to sex with a morphological male demonstrates a fluidity in sexuality not accounted for in theories of "homosexual orientation" or "heterosexual orientation." These men are responding to the femininity of their partner, and the partner's genital equipment is not crucial. Of course, there are significant differences between these instances and a relationship with a berdache. The husband of the berdache knew of the sex of his partner from the beginning, and established a sexual relationship anyway. This genital difference has no bearing on the man's identity.

Since the partner of the berdache is not considered a homosexual,[19] it is easy enough for him to leave the relationship and begin another one with a woman. No matter how long a man is in a marriage with a berdache, there is no stigma that follows him after his male relationship is ended. The man has always been a husband, and the fact that he was husband to a berdache makes no difference to his suitability as a husband for a woman. Heterosexual marriage is thus not ruled out as an option, any more than male marriage is ruled out for men married to women. One of the former husbands to a Klamath berdache was interviewed by an ethnographer in the 1920s, who described him as "a normal old man who has since raised a family of his own" in a heterosexual marriage.[20]

Of course the berdache might resist such a breakup. Among the serially monogamous Mohaves, divorcing an *alyha* is not always an easy matter. Kuwal, a man who had several *alyha* wives, noted that when men try to leave *alyha,* "They are so strong that they might beat you up." This happened to Kuwal himself when he left his *alyha* spouse, who got very angry: "One day he came to the house and beat me so hard it almost laid me out." Later, the *alyha* got in a fight with Kuwal's new wife: "The alyha was stronger than she was, being a man, but he pretended to be a weak woman and fought like women do. He did not use all his strength. He could have beaten up my wife quite easily, but he let my wife throw him several times."[21] What is interesting in this domestic spat is that the *alyha* restrained himself with the wife, but had no inhibitions toward the errant husband. Mohaves of course saw the *alyha*'s resistance to divorce as incredibly funny, because society encouraged breakups.

In this context we can understand why some tribes that accept same-sexuality nevertheless carry the teasing of the husband of a berdache to an extreme. Among the Lakotas, said one of my informants, "the *winkte*'s husband may get some kidding that he will become a *winkte.* Therefore, he will hide his sexual activities—but he will continue in secret, unless he feels so strongly about it that he continues publicly." On the face of it, this explanation makes no sense. Believing as they do that *winktes* are sacred people, and that their androgynous nature is an inborn character trait or a result of a vision, or both, how could they believe that the husband could become a *winkte?*

Actually, this explanation does not express the real reason for the kidding. Traditionally, Lakota culture accepted the *winkte* only as a secondary spouse, to be married after a man already had a female wife and children. Since Lakotas no longer have plural marriages, if a man takes a *winkte* for a spouse that means there would be no heterosexual marriage and progeny. A way to discourage this exclusive homosexuality on the part of men is to make them an object of laughter. The berdache is exempt from the kidding because he is not seen as a man. The culture, after all, is not objecting to the homosexual behavior. If a man wishes to have sexual relations with a berdache, there is no objection among the Lakotas as long as he does not settle into a permanent relationship. What society objects to is behavior that might prevent reproduction. Still, despite this discouragement, some men will go against the norm and marry a berdache.

The laughter among the Mohaves is a case in point. Any kind of sexual matter is an occasion for humor among them, but the jokes about the husband of the *alyha* fly so thick around him that many of the men will eventually leave the berdache. Despite the fact that the berdache provides a stable home and is more likely to be faithful than a female wife, such marriages are not stable.[22] Rather than see the laughter as a condemnation of homosexuality, we should understand it as a balancing mechanism. With all the advantages that marriage with an *alyha* offers for Mohave men (prosperity, stability, luck, sex), if there were not some disadvantages then too many men might marry berdaches and the population growth might be threatened. But by keeping the majority of male marriages short-term, the joking ensures that most men mate with women at some point and have children.

Other cultures accomplish this same goal by restricting male marriages to those men who have already had children. Thus, it is only acceptable for a berdache to become a second or third wife in a polygynous family where the female wife has already reproduced. Among the Hidatsas, berdaches usually marry older men who are beyond their childbearing years.[23] None of these patterns of marriage threatens the reproduction of the population.

The Zapotecs are typical of a culture in which men customarily marry a berdache only after they have married women and produced children. While boys may participate in homosexual behavior before their marriage, by the time Zapotec men are thirty years old almost all of them (not including berdaches, of course) marry women and have children. Yet it is not uncommon for men to leave a heterosexual marriage after a time. According to ethnographer Beverly Chiñas, "A middle-aged man with a grown family may leave his wife and move in with a male lover and generally this scarcely raises an eyebrow. Over the nearly two decades since my fieldwork began several prominent citizens with grown children have left their heterosexual mates to live with same-sex lovers." One case involved a former mayor of the town. People might talk about this for a little while, but they soon adapt to the change in the same way they would to a new heterosexual pairing after a divorce. There is no ostracism of a same-sex couple.[24]

In the case of a wife's death, berdaches will be praised for stepping in to rescue a family. Among the Zapotecs a famous case occurred when a man's wife died while their several children were still young. The man married a *muxe* who became a substitute mother. The berdache cooked, laundered clothes, and did the shopping for the family. Other Zapotecs admired the *muxe* greatly for the sacrifices he made, saying "every one of those children got an education and was sent to school clean and well-fed." He and the widower lived together as a respected couple, until the *muxe*'s death many years later.[25] Zapotecs judged him by his sacrifices for the children, rather than by his sexual behavior.

HETEROSEXUAL BEHAVIOR OF THE BERDACHE

While Zapotecs define *irá muxe* as males who are androgynous and homosexual, there is no stigma against a *muxe* marrying a woman and having children. In this case such a person is the father, the same as other fathers.[26] Given the emphasis on sex with men, such a heterosexual marriage seems an incongruity. Because of instances of berdaches marrying women, recent writers on berdachism have paid much attention to the berdache's supposed heterosexuality. But several of these statements are vague and of uncertain reliability. It is not clear with most cases whether a berdache might have been married to a woman *before* assuming berdache status. Such statements also are based on examples from Indians of the Northwest Coast, where the institution of berdachism seems to have been only sporadically established.[27]

The uncertain sources aside, some berdaches clearly have been married to women. This fact has led some anthropologists to assume that this means those berdaches were heterosexual. If the experience of the Kwakiutl is typical of the Northwest Coast, we cannot make that assumption. A Kwakiutl chief in 1940 remembered that most berdaches in his society did not get married but some did. The chief reported on one who got married, but he and his wife separated after only a year: "She was telling her second husband that this man never touched her [sexually] at all—only by his hands." Another berdache also got married because of pressure from his brother, but "they only lived together one month and then they parted. This woman also tells others this man never touched her."[28] Most of the published sources that speak of the marriage of a berdache to a woman do not describe the sexual behavior of the couple. Since the published sources do not really explain this incongruity, it is necessary to get clarification from Indian people themselves.

During my fieldwork I met a Lakota woman whose grandfather was a *winkte*. He was exceptional in that he not only married but also fathered children. But, she pointed out, he did not have sex with his wife other than for the purpose of procreation. While he was married he continued to have sex with men. He was discreet about his male lovers, and the fact that his wife and other members of the family knew of his homosexual inclinations was not a disruptive factor in his marriage. He died in the 1960s, and his granddaughter remembers him as "quiet, easygoing, effeminate, and very philosophical." He gave people sacred names, and fulfilled a respected *winkte* role on the reservation.

Why would a *winkte* marry a woman, if his sexual desires are largely for men? In traditional Navajo culture, where *nadle* could marry either sex, male marriages come about because of the wishes of the two males; but man-woman marriages are often set up by families as economic arrangements.[29] The desire for children seems to be the crucial consideration. One twenty-seven-year-old *winkte* with whom I stayed for a while in the summer of 1982 has this intention. He has never had a girlfriend or had sex with a woman, and has no sexual attraction toward women. His only sexual experiences have been with men. Yet he says, "I eventually want to settle down and have children." When I asked if this meant marrying a woman he said yes, but his emphasis was on children rather than on heterosexual desire.

This may explain some of the confusion that exists in the published sources. Even where there is marriage to a woman, there is very little hard evidence to suggest that a berdache is entirely heterosexual. In the Navajo language, *nadle* or *nadleeh* can also refer to animals. It is defined as an animal that does not participate in heterosexual reproduction. For example, a male sheep may be observed not to mount female sheep. He is thereby seen as having "feminine characteristics" because he does not participate in heterosexual acts. Nonreproductive sexuality is thus an important element in the definition of *nadle*.[30]

A Lakota berdache explains, "A few *winkte* marry women and have children, and still fulfill the *winkte* role. But most others are not permitted by the spirits to be married. It varies from one person to another. . . . It would be unholy for me to have sex with a woman, or with another *winkte*. That would be wrong, and would violate the role set for me by the Sacred Pipe." Among the Papagos, a common joke was for the men to tease the women that since the berdache was always among women, he had plenty of opportunity for sex with them. The women thought this was great fun, because of the absurdity of the suggestion. In terms of sex, a Papago woman of the 1930s explained, "We have forgotten he is a man."[31] Among the Papago, as with many other tribes, berdaches are either exclusively homosexual or asexual.

Allowing for cultural and individual variation, we can still safely conclude that, in an institution that defines itself around gender role rather than sexual behavior, sex with men is the most obvious erotic behavior of berdaches. It is probably accurate to conclude that most berdaches who are sexually active are exclusively so with men. And for those who marry women, the majority likely have heterosexual contact in order to produce children. It is hard to say how many are asexual, but the amount of direct evidence of homosexual behavior by berdaches leads me to question facile generalizations by heterosex-

sexually identified ethnographers—not based on direct observation of berdache behavior—that berdaches of a tribe are nonsexual.

Many times berdache status itself is seen as defining a person
as nonheterosexual. As an Omaha man explained to me, "A
mexoga cannot be married to a woman, if he is that way." After
describing his sexual experiences with a berdache, a Kwakiutl
chief explained why berdaches do not marry women: "He never
gets married, and neither do most of them. Two of them that
did get married, died soon after. I don't know if it is because
they got married or not."[32] Such statements would function to
inhibit further heterosexual relations by berdaches. But even
when there is marriage to a woman, this does not constitute
"heterosexuality" and should not be taken to imply that the
berdache is avoiding sex with men.

HOMOSEXUAL BEHAVIOR OF THE BERDACHE

Understanding this, it makes little sense to try to discount the
association of berdachism with homosexuality, as some recent
writers have done. In reacting against the view of George Devereux and others that berdachism was "institutionalized homosexuality," Henry Angelino and Charles Shedd defined the institution on the basis of its gender role. This provided an
improved understanding in certain respects, but in so doing
they deemphasized sexual aspects, relegating "homosexual" or
"heterosexual" to mere adjective modifiers.[33] They assumed
transvestism to be an integral part of the role, which I have
shown not to be the case, while implying that homosexuality
and heterosexuality are more or less equal variables.

This tendency to dismiss the homosexual element of berdachism is most evident in a 1980 essay by James Thayer, who
concludes that sexuality "is the least predictable variable concerning their behavior." While correctly pointing out the importance of the religious aspect of berdachism, Thayer makes
the mistake of opposing spiritual issues to sexual issues. This is
a false dichotomy, and it is a vast distortion to claim that sexuality is the *least* predictable variable. Perhaps Thayer's denial of

berdaches' sexual involvement with men is a reflection of homophobia. It certainly seems that way given such language, as when he writes: "A psychofunctional explanation tends to *reduce* the institution to a socially acceptable form of *perverted* sexual activity" (italics added).[34]

More fair-minded essays have recently been written by Harriet Whitehead, and by Charles Callender and Lee Kochems.[35] These writers make the important point that berdaches should not be equated with the idea of "the homosexual" in Western culture, since masculine males might also have sex with berdaches or other males and not be considered berdaches. But Whitehead, Callender, and Kochems go beyond that, to argue that sexuality is a distinctly secondary consideration in berdachism. They overemphasize hetero-homo variation in the berdache's sexuality. As should be clear from the preceding chapters, religious, occupational, and gender roles are extremely important in defining berdache status. But having lived with traditional berdaches, I am aware that it is futile and arbitrary to segregate these roles from a berdache's sexuality. There is no hierarchy of primary and secondary.

Sexual attraction to men is accurately assumed by Indian people to be an important part of berdache status, in the same way that androgyny and spirituality are assumed to be related. I think it instructive that those ethnographers who have had direct fieldwork connections with berdaches (among the earlier generation, Kroeber, Hill, Devereux, Underhill, and others; among more recent fieldworkers, myself, Beverly Chiñas, and Sue-Ellen Jacobs) stress the homosexual aspect of berdaches more than do those anthropologists who have written on berdachism based only on the published literature. Interacting with living people, we see the personalities who give different meanings to the printed accounts. This paean to fieldwork is nothing new to anthropology, but in the case of berdache studies it is time to stress the importance of more fieldwork before additional theorizing engulfs the subject.

What, then, can we conclude about the character of the berdache? By paying more attention to the associations that Indian people themselves make between the various aspects of berdachism, we can bring some balance to the question of the sexuality of the berdache. In attacking the facile equation of homosexuality and berdachism promoted by earlier writers, recent writers have gone to the other extreme in their emphasis that berdaches are not "homosexuals." I am not trying to deny the considerable cultural differences between the status of Indian berdaches and that of American gays. There is no religious connotation in the Western heterosexual and homosexual identities, which categorize people entirely on the basis of their sexual preference. Anglo-American society recognizes only two genders, and "gay people" as a group are not a distinct gender status.

If we must make a comparison, what modern group provides the closest analogy to the berdaches? Harriet Whitehead suggests that transsexuals offer a better comparison than homosexuals. I have explained in a previous chapter why I do not agree with this comparison. Still, Whitehead is on the right track. We cannot make many valid comparisons with Western homosexuals generally, because this category includes many masculine men whose only difference from average men is their sexual involvement with other men. In traditional American Indian societies such a man would more likely be the husband of the berdache.

Cross-cultural comparisons are difficult, but if we attempt to do so for reasons of clarity, it is perhaps more accurate to compare berdaches to a subgroup of homosexuals, those whose character is very androgynous. Since the Indian viewpoint does not divide people by sexual behavior but by character, they view berdaches as comparable only to those gender-mixing males known in the vernacular of the gay community as *queens*. Like berdaches, "drag queens" are known to dress like women, or with a mixture of male and female clothing, but they are still queens even if they dress like men. They often have special occupational choices seldom associated with men, and (most importantly) have androgynous character traits. Masculine gay men are not queens, any more than the berdache's husband is a berdache. In terms of sexual behavior, there might be queens who are celibate, or even involved in some heterosexual behavior, but as a group they are usually homosexual. They are socially defined as gay. Even in Western society, with its rigid sexual distinctions, a man might have sex with a woman and still retain the gay label.

While not denying tribal diversity, the major difference between the berdache and the queen is the religious role of the berdache. But even in Western culture, which at least until recently has systematically denied a respected role for androgynous males, drag queens often exhibit a sense of mystery and a theatricality that is close to the religious role of sacred people. In the Indian view, spirituality is the prime consideration, but this spiritual aspect is reflected in the androgynous character of the berdache. Homosexual attraction is an important aspect of the berdache character, one that Indians do not deny but accept along with the other personality elements in berdachism.

A Navajo woman spoke to me about the homosexual behavior of a *nadle* without hesitation and also without controversy: "Everyone knows that he and the man he lives with are lovers, but it is not mentioned. They help their family a lot and are considered valuable members of the community. Their sexuality is never mentioned; it is just taken for granted." I heard such expressions repeatedly in my interviews with Indian people of different tribes. From 1920s fieldwork, ethnographer C. Daryll Forde concluded that Yuma *elxá* likewise were accepted and their marriage with a man recognized: "Such a pair often remains together permanently. It is considered unwise to interfere with them for the *elxá* has more power than the ordinary man and is thought to have a peaceful influence on the tribe."[36]

Getting berdaches to talk about their sexual acts is sometimes awkward, but not because they are embarrassed to admit to being involved in same-sex relations. Even though sex is seen as humorous, its expression is a private matter. Terry Calling Eagle does not deny his exclusive sexual attraction toward men, but he emphasizes that it is his character that is most important in defining himself. He accepts his sexuality as part of his character.

Once I asked the spirit if my living with a man and loving him was bad. The spirit answered that it was not bad because I had a right to release my feelings and express love for another, that I was good because I was generous and provided a good home for my children. I want to be remembered most for the two values that my people hold dearest: generosity and spirituality. If you say anything about me, say those two things.

Generosity and spirituality, not homosexual behavior, are what underlie the social prestige of the berdache from the Indian viewpoint, but these qualities are emphasized without denying the sexuality of the berdache. Spirituality, androgyny, woman's work, and sex with men are equally important indicators of berdache status. They are all seen as reflections of the same basic character of a person; this is what Indians mean when they talk about berdaches being "spiritually different." This assured sense of balance and interconnectedness has been sadly lacking in writings on the sexual diversity of American Indians. How ironic that homosexual behavior has been either denied, or most emphasized, by the Europeans. The Western fixation on sex has, from the sixteenth century to the twentieth, had a tremendous impact on the American Indian berdache.

Changes in the Berdache Tradition

Since the Coming of the Europeans

Part II

Changes in the Pediatric Tradition

Since the Coming of the Europeans

The Abominable Sin: The Spanish
     Campaign against "Sodomy," and Its
     Results in Modern Latin America

Soon after Christopher Columbus recognized that his voyage across the Atlantic Ocean had not taken him to Asia, Europeans realized that he had discovered a previously unknown continent. To them it was, in a very real sense, a "New World." The peoples they found there were as unfamiliar as beings from another planet, and their history had not prepared them for such extensive dealings with peoples of other cultures. In contrast to Middle Eastern civilizations, which had been at the center of commercial and intellectual interaction from three continents, Europeans after the fall of the Roman Empire had been relatively isolated from outside contact. Accordingly, Europeans held their own cultural values, and were little used to accepting differing viewpoints.

Such intolerance of cultural variation extended to sexuality, and at least since the thirteenth century European thought condemned same-sex relations as a major sin. Despite a tradition of homoeroticism going back to the ancient Greeks, when the Roman Empire adopted Christianity as its state religion it also adopted the antisexual heritage of the Hebrews. Weakened as it was by the otherworldly concerns of Christianity, and divided by sectarian divisions and persecutions within this new state religion, the late Roman Empire began condemning sexual practices that had previously been well accepted.

During the early medieval era a new culture formed, arising from the Greco-Roman-Christian tradition combined with folk cultures from Europe. Some historians have suggested that this medieval culture was not as concerned about condemning homosexual relations, and tolerated emotional expressions of love between people of the same sex. But by the fourteenth and fifteenth centuries, Europe was in the midst of an extremely homophobic outburst. Part of this antihomosexualism was due to Church dogma, and to political opportunism. Jealous political leaders used outlandish rumors to associate homosexual behavior with heresy and treason. By emphasizing the evilness of homosexuality, these factions could justify confiscating the wealth of those accused. The frenzy that resulted also had much to do with simple scapegoating. Europe convulsed itself with mass executions of anyone perceived as different: Jews, Christian nonconformists, woman-centered folk spiritualists known as witches, and "sodomites." The term *sodomy* was taken from the biblical story of God's destruction of the ancient city of Sodom. The original moral of this story is that Sodom was destroyed because of its inhospitality to strangers, but later writers emphasized a sexual interpretation. Especially during the Inquisition the Christian establishment killed and tortured Jews, heretics, witches, and sodomites alike, and not so incidentally confiscated condemned persons' property, thus increasing its own wealth. With this combination of economic, political, and psychological factors, same-sex relations had become a dogmatic issue.[1]

SPANISH HOMOPHOBIA

By the time European explorers landed in America, Europe was more firmly committed than any other culture in the world to persecuting sodomy. While homophobia was typical of Christian Europe generally, the Spanish seemed to be at the forefront of this persecution. In Spain the Inquisition reached sadistic extremes in its suppression of sexual diversity. Sodomy was defined loosely as any nonreproductive sexual act (usually a same-sex act but sometimes anal sex between a male and a female). Sodomy was a serious crime in Spain, being considered second only to crimes against the person of the king and to heresy. It was treated as a much more serious offense than murder. Circumstantial evidence or uncollaborated testimony was easily accepted as proof of the crime. Without any concept of religious freedom, or separation of church and state, sodomy was also considered a mortal sin. Those convicted by the inquisitorial courts were burned at the stake.[2]

Why were the Spanish so morbidly incensed over a sexual act? In what way did it threaten their society so severely as to be classified as more serious than murder? In many ways the Spanish were not much different from other Europeans in their homophobic reactions. Yet they had additional reasons to be upset over sodomy, quite likely growing out of their struggle against the Moors. These North African Muslims had occupied the Iberian peninsula for over seven hundred years, and for just that long the European natives had been resisting. Since warfare depleted the population, Spanish culture encouraged propagation.[3] As in some other societies that emphasized population growth, the Spanish tried to suppress birth control, abortion, and nonreproductive forms of sexuality. In an attempt to regain their homeland—similar to the struggles of the ancient Hebrews—the Spanish emphasized the same pro-population values that they had absorbed from the Jews via Christianity. Moreover, since all Europe had been devastated in the fourteenth century by the bubonic plague, with an estimated loss of half its population, even more pressures were added for maximizing reproduction.[4]

The Spanish had an additional reason for opposing homosexuality. In technology and intellectual thought, the Islamic civilization of the Moors was clearly more advanced than that of the Castilians. If the Spanish were going to challenge their culturally superior Muslim enemy, they were going to have to overcome their sense of inferiority by overcompensating—they had to see themselves as superior. They obviously could not do this in regard to technological or intellectual matters, so they had to turn to ideological values. In short, the Spanish had to create a culture that emphasized its difference from the Moors. Christianity, with its intolerance for other religions, served that function, supplying a unifying theme around which the non-Muslim Spanish could rally and proclaim their superiority. Their religious fanaticism sustained them in their struggles to drive out the Moors, and it left a heritage of intolerance and persecution of nonconformists.[5]

One aspect of Moorish society that clearly stood out as different from the Christians was its relaxed attitude toward same-sex relations. After centuries of continuous warfare, Spanish men displayed contempt for behavior that they associated with their Islamic enemy. When the Spanish regained control of the peninsula by the late fifteenth century, this offered the Church an unprecedented opportunity to impose its rules on the newly conquered lands. By confiscating the property of condemned individuals, the Church could gain a vast base of wealth in Spain as well as eliminate possible competitors for control of the population. This, along with the need for maximizing population growth and differentiation from the Moors, makes it clear why the Spanish treated sodomy as such a serious breach of civil and religious standards. Behind their fanatical condemnation was a striving for economic and political power, and uncertainty about being able to keep their Christian culture free from any taint of Moorish influence. They might not be able to challenge the Moors on technological or intellectual grounds, but they could do so by emphasizing "morals"—social taboos that the Muslims did not share.[6]

THE SPANISH IN THE AMERICAS

Before 1492 the Spanish had so little contact with other cultures, except for their enemy the Moors, that they could not know that homosexual behavior was commonly accepted among many of the world's cultures. But no sooner had they finished the colossal effort to expel the Moors than the discovery of the New World brought them face to face with another cross-cultural struggle. To their horror, the Spanish soon discovered that the Native Americans accepted homosexual behavior even more readily than the Moors. Since this was an inflammatory subject on which the Spanish had strong feelings, the battle lines were soon drawn. Sodomy became a major justification for Spanish conquest of the peoples called Indians.

The Spanish recognized, as would the other Europeans who followed them into the Americas, that the peoples of the New World represented a vast diversity of cultures. Nevertheless, most of the commentators did not often bother to make such distinctions in their rush to condemn Indian eroticism. In one of the least condemnatory accounts of Indian sexuality, for example, Pedro Cieza de León wrote in his "Chronicles of Peru" that the two worst sins of the Indians were cannibalism and sodomy. But he cautioned against condemning all Indians on these grounds:

> Certain persons speak great ill of the Indians, comparing them with beasts, saying that their customs and living habits belong more properly to brutes than to men, that they are so evil that not only do they make use of the abominable sin but also that they eat one another. . . . It is not my intention to say that these things apply to all of them. . . . If in one province they practice the abominable sin against nature, in many others it is regarded as unseemly and is not practiced or indeed may be abhorred. . . . So that it would be an unjust thing to voice a general condemnation of them all.[7]

In his rush to defend Indians, Cieza de León does not question the Spanish antihomosexual consensus, but only points out that not all Indians practiced sodomy. For those who did, he equated them with cannibals, worthy of no defense.

The Spanish did find, however, that same-sex acts were quite common. In many cases this was first observed through native art. Particularly in Mexico and Peru, there was a rich artistic tradition of erotic art. Sexual customs were depicted in detail, including homosexual behavior. For example, Bernal Diaz, on an exploration of the coast of Yucatán in 1517, reported discovering many clay "idols" in which "the Indians seemed to be engaged in sodomy one with the other."[8] Fernandez de Oviedo, the chronicler for the king, wrote about another expedition to a Yucatán coastal island on which Diego Velazquez reported entering a Maya temple and being shocked to see a large wooden statue of two males engaged in intercourse. In Panama in 1515, Oviedo himself saw some of this intricate artwork: "In some part of these Indies, they carry as a jewel a man mounted upon another in that diabolic and nefarious act of Sodom, made in gold relief. I saw one of these jewels of the devil twenty pesos gold in weight. . . . I broke it down with a hammer and smashed it under my own hand."[9] The Spanish melted down untold quantities of Indian artwork in precious metals, but they took a special delight in destroying these "jewels of the devil."

As a result of this systematic destruction, we cannot know the extent to which pre-Columbian art expressed homosexual themes. Unfortunately, this obliteration did not end with the colonial era. Even as late as 1915, a Peruvian art collector knew of many Moche and Vicus ceramic pieces depicting "sodomy or pederasty . . . [which] a misunderstood modesty has led many collectors to destroy." The director of the Peru National Museum of Anthropology and Archaeology points out that such censorship over the centuries continues at the hands of modern "iconoclasts."[10]

The Spanish destruction of art is typical of their refusal to see things in a different light. They did not use this knowledge to gain a wider understanding of sexual diversity, or to question their strange notion that the only function of sexual desire is procreative. Upon no authority other than the Bible, they declared that any other sexual act than that designed to reproduce was "against nature." Accordingly, they could only report in amazement the high incidence of same-sexuality among the Indians. Bernal Díaz del Castillo, accompanying Hernán Cortés during his conquest of Mexico in 1519, commented frequently on the widespread practice of same-sex relations as a well-established custom.[11] The chronicler López de Gomara reported that the Indians "are sodomitic like no other generation of men."[12]

The Spanish were also amazed that homosexuality was often associated with cross-dressing, and that the practice had religious connotations. Cieza de León reported in 1553 that he punished the Indians of Puerto Viejo in Peru because of temple prostitution. He wrote in disgust: "The devil held such sway in this land that, not satisfied with making them fall into so great sin, he made them believe that this vice was a kind of holiness and religion."[13]

Instead of learning lessons about human variability in erotic attraction and gender role, the Spanish used the existence of homosexuality as evidence of Indian inferiority. In his first report to Emperor Charles V, conquistador Hernán Cortés wrote on July 10, 1519, that the Indians of Mexico "are all sodomites and have recourse to that abominable sin." Bernal Díaz del Castillo said Cortés paused in the fighting along the coast near Xocotlan long enough to order his Indian allies: "You must not commit sodomy or do the other ugly things you are accustomed to do."[14]

These matters were emphasized by the Spanish conquistadors and writers for more than just human interest. The Indians' acceptance of homosexuality provided a major justification for the conquest and subjugation of the New World. With their belief that same-sex behavior was one of God's major crimes, the Spanish could easily persuade themselves that their plunder, murder, and rape of the Americas was righteous. They could fight their way to heaven by stamping out the sodomites, rather than by crusading to the Holy Land.

The condemnation of Indian homosexual behavior was a major factor in proving the virtue of the Spanish conquest, and the conquistadors acted resolutely to suppress it by any means necessary. The priests of course tried to convince the Indians to change voluntarily, but sometimes the military leaders did not even give the natives an opportunity to change. For example, the conquistador Nuño de Guzmán recalled that in 1530 the last person taken in battle, who had "fought most courageously, was a man in the habit of a woman, which confessed that from a child he had gotten his living by that filthiness, for which I caused him to be burned."[15] Likewise, Antonio de la Calancha, a Spanish official in Lima, sang the praises of Vasco Núñez de Balboa, who on his expedition across Panama "saw men dressed like women; Balboa learnt that they were sodomites and threw the king and forty others to be eaten by his dogs, a fine action of an honorable and Catholic Spaniard."[16]

Even Francisco de Vitoria, the leading Spanish liberal theologian who argued that the pope and the emperor had no dominion over American Indians, made a few exceptions. The natives, he avowed, could not be legally dispossessed of their lands except for three reasons: cannibalism, incest, and sodomy. The Spanish did not, however, merely take the lands of the Indians.

The Europeans' mere presence led to native decimation in numbers unprecedented in human history. A major reason the Spanish were able to prevail over the Indians was that the Europeans brought with them many deadly germs to which the Indians had no immunity. Europeans at this time had very high levels of pathogens left over from the plague. Diseases that only sickened the hardened white survivors caused the American natives to die in huge numbers. Old World diseases were without a doubt the deadliest weapon of the conquistadors, killing probably ninety percent of precontact populations.[17]

The Spanish did not realize why the Indians were wasting away from disease, but took it as an indication that it was part of God's plan to wipe out the infidels. Oviedo concluded, "It is not without cause that God permits them to be destroyed. And I have no doubts that for their sins God is going to do away with them very soon."[18] He further reasoned, in a letter to the king condemning the Mayas for accepting homosexual behavior: "I wish to mention it in order to declare more strongly the guilt for which God punishes the Indians and the reasons why they have not been granted his mercy."[19]

The Spanish did not understand that the diseases had more to do with the will of microbes than the will of God. With such misunderstandings, the theologian Juan Gines de Sepulveda stated: "How can we doubt that these people so uncivilized, so barbaric, so contaminated with so many sins and obscenities . . . have been justly conquered by such a humane nation which is excellent in every kind of virtue?"[20]

Almost as soon as they were able to establish control, representatives of the Church and the state began imposing their notions of proper behavior on the Indians. As early as 1613 in Florida, Spanish priests were trying to get Timucua Indian men and boys in confessional to admit being "sodomites."[21] A Spanish missionary who saw some "*maricas*" among the Yuma Indians during a 1775 expedition in California condemned them as "sodomites, dedicated to nefarious practices. From all the foregoing I conclude that in this matter of incontinence there will be much to do when the Holy Faith and the Christian religion are established among them."[22]

What happened when the Spanish had a chance to intervene

is seen in an incident that occurred at the mission near Santa Barbara, California, in the 1780s. When a Chumash *joya* and his husband visited another Indian who was a laborer at the mission, the suspicious priest burst into their quarters and caught them "in the act of committing the nefarious sin." The priest reported in indignation that he punished them, but not "with the severity it properly deserved. When they were rebuked for such an enormous crime, the layman [Indian man] answered that the *Joya* was his wife!" What the Indian man stated as a justification for his relationship, the missionary took as an outrage.

After this incident, the priest reported, no more of "these disreputable people" came to any of the southern California missions, "although many *Joyas* can be seen in the area. . . . Almost every village has two or three." Obviously the berdaches and their husbands had quickly learned to avoid the Spanish, but the priests were not satisfied with this. The writer concluded: "We place our trust in God and expect that these accursed people will disappear with the growth of the missions. The abominable vice will be eliminated to the extent that the Catholic faith and all the other virtues are firmly implanted there, for the glory of God."[23]

The Spanish began a concerted effort to wipe out berdachism in California, and by the 1820s a missionary at San Juan Capistrano was able to report that while berdaches were once very numerous among the Mission Indians, "At the present time this horrible custom is entirely unknown among them."[24] Evidently the Spanish were successful in this suppression, because I was able to locate no trace of even a memory of a berdache tradition among Mission Indians today.

With the harsh impact of disease, military conquest, and cultural imposition that the Indians experienced from the Spanish, it is difficult to learn native reactions to the suppression of homosexuality. Yet the Spanish documents do tell us a few things. After stating that most of the Peruvian Indians of Puerto Viejo "publically and openly [practiced] the nefarious sin of sodomy, on which they greatly prided themselves," Cieza de León complimented the local Spanish authorities for having "given punishment to those who committed the above mentioned sin, warning them how our all powerful God is displeased. And they put fear into them in such a way that now this sin is used little or not at all."[25] By 1552 the historian López de Gomora reported that Native American sodomy was being successfully wiped out by the Spanish.[26]

NATIVE RESPONSE

How did the Indians react to the intense suppression of berdachism that the Spanish enforced? It is hard enough to get the Indian viewpoint from the documentary record on any subject, and especially difficult on something like taboo sexual behavior. The Spanish claimed that they had wiped out homosexual practices. Certainly the Spanish got the impression that "sodomy" no longer existed, and without a doubt it was not openly engaged in as it had been before the arrival of the Europeans. But that does not mean that a recognized and respected status for berdaches no longer existed, or that private same-sex behavior vanished.

To find evidence of such continuity is extremely difficult. The researcher must be a detective, searching for a shred of information that might tell how native cultures adapted to these enforced changes on their ways of life. Traditionalist Indians tend not to record their thoughts in written form, and certainly not their thoughts about anything that would only bring them trouble from whites. As a result, there is a large documentary gap beginning with the establishment of colonial control, and it seems unlikely that documents will be found that verify the continuity of accepted and common homosexual behavior among Indians. The lack of documentation requires present-day ethnographers to investigate the position of contemporary Indians, to see if a respected berdache role survives. Such research cannot be done by just any fieldworker, since Indian people long ago learned not to open up to whites on this topic. It requires a person with sensitivity and a feeling of trust developed with informants.

One such ethnographer is Clark Taylor, who had the advantage of being openly gay during his fieldwork among the Zoque

Indians. As a result of his open identity, Taylor's informants confided in him. They reported that among the Zoque, as well as with the Huichol and the Cora Indians, berdaches still play a part in modern-day Indian rituals in springtime. They do not share the *mestizo* values of machismo, and do not think of gender variance and male-male sexual behavior as deviant.[27]

Ethnographic reports on the Indians of present-day central Chile offer a clue to one type of reaction to Spanish suppression. Among the precontact Araucanians, the Mapuche, and probably other peoples, shaman religious leaders were all berdaches. When the Spanish suppressed this religious institution because of its association with male-male sex, the Indians switched to a totally new pattern. Women became the shamans. So strong was the association of femininity with spiritual power that if the androgynous males could not fulfill the role, then the Indians would use the next most spiritually powerful persons. In striving for effective spirituality, they responded in a creative way to Spanish genocidal pressures.

One possible conclusion that might be drawn from this change would be that the Indians merely turned against the berdache priests. But such a sudden and unified move would seem unlikely when considering the previously high status of the shamans. More likely the Indians may have employed a clever strategy to remove the berdaches from a public institutionalized role, to protect them from Spanish wrath. Once the berdaches were no longer in public leadership positions they would not be obvious to the homophobic Spanish officials.[28] Gender variation and same-sex behavior could continue in private, unnoticed by the Spanish overlords.

Such examples may lead us to speculate that once Indians realized how much the Europeans hated sodomy, indigenous groups in various areas of the Americas quickly adapted to colonial control by keeping such things secret. This meant that berdachism would no longer be associated with ceremonialism. We have seen that the religious aspect is an important element in berdachism, but does this mean that without it berdache status would disappear? Evidently it does not. In fact, there are ethnographic reports of certain tribes in which berdache status from the beginning did not involve religious office, and though such cultures were probably rare, they do demonstrate that berdachism is not restricted to a society in which it serves an active religious leadership function.

More recent examples reveal that berdachism can survive without religious connotations. If the religious element of a group's berdache tradition has not survived, what elements do continue? The evidence suggests that the three features most notable in modern Indian groups are an androgynous personality, a woman's or mixed-gender work role, and the passive role in sexual behavior with men. The continuity of a respected social position for such nonmasculine males indicates that these three features are at the core of berdache identity. All three are equally important elements, and are considered to be personality traits that are intertwined. These traits are today more important even than cross-dressing or spirituality.

It was not until after she had been doing fieldwork among the Isthmus Zapotecs of Oaxaca, Mexico, for several years that Beverly Chiñas developed the kind of trust that would allow informants to talk openly with her about this topic. The Zapotec word for berdaches, *ira' muxe,* which means "males who manifest some degree of effeminate behavior," can also be applied to known homosexual or bisexual males, even if they do not display feminine behavior. Chiñas found that Zapotecs do not agree on a precise meaning beyond this, nor on exactly to which individuals it should be applied. But the definition does show a strong connection between nonmasculine personality and homosexual behavior. "*Ira' muxe* are respected by Zapotecs, who emphasize their differences from the general heterosexual population." *Ira' muxe* have no special religious role, but Zapotecs "defend them and their rights to their sexual and gender identity because 'God made them that way.'" Zapotecs reject the idea that *ira' muxe* could choose to be or could be forced into being different from the way they are. Berdachism is seen as a reflection of a person's basic character.[29]

SURVIVAL AMONG MAYAS TODAY

Knowing of the sporadic reports of continued berdache behavior in Latin America, I resolved to investigate a culture about which there was abundant evidence of aboriginal homosexuality: the Mayas. After my fieldwork among berdaches of the northern Plains tribes, I next made a trip to Yucatán to see if I could collect any information on modern Maya berdaches. Since the early Spanish documents contained many references to sodomy among these people, I decided to test my assumptions that such traditions have not disappeared. By luck, I met a man in Key West, Florida, who had previously lived in Yucatán and who had brought back with him a young Mayan as his lover. He had no knowledge of Mayan history, but what he said fit with precontact patterns. He stated, "Maya Indians have a very accepting attitude toward sex; 'If it feels good, do it.' Homosexuality is very open and common, with boys between the early teens to the mid twenties. But after then, men have much social pressure exerted on them to get married to a woman, and to stop dressing effeminately."[30] What he said reflected a remarkable continuity from precolonial Mayan culture, with its institutionalized male marriages of boys and young men.[31]

In trying to understand modern Yucatán folk traditions deriving from the Maya heritage, it is necessary to recognize the unbroken aboriginal influence. Though technological society has made inroads into the daily life of the traditional people, especially in the last decade, when improved transportation made outside access easier, Yucatán retains its separation even from the rest of Mexico.[32] Yucatán is most famous for its surviving archeological ruins, with their large pyramids and intricately carved temples. At several of the ruins, most notably Uxmal, it is difficult to ignore the fascination that the Mayas had with the male penis. Huge stone phallic symbols occupy central positions in the ceremonial grounds.

The situation of homosexually inclined males in Yucatán is much different from that of members of the urban gay subculture of the United States. Because homoeroticism is much more diffuse in the society, there are not separate subcultural institutions for homosexuals. There are, however, known meeting places for males who want to have sexual relations. In small villages, this will usually be a certain area near the central plaza. In the cities, it may be on certain streets. "Cruising" for partners is much easier than in the United States, where the population is polarized between "gay" and "straight" men. In Yucatán, with its more fluid approach to sexuality, there is much more of a chance of meeting someone of the same sex for erotic interests. There is also not a strict separation by age as in the United States, so that even males below the age of eighteen may enter a steam bath. What they do in the privacy of their room is considered no one else's business. Puberty, rather than the arbitrary age of eighteen or twenty-one, is seen as a more proper dividing point concerning sexual matters.

After my arrival in Yucatán, I soon learned that the society provides a de facto acceptance of same-sex relations for males. It did not take long to establish contacts, and my informants suggested that a large majority of the male population is at certain times sexually active with other males. This usually occurs in the years between thirteen and thirty, when sexual desire is strongest, but it also involves men older than that. Marriage to a woman does not seem to have much effect on the occurrence and amount of homosexual behavior.

The limitation that the culture imposes is not to prohibit male-male sexual behavior entirely, but instead to regulate it by placing males in active masculine (*hombre* or *mayate*) or passive feminine (*homosexual* or *loca*) roles. *Homosexuales* are *de ambiente,* having an androgynous ambience. They take the passive role in either anal or oral sex, and are considered the true homosexual. They often share a sense of community with other androgynous males, revolving around drag names, "campy" language, and gender-referenced humor. While they are not seen as "real men," they occupy an accepted position in society and are not subject to homophobic violence as in Anglo-America.

Their masculine sexual partners, the *hombres* (literally "men"), have no sense of identity as homosexuals. As long as they effect a macho demeanor and at least express some interest in getting married to a female at some time in the future, they are free to follow their sexual desires with males. They have no burden of being labeled "abnormal," because in fact their behavior is normal for that society. The surprising configuration of their society is that a particular person might take either role in sex, depending on the particular relationship established with the other partner. Some persons, referred to as *internacionales,* take both roles sexually, but most males identify with one role more than the other and assume either an active or passive role. It is generally assumed that the more masculine of the two will take the active role in sex, but this may vary sometimes. Passive homosexuals have told me of instances when their *hombre* boyfriends played the passive role in sex, but this was done only after a level of trust had been established so that such role reversal would be kept secret. Sex with a male is not something to be embarrassed about, but role reversal is.

Perhaps the best way to explain the social role of homosexual Mayas is to examine the words of particular people. In a small Maya village, it is easy to be introduced to those who are known as *homosexual*. As the man who introduced me said of such persons, "Everyone knows they're homosexual, and accepts them. There are people like that everywhere in the world. There are some homosexuals in every Maya village." With such a matter-of-fact attitude he introduced me to a young man in his mid-twenties who did not seem very feminine but not macho either. He was a typical *de ambiente,* with a pleasant, friendly personality. He was popular with the men in his village, being nicknamed El Sexy. When I met him, I noticed a macho man making a noticeably sexual come-on to him, publicly and without any sense of subterfuge. Later, when he was riding with me in my car, a boy smiled and yelled to him, "I see you have found your husband," referring to me. It was not a negative or derogatory joke, just a relaxed kidding that reflected the general knowledge of the villagers that my informant preferred men. He enjoyed the joke immensely.

The men had no reluctance to be seen with him, and had none of the stiffness so apparent in "straight" males in the United States. When he goes to the village tavern, or *cantina,* the men may dance with him. During carnival time, he dresses as a woman and is especially popular as a dance partner. Everyone accepts him. He says of his respected position:

The other people appreciate me very much. Because I behave properly. *Hombres* will have sex with each other when they get drunk, but

I consider that to be bad. It should only be done with an *homosexual,* then it's alright. I would not have sex with another *homosexual;* I don't consider them to be completely men. They're like a third group, different from men or women.

He never takes the initiative in sex, since the men always come to him. He has had relations with most of the men in his village, from teenagers to the elderly. "They know I'm good," he remarks. The men take him to a place, usually behind the church or in the sports field. Since he lives with his mother, he never brings a man home for sex, although he does do social entertaining there. His mother seems quite comfortable with his male visitors, and had no objection to me staying in their home. Since everyone sleeps in a separate hammock, sex is not usually associated with the bedroom. Sexual acts, male-female as well as male-male, are more likely done outside in the bush. Despite his character and behavior, which in the United States would be defined as gay, "El Sexy" plans to get married to a woman after he is thirty, "so that I won't be alone." He might decide to have children, but otherwise he feels that marriage will not inhibit his sexual activities with men.[33]

A few days later, a young man who was visiting let it be known that he enjoyed sex with males. He does not identify himself as homosexual, but rather as *hombre.* He explained that his *hombre* social role required that he take only the "active" role. To do otherwise (at least where others would know about it) would require a changed social role that he was not prepared to make.

For those who follow the cultural dictates of taking on a clearly defined homosexual role, there is an easy acceptance by society. This can apply even for those who follow the role for their entire lives. In another Maya town in southern Yucatán, I visited a forty-year-old man who dresses in a mixture of men's and women's clothing. He owns a popular beauty shop, and is one of the most prosperous persons in the town. When I and a friend visited him, he was calmly doing a manicure for a middle-aged, proper-looking woman. While I talked with him, the woman's husband continually exchanged erotic glances with the young man who accompanied me. As the beautician sat with his thinning hair in pink rollers, he talked freely about his sex life while continuing the woman's manicure. One cannot even imagine such a situation in the typical Anglo-American beauty parlor. He told me:

Everyone knows I'm *homosexual,* and I am well respected. There are hundreds of *homosexuales* in town, most openly so, but I am the only one who dresses as a woman. The people treat me as a woman, and there are never any problems. I attend mass devotedly; the priest often visits my house for meals because I'm one of the best cooks in town. People respect my good citizenship. The men come to visit me for sex; I have to turn them away. I had a lover for several years, and we walked around town holding hands being completely open. No one objected. I feel no discrimination for being different.

Next I visited a fifty-five-year-old Maya in the same town. He dresses as a man, and is not recognizably feminine. But he has identified as *homosexual* for his entire life, and everyone in his village knows this. He rents out hammock spaces in his house to local high school students, whose parents want them living near the school in a trustworthy environment. He allows men to visit him for sex only during the weekends, when the students are gone.

He had recognized himself as homosexual when he was still a young boy, and had had an open and active sex life with men since his early teens. His family and everyone in town knew, and he had never had any problems. He never felt in danger, and my statements about the attacks against gay people in the United States seemed almost unbelievable to him. He could not even conceive of why someone would want to hurt others merely because they were homosexual. He had not noticed any changes in people's attitudes toward homosexuality since his youth, and stated that attitudes had always been accepting. For those who accept their society's mores and the available roles open to them, there is a recognized and respected position that continues aspects of the aboriginal tradition of the berdache.

MESTIZO MALES

While the Spanish writers were not correct in their belief that they had wiped out the berdache traditions among the Indians, their antisodomy campaign did have a significant impact on the emerging *mestizo* society. Since relatively few Spanish women came to America, most of the early colonists were men. They had sex with Indian women, and produced biracial progeny that were also bicultural. As a result, the *mestizo* culture absorbed opposing notions of sexuality from the aboriginal and Spanish heritages. With Spanish influence being so strong, it is not surprising that homophobia is an element of *mestizo* social attitudes.

In Mexico at least, an antihomosexual feeling may also be a reflection of condemnation of same-sex behavior by the Aztecs. Unlike most of their neighbors, the Aztec conquerers who invaded central Mexico from the north a century before the Spanish seem to have had taboos against homosexuality. Like the Spanish, the Aztecs were a militarized conquering people, and both societies pursued an ideal of absolute machismo that condemned effeminacy. The modern Mexican *mestizo* identifies with the Spanish or the Aztecs, rather than with the more traditional civilizations of classical Meso-America. Those other cultures, with their easy acceptance of homosexuality, are seen as weak.

Many people do not publicly admit to being Indian, and claim not to understand a Native American language when in fact they do. This acculturative pressure, which is just beginning to be felt in more remote areas, has existed in central Mexico for centuries. The process of acculturation has caused tremendous problems in personal identity that have an impact on sexual behavior. With such conflicting cultural values in *mestizo* society, there are contradictory messages for homosexually inclined individuals.

The major impact that the Spanish campaign has had on modern *mestizo* culture is a decline in status for androgynous males. These individuals have lost the respected status they had in many traditional cultures, and instead are often criticized as being traitors to the macho ideal. Yet, even in *mestizo* culture, the Spanish were not able to wipe out the behavior they so detested. Ironically, what emerged was a kind of de facto cultural approval for masculine males who wish to have sex with these *homosexuales*. Establishing who is *homosexual,* however, leads to a confusion of roles. Erskine Lane, a gay man from the United States who has lived in Latin America for several years, expresses this confusing situation: "The gay gringo who lingers for awhile in Spanish America soon comes to understand how Alice felt when she fell down the rabbit hole. Disorientation in a topsy-turvy wonderland where many old familiar standards of sexual behavior no longer apply at all and most of the others have been reversed. Who is gay? What is gay? For a while you're not sure any more."

Lane characterizes *mestizo* males as almost completely bisexual in their behavior. Yet, they manage to avoid defining themselves as such. By their view, manhood is defined as one who takes the active role in sex. The sex of the person he sleeps with is less important than the position he takes in the sex act. "The macho can actively court and pursue other males; he can even, in some circumstances, admit to a preference for males, all without compromising his heterosexuality." He can do this, however, only as long as he plays the inserter, or "man's," role.[34]

This feeling is illustrated by one *hombre* who would take only the active role in sex, saying "If I let him fuck me I'd probably like it and then I'd do it again. And then I'd be queer." This fear of the enjoyment of anal sex partly explains the strict separation of active and passive roles in *mestizo* society. Lane asked some of his macho male sexual partners which sex they really preferred. This kind of question was puzzling to them, and they had to think about it before giving an answer. One responded: "It really wouldn't matter to me . . . I guess I really have no preference, but sometimes I think it feels better with a man." The North American writer concluded: "The pansexuality of some guys here amazes me. Male, female, fat, skinny, tall, short, young, old, whatever. No apparent preference. Or, if they have a preference, it is overridden by the supreme macho mandate, which simply says Fuck!"[35]

A similar pattern has been observed by Paul Kutsche, an anthropologist who did fieldwork in Costa Rica. He speaks of the relaxed attitude about sex that is common among mestizo males, and explains it as due to their general approach to life:

"Latins are less prone to pigeonhole other individuals or themselves, and more prone to approach each event existentially without [having categories determined by] the foregoing events."[36] Though it is easy to see the continuities of aboriginal culture in these sexual patterns, among modern *mestizos* the androgynous male has lost the high status and religious association that was formerly held by Indians. The pejorative term *maricón* means effeminate, swish, but not homosexual per se. So while a masculine man who has sex with other males is not an object of concern, the androgynous male is the brunt of jokes.[37]

Just as the status of women has declined with the imposition of a misogynist Spanish culture, so too has the status of non-masculine males. There are many similarities between these two groups, in that the social position of both is contradictory. There is the *madre,* who is saintly and sexless, but there is a contrasting species of female, the *bicha.* These social constructs are models of femininity, and an androgynous male fits into this pattern. Lane concludes, "He may be treated with something resembling tenderness or with something bordering on contempt. Or, more probably, with a strange mixture of the two. Just as the woman is treated."[38]

In such a cultural context, specifically "gay" establishments—like bars where homosexuals congregate—are rare. Until recently at least, attempts to organize a separate subculture were met with repression. Police may arrest customers if an openly gay bar opens, and an attempt to start a gay newspaper would most assuredly meet with police opposition. But the focus of such repression would not be against the sexuality itself, as it would be in the United States. It would be against the political implications of the rise of a separate gay subculture. Since same-sex contacts can occur in just about any location, there is little need for separate subcultural institutions. As a consequence, people are not polarized into opposite identities based on sexual behavior. So the irony is that while the androgynous male may be derided, as women are derided, there is still a place in society for him. Lane contrasts the situation in Anglo-America, "where a flamboyant painted queen wandering into a straight bar by accident may get thrown out, beat up, or abused.

Here he will more likely be invited to dance by some admiring macho."[39]

Since Latin American *mestizo* cultures are the product of two cultures with such opposing attitudes toward gender variation and same-sex behavior, it is understandable that they should have contradictory and confusing tendencies. The fieldwork in Latin America reported in this chapter indicates that in areas where a precolonial berdache tradition existed, and where the Indian traditions are still followed, berdaches continue to be respected. Such is also the case in North America. But for *mestizos,* the contradictory position of homosexually inclined males, whether feminine or masculine, is a product of the historic changes forced on Native Americans by the Spanish. It is part of the heritage of cultural genocide.

8   Seafarers, Cowboys, and Indians: Male Marriage in Fringe Societies on the Anglo-American Frontier

Before the mid-nineteenth century, Anglo-American culture seems to have had little impact on the berdache tradition in Native American societies. The English were latecomers to the New World, and their involvement in North America and the Caribbean was initially concerned with establishing colonies populated by Europeans and Africans. Rather than ruling Indian populations in an empire, as the Spanish did in Latin America, the English pushed the natives out of the way.

It was the existence of a frontier that at least allowed most Indian tribes to preserve their self-government for the next two centuries, even if eventually they had to leave their homelands because of the advancing frontier of white settlement. And it was the frontier that provided the setting for the emergence of all-male societies on the fringes of English occupation, first in the Caribbean and later in the Western interior. White men who participated in these fringe societies in the West interacted, and in some cases probably established relationships with berdaches.

Since we do not have documents in which a frontiersman admitted to an affectional relationship with a berdache, these suggestions are speculative. Given the attitudes of Anglo-American society, it is unrealistic to assume that a man would disclose such stigmatized behavior, especially in print. There were few white men who would even admit in print to sexual involvement with an Indian woman, yet the number of light-skinned "mixed bloods" in nineteenth- and twentieth-century Indian communities attests to its commonness. Since homosexual involvement does not produce offspring, and male-male marriage is not legally recognized, tangible evidence is difficult to find.

Those who insist on documentation may want to skip over this chapter, but existing evidence, though sparse, indicates a basis for at least sketchy generalization. My approach in this chapter is based on the reasoning that all-male fringe societies are not asexual, and that individual men who had less need for women would be precisely the type of men who would gravitate to male fringe groups. What follows should be taken as a tentative hypothesis, which I hope future research on the Old West can amplify.

PIRATES

The first all-male society in the New World originated in the Caribbean, where the Spanish lost control of their original claims. Other Europeans made competing claims to islands, promoting a state of confusion that was close to anarchy. In this climate, no one nation was in control. Lawlessness reigned, and individual groups of seamen found that they could profit handsomely by raiding the ships that were transporting huge amounts of wealth taken from the Indians. Thus were born the buccaneers. By the end of the sixteenth century, piracy had turned the Caribbean into the first of a series of "Wild West" areas, outside the control of established authority.[1]

A frontier, on which individuals could operate outside the controls of a national government, offered a revolutionary opportunity for male Europeans. From what we know, pirates generally came from lower-class families. As adolescents they often joined wandering bands of male youths, surviving by petty theft. Scouted by the law, these bands would usually stay isolated, camping in forests and hiding from people.

As a consequence, these boys went through their awakening years of sexual feeling in an all-male group without adult supervision. These boys, without an authority repressing their sexuality, no doubt learned their sex from the older boys. They seldom had association with females, and even less chance for heterosexual contact. So unless we assume that they were totally asexual, we can reasonably suggest that these boys were socialized into an all-male form of sexuality.[2]

Older boys in such bands were often captured by the law and pressed into service in the Royal Navy. There they learned seafaring skills, but they chafed at the authority and excessive restraints placed on them aboard a naval cruiser or a merchant ship. It was these men who most likely deserted to pirate bands. They were attracted to the democratic nature of pirate society, in which practically all of the members were from lower-class backgrounds like themselves. In contrast to their bitter memories of the navy, they gloried in the freedoms they enjoyed as buccaneers.

In these fringe all-male societies, existing outside the control of the church and the state, men had the choice of being sexual with another male or of being abstinate. Buccaneers rarely had opportunities to be around women, and evidence suggests that they seemed uncomfortable when associating with females. They did not keep women captives for sex, and reports of rape attacks by pirates were rare. Pirate folklore stressed that it was unlucky for them even to be around women.[3] For those men who stayed with a pirate band, homosexual behavior was not a variant option in their life; it was their sole sexual activity other than masturbation. Those who had grown up in vagrant bands had little or no opportunity to acquire heterosexual socialization. Sex with another male was the ordinary and acceptable way of engaging in erotic pleasure.[4] In contrast to the androgyny of the berdaches, the pirate form of homosexual activity emphasized masculinity.

There is very little direct evidence for this homosexual activity.[5] We know that officials often complained that Port Royal, Jamaica, a favorite pirate safe harbor, was "filled with sodomites."[6] And we know that when England began strictly enforcing sodomy laws, sailors were prominent among the accused and that their usual defense was that they did not know it was wrong.[7] Long-distance sailors have long had a reputation for same-sex expression. As recent as the early 1900s a British naval officer remarked, "Homosexuality was rife. . . . In some services (the Austrian and French, for instance) nobody ever remarks about it, taking such a thing as a natural proceeding. . . . To my knowledge, sodomy is a regular thing on ships that go on long cruises. In the warships, I would say that the sailor preferred it."[8]

This acceptance of homosexual behavior may have declined in the twentieth century, but the reasons for its decline specify why it was likely to have been common among the pirates. A sexologist writing in 1914 declared that informants who were exceptionally knowledgeable about seafarer life-styles stated that "homosexual practices among sailors had decreased in recent years to a notable extent." The main reason for this decline was the change in the speed of steamships. Vessels were seldom at sea for more than two weeks, in contrast to the long sailing voyages which would take men away from land for several months at a time. This writer suggested that another reason for the decrease in homosexual behavior was a recent "rise of public sentiment, condemning it, among the men. This would operate, of course, to put a check on the conduct of individuals."[9] Obviously, such behavior had been more common earlier. With the pirates' backgrounds, their very long periods isolated at sea, and their rebellion against conventional society, we can hypothesize that they likely found male-male sex preferable to celibacy.

Another way to explain pirate sexuality is to argue by analogy from other all-male fringe groups, in which there is direct evidence of widespread homosexual behavior. One such group is hoboes. This group was a product of the era of railroading in the United States when unemployed males discovered that they could ride cross-country as uninvited guests on freight trains. From the Civil War to World War II, these men created a fringe society that, while not as independent and physically isolated from general society as pirates, did depend on long-distance traveling (but on rail instead of ships). By doing this, they isolated themselves from women and lived in all-male groups. Like pirates, many hoboes were from lower-class families and as youths had run away from home and grown up in the hobo group. From the 1870s to the 1930s, hobos were the kind of economic and social rebels that pirates had been earlier.

Two major studies of the social world of the hobo, in the 1890s and in 1919–20, both found that many hoboes accepted and indeed defended male-male sex. In rebelling against Victorian social norms in general, they were more tolerant of sexual variance as well. These studies found that sexual interaction was almost entirely anal or between-the-thighs intercourse. Rather than promiscuity, the usual pattern was a pair-bonded couple— often an adult man with a teenager—who were devoted to each other and would stay together for years.[10]

While there may not be much evidence for what pirates did sexually, we can observe a pattern of pair-bonding that is very similar to what existed in hobo homosexual relationships. When buccaneers captured a ship, the only captives they would take with them were sailors and boys past about age ten. A boy was assigned to an individual, either as cabin boy for the captain, or as an apprentice for one of the ship's artisans. From evidence in court records of pirates' trials, these boys became very attached to their mentors.[11] Among the regular sailors, two men paired off with each other as "mates." If one of these men died, the rule within pirate society was that all of the man's property and share of the booty was inherited by his mate. In battle the two mates would fight as a team, and there are numerous stories of a pirate dying while trying to save his mate.[12] These were devoted, loving relationships; they were de facto male marriages.

Conceding the idea that pirates were sexual with each other, it might be claimed that pirate sex was no more than the "situational homosexuality" so well known among contemporary prisoners. This comparison is faulty, because of several critical differences. Prisons are heavily regulated, with rigid rules imposed by outsiders. These rules are antipathetic both to prisoners and to homosexual expression. Most prisoners regard their imprisonment as temporary, and their homosexual behavior as a temporary adjustment due to the lack of women. Prisoners have little unsupervised time together, and are subject to being transferred at any time. All of these things make for sexual behavior which is different from the marriage patterns that evolved in buccaneer communities during the seventeenth century.[13]

Though some of the pirates originally joined their crew as captives, those who chose to remain with the pirates made a conscious decision to live in a society without women. Many of them coupled with another male on a permanent basis. Pirates, of course, had nothing to do with Indians. But they did evidence a pattern that repeated itself in later centuries. By the early 1700s the colonial governments had wiped out the Caribbean pirate communities. The only place that males could now go to avoid the oppressive rules of church and state was the Western frontier.

COWBOY SEXUALITY

With the exception of those men who married Indian women, males who remained on the frontier were those who—like buccaneers—were comfortable living outside of established rules and without women. They may not have originally gone to the frontier because of homosexual preferences (though some undoubtedly did), but they did not stay if they had strong heterosexual needs. The frontier was largely populated by men who were content to be asexual for long periods or who had sex with other males.

Looking at cowboys, a later group of frontiersmen, it is hard to imagine them as asexual. In 1871 the *Topeka Daily Commonwealth* printed a description of cowboys: "Life with them is a round of boisterous gayety and indulgence in sensual pleasure." [14] The cowboy is usually thought of in terms of his philandering with showgirls and prostitutes. A former cowboy acknowledged that most of them had venereal disease. [15] That is not a sign of abstinence. But can we attribute this solely to prostitutes?

What about when cowboys were not in the cow towns? Other than their brief annual or semiannual payday flings, most of their time was on the range or in the camps where women were conspicuously absent. Out on the range, isolated from mainstream society, there was no outside authority checking on them. The range boss was a senior cowboy himself. In this situation, cowboys paired off. A deep personal relationship often developed between two "partners" or "sidekicks." A poem published in 1915 by a ranch hand who had lived in South Dakota and Arizona illustrates a cowboy's feelings after his partner's death.

> I hate the steady sun that glares, and glares!
> The bird songs make me sore.
> I seem the only thing on earth that cares
> 'Cause Al ain't here no more!
>
> And him so strong, and yet so quick he died,
> And after year on year
> When we had always trailed it side by side,
> He went—and left me here!
>
> We loved each other in the way men do
> And never spoke about it, Al and me.
> But we both *knowed,* and knowin' it so true
> Was more than any woman's kiss could be.
> ....
> The range is empty and the trails are blind,
> And I don't seem but half myself today.
> I wait to hear him ridin' up behind
> And feel his knee rub mine the good old way.[16]

Are we to believe that for most of the year this cowboy, who had such deep emotional ties to his partner, was totally asexual? While the autobiographies on which the cowboy literature is based do not of course mention sex among men, cowboy humor suggests a different view. In some limericks gathered from elderly cowboys, two suggest homoerotic elements:

> There was a cowboy named Hooter,
> Who packed a big six-shooter,
> When he grabbed the stock
> It became hard as a rock,
> As a peace-maker it couldn't be cuter.
>
> Young cowboys had a great fear,
> That old studs once filled with beer,
> Completely addle'
> They'd throw on a saddle,
> And ride them on the rear.[17]

Obviously such things were not unknown among cowboys. But for someone raised during the Victorian era, it was a rare event that he would reveal his private sexual behavior. Yet there are a few such documents. One early twentieth-century Oklahoma cowboy, who decades afterward moved to California and became a sailor, later recalled how the trail boss urged each cowboy to pair off with one other man: "Always take another puncher along," urged the boss, "In a cow outfit, you and your fellows are members one of another." In his private correspondence, this cowboy confessed that these partnerships often eventually became sexual: "At first pairing they'd solace each other gingerly and, as bashfulness waned, manually [i.e., mutual masturbation]. As trust in mutual good will matured, they'd graduate to the ecstatically comforting 69 [mutual oral sex]. . . . Folk know not how cock-hungry men get." He pointed out how sex on the range was mostly mutual masturbation and oral sex, but it was not limited to what he called "cockulation." Attraction for another cowboy, he wrote, "was at first rooted in admiration, infatuation, a sensed need of an ally, loneliness and yearning, but it regularly ripened into love." [18]

Another man remembered that in his youth in the early 1900s he worked in an isolated all-male Western logging camp. Unlike the open range, here the group of nine men were snowed in for months during the severe winter. He wrote, "not one of us could be considered effeminate, neurotic or abnormal. Yet all but two engaged in homosexual activities. . . . The popular method, preferred by the majority, was sodomy, and it was in this logging camp that I was initiated into the discomforts, adjustments and ecstasies of this form of sexual activity." He continued:

After the logging experience followed two years in a gold mining camp where some 55 men were employed. . . . Restlessness among the crew evidenced itself by a raid on the vaseline supply in the first aid cabinet, of which I was custodian. Here again, I was to learn the error of assuming that those engaged in homosexual activities were of a specific type. Out of the 55 men in camp, conservatively over half were getting relief from one another. The brawny, ultra-masculine types invariably started out increasing their sociabilities, taking booze with them when dropping in on different buddies throughout the camp. My time was pretty well monopolized in the evenings by first one and then another of those inclined towards homosexuality.

Two of the most masculine of the crew (a tram operator and a jackhammer man) soon started pairing off exclusively, moving into a cabin together, even ordering exact duplicates of clothing out of the Montgomery Ward catalog. They were the envy of a number of us.[19]

While it may be questioned how accurate this one man's perception is, this remembrance rings true. In his massive survey of American male sexual behavior in the 1940s, Alfred Kinsey suggested that this type of experience was common. Kinsey pointed out that the highest frequencies of homosexual behavior his research team found anywhere in America were in isolated rural communities in some of the remotest sections of the West. This contrasted with the lowest rates among settled small farming communities, which are much more family oriented than the all-male fringe communities. The Kinsey report concluded:

There is a fair amount of sexual contact among the older males in Western rural areas. It is a type of homosexuality which was probably common among pioneers and outdoor men in general. Today it is found among ranchmen, cattle men, prospectors, lumbermen, and farming groups in general—among groups that are virile, physically active. These are men who have faced the rigors of nature in the wild. They live on realities and on a minimum of theory. Such a background breeds the attitude that sex is sex, irrespective of the nature of the partner.[20]

Among such men, Kinsey added, "There is a minimum of personal disturbance or social conflict over such activity."[21] They were men living in a single-sex environment, and most of them were not asexual. They established full relationships, which were evidently no more restricted than male-female relationships in the mainstream of Western culture.

BACHELORS OF THE FRONTIER

How such male relationships operated on the frontier, and even later were accepted as part of society in the rural West, is suggested by an interview I conducted with an elderly woman in

Interior, South Dakota. She has lived her entire life on the homestead that her parents settled in the 1890s. When asked if she remembered any of the pioneer bachelors, she said, "Oh yes, there were many bachelors in the area, especially earlier when the area was newly settled. They never married. Some had a reputation of being a little weird, with very strange ideas." When asked if people thought it strange that they never married, she replied, "Everybody had a 'do your own thing' attitude so people respected each other's individual choice. There weren't that many women around, so it wasn't thought about if they didn't marry, or even show an interest in women."[22]

She then told about Charles Brown (c. 1880–c. 1960) and his roommate, George Carr (c. 1875–1958), neither of whom ever married. Both of them were originally from Iowa. Charles came to homestead when he was about age twenty-nine, bringing his parents with him. George came west by himself, and soon moved onto the Brown farm. They lived together for many years, until Charles moved to California because of bad health in 1936. George stayed another twelve years on the homestead by himself, but eventually got lonely and moved away. The sod house that they lived in has been preserved, and is now a South Dakota historic landmark. My informant remembered Charles as being "a loner," who did not associate much with others beyond his parents and his roommate. George, on the other hand, "was the best cook in the area, and he loved children. In winter he would take neighbor children on sled rides and cook big fried chicken dinners for them. All the neighbors loved him. He was like family, and we respected his different ways." This description is remarkably similar to descriptions in the literature about berdaches.

After talking about George Carr and Charles Brown for a good bit, she thought awhile and said, "The story of these bachelors has never been told." Up to this point I had not mentioned anything about sex, but I gingerly introduced the topic. I expected that a person of her generation might have reacted negatively, but when I asked if these bachelors might have had a homosexual relationship, she answered very matter-of-factly: "People back then didn't talk about *any* kind of sex. So they wouldn't think anything of it." I suggested that if they did have sex together, such behavior would not have been known about simply because people accepted their living together in a relationship. After a long pause she said, "Now that I think about it, many of them probably were that way. We didn't talk about such things then. It was better than today, when everyone is paranoid about it."

Do we have documentation that George Carr and Charles Brown had a sexual aspect to their relationship? No. How do we prove that homosexual acts actually occurred in these male marriages? To hope to find proof is unrealistic, because private sexual behavior between consenting individuals rarely shows up in the historical record. There were no social scientists scouring the Caribbean and the West doing surveys of the pirates' and frontiersmen's sex lives. We cannot expect more of the historical record. There is, in fact, as the historian Martin Duberman points out, "only a tiny stockpile of historical materials that document the existence of *heterosexuality* in the past. Yet no one claims the minuscule amount of evidence is an accurate gauge of the actual amount of heterosexual activity that took place." [23] The "proof" of genital contact that is wanted to confirm a male marriage is not asked of historians discussing the heterosexuality of women and men who live together for many years, or even of women and men who have ephemeral love relations. The documentation that does exist for these bachelor couples is the same as that for heterosexual couples: These pairs of men on the frontier chose each other as their life companion, and lived with each other devotedly. That is what the historian can demonstrate. [24]

Beyond all this, it is also true that some men went to the frontier specifically *because of* homosexuality. Escaping to the frontier was a common reaction for individuals who were accused of any kind of crime. It was easier to leave than to face a possible jail sentence in their hometown. Someone accused of sodomy, or any related charge like "lewdness" or "gross immorality," would probably behave no differently.

In the earliest settlements, the English colonies enacted sodomy laws. The law code of Virginia in 1610, to cite the earliest case, specified a long list of capital crimes including impious or treasonous speech, blasphemy, sacrilege, theft, and the "sins of Sodomie." In 1624 Richard Cornish was tried and found guilty of a homosexual attack on another man. Against the protests of a number of the other original (all-male) settlers at Jamestown, the authorities executed him.[25] Cornish was the first of many to die in the English settlements for committing "the sin not to be named among Christians."

Others survived, but only after being tortured by the government. In 1637 in the Plymouth Colony, the first known case of same-sex persecution in New England involved John Allexander and Thomas Roberts. They were convicted of "lewd behavior and unclean carriage one with another, by often spending their seed one upon another, which was proved both by witness & their own confession." Roberts, a servant, was severely whipped, but the instigator Allexander was sentenced "to be severely whipped, and burnt in the shoulder with a hot iron, and to be perpetually banished."[26] Perhaps some of these banished men, as well as the many others accused or even suspected of male-male sex, escaped to join the Indians rather than face the draconian laws of white society.

The historian Jonathan Katz has collected a number of nineteenth-century documents of European men who were exposed as homosexuals in their home countries, and whose response was to escape to the United States. One wrote back to Europe a letter describing his ordeal, and concluding: "In consequence of the disgrace which came upon me in my fatherland I am obliged to reside in America. Even now I am in constant anxiety lest what befell me at home should be discovered here and thus deprive me of the respect of my fellow-men."[27] Another wrote to his brother on the eve of his departure from Denmark, "My nerves have been very bad. . . . I am not heartless, but you will understand how hard it is for me to see any of my family."[28] No doubt some of those accused similarly in the United States went to the frontier, beyond the reaches of the law.

But it was not even necessary that accusations of sodomy be lodged against a person for them to go west. The Danish man just quoted, who had admitted in court his participation in a homosexual act, first settled in a small town in Illinois, where he was quite unhappy. He wrote back to his brother in disgust:

"So far the young ladies have been desperately wooing me in a very energetic American way. . . . I shall never really be at ease in this place. The town is too small, people are too inquisitive and prying and—there is too much religion. . . . I demand peace in my own territory. That I shall never get here. . . . I keep as much to myself as possible, but sometimes it is undeniable that I feel a little closed in." Reacting against the oppressive conformity of small-town life in the Midwest, like so many others this man went west. He eventually settled in San Francisco, but he wrote late in his life about his past years in the United States: "I have been cast from the Atlantic to the Pacific, from the Mexican Gulf to the border of Canada."[29] It was natural for someone with something to hide to move to the transient areas on the frontier.

FRONTIERSMEN'S CONTACTS WITH BERDACHES

Having established that male-male sex occurred on the frontier, it is reasonable to conclude that some of the frontiersmen who made contact with American Indians most likely had more than a passing interest in berdaches. From early Spanish and French accounts, knowledge of berdaches had already spread among frontiersmen. These accounts, as we have seen from previous chapters, associated berdachism with sodomy. One of the earliest references in English to the direct observation of berdaches was written by Nicholas Biddle in an official journal entry of the Lewis and Clark expedition. On December 22, 1804, he noted that they saw "men dressed in squars [squaws'] clothes" among the Mandan Indians. Biddle later wrote, in explanation of this practice among the Hidatsas, that "If a boy shows any symptoms of effeminacy or girlish inclinations he is put among the girls, dressed in their way, brought up with them, and sometimes married to men. They submit as women to all the duties of a wife. I have seen them—the French call them Berdaches."[30]

In the years after the Lewis and Clark expedition, there was an intense interest in the new lands acquired in the vast Louisiana Purchase. Most of the information that Americans received about Western Indians came from the French sources, and the

accounts that mentioned berdachism emphasized same-sex behavior. The translated account of La Salle's expedition, published in 1814 in New York, characterized Indian men as having
"a brutish sensuality," loving "boys above women."[31] A white
explorer who had spent some time among the Kansa Indians
reinforced this view in 1819. He wrote that "Sodomy is a crime
not uncommonly committed; many of the subjects of it are
publically known, and do not appear to be despised, or to excite
disgust. One of them was pointed out to us." The explorer described this person as dressing like a woman, having long hair,
and doing woman's work.[32]

The early comments usually express a matter-of-fact acceptance and a curious interest in berdaches. Thomas McKenny,
founder of the United States Office of Indian Affairs, had
learned all about berdachism from frontiersmen even before he
went west. The fact that McKenny was so well informed indicates that frontiersmen knew quite a bit about berdachism. In
1824 he wrote about the Chippewa "man-woman." From a
dream, he explained to readers of his book, such a person "considers that he is bound to impose upon himself, as the only
means of appeasing his manito [guiding spirit], all the exterior
of a woman. . . . It [is] impossible to distinguish them from the
women . . . and [they] even go through the ceremony of marriage! Nothing can induce these men-women to put off these
imitative garbs. . . . [They] live, and die, confirmed in the belief
that they are acting the part which the dream . . . pointed out
to them as indispensable."[33]

Another widely read author of life among Native Americans
was Alexander Maximilian, a prince from the German state of
Wied who traveled in the West from 1832 to 1834. He wrote
that all Indian tribes had berdaches, and that the Crows in particular had many of them. From his time spent among this tribe
he concluded that the Crows "exceed all the other tribes in unnatural practices."[34]

An even more famous writer was George Catlin, whose eight
years' travel in the West, as well as his paintings of Indian scenes,
gave his writings a particular authority. Catlin's book on Indians
was so popular that by the 1860s it had gone through ten edi-
tions, and even to the end of the century was one of the main

sources by which people learned about aboriginal Americans. Among the Sauk and Fox in the 1830s, Catlin's attendance at the "feast of the Berdache" publicized the custom. After making it clear that the warriors doing the dancing were the sexual partners of the berdache, Catlin concludes his description with a suddenly vehement comment: "This is one of the most unaccountable and disgusting customs that I have ever met in the Indian country. . . . For further account of it I am constrained to refer the reader to the country where it is practiced, and where I should wish that it might be extinguished before it be more fully recorded."[35] Whether these sentiments were Catlin's personal views is uncertain, since he might have felt constrained to insert a negative comment to prevent controversy. Nevertheless, he did emphasize the berdache by drawing a sketch of the dance in his book, and he had practically invited homosexually inclined men to go west and see berdaches for themselves.

Another traveler, who made similar records of his travels but in a more positive vein, was William Drummond Stewart. Visiting the Blackfoot and Crow in the 1840s, he openly admired "a handsome youth, who was attached to the service of the rest. Having refused to take part in the warlike feats of the men, he had previously been consigned, under the name of Broadashe, to the society, the duties, and the dress of the women. There are youths of this description in every camp, resembling in office the eunuchs of the seraglio. Enjoying the flavor of the partisan, Broadashe was a follower, together with two squaws, of this band."[36] This last sentence described the berdache's sexual role, of which the admiring white visitor was well aware.

Throughout the frontier era, references to berdaches continued to appear. Some of these reports were from army officers. Henry Schoolcraft's survey of all of the tribes in the United States includes a reference indexed under "hermaphrodite" from a United States Army surveyor in 1849. Referring to a berdache who was most likely Papago or Yuma, a Lieutenant Whipple mentioned on meeting this person that "she cohabits with a man."[37]

Another army officer, William Hammond, disabused his readers of the idea that berdaches were physically hermaphroditic. In 1851, when he was stationed in Laguna Pueblo, he met a person called by the Indians *mujerado* (Spanish for "womaned"), and when he visited Acoma Pueblo he met another one. The medical doctor did a physical inspection of both berdaches, and reported them both to have normal male genitals which were, however, somewhat "atrophied." Hammond claimed that the Indians intentionally demasculinized these individuals so that they would receive anal intercourse: "A *mujerado* is an essential person in the saturnalia or orgies, in which these Indians . . . indulge. He is the chief passive agent in the pederastic ceremonies, which form so important a part in the performances. These take place in the Spring of every year." Every pueblo, he was told, had at least one *mujerado,* and toward them "the Indians observed a great deal of reserve and mystery. . . . He is protected and supported by the pueblo, is held in some sort of honor, and need not work unless he chooses." He performs his daytime activities with the women instead of the men, "but this is more in accordance with his wishes and inclinations than from any desire on their part to avoid him."[38]

Stephen Powers was another popular writer who emphasized that berdaches were physically normal males. In a series of articles on California Indians in the popular magazine *Overland Monthly* in 1871–72, Powers indicated that whites commonly knew of the tradition. Frontier settlers advanced several theories to him to account for the phenomenon, including that the *i-wamusp* were forced to dress like women as a penalty for cowardice in battle, or that it was a punishment for "self-abuse." Powers pointed out that those theories were not true. Instead, he wrote, "All this folly is voluntary; that these men choose this unnatural life merely to escape from the duties and responsibilities of manhood." It is, he concluded, "another illustration of the strange capacity which the California Indians develop for doing morbid and abnormal things."[39]

Since white visitors easily learned about berdaches and about the acceptance of male-male sexual relationships among Indians, it is obvious that there might develop deep associations between berdaches and frontiersmen who actually lived with a tribe. The earliest evidence of this close association is from Peter Grant, a frontiersman who lived among the Sauteux Chippewa at the beginning of the nineteenth century. He admitted in his memoirs that he had known several berdaches. He did not denounce them, but on the contrary mentioned the Indian view that they were "respected as saints or beings in some degree inspired." Grant evidenced a cheerful demeanor toward them, remarking that they were "stout strapping fellows."[40] John Tanner, a white man living among the Chippewa in the 1820s, even admitted to being sexually approached by a berdache! He met one of these *a-go-kwa,* whom he defined as men "who make themselves women." He reported, in his widely read autobiography:

There are several of this sort among most, if not all the Indian tribes. . . . This creature, called Ozaw-wen-dib (the yellow head) was now near fifty years old, and had lived with many husbands. . . . She soon let me know she had come a long distance to see me, and with the hope of living with me. She often offered herself [sexually] to me, but not being discouraged with one refusal, she repeated her disgusting advances until I was almost driven from the lodge. . . . [Another Indian] only laughed at the embarrassment and shame which I evinced. . . . At length, despairing of success in her addresses to me, or being too much pinched by hunger, which was commonly felt in our lodge, she disappeared.

Four days later, Yellow Head returned with food for the hungry lodge, and Tanner was not too reluctant to accompany the berdache on a two-day journey to another lodge. Tanner continued his narrative upon the arrival at Wa-ge-to-te's lodge, where he ate as much as he wished.

Here also, I found myself relieved from the persecutions of the A-go-kwa, which had become intolerable. Wa-ge-to-te, who had two wives, married her. This introduction of a new intimate into the family of Wa-ge-to-te, occasioned some laughter and produced some ludicrous incidents, but was attended with less uneasiness and quarreling than would have been the bringing in of a new wife of the female sex.[41]

Another writer who reported being approached sexually by Indians was Victor Tixier, who lived with the Osages in 1839–40. When bathing in the river with Osage men, Tixier reported, "The warriors bothered us with indiscreet questions. . . . If we swam along beside them, they asked us to let them examine our bodies; we had to tell them very sternly to be of more decent behavior." Tixier was quite irritated by their "habits of sodomy, which their curiosity seemed to announce and which they exercise, according to what they say, on their prisoners. These sons of nature are extremely lascivious."[42]

Popular writers like Tixier, Tanner, and Catlin, even if critical of berdaches on the surface, created an awareness among homosexually inclined men in the United States that they could find a life of acceptance and affectional fulfillment by joining the Indians. Beyond this, fictional literature stressed themes of intimate association between frontiersmen and Indians. No books of fiction were more widely read in the nineteenth century than James Fenimore Cooper's Leatherstocking Tales. The main character, Natty Bumppo, avoided women and felt more comfortable living isolated from them on the frontier. He gave his devotion to his male Indian companion Chingachook. While their relationship was of course presented as chaste, it is not a distortion to say that it was an Indian–white male marriage.[43]

The popularization of this Indian-white companionship, combined with the factual statements about berdaches in the press, cannot be totally discounted as a motive for at least some unmarried young men who went west. Demographers who study migration movements analyze them in terms of "push-pull" factors. A male who was erotically attracted to another male might be "pushed" out of his settled hometown because of fears of discovery by relatives and townfolk, and because of frustration at not being able to establish a relationship with another male. He might be "pulled" to the frontier by the knowledge that it was almost completely an all-male fringe society, and that "sodomy" was associated with the Indians. This is not to suggest that most men went west with these more or less conscious notions. But it does suggest that those historians who do not consider this motivation ignore an important facet of frontier life.[44]

BERDACHES' ATTRACTION TO NON-INDIANS

If we can conclude that white men desiring all-male associations may have been pushed in the direction of the frontier, there were also factors leading Indian societies to absorb them. During times when there was no warfare with whites (and sometimes even when there was), Indian peoples often adopted escaping settlers. Faced with their own declining populations because of the ravages of warfare and disease, many groups welcomed the addition of healthy adult men of any race. Given the liberality of native customs of adoption, tribes were able to absorb outsiders into the kinship system.[45]

Again, this kind of phenomenon is hard to document. If they lived out their lives with the Indians, such persons were lost to the historical record. The main way that they showed up again was if whites recaptured them. Many of these recaptives fiercely resisted being taken back to U.S. society.[46] And if they did come back into white society, they would not admit that they had been married to an Indian (which was bad enough) who was a male (which was worse!). The same thing would apply to white traders who lived among the Indians. Men who joined a tribe either married an Indian woman or perhaps took a berdache as a wife (or maybe both).

A berdache provided, in fact, a very attractive situation for an outsider joining a new culture. As noted earlier, the berdache's prosperous household offered the comforts of home, and a willing spouse. Berdaches may have become more prosperous by having sex with white men for money. By the 1930s berdaches among the California Pomo were charging twenty-five cents for sex. While the source does not state who their customers were, we can speculate that Indians were not the customers since cash was not often used among them. We may surmise that the berdaches, like prostitutes anywhere, got their business from men with money.[47]

Berdaches had an extra incentive to marry outsiders. Since the husband of the berdache often got a lot of kidding, the outsider would be somewhat insulated from this and thus would more likely stay with a berdache. I could see this operating in my own case during fieldwork, as berdaches became attracted to me. Because I did not have relatives on the reservation, it would be easier for me to dismiss any gossip or joking that came with my association with a berdache. Some of my berdache informants made a strong case that I should stay with them on the reservation. In the case of one person it was quite difficult for me to convince him that I had to leave.

If berdaches tried so diligently to attract me as a husband, with the same kind of persistence that so exasperated John Tanner, I surmise that our two experiences are part of a continuum. I know of berdaches now having relationships with non-Indian men, living as couples on reservations and accepted by their families. I would be surprised if they are the first generation to do so.

The best existing documentation of a love relationship between a frontiersman and a male Indian goes back much further than the present, and even long before the Leatherstocking Tales. In northeast Florida, a truly tragic tale unfolds in the Spanish record of 1566. The Spanish there were dependent on a Frenchman to interpret the language of the Guale Indians. How this man came to reside among the natives is unclear, but he lived with the eldest son of the chief. He knew their language better than the Spanish initially did. Though the Frenchman was paid by the Spanish, there was no love lost between him and the colonial authorities. The Spanish referred to him as "a great Sodomite."

Relations reached a low point when the Spanish discovered that the Frenchman was warning the Indians not to convert to Catholicism. He had, according to a report by the Spanish governor, "spit on the cross many times before the Indians, scoffing at the Christians." The Spanish therefore decided to have him killed. But they did it secretly because "the son of the cacique [chief] had more authority than his father, and loved that interpreter very much." The Spanish knew that if they killed the beloved interpreter, the Indians would be angered and might renew their resistance to colonial intrusion.

The Spanish concocted a plot, telling the interpreter that they would pay him well if he went with them for a few days as interpreter in another area. The governor also issued a secret order, commanding the soldiers on the journey to "have that interpreter killed with great secrecy, as he was a Sodomite." Though the interpreter agreed to go, upon his departure "the son of the cacique showed much sorrow because the interpreter was going, and prayed him, weeping, to return at once."[48]

The tragedy of this man's death is directly attributable to the authority of the Spanish government. To survive, male-male relationships had to exist away from colonial control. It is precisely this fact that explains the scarcity of historical evidence of Indian-white male marriages on the frontier. In the late eighteenth century, however, the English frontier explorer James Adair mentioned one of these. He heard from the Creek Indians about "a lusty young fellow, who was charged with being more effeminate than became a warrior." This young tribesman closely associated with a white man who lived nearby, "an opulent and helpless German, by whom they supposed he might have been corrupted."[49] Who this German was, how he got to the frontier, and what his life was like with his effeminate Indian friend is lost to the record. The Creeks, who did not have a recognized berdache status and who disliked this behavior, reported it to the visiting white man. But for tribes who respected berdachism, how many would report such a relationship?

More often, people simply did not write about such involvements. One cowboy included in his reminiscences, written in 1903, a mysterious statement about an incident with a group of cowboys in the 1880s. He wrote simply, "The four of us left with the cows became occupied by a controversy over the sex of a young Indian—a Blackfoot—riding a cream-colored pony . . . distinguished by beads and beaver fur trimmings in the hair. . . . The young Indian was not over sixteen years of age, with remarkable features." The cowboy thought this person might have been a female, but since they were not sure another cowboy "took exception to the decision and rode alongside the young Indian, pretending to admire the long plaits of hair, toyed with the beads, pinched and patted the young Blackfoot."

The others worried that the Indian might take offense at these erotic suggestions, but the Indian did not resist. Instead, when the cowboy asked if the youth wanted to be "his squaw," the Indian gave "a broad smile, and in fair English said, 'Me buck.'"[50] To what extent did the cowboys become "occupied," and why would one of them remember this incident decades later, if it involved a merely casual encounter? Was this the author's way of relating a sexual episode he might have had with this attractive Indian "with remarkable features"? The sources do not reveal, but they at least suggest how easy it was for white males on the frontier to meet berdaches. The berdache's smile indicated a friendliness toward the cowboys that might have ripened into a relationship.

Ironically, the best description we have of how one of these relationships might have begun does not involve an American Indian. It concerns Hawaiians, another native people whose *mahu* tradition is similar to the berdache. Charles Warren Stoddard, a young San Francisco writer who communicated his love for males to Walt Whitman, went to Hawaii in the 1860s. In 1869 he published a short story in the *Overland Monthly* that, as is clear from his letters to Whitman, is based on his personal experience in Hawaii. It is remarkable that such a homoerotic tale as "A South Sea Idyl" was accepted in so prominent a magazine. To get the flavor of his feelings, his story bears reprinting in part. Immediately upon meeting a young man named Kanaana, Stoddard recalled,

I knew I was to have an experience with this young scion of a race of chiefs. Sure enough, I have had it. He continued to regard me steadily, without embarrassment. He seated himself before me; I felt myself at the mercy of one whose calm analysis was questioning every motive of my soul. This sage inquirer was, perhaps, sixteen years old. His eye was so earnest and so honest, I could but return his look. I saw a round, full, rather girlish face; lips ripe and expressive . . . eyes perfectly glorious—regular almonds—with the mythical lashes "that sweep," etc., etc. The smile which presently transfigured his face was of that nature that flatters you into submission against your will.

Having weighed me in his balance—and you may be sure his instincts didn't cheat him (they don't do that sort of thing)—he placed his two hands on my two knees, and declared, "I was his best friend, as he was mine; I must come at once to his house, and there live always with him." What could I do but go? He pointed me to his lodge, across the river, saying, "There was his home, and mine."

. . . .

Thereupon I renounced all the follies of this world, actually hating civilization—feeling entirely above the formalities of society. I resolved on the spot to be a barbarian, and, perhaps, dwell forever and ever in this secluded spot. . . . How strangely I was situated: alone in a wilderness, among barbarians; my bosom friend, who was hugging me like a young bear, not able to speak one syllable of English, and I very shaky on a few bad phrases in his tongue. . . . [Yet,] if it is a question how long a man may withstand the seductions of nature, and the consolations and conveniences of the state of nature, I have solved it in one case; for I was as natural as possible in about three days.[51]

For reasons that he himself did not understand, Stoddard later returned to San Francisco. In 1870 he wrote to Whitman, "I know there is but one hope for me. I must get in amongst people who are not afraid of instincts and who scorn hypocrisy. I am numbed with the frigid manners of the Christians; barbarism has given me the fullest joy of my life and I long to return to it and be satisfied."[52] Stoddard's testimony deserves attention because it explains the reactions that a young man joining the Indians might have felt. If Stoddard had truly fit into Hawaiian society, he would have disappeared and we never would have read "A South Sea Idyl." But the feelings he expressed give us some perception of what might have occurred on the American frontier.

It is realistic to conclude from the available evidence that some of the frontiersmen who interacted with Indians also interacted affectionally with berdaches. If frontiersmen could have adapted to a marriage with another masculine man, then surely it would have been less psychologically difficult for some of them to adjust to being the husband of an androgynous berdache wife. Such experiences were a transitory possibility, however, with the establishment in the West of the authority of church and state.

9   *Of Bibles and Bureaus: Indian*
     Acculturation and Decline of the
     Berdache Tradition

Male marriages, and berdaches themselves, could not survive undisturbed when representatives of the established social order arrived. Their history after the frontier era is part of the wider story of the effect of Anglo-American dominance on American Indian cultures generally. It is a story of cultural repression by the church and the state, leading to the decline of the old ways, and an acculturation to the new alien values. But it is also a story that is marked by a surprising continued persistence of Native American traditions, even into the contemporary era.

During the 1840s the United States established its clear title to the West by forcing Britain and Mexico to give up their claims to the vast area between Texas and the Northwest Coast. California and Oregon were the real prizes. Especially after the discovery of gold, white settlers began crossing the Great Plains to get to the Pacific coastal regions. Unlike the earlier period, when individual whites went to live or trade with the Indians, by about 1850 massive numbers of settlers were moving to the far West. In the decades following, the interior gradually came under white control as successive waves of miners, ranchers, and farmers sought to possess the land.

This invasion of their lands led Western Indians to react in much the same way as eastern Native Americans had done in the previous century: by armed defense of their homelands. Such clashes were usually settled not by total military defeat of an Indian group, but by a negotiated settlement between the United States and the tribal government. These settlements were certified by treaties, which gradually restricted Indian lands to areas called reservations. In return, treaties guaranteed that tribes retained most rights of self-rule within their remaining reservation lands.

By the 1870s, after most Western tribes had been settled on reservations, the government began to cancel promises made in the treaties. Congress stopped making new treaties with Indians in 1871, and the Supreme Court ruled that Congress had the right to contradict treaties—without getting the consent of the tribes. Government officials threatened to abrogate the treaties altogether, leaving Indians with no protections at all. Though Congress did not do so, in 1885 it did grant federal courts the right to prosecute major crimes that occurred on reservations. This abolition of the power of tribes to maintain their own justice systems violated numerous treaties. The Supreme Court ruled in *United States v. Kagama* (1885) that Indian tribes were not states or nations, only "local dependent communities." Such a change was a significant demotion of status from the national recognition and powers of self-government promised in the treaties.[1]

In 1887 Congress passed the Indian Allotment Act, by which it hoped to do away with reservations by dividing the remaining lands into individually allotted plots. Since land was allotted to male "heads of households," this meant that women and berdaches lost ownership rights. Non-citizen Indians became almost totally powerless without the protection of their treaty guarantees and their tribal governments. They were left with a legal status called "nationals," which meant they were dependent wards under the paramount authority of Congress. By the end of the nineteenth century the federal government held virtually unlimited power over American Indians. Indians' position was in fact that of colonial subjects.[2]

Allotment and forced assimilation became the hallmarks of United States Indian policy, and as more land was lost each reservation became smaller and its resources overtaxed. The resulting poverty and despair within the reservations justified treating Indians as helpless and dependent wards of the government. The power of the federal bureaucracy over the daily lives of native peoples became virtually unchallenged. Native religions were outlawed, and though this violated the First Amendment's provision for freedom of religion, Indians were not citizens and so had no protection. White social and economic mores were enforced, and children were forcibly taken away from their families to be placed in distant boarding schools. Such policies were rationalized on the grounds that the only solution for the "Indian Problem" was for Indians to be absorbed into the United States' melting pot and eventually to become citizens just like everyone else. The policy of forced assimilation ignored the fact that Native Americans had never asked to be assimilated.

Year by year, tribal governments were allowed less and less power, while local agents of the federal Office of Indian Affairs exercised more complete control. Pioneer ethnographer George B. Grinnell attested to the reality of life on the reservation when he wrote in 1899: "An Indian agent has absolute control of affairs on his reservation . . . more nearly absolute than anything else that we in this country know of. . . . The courts protect citizens; but the Indian is not a citizen, and nothing protects him. Congress has the sole power to order how he shall live, and where."[3]

GOVERNMENT SUPPRESSION OF BERDACHES

One of the aspects of American Indian life that the assimilationist program attacked was sexuality. In order to "civilize" the Indian, it was felt necessary to enforce the same standards as in white communities. United States government officials mirrored the anti-sexual attitudes of missionaries and public opinion, and they had the power to enforce changes. For example, in describing some sexually explicit ceremonial dances among the Hopi Indians, the government superintendent, P. T. Lonegran, wrote to the commissioner of Indian affairs on December 7, 1915, saying "These dances are too loathsome and repugnant for me to describe. . . . They are vulgar and I am almost shamed to send them through the mails." Prominent in these dances were the antics of the clown dancers, who used both homosexual and heterosexual humor as a way of providing comic relief in the otherwise serious ceremonies. Since the Hopi did not see sex as dirty or antireligious, and did not separate humor from ceremony, they must have been confounded by the whites' suppression of sex.

This confusion can be discerned in a Hopi clown's reactions to the arrogant actions of Emory Marks, the government principal of Oraibi School on the reservation. Marks wrote to the commissioner on December 11, 1920, recounting with pride how he had interrupted a dance. When he saw a Hopi clown display a huge artificial penis, to the merriment of the crowd, "I went up to him and stopped the performance . . . and told him that if he ever did a thing like that again, I would put him in jail. He told me that he did not know it was wrong, that it was a Hopi custom."[4]

Berdaches were also a target of this suppression. Since in many tribes berdaches were often shamans, the government's attack on traditional healing practices disrupted their lives. Among the Klamaths, the government agent's prohibition of curing ceremonials in the 1870s and 1880s required shamans to operate underground. The berdache shaman White Cindy continued to do traditional healing, curing people for decades despite the danger of arrest.[5]

But the government also reacted specifically against the berdaches. Probably the most direct attempts to force berdaches to conform to standard men's roles can be seen in actions by the government Indian agents. As early as the 1870s the agent among the Hidatsas forced a berdache to wear men's clothing and cut his hair short like a white man's. The berdache fled to the Crow reservation, where he found sanctuary.[6] Even the Crows, who had consistently been allies of the United States, were not safe from these governmental intrusions. Dr. A. B. Holder, the reservation physician, wrote in 1889 of the *badé* producing "sexual orgasm by taking the male organ of the active party in the [*badé's*] lips. . . . Of all the many varieties of sexual perversion, this, it seems to me, is the most debased that could be conceived of."

Holder knew of at least five berdaches at the Crow reservation headquarters. One boy at the agency boarding school was repeatedly discovered wearing female attire, and the officials punished him. But rather than conform, he escaped from the school and lived among traditional Crows as a berdache. Holder refused to believe the berdache had high status, but only attributed the other Crows' toleration to their "debased standard . . . showing that there is no bottom to the pit into which the sexual passion, perverted and debased, may sink a creature once he has become its slave."[7]

Such attitudes were reflected in policies of the local government agent. In 1902, an anthropologist who visited the Crow reservation briefly mentioned that a few years previously an Indian agent tried without success to force *badés* to wear men's clothing.[8] Another anthropologist, arriving five years later, met the Crow Osh-Tisch ("Finds Them and Kills Them") and described this fifty-year-old berdache: "Dressed as a woman, he might have passed for one except for his affectedly piping voice. Agents, I learnt, had repeatedly tried to make him put on masculine clothing, but the other Crow protested, saying it was against his nature."[9]

Such offhand comments, typical of the brevity often accorded the topic in ethnographic accounts, leave one yearning to know more about these historic events. Fortunately, I was able to discover fuller accounts by interviews with Indian people themselves. Joe Medicine Crow, an elder in the Baptist church on the Montana reservation of the Crows, is also keeper of the tribal history among traditionalists. He remembered Osh-Tisch, who died in 1929 when Joe was seven years old. When I asked about the controversy over Osh-Tisch's clothing, he did not answer but told me to meet him the following day on the grounds of the Bureau of Indian Affairs offices. I arrived the next day and observed that the BIA building was surrounded by huge oak trees. As we walked among the trees I realized why Joe had asked me to meet there. He explained the incident with the BIA agents:

One agent in the late 1890s was named Briskow, or maybe it was Williamson. He did more crazy things here. He tried to interfere with Osh-Tisch, who was the most respected *badé*. The agent incarcerated the *badés,* cut off their hair, made them wear men's clothing. He forced them to do manual labor, planting these trees that you see here on the BIA grounds. The people were so upset with this that Chief Pretty Eagle came into Crow Agency, and told Briskow to leave the reservation. It was a tragedy, trying to change them. Briskow was crazy.[10]

Considering how little power Indians had on their reservations at the beginning of the century, the strength of the Crows' protest, forcing the agent to resign, is remarkable. The fact that the Indians saw an attempt to force the berdache to change as "crazy" tells us much about the high status Osh-Tisch held.[11]

Such native pressure could not be brought to bear when Indian youth were taken off the reservation to boarding schools far from their homeland. In an effort to wipe out Indian culture before children matured, government educational programs focused on teaching students to be like white people. What happened to a berdache in boarding school is indicated by a Navajo woman who remembered being taken to Carlisle Indian School, in Pennsylvania. Her cousin, a *nadle,* was also taken there. Since he was dressed as a girl, school officials assumed he was female and placed him in the girl's dormitory. The Navajo students protected him, and he went undiscovered.

Later, however, there was a lice infestation. The white teachers personally scrubbed all the girls, and were shocked when they found out that the *nadle* was male. The Navajo woman said, "They were very upset. He was taken from the school, and he never returned again. They would not tell us what happened to him, and we never saw him again. We were very sad that our cousin was gone." The family still does not know if the boy was sent to another school, or to prison, or was killed. After all these years, the Navajo woman gets upset thinking about her cousin who was taken away.[12]

Contemporary Indian androgynous males who were taken to government schools remember being forced to participate in boys' games and activities, and to dress like other boys. They recall this coercion by the teachers as one of the worst things about growing up.[13]

The Canadian government also made attempts to wipe out the berdache tradition. A Kwakiutl chief in British Columbia remembered what happened when his berdache lover was forced to take on a man's role about 1900: "The Indian agent wrote to Victoria [the provincial government], telling the officials what she was doing [dressing as female]. She was taken to Victoria, and the policeman took her clothes off and found she was a man, so they gave him a suit of clothes and cut off his hair and sent him back home. When I saw him again, he was a man. He was no more my sweetheart."[14] The change from feminine

to masculine pronouns indicates that the forced change of clothing and social role could cause the berdache to lose sexual partners as well as social status. Though this chief did not hesitate
to detail his love life with the berdache when she was cross-
dressing, he did not feel it appropriate to continue the relationship after she took on a man's role. The government's policies
thus had a social as well as a sexual impact on the berdache.

MISSIONARIES' IMPACT ON BERDACHES

The emotional torment of the berdache must have been severe.
Among some tribes, the condemnation by whites led berdaches
to commit suicide.[15] Indians could not help but be affected when
they heard whites refer to berdachism as "the most repugnant
of all their practices," or "a shameful custom,"[16] or, as a traveler
among the Papagos in 1909–10 alluded to it, an "unnatural
vice." That writer recounted that "Several startling instances
were told me. . . . Even a married man with full grown daughters was subject to this depravity."[17] But whatever the influence
of whites in general, it was missionaries who had the greatest
impact on Indians.

Along with the government agent, it was the missionary on
a reservation who held the real power over Indian people's lives.
These clergy had a stern sense of Christian duty, and endeavored
to lift the unconverted to what they felt was a higher and better
plane of spiritual life. The missionaries were characterized by a
strong belief in the superiority of their own way of life. Unlike
the frontiersmen, who often came west to get away from the
restrictions of Euroamerican culture, the missionary came as its
exemplar. They remained so convinced of the need for Christian
civilization that they sought to spread their culture to non-
Western peoples everywhere.

This meant that the missionary actually went into Indian
areas with two goals: to teach the Christian religion, and to
westernize the way of life. In its most extreme ethnocentric
form, everything Western was sanctioned as the will of God,
while everything belonging to the indigenous culture was evil.
A Christian mission, therefore, could bring great disruption

into a non-Western society. It was in many ways a deliberate
means of political control, an efficient means of controlling colonial peoples. The introduction of Western values, technology,
and material culture rapidly challenged the traditional order of
life. Native American populations split into factions as those
who converted to Christianity began to condemn traditionalists.[18]

Beginning with the early French presence in North America,
missionaries tried to prevent male–male sex. They even attacked
the close special friendships among native men, in which, according to one Jesuit writer, "there is, or may be, much real
vice. . . . Missionaries suppressed attachments of this kind on
account of the abuses which they feared would result."[19] As
with the Spanish, those few missionaries who generally took an
understanding view of native culture still condemned berdachism. For example, the Baptist missionary Isaac McCoy, who
expressed much more sympathy for Indians than most other
clergy, in 1840 described meeting a berdache among the Osages
thusly: "One of these wretches was pointed out to me. He appeared to be about twenty five years of age, was tall, lean, and
of a ghost-like appearance. His presence was so disgusting, and
the circumstances of the case so unpleasant, that I spoke not a
word to him, and made few inquiries about him. He was said
to be in a declining state of health, and certainly his death would
not have been lamented."[20]

A Lakota medicine man told me of the pressures put on
winktes in the 1920s and 1930s:

When the people began to be influenced by the missions and the
boarding schools, a lot of them forgot the traditional ways and the
traditional medicine. Then they began to look down on the *winkte*
and lose respect. The missionaries and the government agents said
winktes were no good, and tried to get them to change their ways.
Some did, and put on men's clothing. But others, rather than
change, went out and hanged themselves. I remember the sad stories
that were told about this.[21]

Likewise, another Sioux traditionalist reported:

By the 1940s, after more Indians had been educated in white schools,
or had been taken away in the army, they lost the traditions of re-

spect for *winktes*. The missionaries condemned *winktes,* telling families that if something bad happened, it was because of their associating with a *winkte*. They would not accept *winktes* into the cemetery, saying "their souls are lost." Missionaries had a lot of power on the reservation, so the *winktes* were ostracized by many of the Christianized Indians.[22]

Among the Crows, missionaries also had an impact. The leading elder medicine man of the Crows, Thomas Yellowtail (now in his eighties), told me: "When the Baptist missionary Peltotz arrived in 1903, he condemned our traditions, including the *badé*. He told congregation members to stay away from Osh-Tisch and the other *badés*. He continued to condemn Osh-Tisch until his death in the late 1920s. That may be the reason why no others took up the *badé* role after Osh-Tisch died."[23] Perhaps the most dramatic change occurred among the Navajos, where traditionally berdaches received such high respect. As early as the 1930s, when anthropologist W. W. Hill recorded numerous reverent praises of *nadle,* he also noted one informant saying, "The *nadle* are not so much respected nowadays. The older attitude is giving way to one of ridicule. . . . In recent times some of the school boys made fun of the woman's dress of Kla [a *nadle*], and he put on his pants"—began to dress as a man.[24]

Navajo *nadle* were beginning to realize that white society considered them "queer," and the object of jokes rather than respect.[25] By the late 1940s anthropologists were reporting that the remaining berdaches were all middle-aged or older: "It may be that the bachelors in their thirties who live in various communities today are [secretly berdaches] . . . who fear the ridicule of white persons and so do not change clothing."[26]

INDIANS STOP TALKING ABOUT BERDACHISM

How did berdaches respond to such drastic cultural changes forced on them? One of the most obvious reactions was to stop talking to white people about the tradition, and to do everything possible to avoid mention of the subject. One of W. W. Hill's Navajo informants was a well-known *nadle* named Kinipai. While Kinipai answered questions "cheerfully and readily" about Navajo culture in general, when Hill asked about *nadle,* "The result was that the informant gave instant evidence of acute emotional distress. She was visibly upset, very nervous, kept her eyes on the ground during the whole recital, kept rubbing her hands together, and squirming. She lost her voice completely for a few moments and when she began to talk, spoke in a whisper, and her accounts and her answers were so incoherent that the interpreter had trouble in getting the sense and was forced to question her repeatedly."[27]

Indians being questioned by anthropologists sometimes complain that the nosy whites cannot take an obvious hint to avoid certain subjects. One particularly insensitive interviewer was Leslie Spier, who did fieldwork among the Klamaths in 1925 and 1926. Not only did Spier snidely characterize berdaches as "psychologically abnormal," but he was arrogant as well. One of Spier's informants, then in his sixties, had been a berdache in his teens and twenties, but had given up dressing as a berdache by the 1890s (Spier did not think to ask why). In response to Spier's inquiries, the Klamath falsely claimed that he had once been married to a woman, and his wife had died twenty years ago. It evidently did not occur to the anthropologist that the Indian might have lied to prevent further questioning. When Spier asked why he had never remarried, the Indian replied simply, "Some men like it that way."[28]

Spier's insensitive and nonproductive questioning leaves his conclusion, that berdaches were scorned and taunted by other Klamaths, open to question. Either he did not recognize that Klamaths might have changed their attitudes as a result of white influence, or he did not see that his own obvious antipathy for berdaches might have influenced the responses he received.[29] Even with a group like the Yumas, who clearly respected the berdache's spiritual gift from the dream world, Spier slanted his report by stating that berdachism came about due to "too much dreaming."[30]

This type of prejudice typifies the writings of some other researchers.[31] Even some ethnographers who appreciated the social utility of berdachism still used negative terminology and concepts. George Devereux referred to Mohave homosexuality as "a social disorder," when his data showed it was far from that. Robert Lowie remarked that the Crows won "the championship in unnatural practices." Other researchers, either through ignorance, embarrassment, or outright prejudice, simply never asked the right questions. Too often, ethnographers either ignored evidence of homosexuality, or only briefly mentioned it as if it were a perversion.[32] In my own research, as I interviewed ethnographers who had spent time among Indians, on more than a few occasions my questions concerning berdaches were met with visible embarrassment.

Another problem is that anthropologists who have gathered good data on sexuality have been reticent to put it in print. This is typified by the writings of Matilda Coxe Stevenson, who ably described the social position of berdaches during her fieldwork at Zuni in the 1890s. Yet when she addressed the question of the berdaches' relationships, she could not bring herself to use such terms as "husband" and "marriage." She would only go so far as to mention that the *lhamana* "allied himself to a man" and remained with him for many years. Yet rather than pursue the nature of this de facto marriage, Stevenson said, "There is a side to the lives of these men which must remain untold. They never marry women, and it is understood that they seldom have any relations with them."[33] Why their relationship "must remain untold" reveals more about Western inhibitions concerning homosexuality than about berdachism itself.

It is not surprising that the Zuni, having been exposed to such attitudes, learned not to mention such things around whites. When Elsie Crews Parsons went to Zuni later, in 1916, she did try to get more information about one of these marriages between a berdache and a man, and reported, "The 'marriage' was discussed with me as an economic arrangement, and with not the slightest hint of physical acts of perversion on the part of either 'husband' or 'wife.' . . . It is not at all unlikely that this oblivious manner was assumed to check further discussions— for reasons I do not know."[34]

Even as early as the 1850s, the Pueblo Indians had learned to keep secret from whites the ceremonies in which sex was involved. Having investigated the subject of the *mujerado* in Laguna and Acoma pueblos, Dr. William Hammond reported some "pederastic ceremonies" that "are conducted with the utmost secrecy, as regards the non-Indian part of the population. . . . I could not ascertain, with any degree of certainty, whether the *mujerados* were public property for pederastic purposes at any other times than at the annual orgies, but I am inclined to think that the chiefs or some of them have the right so to employ them, and that they do avail themselves of the privilege. They avoided all reference to the subject, and professed the most complete ignorance of the matter when I questioned them directly thereon."[35]

In the twentieth century, as Indians have become still more aware of white attitudes, they have become more secretive. Even when a researcher tries to get accurate information, the heritage of Western homophobia makes it difficult to get modern Indian people to talk about the berdache tradition. Among many modern tribes, after years of missionary indoctrination, sexuality is not discussed. By the late 1920s, an ethnographer doing fieldwork among the Yokuts Indians of California could locate only one informant who would acknowledge the existence of berdachism, though berdaches had an important role in Yokuts funeral ceremonies. Similarly, when Nancy Lurie did fieldwork among the Winnebago in 1945–47, she reported that informants "tended to be reticent to discuss the matter of the berdache. Their embarrassment may indicate that knowledge of the subject was withheld." One seventy-year-old woman, when asked about berdache, "became very angry and said in Winnebago, 'Why did you ask about that? That is something we want to forget and not talk about!'"[36]

The information that modern researchers such as Lurie have received from informants about aboriginal berdache traditions is a tribute to the closeness and trust developed in dealing with a delicate topic. Even more delicate is the question of the continuation of a berdache tradition in contemporary times. As one Lakota *winkte* told me, "Indians don't want to be mocked any more by the outside white world, it has happened so many times. So, we keep it secret about *winkte*." The experience of an ethnographer at Hopi in the 1970s is instructive about ways in which Indians keep berdachism hidden. Informants talked freely about a teenage boy in their family, without mentioning sexuality and gender role. When the ethnographer later met the boy and recognized obvious berdachelike behavior, and tried to get an informant to talk about the boy, "he was very reticent to discuss anything about him. . . . It seems clear that he's figured out that I understand the boy's situation and is now being quite protective. All he would say was that ——— has a special friend who takes care of him by supplying many of his material needs."[37]

Because modern Indian people distrust any outsider whom they fear might approach berdachism from a disrespectful position, they will often claim when asked that berdachism has completely disappeared. Though Alfred Kroeber early pointed out the impact on research of Western condemnatory attitudes, some modern anthropologists accept statements of denial at face value. As lesbian researcher Paula Gunn Allen (herself an Indian) points out, many recent anthropologists have misperceived berdachism, and assumed it has died out; "Perhaps this is so because it is felt—at least among ethnographers' tribal informants—that it is wise to let sleeping dogs lie."[38] Because of these factors, openly gay or lesbian researchers have obvious advantages in obtaining accurate information. Over and over again in my research, berdaches mentioned that they would not be disclosing this information had I been heterosexual. It was because of a sense of trust developed out of what they saw as a connecting link between us that they were relaxed enough to talk openly.

ACCULTURATION AND INDIANS' NEGATIVE ATTITUDES

While the suppression of the berdache tradition originated from the prejudices of white government officials and missionaries, ultimately the changing ideals of Indian people themselves have had the most direct impact on berdaches. Under the devastating impact of the church and the state, traditional religious ceremonies were suppressed and ideology revolutionized. When Indians converted to Christianity, many absorbed Christian notions about the evilness of sex, and disrespect for the shamans and their ceremonies. By internalizing white ideals, they undercut the basis for respect of things they had previously accepted.

When U.S. officials suppressed the Hopi dances in 1920, for example, they included in their report affidavits from several Christian converts. One man named Talasnimtiwa dictated his story, saying, "I am telling these awful things about the old ways of the Hopi Indians only because I have become a Christian and I want these evil things known to the Government in order that they may be stopped among my people." Another, Kuanwikvaya, said, "There is nothing good in the Hopi religion. It is all full of adultery and immorality. I cannot tell all the dirt and filth that is in these ceremonies." And a third, Tuwaletstiwa, offered, "Before I became a Christian, my life was unspeakable evil. . . . When a Hopi becomes a Christian he quits attending these dances. He knows the evil in them is so great."[39]

In 1944 an ethnographer among the Hopis reported that while homosexuality had formerly been quite common, it was infrequent by the 1930s because of white influences. Another fieldworker among the Hopis forty years later was told by informants that while same-sex behavior is considered normal for boys and young men, "lifelong homosexual orientation is highly frowned upon." By the time males are in their twenties it is expected that they will "grow out of it." An androgynous young man is seen as "an embarrassment to his family and he wouldn't be able to find someplace to live [as part of the Hopi community] unless he changed and got a wife, even if he did continue to have men come to see him."[40]

Any tradition that combined both sexuality and traditional religious ideas, like berdachism, received much genocidal pressure. When people no longer respected the vision quest, or sought their individual life role in its guiding spirit, then the days of respect for the berdache were numbered.

Peggy Sanday has demonstrated cross-culturally the importance of religious mythology in justifying the consideration of women as equals of men. Gender egalitarian societies often have creation stories which give important roles to women. Without the active explanation in myth, there is no ideological underpinning for a high female status.[41] The same may be true for the berdache. In cultures where berdaches have high status, there is usually mythological justification for the practice. It is not enough that the religion be neutral or tolerant. It must actively explain the phenomenon in a positive manner.

Just as the status of Indian women declined with the adoption of patriarchal Christianity, so did berdaches. Since Christianity views men as superior, with a creation story specifying a male god creating a masculine being and only later taking the female from the rib of the male, then the berdache is likewise inferior because he is "less than a man." No longer is he combining the power of both women and men; in Christianity he is seen as subverting his natural male superiority to take an inferior female form.

Non-Western peoples who come under colonial control often feel disillusioned with their traditional religion, because it did not protect them from conquest, or in the case of American Indians, from the ravages of disease. The religion of the conqueror seems more powerful, and therefore is attractive as a means of absorbing some of the power of the white man. Religious justification of the berdache's vision quest was rejected in favor of the Bible, which as translated offered no explanation for the existence of gender or sexual variance. The only words of guidance came from the list of taboos in Leviticus 18:22, "Thou shall not lie with mankind, as with womankind; it is abomination," and Deuteronomy 22:5, "A woman shall not be clothed with man's apparel, neither shall a man use woman's apparel; for he that doeth these things is abominable before God." With the collapse of native ideology justifying berdachism, there was no defense against these new taboos.[42]

Under such influences, it is not surprising to hear stories such as that recorded about the Winnebagos, who had previously treated berdaches as highly honored and respected persons, but who had "become ashamed of the custom because the white people thought it was amusing or evil. By the time the last known berdache attempted to fulfill the role [about 1900] his brothers threatened to kill him if he 'put on the skirt.' This berdache then affected a combination of male and female clothing, fearing that he would die if he did not at least attempt to follow directions given him in his vision of the moon." By the 1940s, the Winnebago word for berdache, *siange,* was used "as an insult or teasing epithet."[43] According to a Lakota berdache informant, the Christian "Holy Rollers" consider him to be "possessed by the devil." Another said his grandmother wanted to accept him but felt that her Christian belief told her he should be heterosexual. His grandfather (who was not Christian) was accepting.

The emasculation of Indian men's roles also led to a decline of berdachism. Especially in societies like the Lakotas, men got much of their status from participation in warfare. Their other major contribution to society was through the hunt. Once a tribe was restricted to a reservation, and game was depleted, a man was left with little to do. Forced settlement had a dramatic impact on men's roles, and many responded by retreating into a cynical defeatism that they could relieve only with alcohol. Men could no longer go off on the hunt or the raid. In many cases Indian peoples were actually forcibly prohibited from ever leaving the reservation. At least women had more continuity in their domestic work. Men had no choice but to begin farming, which among Plains Indians was previously considered women's work. In such a situation, there was not as much contrast between women and men. The berdache's role as mediator between two clearly separate spheres waned. Conceivably, without warrior-hunter roles berdaches could have become more prestigious, but the absorption of European values through Christianity prevented this.

Being taken away into the armed forces in World War II and the Korean War, and taking off-reservation jobs, immersed Indians into white society as never before. A Cheyenne man says, "My generation, growing up in the 1930s, '40s, and '50s, did not get a knowledge of the traditions. There was a lack of appreciation for the native culture then. Because of television and the automobile, many Cheyennes have similar attitudes as whites." An Arapaho traditionalist elder says plainly that a-whock died out by the 1950s "because young people did not continue the old tribal traditions."[44]

In this context, hostility toward berdaches grew. Even some Indians who claim to be traditional have absorbed homophobic attitudes. For example, in a statement ignorant of historical fact, writers from Sinte Gleska College on the Rosebud Sioux reservation had this to say about homosexuality: "Socially deviant persons neither were honored, nor would a ceremony ever be allowed for them. In fact, our past society was so well-organized that the phenomenon of a 'sexually warped' person is almost nonexistent. The moral codes of the Lakota people did not allow for oral sex." Having talked with some of the authors of this statement, I know that they are aware of the sexuality of *winktes*. Perhaps their denial can be explained by another statement in the same pamphlet: "such assertions [about homosexuality] are seriously damaging to the image that the [white] American people have of all Indian tribes." [45]

This new homophobic myth is reflected in a statement by Mike Myers, speaking for the Indian newspaper *Akwesasne Notes* in 1978. Reacting to publicity about Indian homosexuality, he stated, "We have asked traditional people of the Nations most often cited to us (Navaho, Sioux, Cheyenne) if gays existed in their cultures. In all cases the answer has been NO." Asking elder Indians about "gays" distorts the meaning of such a question, because it does not account for the aboriginal ceremonial function of berdaches. If Myers had instead asked about *nadle* or *winkte,* or used other native language terminology instead of a Western concept based wholly on homosexual acts, he would have received very different answers. [46] Myers reflects the homophobia absorbed from white sources. Such is the loss of memory after the spiritual basis of berdachism is removed.

One Lakota man I interviewed who claims to be traditional told me he considers *winktes* to be lower in status, saying it is not good for a man to act like a woman. He seemed uncomfortable talking about the subject, and it is this type of response that has led some anthropologists to get a distorted view of the aboriginal tradition. Yet even this man did not condemn homosexual behavior. His complaint about *winktes* was against their androgyny. When I later mentioned this condemnatory attitude to another traditionalist who knew this man, he replied only, "Some who claim to be traditional really have absorbed white attitudes."

The best summary of this new homophobia is offered by the contemporary gay Mohawk poet Maurice Kenny:

The modern Indian has been programmed by white society so that his former mores and measurements have been changed to fit his ever-assimilating environment. With the loss of his religious rites, culture, there is probably no place for the contemporary berdache within that social structure. There are no warriors to entertain on the warpath; no scalps to dance over; no mountaineers to court, subdue and copulate with; and certainly no ceremonial dances exclusively devoted to the berdache. Many 'traditionalists' have become racists, sexists, and are generally disquieted when among homosexuals. Hollywood, T. V. and the Church have had a heavy influence on the changing attitude of Indian thought.[47]

Despite the accuracy of Kenny's statement, any generalization about twentieth-century Indians must include many exceptions. While a more homophobic reaction is perhaps found among acculturated Indians, their attitudes vary from condemnation to indifference to acceptance. Still, as a general rule, Indians are more accepting of other people's differences than are white people. It is because of this acceptance, and the continuing influence of traditionalism, that the berdache role has survived in some tribes.

SURVIVAL OF BERDACHE SHAMANISM

How could the berdache tradition survive under such pressure? It has endured in the same way that other aboriginal traditions of Native Americans have survived. The old ways persist thanks to attitudes and thoughts of a core group of cultural conservators. Yet, each generation adapts to different circumstances, and the traditions are modified in response. Traditions are vibrant and alive; they are part of life. Within this process of change, however, enough of the essence of the old idea continues, so that cultural continuity is maintained. Most Indians who have kept their traditions and ceremonies also seem to have kept the respect for the berdache.

Since berdaches were often associated with shamanism, the strength of their prestige often kept them protected. In 1883 the United States Department of the Interior set up Courts of Indian Offenses, run by cooperative Indians, as a means of handling minor crimes. These courts handled the majority of cases on reservations in the late nineteenth and early twentieth centuries. Court records abound with cases relating to hetereosexual acts—adultery, polygamy, cohabitation, licentiousness, bastardy, and fornication are some of the case labels appearing most frequently.[48] Yet, as long as this court system was Indian-operated "sodomy" cases were notably absent.[49]

Also absent were cases involving the arrest or sentencing of shamans. Even cooperative Indians feared the supernatural powers of the shamans, so shamans were left alone by the colonial court system.[50] Among the Klamaths, for example, though the government agents made a major campaign against shamanism in the 1870s and 1880s, the ceremonies continued. If people believed that their health and indeed their whole continued existence as a people were dependent on the enactment of certain ceremonies, they would risk punishment to participate in them. Many of the ceremonies dealt with health, and berdaches were notable for their curing ceremonies.[51]

Perhaps the fact that berdaches were holy persons meant that they, like shamans, were left alone. Respect for the berdache's ability to help a person was balanced by fear of the berdache's ability to harm. Contemporary berdaches still believe in this power. Terry Calling Eagle says with quiet confidence, "If someone ever makes fun of me, something bad will happen to them. Once a half-breed woman said I was a disgrace to the Indian race. I told her that a century ago, I would have been considered that much more special. She died shortly after, and I think it was because she had insulted *winkte*. The spirits take action when sacred things are insulted."[52] For Indians who held this belief, it was a powerful incentive to help protect berdaches and keep them hidden from outsiders.

Another possible means of survival was simply for the berdache to dress always as a woman, and be accepted by whites as such. Even aboriginally many berdaches would dress as women (or at least close enough that white observers thought they were women). A Russian official in Alaska in the early nineteenth century reported confidently that *shopans* among the Kodiak Islanders were "formerly so prevalent that the residence of one of these monsters in a house was considered as fortunate; it is, however, daily losing ground" because of the interference of the

Russians. But he also reported that they were so much like women that white observers did not realize they were males. He mentioned the case of a Russian Orthodox priest who nearly married one of them to a man, before another Russian happened to learn that the bride was a *shopan*. By such tactics, others were able to pass as women. Despite the Russians' projections of berdachism's imminent disappearance, a full century later observers reported that *shopans* continued to be fairly common.[53]

Matilda Coxe Stevenson reported of the Zuni *lhamana* We'wha: "so carefully was his sex concealed that for years this writer believed him to be a woman." Later, We'wha started doing laundry for whites and "ultimately became as celebrated as a Chinese laundryman, his own clean apparel being his advertising card, and was called upon not only by the officers' families at the [Fort Wingate army] garrison but the white settlers near and far." While visiting Washington, D.C., for a six-month period We'wha had full run of the women's bathrooms, and reported back gleefully to the other Zunis that white women were all frauds: We'wha saw them remove their wigs, false teeth and bosom padding. The Zunis reportedly got much entertainment from the fact that this "woman" became such a social hit among the government elite, including Speaker of the House John Carlisle and President Grover Cleveland.[54]

Though contemporary Zunis do not talk much about *lhamana*, We'wha is still referred to reverently as a cultural hero.[55] In other tribes, such cross-dressing has continued up to the present. A white educator living on the Northern Cheyenne reservation reported his surprise upon learning that the "woman" living across the street from him for two years was really a male.[56]

The cross-dressing may be selective, as with a Crow *badé* today who usually dresses androgynously on the reservation, but if he wants to go into the white towns nearby with his women friends, he will dress as a woman. By doing this, he can act femininely without causing notice from whites. Another berdache, a Lakota *winkte,* fell in love with a white man in the Air Force. Realizing they could not be together as two men, he began to dress as a woman. He lived with the airman as his wife for sixteen years. He brought along his two Indian adoptive children and they became a typical military family. Though he participated in social events in the base town, including attendance at military dances, no Air Force authorities ever realized he was male.[57]

In order to survive, many berdaches stopped cross-dressing altogether. One Navajo *nadle* in the 1930s, a popular singer for the Blessing Way ceremonies, blended in by dressing always as a man. But his name, Stick Bounder, was suggestive of his berdachism to those who were familiar with the woman's gambling game it referred to. Navajos characterized him as being noted for his "feminine accomplishments, but also practice[d] pederasty." But whites did not understand the subtle clues of his social status as a berdache. Another anthropologist wrote of a masculinely dressed berdache, "Had there been no rumors or whispers, no white person would have picked him out of a Navajo crowd as abnormal."[58]

Even in the 1970s, Navajo *nadle* continued to wear a few articles of distinctive clothing [for example, a special type of sash] with their men's dress, so that other Navajos would be able to recognize them as berdache while whites would be ignorant of the distinction.[59] The popularity of unisex clothing in the 1960s allowed more flexibility in men's dress, so that a berdache might not stand out as much.

Since many Indian people continued to think of berdachism, and also of homosexual desire, as personal inclinations that individuals had a right to express, they naturally worked to keep the white legal system from interfering with berdaches.[60] A contemporary Lakota points out that it was not difficult to keep things secret from the white authorities, because government officials and missionaries were too few in number to keep tabs on the traditionalists throughout the reservation. Most whites, he remarks, "didn't really care very much about anything other than getting the Indians' land and wealth. Indians just keep things like this unknown to whites who don't understand our sacred ways."[61]

Even when whites knew about berdachism, the Indians sometimes used clever rationalizations for the practice which would justify it in Western eyes. In the 1840s a Catholic missionary near Vancouver recorded a statement about an Indian named Rose Thrael Nisqually (1797–1847), presumably of the Nisqually people south of Puget Sound, who was "disguised as a woman for a long time past." The missionary wrote, "For a man to disguise himself as a woman was not unusual among natives, who claimed the ruse offered them greater safety in travel and in spy activity."[62] While it is not clear why missionaries believed this explanation, it does indicate the ability of the Indians to keep their customs intact by manipulating white authorities.

CONTINUED RESPECT BY TRADITIONALISTS

Traditionalism survives among modern American Indians by more than manipulation. Religious ideology is often the slowest part of culture to change, and among Native Americans it is often the last thing left that is not dominated by whites. The Euroamericans took or destroyed the physical things Indians possessed: the land, the wealth, people's physical freedom, and even control over children's education. Many Lakota traditionalists, the followers of Red Cloud's way, feel there is little possibility of challenging this white control. It only brings grief to try.

Faced with such outside domination, many people might despair. But the Lakota shamans and berdaches with whom I spoke do not. Their comfort is that white domination is limited. It is restricted to the rational world of the here and now. They feel that they can survive as a people if they can retreat into the other world, the supernatural aspect of life that transcends and goes beyond the limits of rational reality. Shamans and those sacred people like the berdaches possess the only kind of knowledge not challenged by Western culture, the knowledge of a distinct other world outside of rationality. Traditionalists feel that whites, with their emphasis on the rational, are not capable of exploring this other world. Reflecting the limits of their rationalist thought, whites do not know that such a world exists.

Traditionalist Indians do not isolate themselves from the elements of the here and now. As long as they recognize that there is a world beyond the rational, they may partake in the day-today aspects of modern life in the same way that a person without spiritual insight would. For example, an Omaha *mexoga* I visited considers himself, and is considered by others to be, a traditionalist. Yet he served in the army during World War II, traveled to North Africa and Europe, and after the war lived in the city of Omaha for two decades before retiring to the reservation. His traditionalism is not judged on the basis of his exposure to modern rational ideas and ways of doing things, but on his awareness of another realm.

The evolution of berdache status in modern times and its relationship to traditionalism can be seen with the Pueblo Indians. While the Pueblos have been affected by Christianity, Hispanic machismo, and off-reservation jobs since 1940, the older population continues the old ideas. Berdaches do not dress differently, but they are still respected. In the early 1970s, three of the traditional Pueblo governors were berdaches.[63]

One of these respected elderly berdaches was interviewed in his New Mexico pueblo about 1978. He does not appear effeminate, but always plays the passive role in sex with the "straight" men of the pueblo. His behavior lies comfortably within the norms of this culture, and his place in the community is so secure he feels no need to question it. Younger Indians, however, do not feel this sense of tranquility. They have absorbed Chicano ideas about machismo and Anglo ideas about sexual orientation, and the result is stress and confusion.[64]

There are often generational differences within families, with the more traditional older people challenging their acculturated children. A Crow *badé* recalls how when he was six years old he enjoyed playing house with girls and dressing up like a girl, but his acculturated mother and mother's brother punished him for this. "But I sneaked around still, and did it secretly. I've been like this as long as I can remember. I practiced the baton with girls, and became so good that by seventh grade they asked me to perform at basketball games. No boy had ever done baton before, but I was even better than the girls. My uncle walked out ashamed, and later beat me for this. But my grandfather intervened, and told me about the old days when people respected the *badé*. After that my uncle and mother laid off me."[65]

Such generational differences, a response to the conflicting messages being received by modern Indians from two different cultural traditions, make for a confusing situation. As early as 1916 Elsie Clews Parsons reported from Zuni: "I got the impression that in general a family would be somewhat ashamed of having a *la'mana* among its members. In regard to the custom itself there seemed to be no reticence in general and no sense of shame."[66] What are we to make of such a statement, which on its face seems contradictory? We could claim, as some anthropologists have done, that this represents an ambivalent attitude on the part of traditionalists. Or we can see it as a reluctance to talk about such a family member in front of white people, or even as a possible response to the impact of Western culture on twentieth-century Indian societies. Weighing all of the evidence about berdachism, I favor the latter interpretation.

Among those Indians who have lost faith in the old ways, the topics of gender nonconformity and homosexuality may evoke confusion and a sense of tragedy. But traditionalists exhibit no such disturbance. The Sioux medicine man Lame Deer remembered a conversation he had with a *winkte* in 1971: "I wasn't even sure of whether I was talking to a man or to a woman. . . . To us a man is what nature, or his dreams, make him. We accept him for what he wants to be. That's up to him. . . . There are good men among the *Winktes* and they have been given certain powers."[67]

A *winkte* who continued dressing androgynously even in the 1970s was reported being fully accepted as a respected member of the community and was only rarely ridiculed by the acculturated Indians—but never by traditionalists.[68] An elder Lakota woman told me, "We consider *winktes* to be sacred persons, still today. We're not like white people who don't accept half-and-half people. The attitudes of the traditional people toward *winktes* have not changed. The whites did not mess with *winktes* because they did not recognize them."[69]

Omaha traditionalists expressed to me the same feeling; there is no change for those who respect the old ways. There is a need for more fieldwork among different tribes to assess the feelings of traditionalists. It would not be surprising if more continuity is found than studies of acculturation suggest. When Ruth Underhill could report about Papagos in the 1930s that berdaches were accepted "entirely without opprobrium," would we expect that feeling to have disappeared totally today?[70] Students of modern American Indians are beginning to realize that the disappearance of Native American culture has been overemphasized; Indian people hold on to their ideas more thoroughly than their outward appearance suggests. While acculturation occurs, cultural persistence is an equally important theme in recent Indian history. The survival of cultural elements among Indians of eastern North America, who have been in intensive contact with Euroamericans for hundreds of years, leads one to think that such continuities exist for Indians of the West as well.[71]

We can see such continuities among the Navajo. As anthropologists earlier noted that *nadle* were common among the Navajo,[72] so this heritage has not disappeared today. A middle-aged *nadle* today reports his awareness of a sharp contrast between the way he is treated when he is off the reservation, where he is not respected, and the way he is treated by traditional Navajos. He is paid respect, he says, because it is the *nadle* who keep the men and women together as a unit.[73] A white gay man who lived among Southwestern Indians for nearly a decade, and who well understands the traditional ways, reports a gathering in 1978 of over 250 *nadle* in a sacred area of the reservation, and thinks *nadle* are increasing as more Navajos revitalize their culture. Though Navajos will not talk about berdachism to nongay whites, he reports that *nadle* have a special ceremonial role in the night dances before the winter solstice.[74]

This man stresses that the following sentiments, expressed by an educated Navajo who still values her old-style upbringing, are typical among traditional Navajos. She speaks with pride about her uncle who is a *nadle*.

Even today among traditional people, especially in the isolated rural areas, *nadle* are well respected. . . . One that I know is now a principal of a school on the reservation. Everyone knows that he and the man he lives with are lovers, but it is not mentioned. . . . Missionaries and schools had a bad effect on stigmatizing homosexuality among more assimilated Indians, so it's not as open as in the past. But among traditionals *nadle* never even went underground. It has just continued; they are our relatives—part of our family.[75]

This form of social continuity is remarkable given the extent to which Western culture is antagonistic to berdachism, and it tells us much about the strengths of cultural persistence when families support berdaches.

Because the berdache institution has been subjected to extreme repression, it has declined in the twentieth century. Berdachism may have gone underground, and it may have lost a religious role, but it has not disappeared. If white suppression of berdachism is a case study of cultural genocide, the continuation of the practice is an example of the strength of cultural persistence among contemporary Indian peoples. This persistence has had a surprising effect on modern Western society as well.

10 Survival and Pride: The Berdache Tradition and Gay American Indians Today

The berdache tradition has not only survived, but knowledge of it has had a significant impact on the rise of the gay liberation movement in Western culture. That movement has in turn had an impact on younger contemporary Indians. With this two-way cultural exchange, the status of gay people and the status of American Indians have some interesting parallels in the United States today. An examination of the origins of gay liberation in Europe and North America helps us understand these parallels.

A strong homosexual rights movement began in Germany in the late nineteenth century, and quickly spread to England. One of the techniques this movement used to provoke questioning of social norms was to publicize the acceptability of homosexual behavior in other cultures. The earliest substantial, nonjudgmental account of Native American berdaches, in a chapter called "Homosexual Love," appeared in a book by Edward Westermarck in 1908. This anthropology professor at the University of London, who was most likely homosexual, documented worldwide manifestations of same-sex relations.[1]

Soon after that, Ferdinand Karsch-Haack, a professor at the University of Berlin, published a massive compilation of source materials on same-sex relations among the peoples of Native America, Oceania, Southeast Asia, and Africa. *Das Gleichgeschlechtliche Leben der Naturvölker* (1911) has never been equaled in its comprehensiveness for cross-cultural information about homosexual behavior. Karsch-Haack was a member of Dr. Magnus Hirschfeld's homosexual emancipation organization, the Scientific Humanitarian Committee. The cross-cultural emphasis on berdachelike institutions in various areas of the world helped form Hirschfeld's ideas on homosexuals as constituting a "third sex."[2]

Unfortunately, the Native American concept of a mixed-gender or alternative gender role became confused with the Western tendency to emphasize physical aspects of biological sex. Hirschfeld's writings are filled with references to the soft feminine bodies of individuals with male genitals. By equating these "intersexed" people with "homosexuals," such an approach ignored the fact that a masculine man could also be exclusively homosexual in his behavior.[3] In looking for a biological foundation to justify homosexuality, this view distorted the Native American emphasis on a berdache's spirit as more important than his physical attributes.

The notion of a different "spirit" of homosexuals, however, also existed. By the late nineteenth century pioneer homosexual writer Karl Ulrichs had begun to write about the people that he called "Urning," as a distinct class of person. His ideas spread to Britain, and influenced the rise of the idea of "the intermediate sex" in the writings of Edward Carpenter. This pioneer English homosexual emancipationist published a book in 1914 titled *Intermediate Types among Primitive Folk,* which became the major source of ideas on American Indian berdaches for the founders of the homophile movement in the United States.[4]

The most influential theorist in the founding of the modern U.S. gay activist movement is Harry Hay (at certain periods of his life he has also been known as Henry Hay). Born in 1912, he has lived most of his life in Los Angeles and was to a great extent responsible for the emergence of gay activism in that city. During his youth Hay often spent his summers on a relative's ranch near Yerington, Nevada, next to a Washo Indian settlement. He became fascinated by Indians and attended traditional Washo dances. At age thirteen he was blessed by the elderly Paiute prophet Wovoka, whom Hay remembers as a very old man, blind and with a heavily wrinkled face. The Ghost Dance prophet touched the boy and said a prayer in his native language. Hay later recalled that the Indians told him Wovoka had said that "we should be good to this boy, for he will be a friend to us later."[5]

This incident, as well as Hay's fascination with some Hopi

dancers whom he later met, had a dramatic impact on Hay in his later years. In 1951 he and others founded the Mattachine Society, named after a French fraternity of unmarried men who conducted dances and rituals during the Renaissance. His idea, he later recalled, was to base the organization on "a great transcendent dream of what being Gay was all about. . . . Organizing the Mattachine was a call to me deeper than the innermost reaches of spirit, a vision-quest more important than life." Hay's emphasis on spirituality was likely a reflection of the impact of American Indian thought on the formulation of his identity as well as his language. He had proposed "that it would be Mattachine's job to find out who we Gays were (and had been over the millennia)."[6]

Such an emphasis meant that historical and cross-cultural investigation would be the focus of this search. Hay presented several papers on berdachism. In 1953 conservative leaders, without the founder's vision, took over the Mattachine Society and abandoned these investigations. Hay and other activists who favored a more radical perspective withdrew from the organization and focused on a gay group that had begun publishing *ONE Magazine*. Within a few years ONE Institute was sponsoring classes and educational seminars as well. Harry Hay's influence at ONE Institute emphasized the Indian view of homosexuality. In 1956 he began visiting the Pueblo Indians in New Mexico, establishing contact with gay Indians there.[7]

Hay encouraged Jim Kepner, an active writer in ONE, to offer anthropology classes that would emphasize berdachism. Kepner based his 1956 class on the writings of Carpenter, Westermarck, and other anthropologists. He recalls that more conformist homosexuals did not want to identify with "savages," or to confront the fact that they might be "different" in more ways than sexual behavior. Says Kepner, "They were trying to blend in by claiming that gays were no different than anybody else, except for what they did in bed."

The intellectually oriented activists at ONE Institute, influenced by the anthropological findings on berdachism, and by theories of an intermediate sex, emphasized the androgynous character of the person. Hay had rejected the word *homosexual* in favor of *homophile*. Kepner says, "The berdache was a symbol that we were there from very earliest times and had specific honored roles." Activists at ONE, building on early Mattachine ideas, were asking homosexuals to question: "Does this androgyny give us a different vision, a double vision, that enables us to see things differently and creatively? Do we have special talents? How can we best contribute these talents to society? Are the gay contributions in art and creative thought similar to those of the berdaches to their societies?"[8]

In 1959 W. Dorr Legg wrote an article called "The Berdache and Theories of Sexual Inversion" that was published in the *One Institute Quarterly*.[9] Legg, a leader at ONE Institute, recalls: "We in the early movement were very familiar with berdache as an institution." He felt that Clellan Ford and Frank Beach's 1951 book, *Patterns of Sexual Behavior,* had a tremendous impact, since it concluded that a majority of non-Western cultures accepted some form of same-sex eroticism as normal. This finding, Legg emphasizes, "placed the homophobia of Western society in a different perspective."[10]

Inspired by such an approach, Donald W. Cory's book *Homosexuality, A Cross-Cultural Approach* reprinted Westermarck's essay "Homosexual Love" and George Devereux's essay on Mohave homosexuality. Dorr Legg felt that American Indian berdaches "were especially significant because they are an American source, not something so easily dismissed as a strange exotic practice from the opposite end of the world. It showed that homosexuality is not alien and foreign, but was right here in America, from a very early date. We recognized that berdachism was not exactly the same as a modern gay identity, but it was part of the larger homosexual question."[11]

Meanwhile, interest in berdachism was growing in homophile publications. In 1959 (inspired by Hay's papers and Legg's article) the Denver chapter of the Mattachine Society invited the anthropologist Omer Stewart to speak on berdachism. *Mattachine Review* published his speech soon after. In 1963 Harry Hay wrote an essay on Pueblo berdachism in *One Institute Quarterly*. And, inspired by that article, another ONE writer went to the Mohave reservation to interview a modern homosexual Indian.[12]

By the late 1960s Hay and his lover, John Burnside, decided

to devote their lives to the Pueblos, and to spread ideas of gay liberation to the Indians. They left Los Angeles in 1970 and moved to a Tewa Pueblo as permanent residents. Omer Stewart had assigned one of his graduate students, Sue-Ellen Jacobs, to do research on berdachism, and referred her to Hay's essay. As luck would have it, Jacobs passed by the Pueblo in 1970, just three months after Hay moved there, and they began a close association. Jacobs's paper, published in the *Colorado Anthropologist* in 1968, soon circulated among gay academics—especially among anthropologists who were seeking to establish a gay study group within anthropology. Jacobs sent out many reprints upon request, including one to Jonathan Katz, who was collecting documents on Native Americans for his book *Gay American History.*[13]

Katz was aided by several gay historical researchers, most notably Stephen W. Foster and James Steakley, a specialist on the early German homosexual movement. The two main sources of knowledge about berdaches, the anthropological reports and the earlier historical documents collected by the European homosexuals, thus found their way into *Gay American History.* Katz's 1976 documentary collection ensured that berdaches would become a well-known aspect of the gay movement's sense of its past. By the 1970s non-Indian Americans were taking a more respectful attitude toward Native American cultures, and this was reflected in the gay movement.

In his introduction to *Gay American History,* Katz wrote that the existence of acceptable same-sex behavior among Indians holds a special fascination for "Lesbians and Gay men who are today beginning to repossess the national and world history of their people—part of their struggle for social change and to win control over their own lives." The attempt by the European conquerors to wipe out "sodomy" was, he concluded, "a form of cultural genocide involving both Native Americans and Gay people. Today, the recovery of the history of Native American homosexuality is a task in which both Gay and Native peoples have a common interest."[14] Writings about berdaches appeared repeatedly in 1976. Maurice Kenny, a Mohawk poet, wrote an essay in *Gay Sunshine* about the berdache tradition, while the national gay newspaper *The Advocate* proclaimed: "Gay Was

Good with Native Americans." Two bestselling gay books, Arthur Evans's *Witchcraft and the Gay Counterculture* (1978) and Mitch Walker's *Visionary Love* (1980), emphasized the berdache.[15]

In 1979 the Quebec gay movement even named its magazine *Le Berdache*. Its lead article suggested that the Indian view was superior because it integrated the berdache into society, not as a barely tolerated marginal anomaly, but as a valued spiritual entity. The emphasis in these articles was on the spiritual message of the berdache tradition. The most recent essay along this line is by J. Michael Clark in the gay magazine *RFD,* which argues that gay people should reject the homophobic Christian church, because its denial of gay spiritualism has left gay people as "sexually aberrant, soulless" marginal persons. But in rejecting Christianity, Clark argues, gays should not abandon a spiritual quest: "The challenge instead is to discover alternative resources for spirituality that are appropriate to our existential standpoint as gay and exiled persons." Clark sees the berdache as an alternative, which "can remind gays of a forgotten, primordial past and of the demand to fulfill a sacred destiny."[16]

The impact of the knowledge of such a destiny has been dramatic in the emergence of a proud gay identity. Judy Grahn, a leading poet in the lesbian and gay community, recalls her feeling upon first learning of the respected position of the berdache: "I put my face into my hands and sobbed with relief. A huge burden, the burden of isolation and of being defined only by one's enemies, left me on that enlightening day. I understood then that being Gay is a universal quality." When Grahn later wrote her worldwide survey of words related to homosexuality, *Another Mother Tongue: Gay Words, Gay Worlds,* the berdache was prominently highlighted.[17] Will Roscoe, a gay writer, expresses the attraction of the berdache as a model.

I have chosen not to see in these dress-wearing men (and warrior-hunter women) a ridiculous or pathetic figure, but a life devoted to a unique and specialized role. I think of the marvelous blackware pottery of the Rio Grande Pueblos, its gleaming, polished surfaces smooth and cool to the touch—and I have no difficulty imagining the rationale and the rewards of specializing in a work otherwise considered female. My own consciousness has thus absorbed the berdache.[18]

To Roscoe and others, knowledge of berdachism supplies a sense of roots, a feeling of being part of a long tradition in America, "to know you're not alone and not the first; to know you have, like the [Cheyenne] *hemaneh*, sources of inner strength to overcome obstacles and to do it, in gay fashion, with a flair."[19]

URBAN GAY INDIANS

Knowledge of the berdache tradition has had a significant impact on the development of gay liberation, but within the last two decades the gay movement has had a strong impact on younger Indians. The situation of modern gay people and modern Indians is similar in many ways. Individuals of both groups happened to migrate to the big cities as a result of the massive draft and defense industry during World War II, with urban Indian communities and gay communities emerging about the same time.

There are major differences between a culture one is born into, with a family that socializes one from infancy, and a subculture that individuals enter later in life. Still, both gays and Indians share a sense of being different, of being something other than what white America says is proper. In the same way that Indians were stigmatized as inferior savages, homosexuals were stigmatized as sick and sinful. As a result of this stigma, many individuals of the two groups found themselves lost in the mainstream culture, with high rates of alcoholism and suicide reflecting this low self-esteem.

Militant action by the American Indian Movement paralleled that of the Gay Liberation Front, while both had been inspired by the Black Power movement of the 1960s. Indians and gays both came to realize that in order to gain their rights, they had to fight discrimination by the mainstream and also attack the low self-esteem of their own group's members. Problems like alcoholism and suicide have dramatically declined in recent years, due to the cultural renaissance of Pan-Indianism, and the rise of Gay Pride. As Indians and gay people have built resources for a positive self-image, they have begun to build their communities constructively and to take control of their lives.

Many young Indians have recognized these parallels, first in a personal sense and later in a political sense. We can see the personal impact of gay liberation on younger Indians especially in the social evolution of an individual from a berdache pattern to a gay pattern. A Papago man who today identifies as gay recognizes elements of the berdache tradition in the way he was treated on the reservation. Born in 1955, he was of slight build and nonmasculine character as a child. He had always felt different from the other children, tending toward artistic concerns. When he was eleven years old, his older brother introduced him to sex. In his teen years he always took the passive role in anal sex, and was always attracted to older, masculine men. He absorbed his culture's notion that the passive role "was the only role for someone like me. I did not feel restricted by it, but that was just the way it was done and so that is what I wanted to do." He sometimes dressed in women's clothing, and his family accepted his inclinations. Everything pointed toward a berdache role for him.

When he was still in his teens, however, his parents left the Papago reservation and moved to Phoenix. By the time he was eighteen, he connected with the urban gay subculture. He learned to enjoy taking the inserter role in sex, and is now much more versatile in his sexual behavior with men. But though he has been influenced by the more flexible standards of gay life in a social as well as sexual sense, there are continuities from his past. He continues to be attracted to older masculine men, feels a strong sense of spiritualism, and places a high value on family relationships. He feels that life will not be complete if he does not raise a child, so he is looking forward to adopting children and would even consider having sex with a woman in order to have children.[20] As with many urban Indians, his life represents a gradual and partial adjustment to urban patterns, rather than a total break from his tribal culture.

The impact of Western culture is often felt in the families of acculturated Indians whose children have homosexual experiences. In an incident not that different from what happens to many white gay youth, a controversy emerged in Laguna Pueblo in 1978. A westernized father found out that his teenage son was in a relationship with another adolescent boy. He severely beat the boy, and then ordered tribal police to put the son in jail. A Pueblo gay man who lives in Albuquerque rescued the boy from jail and, to prevent the boy from being returned to the abusive father, took guardianship of the teenager. In Albuquerque the boy finished high school and later became a top Indian student at the University of New Mexico.[21]

Though this is an extreme example, it does point out the contrast between the respect given to berdaches in traditionalist families, and the abuse heaped on many young homosexual Indians by their Christianized parents. In the one case, families remain loving and unified, while in the other the family is discordant and fragmented. Many such young Indians leave their communities and migrate to the cities. By the early 1970s, Harry Hay reports, this trend was common among many young non-macho Pueblos who did not want to be stuck with a set role. They thought of themselves as different from regular men, and were attracted to masculine gay men. But they have been influenced by the gay lifestyle to be more open, and are facing the rejection of the more acculturated Indians. They have an open gay consciousness, and want to have a full relationship with a man, without the strict role definitions of the berdache tradition.[22]

Hay himself felt a certain disillusionment with the contemporary Pueblo attitude. "The gay must be passive and humble himself, and not show intimate contact in public while still having sex in private." With his liberationist values of publicly expressing relationships with other men, Hay reacted against the secretiveness of Pueblo "straight men who want a woman-substitute." Despite his awareness that berdaches were respected for their ceremonial roles, Hay understood why younger gay Indians would want to leave the reservation.[23]

For other urban Indians, especially those born in the city and not influenced by a reservation, there has been a sharp divergence from their ancestors' customs. Many younger Indians who are homosexually inclined have never been exposed to any alternative except the urban gay identity. I have interviewed Navajo men in gay bars in places like Salt Lake City and Denver who have never even heard of *nadle*. If their family left the reservation, and especially if they converted to Mormonism or other Christian religions, knowledge of such traditions would not be transmitted. Cut off from a sense of tradition, young homosexual Indians are left, like gay non-Indians, with only their sexuality as a means of defining themselves. If they are cast out of their urban Indian family and community on the basis of their sexual differences, it is a fatal blow for many. With racism still strong in many areas, the general society is seen as more threat than refuge. And so a rejection from the Indian community hurts all the more.

Even if a notion of the berdache tradition were transmitted, it might not be with the same respect as on the reservation. Certainly this is due to Western influences, but it is also because many Indians do not consider their traditional religion to apply when they are outside their homeland. Ronnie Loud Hawk says, "People are afraid to criticize *winkte,* because they fear the *winkte* spiritual power. . . . People know that on the reservation the spirit of Big Bull is watching them, so they cannot criticize *winkte*. But if they were away in the city, away from the kin groups, then they might be antigay. That is a different thing."[24]

Gay Indians have to deal with both homophobia, from Indians and non-Indians, and racism, from gays and nongays. In response to this double isolation, young gay Indians in San Francisco organized in 1975. Gay American Indians (GAI) was founded by Randy Burns (Paiute) and Barbara Cameron (Lakota). "We were first and foremost a group for each other," Cameron said. "Bringing together gay Indians is our most important current task." Burns came to the city by himself to attend college, and did not know anyone, gay or Indian. He read an article in a gay newspaper about the respected place of berdaches in many traditional Indian societies. This helped to inspire him to get together with other gay Indians.[25]

San Francisco was a city with a large Indian population, as well as a highly visible gay community. At first Gay American Indians met some resistance from the general Indian community. The director of the city's American Indian Center suggested that they would be offending people by putting up GAI posters, but Burns and Cameron continued anyway. They found that the older traditionalists were not condemnatory, but many of the middle-aged Indians wanted to keep the topic of homosexuality from being talked about. Given the government's earlier attempts to use "sexual perversity" as an excuse for taking Indian children away from their parents, such reluctance is understandable. GAI members felt, however, that it was time for Indian people to stand up for their past traditions rather than to hide them. Randy Burns says, "In the Indian community, we are trying to realign ourselves with the trampled traditions of our people. Gay people were respected parts of the tribes. Some were artists and medicine people. So we supply speakers from the group to appear at Indian gatherings. Sometimes we are booed or jeered, but it doesn't last long."[26]

More young gay Indians continued to migrate to San Francisco in the 1970s, attracted (like gay non-Indians) to the visible gay community. Many young people arrived there with little besides their hopes for the future. GAI members helped them get referrals for housing and jobs or student loans, and provided social opportunities in a mutual support group. The younger Indians tended to have more formal education than the general Indian population, with the result that they adjusted well and advanced in their new home. Within five years of its founding GAI had 150 members and was earning the respect of the Indian community. I met Randy Burns in 1980, and he was proud of the achievements of the organization. "At the beginning straight Indians snickered at us, but since the gay movement has made strides and since more gay Indians have come out, they now treat us respectfully."[27]

GAI members are proud of their heritage, and they are aware of the berdache tradition. Though he is a Paiute, Burns tells the accounts of *nadle* in the Navajo creation story. He sees the message of the berdache as important no matter what tribal background a person comes from. He wants to prevent the sense of isolation and despair that faces some teenage gay Indians, who react by committing suicide when they recognize their homosexuality. If their family knows and accepts them as gay, then suicide seldom occurs. GAI members feel a sense of responsibility to help others adjust when they are lost and do not know where to turn. They have celebrated their tenth anniversary as an organization, and have grown to over six hundred members nationwide. They have published a bibliographical guide to berdachism, and are planning an anthology of essays, short stories, and poetry.[28]

YOUNG INDIANS ON THE RESERVATION

Through both GAI and gay people's increasing presence in the media, gay liberation is reaching young Indians on the reservations. One of those who migrated to an urban gay community is Michael One Feather, who was born in 1958 on a South Dakota reservation, and was raised almost entirely by his grandparents. Though he now makes his home in Los Angeles, he retains many ties to the reservation. Typical of the two worlds that contemporary gay Indians must straddle, he is both a sophisticated urbanite and a Lakota traditionalist. A gentle person, Michael is proud of his androgynous manner and of his respect for Indian traditions.

When he was growing up, Michael remembers that he always saw himself as different. Long before any sexual urges led him to identify as gay, he knew that he was not like the other children. He enjoyed designing flamboyant clothing and artistic things as a child, and generally isolated himself from others his age. He preferred to spend time with his grandparents, or by himself. He has been sexually active since he was ten years old, always with men who were older than he.

When he was twelve years old, other kids called him *winkte*. He recalls: "I asked my grandmother what it meant, and she didn't tell me but said not to listen to them." Later, other boys in his school explained it to him: "they used the word *winkte* for what we call gay." Because the kids at school were using *winkte* as a word of ridicule, he took "gay" as a more positive term. He used the word *gay* to describe himself, not *winkte*. "I had seen references to gays in magazines, and had an Indian friend who was raised in a nearby town, and he showed me a copy of the gay newspaper *The Advocate*. He connected me to the gay world, and told me what it was all about."

He did not know much about *winkte,* beyond the jokes of his age-mates. "I didn't know about its spiritual role until I took an American Indian studies class in high school. The teachers said that *winktes* were holy people who should be respected. A long time ago they went on the warpath with the warriors and took care of them and nursed them." When Michael mentioned this to his grandparents, his grandfather did not react negatively but his grandmother, with her Christian beliefs, told him that he should not be that way. This did not faze him because, Michael recalls, "I never took my grandmother's statement seriously. At age fourteen I just decided to do things the way I wanted to do it."

By the age of fifteen he was ready to leave the reservation. "I was looking for my freedom to be gay. The only way I could see to do that was to work my way into school fieldtrips and go off to other cities." On a summer school trip to Minneapolis after a teacher pointed out a gay bar, "I snuck out of the hotel room and went down there. I met two Sioux Indian drag queens on the street, and they got me into the bar. I liked it and wanted to go back." Returning home from the trip, he stayed at his grandparents' for only a week before deciding to go back to Minneapolis. He had saved some money from a part-time job, which he used to buy a one-way ticket to Minneapolis.

Once he got to the city, the two Sioux he had met earlier let him stay with them. "They showed me the drag scene, and introduced me to a wonderful world that I enjoyed a lot. I started dressing as a woman, and earned money by giving blow jobs to straight guys who thought they were buying a woman. One time a guy discovered I was male and that was kind of scary, but usually it was quickies in their car so they never knew. I worried a lot about getting arrested by police, though."

When he was still sixteen Michael met a thirty-two-year-old white construction worker at a nightclub. "We fell in love and I moved in with him. It was a good relationship. He enjoyed tak-ing me out to straight places with me dressed as a woman. We got a kick out of fooling the straights." But later both of them started drinking too much alcohol and the relationship went downhill. "After we were together six years, he left me for a woman. That hurt me. So in 1981 I left Minneapolis and returned to my grandparents. But then after a little while my lover drove all the way out to the reservation to make up with me. He apologized and begged me to come back with him. It was so romantic. We both drove back to Minneapolis to try to make our relationship work. But unfortunately it didn't, so I came back to the reservation again."

On his return Michael was asked to join a small Indian dancing group, since he was known as a very good "fancy dancer." Under his leadership the group became famous throughout the Plains for competition at international powwows. To support himself and the group he applied for Native American culture grants, a skill he had learned in high school. "I had a knack for writing things about my heritage and my culture, and putting it into a grant. Our grants always got accepted. I always put in for far places, since I liked to travel." This dance group became known for the accuracy of their dances, with his grandparents and other elders serving as advisors.

Most people knew about Michael being gay, but it was not discussed. What they noticed were his efforts to keep alive an important aspect of their culture. Another gay Indian dancer, who had been in California, told him about the well-developed gay communities there. By that time Michael was feeling restless: "I had accomplished everything I wanted in the dancing. There was no more excitement. So then I answered an ad in the *Advocate* from a guy in West Hollywood, and he paid for my ticket to Los Angeles. Social life on the reservation was not too exciting, so I left."

Michael came to Los Angeles and stayed at the man's house for three months. Disoriented by the move, he began to drink too much. Finally, his roommate asked him to leave. He had to look for a new apartment and a job. "It was hard, but I knew when I was out here I was free. When I see how many gay people there are in Los Angeles, with its own gay city now in West Hollywood, I knew I had found my home. It is a place to go and be accepted. I have no desire to go back to the reservation to live."

But he does go back to visit, and regularly talks with his

relatives on the telephone. His grandparents did not want him to move so far away from home, "But they understand why I like it out here. I let them know that I finally became self-supporting." He is proud that he has not touched a drop of alcohol for three years. He likes his job, and spends his free time working for the International Conference for Lesbian and Gay People of Color. "I'm happy to be able to take care of myself, to be able to start to grow." His pride and self-confidence have never been greater.

In the last few years, since Michael left his reservation, gay liberation has been having more of an impact there. Michael says, "Today on the reservation there are so many gays and lesbians emerging more visibly, and more rumors about who slept with whom. People are becoming more open-minded, due to the impact of the urban gay rights movement. Since more young Indians are influenced to come out as gay, their openness forces other Indians to change their attitudes and accept gays."[29]

BERDACHISM AND GAYNESS

Differences

While both berdachism and gayness involve sex with men, there are dissimilarities. Part of the difference between berdache and gay roles is in terms of gender identity. Some homosexually inclined Indians today, especially those who have been exposed to urban gay communities, may not wish to make a choice between being a berdache or a masculine man. They see themselves as gay, not berdache, and do not want social acceptance if it means they will be treated like a halfman-halfwoman. They want to be treated as men.

In traditional Indian values, men who are not berdaches are expected to marry women. With some signifcant exceptions, many tribes put pressure on men not to marry a berdache but only to visit him for sex. There was not a recognized way for two masculine men to become formally married. In rejecting a berdache role for themselves, some younger homosexually inclined men also reject family pressure to take a wife.

These men want a full-time relationship with another gay-identified man, rather than always being propositioned by masculine men for secret sexual encounters. And they do not like exclusively taking the passive role in sex. They were socialized in the gay subculture to expect a flexible exchange and blending of roles with their partner.

These issues point up the differences between a berdache role, overlaid with its alternative gender traditions, and the idea of two masculine males having a gay relationship. But the differences should not be overstated. While most people tend to follow the accepted pattern in which they are socialized, long-term relationships between a berdache and a man do offer the privacy and trust within which sexual flexibility can take place. Homosexual behavior might be the same as in Western society, but the meanings that society constructs around these relationships differ considerably.

Still another difference is that a separate gay community arose largely as a refuge from the persecutions of an antagonistic culture. Individuals migrated to such a community to escape a home from which they were often alienated. When berdaches had an accepted role within the family and the community, there was no reason to migrate to a separate urban subculture. A berdache might share a sense of sameness with other berdaches, but there was no estrangement from the general society.

One *winkte* I interviewed said he did not think he would be a good gay lover. He did not mean in terms of sexual behavior, but in terms of his commitment to family, his love for children, and his desire to remain on his reservation. Living in a separate community of people like himself was not his goal in life. He did not even have a desire to visit the city, where he imagines a faceless anonymous mass of people lost without their extended family connections and their communion with nature and the spirit world.[30]

For their part, some white gay men resist the analogy to berdachism. In many ways modern gay subculture is more similar to frontier male fringe societies, in which two masculine men paired up, than it is with the gender-mixing berdache tradition. In a letter attacking the Quebec gay magazine for taking the name *Le Berdache,* a gay writer complained that the name implies an integration into society rather than a separate gay sub-

culture. More importantly, the berdache represented too feminine and mystical a role, which this writer felt was not what
male homosexuality was about. He preferred to emphasize pairings of masculine men with each other, not a masculine man
with "a parody of a woman."[31] Given the trend in the gay community toward a more macho image, and the consequent dis-
paragement of drag queens, it is surprising that the berdache
model has been as popular as it has.

Traditionalist Indians see the mystical and gender aspects as
the greatest strength of the berdache. I asked a Lakota *winkte* if
a certain gay-identified Indian we both knew would be considered a *winkte*. He said no, because the man was not androgynous
enough and was not spiritual: "*Winktes* are very spiritual. When
Indians say *winkte,* they mean a male who is effeminate, like a
woman. 'Gay' and *winkte* are different. *Winkte* is a gay with ceremonial powers."[32] Because of this lack of spirituality traditional
Lakotas sometimes look down on gay-identified people. One
says:

Winktes at one time were regarded as sacred, but that has declined,
and today it is like gay—like in California. Even today elderly
winktes are respected as holy persons, especially by elderly and traditional people, and feared because of their spiritual power. They could
put a curse on people, so you had better respect them. Younger
people will call other youngsters *winkte* but I don't think they are
really *winktes* because they have no spirituality. They are just gay;
there's a difference. Maybe they got that way from drinking or
smoking. Most of them don't even know about the *winkte* tradition.
If they did they wouldn't drink.[33]

Gays are not condemned by traditionalists because of their sexual behavior but because they are not fulfilling their spiritual
role in life. A woman whose uncle is a *winkte* says, "People who
don't respect their Indian traditions criticize gays, but it was part
of Indian culture. It makes me mad when I hear someone insult
winktes. A lot of the younger gays, though, don't fulfill their
spiritual role as *winktes,* and that's sad too."[34]

Spiritual justification is the crucial element underlying a respected role for *winktes*. A shaman admits that people currently
define someone as *winkte* on the basis of their homosexual re-

lationships and androgynous character, but "today it is hard to know really who are *winkte*" because so many do not fulfill their spiritual powers. As Terry Calling Eagle says, "Some *winktes* today are not dependable, to help others spiritually."[35] Even though he would be classified as exclusively homosexual if he were in white society, Terry does not identify as gay. He sees his spiritual role as more important in his self-identity than the fact that he has sex with men.

I am most indebted to this forty-six-year-old *winkte,* with whom I lived in the summer of 1982, who led me to understand this distinction. He patiently explained Lakota culture while preparing me for participation in some of the most sacred ceremonies: sweats, smoking of the sacred pipe, Yuwipi, and my own vision quest. At the Sun Dance I attended, it was he who led the prayers blessing the Sun Dance pole, as it was placed in the ground. He and the medicine man who guided my learning, helped me appreciate as never before the intense spiritual role of berdache.

Terry Calling Eagle talks continuously about spiritual matters, and spends his days helping people prepare for ceremonies. He also helps people in very practical matters—visiting with the infirm, taking them to the doctor, helping them sell beadwork, conveying messages for people without telephones, cooking for them, and doing a multitude of other small tasks. He says, "If I practice the *winkte* role seriously, then people will respect me. I've worked as a nurse, and a cook in an old age home. I cook for funerals and wakes too. People bring their children to me for special *winkte* names, and give me gifts." I observed some of this gift giving, in which people brought him things informally as well as in "giveaway" ceremonies. He always had a large pile of blankets and gifts piled in the corner, which he would in turn give as presents to those in need. When I asked him why he did all this, he replied, "If I show my generosity, then others help me in return."[36]

As we sat in his room, with pictures of his smiling adoptive children hanging on the walls, along with posters from the American Indian Movement and souvenirs from his participation in the 1973 Wounded Knee occupation, I saw that he is indeed different from the average man. He defines his existence around his helping role and his intense spirituality.

Both Berdache and Gay

The relationship between a berdache identity and a gay identity can be seen especially in the case of present-day individuals who have switched back and forth between the two. A traditionalist Kiowa berdache, when he moved to San Francisco in the early 1960s, wore a mixture of men's and women's clothing, and wore his hair long like a woman. But in the city he gradually stopped identifying as a "male-female," and was influenced by his urban friends to begin identifying as "gay."[37]

In some respects, a gay identity is closer to a traditional berdache role than is a transvestite identity. A Hupa berdache who left his reservation in his late teens began dressing entirely as a woman and passing as a female. His previous role on the reservation was different—more androgynous than feminine. After several years living as a woman in mainstream American society, he decided, "I wanted to identify as a male. I was tired of people reacting to me as a woman. I liked the feeling, but I got tired of it. So I decided I would be gay." He cut his hair short, and started socializing in the gay community. "I had to be comfortable that society accepted me, and I figured that being gay would be more acceptable. Everything before then I had geared as female, but I accepted that I don't have to go into a lot of role playing, and can do anything as gay. I could go to work and be comfortable. As a woman I only knew how to be taken care of by a man."[38]

It is interesting that, on moving into Anglo-American culture, with its notions that there are only "two opposite sexes," this berdache first chose a woman's status. Later, he chose a man's status. Finally reacting against the either/or choice forced on him, a gay identity offered him a more flexible androgynous role. For him, gay identity seemed closer to what he had experienced during his years on the reservation than had been the transvestite life-style he lived in the interim. Today he seems not particularly feminine, being more accurately characterized as a gentle man.

Such identity changes can occur more than once in a person's life. A Yaqui Indian now in his thirties, who was raised as a berdache, was respected as a dreamer and a mediator between the genders. He did a mixture of women's and men's work, and was sexually active with men. About 1970 he migrated to Los Angeles, where he merged into the gay community. He continued to gravitate to androgynous work, becoming a florist and later an owner of a unisex clothing boutique. Though he was successful in the city, he missed the spiritual element that had been so important in his life. In 1982 he gave up all his material gain to return to his people. Today he is an apprentice to an elderly berdache, training to be a healer. He has sex only with males, similar to his behavior when he was in the city, but the emphasis in his life now is on his spirituality. He again identifies, and is identified by his community, as a berdache.

Since such individuals have clearly not disappeared, we cannot say that the berdache tradition has died. The degree to which berdachism overlaps with gay identity depends on the particular tribe, of course, but it also depends on how the tradition is conceived. During her 1930s fieldwork on the Potawatomi reservation, Ruth Landes knew two young men in their twenties who were "potential berdaches, now frustrated by cultural changes." Landes suggested that the demise of the tradition was due to Western influences: "the berdache could not survive fundamentalists' outrage in the general American world." Yet even though she described them as "incomplete berdaches," the characteristics she mentioned lead one to wonder just what had changed.[39]

Landes portrayed these individuals as "rather delicate. . . . He walks like a woman, he talks like one, he likes housekeeping . . . his manners rather mincing, unlike the other boys." They were skilled beadworkers, excelling in a craft that only women normally pursue. These "berdache-seeming young men were assumed to be visionaries" and were well respected as "supernatural, extraordinary." An elderly Potawatomi woman described such a person as "something unusual the Good Spirit put here for a purpose." If such persons had been taught the traditional Indian ways, this woman said, "then we would have heard something extraordinary" from them.[40]

So even though the customs had changed, the type of person was seen as the same. One such Potawatomi was remembered in terms that seem typical of descriptions of berdaches. His name was Louis Nowgizhik, but he preferred Louise. He was known for his cleanliness, his hardworking productivity, and his sewing. Because he was such a good cook, a prosperous Potawatomi family hired him. One of the daughters in this family later described him fondly: "He made a strawberry pie with the loveliest crust. His rhubarb pie was wonderful!" Louise started off wearing a big apron over his pants, but later got rid of the pants in favor of dresses. After that he began to style his hair like a woman and to wear fancy combs in it. Landes's informant recalled:

We laughed but told him he looked nice. He was pleased. . . . He was crazy over my brothers. . . . He joked and giggled around boys like a boy-struck girl. . . . At my father's dances, he danced like a woman, with a man partner. . . . People used to come and stand around watching him. He was a curiosity, but they respected him. He didn't seem to mind; he seemed to like the attention. . . . He or 'she'—Louise liked the 'she'—was so tall, taller than most men, that he didn't look much like a woman . . . [but] his manners were beautiful.

When Louise died in his old age, the Indians respected his wish to be buried in women's clothes. "No indeed, the Indians never made light of him. They thought 'she' had some great 'power.'"[41]

Similarly, some Hopi women interviewed in 1965 about a modern male Indian expressed sentiments that are practically the same as statements of a century ago. They emphasized that such androgynous males were hard workers and owned a lot of cattle. About his character these women said, "his actions want to be like that of a woman, he acts like a woman, and he talks like a woman. . . . We liked him. . . . There's nothing the matter with them. It's just their actions. . . . We don't care. We tease him about it, but he doesn't care either."[42]

A psychologist who in 1976 interviewed another such male of a Southwestern tribe described him as "a gay man." Yet the way his family and tribe reacted to him was more like that of a berdache. He was comfortably accepted in the tribe, never suffering humiliations or attacks, nor had any restrictions been placed on his nonmasculine behavior. He was considered the best basket maker and sewer in the tribe. Typical for berdaches in the Southwest, his skills in woman's work were an object of praise by all. The psychologist wrote his reactions, "His appearance is neuter, not feminine, effeminate, or masculine." The interviewee was not uncomfortable discussing his sexual behavior with men or his gender variance. "There were no signs of psychosis . . . nor was there the impression of a person afflicted with chronic anxiety, depression, or their transformations."[43]

Clearly there have been major changes in the berdache tradition, but we must look at these modifications as part of an ongoing process of culture change. Native American cultures were not static before the coming of Europeans, and it is unrealistic to expect them to have remained unchanged since colonization. The changes occurring in this century should not be seen as a sudden transposition foisted on a static institution. Instead, we must look for continuities within the context of change. In this respect, there is much continuity from the past, in American Indian cultures generally and in the berdache role in particular, even up to the present.

Though some young Indians identify as gay and not as berdache, because they are not involved in the traditional ceremonies,[44] others see the two categories as essentially similar. This similarity is evidently not something that has existed just since the emergence of gay liberation. During her fieldwork among the Omahas in the 1930s, Margaret Mead recalled that she was visited by a white friend "who had been living an avowed homoerotic life in Japan, who was not a transvestite but who had a complete repertoire of homosexual postures. Within an hour of his arrival, the single berdache in the tribe turned up and tried to make contact with him."[45] The berdache's interest indicates that he saw a commonality with the white homosexual, beyond cultural definitions.

This cross-cultural commonality is not restricted to Anglo gays. A Hupa berdache who moved to San Francisco in the 1970s began to associate with a group of Hawaiian migrants who identify as *mahu,* a traditional gender-variant role in Polynesian culture that is similar to berdachism. They felt a close sense of "sisterhood." In 1979, he recalls, "I took a troup of Hawaiian queens back to the Hupa reservation. Everyone treated them with a lot of respect, and cleared a special place for them to do the traditional Hawaiian dances. People on the reservation went wild over this."[46] He was not the only one who saw cross-cultural similarities based on their similar gender and sexual identities; the Indian community responded likewise.

Many contemporary Indians, when asked to define their word for berdache, interpret it as "gay" or "homosexual."[47] "You can easily recognize *winktes,*" a Lakota man told me before I visited his reservation. When I asked how, he replied, "The same way you recognize a gay, very open and flamboyant. *Winkte* went underground a few decades ago, but has now re-emerged as openly gay."[48] When I was on the Cheyenne reservation, and I would ask people to define *he man eh* (sometimes pronounced as "hoim-a" or "e hi e mun"), they translated it as "a male who acts like a female." Knowing that I was going to Los Angeles, they said, "You'll see a lot of people like that out there."[49] Among tribes that no longer have a ceremonial role for berdaches, modern Indians equate berdaches with androgynous gay men.

It took a long while to figure out that when they said "gay" they did not mean it in exactly the same way that whites use the term to apply to anyone who is homosexual. When I first arrived on reservations, I was surprised that elderly Indians generally preferred to use the word "gay" rather than "homosexual." They see the latter term as focusing on sexual behavior, whereas their focus is on a person's character. "Gay," with its connotations of life-style beyond sexual behavior, seems to fit in more closely with an Indian understanding. The Indians use "gay" to apply only to those who are not stereotypically masculine. A young Omaha man remembers asking his elderly uncle why he was not like other men. The uncle replied, "Because I am *mexoga*—I am gay. That's just the way I am." This young man defines *mexoga* as "a very gentle man, but not a woman."[50] Using gay in this way, they would not count masculine-acting homosexuals as part of this status. They assume that berdaches will be involved sexually with men, but that is not as important in defining them as their character.[51]

An elder Crow traditionalist explains that Osh-Tisch was the last *bade'* to dress differently. "Since then the younger ones dress like men and blend in more. There are some today, transvestites, homosexuals, or gays you call them, but they don't have any ceremonial role." I asked what was the difference between *badé* and "gay" and he said they were the same.[52] When I asked other Crows about *badé* (without mentioning any association with homosexuality), they consistently said it meant "gay."[53] Russell Means, a leader in the American Indian Movement, likewise compared gays and berdaches: "The Indian looked upon these unique individuals as something special the Great Mystery created to teach us. These people had something special to tell us."[54]

BERDACHISM AND THE REVIVAL OF TRADITIONAL VALUES

There is an association between respect for the traditions and respect for berdaches. Crow people point out that there was a sharp decline in respect for the old ways in the 1920s, which was the decade that *badé* status seems to have waned. Today there are no *badé* who reached puberty (the age at which berdachism usually becomes manifest) before 1960. Since 1960 there has been a cultural revitalization among the Crows, and a more respectful attitude toward berdaches emerged. A Crow man told me that berdachism comes from "the same causes as homosexuality in other cultures" but the difference is how the larger society reacts to it. If an individual has an androgynous personality, then "Indian people tend to be more accepting than whites."[55]

Ronnie Loud Hawk says, "I get my holiness from the Sacred Pipe. From that holiness the Sioux people show respect. In the last few years, respect for *winkte* has increased, more than it had been, as more people return to respect for the traditions. Some mixed-blood Indians condemn 'queers,' but the traditional people stick up for them."[56] This new pride in the traditional heritage has meant that the cultural renaissance for American Indians has also brought with it a renewed sense of self-confidence for those who identify as berdaches and as gay. A woman who is half Navajo and half Lumbee remembers when her cousin came out as gay in the late 1960s. The Lumbee side of the family, who did not have a berdache tradition, condemned the cousin. But the Navajo side was consistently supportive. The Navajo grandmother told the children not to be upset, because their respected great-uncle, a *nadle,* was "also like that."[57] The grandmother saw *nadle* and *gay,* in their essence, as the same.

Younger gay Indians, upon coming out to their families, will sometimes have an elderly relative who takes them aside and tells them about the berdache tradition. A part-Choctaw gay man recalls that his full-blood Choctaw grandmother realized he was gay and told him how people like him traditionally worked closely with the medicine men: "What she told me made all the difference in my acceptance of myself. She said many of the holy men were gay and it was totally acceptable. They were almost seen as belonging to the tribe as a whole"— that is, as kin to everyone.[58]

This respectful attitude eliminates the stress felt by families that harbor homophobia. As a consequence, berdaches feel very close to their relatives. Michael One Feather says:

My grandparents accept my being gay, and we have a really good relationship. My grandmother got over her Christian prejudices, and like others has returned more to the traditional Indian way of looking at it. She told me that one male out of every generation in our family is a *winkte* and she had to accept it. She explained that in the old days people let them live and did not ridicule or bother them. There was the Indian belief that if anyone treated them badly then something bad would happen to them. Even in her Christian days she never tried to stop my homosexuality, or try to make me get married. It helps me to know of the *winkte* tradition.

Michael One Feather's elders prominently mention several *winktes* in their recounts of the family's history. They are descended from the famous Lakota leader Sitting Bull, and it is mentioned in family stories that Sitting Bull had a *winkte* wife.

There is no embarrassment in these stories, and no sense that this is a skeleton in the family closet. Instead, such stories stress that *winktes* are the holy people chosen to do sweat lodge ceremonials in association with medicine men. How different it must be for a nonmasculine boy growing up to hear family stories about respected ancestors who shared his gender identity, as opposed to a youngster who feels that he is the only one in the world like himself.

When Michael One Feather returned to live on the reservation as an adult, traditionalists recognized his spiritual gifts. He was widely respected for his devotion to the traditions in his leadership of the dance group. He also studied with a prominent medicine man, who paid particular attention to him. The shaman, according to Michael,

talked to me a lot and interpreted dreams of mine. He said I could foretell the future. I've often predicted things that would happen, so people realize that I am a seer. Though the Christianized Indians ridicule it, the older generation understands the proper meaning of *winkte* and respects it. The medicine man respects me as a *winkte*. If an older person calls me a *winkte,* I would take it as a compliment. I identify both as a *winkte* and as gay. They are the same.[59]

From this perspective, differences in the behavior of the berdache and the gay man should not be overstated. Berdaches were socialized into a culture where they were expected always to take the passive role in sex. Michael One Feather did that, and never felt sexually restricted by such a role. But after he moved to the city, and became more experienced in urban gay sexual behavior, he has learned to enjoy taking the active as well as the passive roles in sex. Today he has modified his sexual behavior, just as he has modified his dress. At times he will costume himself in a dress, but is as likely to wear a muscle shirt and blue jeans, though he usually wears stylish androgynous clothing.

Michael likes the flexibility of his urban gay lifestyle, but he has added that to his Lakota traditional *winkte* role rather than denying it. He has inventively adjusted, bringing his bicultural background to a rich self-identity as *winkte* and gay. He sees different styles in both traditions, but no contradiction in either role as a particular culture's expression of what he sees as a basic aspect of his character. The gift of tribal spirituality, combined with the flexibility of urban life-style; that is the potency of his dual identity.

Members of San Francisco's Gay American Indians also have combined these identities. GAI co-founder Randy Burns says, "We are living in the spirit of our traditional gay Indian people. The gay Indian person is probably more traditional and spiritual and more creative than his or her straight counterpart because that was the traditional role we played. The old people will tell you that. . . . We were the Go-Betweens. Because of our skill and our education today, we are the go-betweens, between the Indian community and the governmental bodies."[60] In San Francisco, with their contacts with the politically influential gay establishment, GAI uses their position to aid the Indian community in general.

Service to the community is an idea that continues to be emphasized for berdaches on a number of reservations. Joseph Sandpiper, a Micmac man who is identified as *geenumu gesallagee* ("he loves men"), told me that there are a number of prominent Micmac leaders who are like himself. They wear men's clothes, but will often wear a woman's sash as symbol of their status. Joseph served two terms as chief of his reserve, and he is now putting himself through college in public administration so that he may return with new skills to help his tribe. He is the Go-Between for his people, mediating with the outside world. Though everyone on his reserve knows that he is sexually active with men, he has never felt any prejudice on the basis of his sexuality. The only time people got upset with him was when he decided to leave the community to go to school. They felt he was abandoning them when they needed his leadership.[61]

Respected leader Salyoqah Channey (Seminole) expresses appreciation for the work that GAI members do for the San Francisco Indian community, saying, "They're being very, very helpful because they're enlightening non-Indians to our needs. They're doing a real civic duty. They're trying very hard to help our people." Randy Burns responds with pride, "When you have elders coming to us, asking us to be part of their ceremony, that's spiritual, that's cultural, that's Indian."[62]

Those who favor the revitalization of traditional culture point out the wisdom of berdachism as a benefit for Indian society generally. Not only does this respect prevent family disunity when a family member becomes berdache and/or gay, but it also helps to ensure that the member will actively contribute to the well-being of his relatives and his community. Poet Paula Gunn Allen (Laguna Pueblo) points out that the berdache role as Go-Between for women and men also fulfills a valuable social function. With a respected person to serve as mediator between the sexes, marital discord is inhibited in Indian families.

"If you make people hate berdaches," Paula Gunn Allen states, "they will lose their Indianness. The connection to the spirit world, and the connection between the world of women and men, is destroyed when the berdache tradition declines." The adoption of Western prejudices by modern Indians is, she concludes, an important aspect of "psychological colonization. If you hate the traditions, you hate part of yourself as Indian. If you hate yourself, that weakens your resolve to oppose white colonization. If we could stop Indian homophobia, other aspects of cultural revival can occur. We must recolonize ourselves. The issue of self-determination for Indian people means acceptance of lesbians and gays is central to accepting ourselves as Indian."[63]

Traditionalists' respect toward berdaches is suggested by another leading Indian poet, Maurice Kenny (Mohawk), in his 1979 poem that he titled "Winkte."

> We are special to the Sioux!
> They gave us respect for strange powers
> Of looking into the sun, the night.
> They paid us with horses not derision.
> ....
> For the people of the Cheyenne Nation
> There was space for us in the village.
>
> And we were accepted into the fur robes
> Of a young warrior, and lay by his flesh
> And knew his mouth and warm groin;
> Or we married (a second wife) to the chief,
> And if we fulfilled our duties, he smiled
> And gave us his grandchildren to care for.

We were special to the Sioux, Cheyenne, Ponca
And the Crow who valued our worth and did not spit
Names at our lifted skirts nor kicked our nakedness.
We had power with the people![64]

An Indian from Arizona states, "Among my people, gay is a special status. . . . The more unique someone is, the more valuable they are, the more unique their vision, the more unique their gift, their perspective, everything they can offer is something that other people can't offer. . . . The thing that's different about where I come from, is that all human beings are respected because all human beings have potential, all human beings have value."[65]

Examined from the perspective of two traditions, Indian society and the Western gay subculture, American Indian berdachism today demonstrates that despite intense pressure from white people, Native American culture has not succumbed to cultural genocide. This tradition had to change and even go underground, but it has not vanished. By creatively adapting, berdaches—like American Indians generally—must be seen not as the vanishing American, but the persisting American. It has managed to survive because of the respect that traditionalist Indians feel for the strength and the magic of human diversity. Some of this strength can be discerned in a 1964 statement by a Mohave berdache, which is perhaps the most important message of all.

I don't think I would like to change. I guess I'm just on my own personal little warpath—not against whites but against heterosexuals who think that everyone should be like them. I'm not always happy, but I'm always me. And they can like it or lump it. Life's too short to spend your time being something you don't want to be. Like the old saying, "To thine own self be true." I'm true to my self and my own nature. I think that's all anyone has a right to ask of me.[66]

Part III

Toward a Theoretical

Understanding

of Gender and Sexual Variance

11   Amazons of America:
Female Gender Variance

When Pedro de Magalhães de Gandavo explored northeastern Brazil in 1576, he visited the Tupinamba Indians and reported on a remarkable group of female warriors.

There are some Indian women who determine to remain chaste: these have no commerce with men in any manner, nor would they consent to it even if refusal meant death. They give up all the duties of women and imitate men, and follow men's pursuits as if they were not women. They wear the hair cut in the same way as the men, and go to war with bows and arrows and pursue game, always in company with men; each has a woman to serve her, to whom she says she is married, and they treat each other and speak with each other as man and wife.[1]

Gandavo and other explorers like Orellana were evidently so impressed with this group of women that they named the river which flowed through that area the River of the Amazons, after the ancient Greek legend of women warriors.

To what extent did this recognized status for women exist among Native Americans? The sources are few, since European male explorers dealt almost entirely with aboriginal men. Most documents are unclear about anything to do with women, and as a result it is difficult to make conclusions about those females who took up a role similar to that of the Tupinamba Amazons. But we can begin by making it clear that this institution was not the same as berdache. As specified earlier, the term *berdache* clearly originated as a word applying to males. Anthropologist Evelyn Blackwood has done a thorough search of the ethnographic literature and found mention of a recognized female status in thirty-three North American groups. Because she sees it as distinct from berdachism, she does not use the term "female berdache" but instead calls this role "cross-gender female." She notes that it was most common in California, the Southwest, the Northwest, and the Great Basin, but she also notes a few instances among peoples of the Subarctic and the northern Plains.[2]

Because I have some disagreement with the concept of gender crossing, and also because "cross-gender female" is linguistically awkward, I prefer the word *amazon*. This term is parallel to berdache, but it is a status specific to women that is not subservient to male definitions. American Indian worldviews almost always recognize major differences between amazons and berdaches. With the single exception of the Navajo, in those cultures that recognize alternative roles for both females and males, have distinct terminologies in their languages that are different for each sex. The Papago word translates as "Light Woman," and such women even up to the 1940s were considered simply socially tolerated variations from the norm.[3] Among the Yumas of the Southwest, berdaches are called *elxa'*, while amazons are called *kwe'rhame*. They are defined as "women who passed for men, dressed like men and married women." There is no ceremony marking their assumption of the role, as there is for the *elxa'*.[4]

The parents of a *kwe'rhame* might try to push her into feminine pursuits, but such a child manifested an unfeminine character from infancy. She was seen as having gone through a change of spirit as a result of dreams. In growing up she was observed to hunt and play with boys, but she had no interest in heterosexual relations with them. According to Yuman informants in the 1920s, a *kwe'rhame* "wished only to become a man." Typical of amazons in several cultures, she was said to have a muscular build and to desire to dress like a man, and it was also claimed that she did not menstruate. A Yuman *kwe'rhame* married a woman and established a household with herself as husband. She was known for bravery and for skillful fighting in battle.[5]

RAISING A FEMALE HUNTER

While there are parallels between berdaches and amazons, female amazons are also very different from male berdaches. Among the Kaska Indians of the Subarctic, having a son was extremely important because the family depended heavily on big-game hunting for food. If a couple had too many female children and desired a son to hunt for them in their old age, they would simply select a daughter to "be like a man." When the youngest daughter was about five years old, and it was obvious that the mother was not going to produce a son, the parents performed a transformation ceremony. They tied the dried ovaries of a bear to a belt which she always wore. That was believed to prevent menstruation, to protect her from pregnancy, and to give her luck on the hunt. According to Kaska informants, she was dressed like a male and trained to do male tasks, "often developing great strength and usually becoming an outstanding hunter."[6]

The Ingalik Indians of Alaska, closely related to the Kaska as part of the Dene culture, also recognized a similar status for females. Such a female even participated in the male-only activities of the *kashim,* which involved sweat baths. The men ignored her morphological sex in this nude bathing, and accepted her as a man on the basis of her gender behavior.[7] Other notable Subarctic amazons from the eighteenth century included the leader of the eastern Kutchin band from Arctic Red River, and a Yellowknife Chipewayan who worked for peace between the various peoples of the central Subarctic.[8]

Among the Kaskas, if a boy made sexual advances to such a female, she reacted violently. Kaska people explained her reaction thus: "She knows that if he gets her then her luck with game will be broken." She would have relationships only with women, achieving sexual pleasure through clitoral friction, "by getting on top of each other."[9] This changed-gender demonstrates the extreme malleability of people with respect to gender roles. Such assignment operates independently of a person's morphological sex and can determine both gender status and erotic behavior.

TRANSFORMATION INTO A MAN

In other areas, becoming an amazon was seen to be a choice of the female herself. Among the Kutenai Indians of the Plateau, for example, in what is now southern British Columbia, such a female became famous as a prophet and shaman. She is remembered in Kutenai oral tradition as being quite large and heavy boned. About 1808 she left Kutenai to go with a group of white fur traders, and married one of them. A year later, however, she returned to her people and claimed that her husband had operated on her and transformed her into a man. Kutenai informants from the 1930s told ethnographer Claude Schaeffer that when she returned she said: "I'm a man now. We Indians did not believe the white people possessed such power from the supernaturals. I can tell you that they do, greater power than we have. They changed my sex while I was with them. No Indian is able to do that." She changed her name to Gone-To-The-Spirits, and claimed great spiritual power. Whenever she met people she performed a dance as a symbol of her transformation.[10]

Following her return, she began to dress in men's clothes, and to carry a gun. She also began to court young women. After several rebuffs she met a divorced woman who agreed to marry her. "The two were now to be seen constantly together. The curious attempted to learn things from the consort, but the latter only laughed at their efforts." A rumor began that Gone-To-The-Spirits, for the pleasure of her wife, had fashioned an artificial phallus made of leather. But whatever their sexual technique, the wife later moved out because of Gone-To-The-Spirits's losses in gambling. Thereafter, Gone-To-The-Spirits changed wives frequently.

Meanwhile, she began to have an interest in warfare and was accepted as a warrior on a raid. Upon coming to a stream, Kutenai oral tradition recalled, the raiders would undress and wade across together but she delayed so as to cross alone. On one of these crossings, her brother doubled back to observe her. He saw her nude and realized that her sex had not been changed at all. Seeing him, she sat down in the water and pretended that her foot was injured. Later, trying to protect her reputation, she told the others that she was injured in the stream and had to sit. She declared that she hereafter wished to be called *Qa'nqon ka'mek klau'la* (Sitting-In-The-Water-Grizzly).

Her brother did not tell what he saw, but refused to call her by her new name. Later, she took still another wife, and as she had done with previous wives eventually began accusing her of infidelity. Qa'nqon was of a violent temper, and when she began to beat this wife, the brother intervened. He yelled out angrily, in the hearing of the entire camp: "You are hurting your woman friend. You have hurt other friends in the same way. You know that I saw you standing naked in the stream, where you tried to conceal your sex. That's why I never call you by your new name."[11]

After this, according to Kutenai informants, all the people knew that Qa'nqon had not really changed sex. It is conceivable that the community already knew about her sex before this pronouncement since Qa'nqon's ex-wives must have spread the truth. The oral tradition does not explain why women continued to marry the temperamental Qa'nqon. Soon after this incident, evidently, she and a wife (whether the same woman or another is unknown) left to serve as guides for white traders. The couple seemed to get along fine once they arrived at Fort Astoria on the Columbia River in 1811.

One trader named Alexander Ross characterized them as "two strange Indians, in the character of man and wife." "The husband," he said, "was a very shrewd and intelligent Indian" who gave them much information about the interior. Later, this trader learned that "instead of being man and wife, as they at first gave us to understand, they were in fact both women—and bold adventurous amazons they were." Qa'nqon served as guide for Ross's party on a trip up the Columbia to the Rocky Mountains. Ross recounted that "the man woman" spread a prophesy among the tribes they passed, saying that the Indians were soon going to be supplied with all the trading goods they desired.

These stories, so agreeable to the Indian ear, were circulated far and wide; and not only received as truths, but procured so much celebrity for the two cheats, that they were the objects of attraction at every village and camp on the way; nor could we, for a long time, account for the cordial reception they met with from the natives, who loaded them for their good tidings with the most valuable articles they possessed—horses, robes, leather, and higuas [?]; so that, on our arrival at Oakinacken [Okanagon, near the present-day border of British Columbia and Washington State], they had no less than twenty-six horses, many of them loaded with the fruits of their false reports.[12]

Another white traveler in the area nearly a decade later heard the Indians still talking about Qa'nqon, whom they referred to as "Manlike Woman." She had acquired a widespread reputation as having supernatural powers and a gift of prophesy. Her most important prediction was that there would soon be a complete change in the land, with "fertility and plenty" for all tribes. According to this traveler, writing in 1823, she had predicted that the whites would be removed and a different race of traders would arrive "who would supply their wants in every possible manner. The poor deluded wretches, imagining that they would hasten this happy change by destroying their present traders, of whose submission there was no prospect, threatened to extirpate them."[13] What we can see from these stories is that Qa'nqon sparked a cultural movement similar to "cargo-cults" that twentieth-century anthropologists have observed among Melanesians and other tribal peoples coming in close contact with Western trade cargo goods. This movement also reflected the dissatisfaction the Indians felt with the white traders.

After establishing her fame, Qa'nqon returned to settle with the Kutenai and became noted as a shamanistic healer among her people. A twentieth-century elderly headman named Chief Paul remembered his father telling stories of her curing him of illnesses when he was a child. In 1825 she accompanied a Kutenai chief to the Hudson's Bay Company post among the Flathead Indians, taking the role of interpreter. The company trader described her as "a woman who goes in men's clothes and is a leading character among them. . . . [She] assumes a masculine character and is of some note among them."[14]

In 1837 she was traveling with some Flatheads when a Blackfoot raiding party surrounded them. Through her resourcefulness the Flatheads made an escape while she deceived the attackers. The Blackfeet were so angry that they tried to kill her, but after several shots she was still not seriously wounded. They then slashed her with their knives. But according to Kutenai oral tradition, "Immediately afterwards the cuts thus made were said to have healed themselves. . . . One of the warriors then opened up her chest to get at her heart and cut off the lower portion. This last wound she was unable to heal. It was thus Qa'nqon died." Afterward, the story goes, no wild animals disturbed her body.[15]

This story, which was passed down among the Kutenai for over a century, signifies the respect the Indians had for the shamanistic power of the "Manlike Woman." Even the animals recognized this power and respected it. It should be noted that the Kutenai did not recognize a berdache status for males. A tribe that had an alternative gender role for one sex did not necessarily have another role for the other sex. Native Americans did not see the two roles as synonymous so equating amazons with berdaches does not clarify the matter.

MANLIKE WOMAN

The Mohaves, like other cultures, have different words for berdaches and amazons. *Hwame* girls are known to throw away their dolls and refuse to perform feminine tasks. It is said that they dreamed about their role while still in the womb. Adults recognize this pattern and, according to ethnographer George Devereux, make "occasional half-hearted and not very hopeful attempts to discourage them from becoming inverts. When these efforts fail, they are subjected to a ritual, which is half 'test' of their true proclivities and half 'transition rite' and which authorizes them to assume the clothing and to engage in the occupations and sexual activities of their self-chosen sex." Adults then help the *hwame* to learn the same skills that boys are taught.[16]

Mohaves believe that such females do not menstruate. In the

worldview of many American Indians, menstruation is a crucial part of defining a person as a woman. Some amazons may have in fact been nonmenstruating, or, since they wished to be seen as men, if they did menstruate they would hide any evidence of menses. The other Indians simply ignored any menstrual indicators out of deference to their desire to be treated like men.[17]

Mohaves also accept the fact that a *hwame* would marry a woman. There is even a way to incorporate children into these female relationships. If a woman becomes impregnated by a man, but later takes another lover, it is believed that the paternity of the child changes. This idea helps to prevent family friction in a society where relationships often change. So, if a pregnant woman later takes a *hwame* as a spouse, the *hwame* is considered the real father of the child.[18]

George Devereux, who lived among the Mohaves in the 1930s, was told about a famous late nineteenth-century *hwame* named Sahaykwisa. Her name was a masculine one, indicating that she had gone through the initiation rite for *hwames*. Nevertheless, she dressed more like a woman than a man, proving that cross-dressing is not a requirement for assuming amazon status. While she was feminine in appearance and had large breasts, Mohaves said that she (typical of others like her) did not menstruate. As evidence of this, they pointed out that she never got pregnant, despite the fact that she hired herself out as a prostitute for white men.

Sahaykwisa used the money that she received from this heterosexual activity to bestow gifts on women to whom she was attracted. With her industriousness as a farmer (a woman's occupation) and as a hunter (a man's occupation), she became relatively prosperous. She was also noted for her shamanistic ability to cure venereal diseases. Shamans who treated venereal diseases were regarded as lucky in love. This fame, plus her reputation as a good provider, led women to be attracted to her.

Sahaykwisa's first wife was a very pretty young woman, whom many men tried to lure away from her. Motivated by jealousy, they began teasing her, "Why do you want a *hwame* for a husband? A *hwame* has no penis; she only pokes you with her finger." The wife brushed off the remark saying "That is alright for me." But then later the wife eloped with a man. Such

a breakup was not unusual, given the fact that heterosexual marriages among Mohaves were equally subject to change. After a
time the wife returned to Sahaykwisa, having found the man
less satisfying. People referred to Sahaykwisa by the name Hith-
pan Kudhape, which means split vulvae, denoting how the
hwame would spread the genitals during sex. This part of the
oral tradition indicates that the Mohaves were well aware that
an amazon role involved sexual behavior with women.

While accepting these relationships, Mohaves nevertheless
teased Sahaykwisa's wife unmercifully. While teasing is quite
common in American Indian cultures generally, in this case it
was done so much that the woman left a second time. Sahaykwisa then began to flirt with other women at social dances, soon
easily attracting another wife, and then a third one later on.
Mohaves explained this by the fact that Sahaykwisa was, after
all, lucky in love. Her reputation as a good provider was also an
obvious factor. But after the third woman left her, and returned
to the man from whom Sahaykwisa stole her, the man attacked
the *hwame* and raped her. Rape was extremely uncommon
among the Mohaves, so this incident had a major impact on her
life.

Sahaykwisa became demoralized and an alcoholic, and ironically began having wanton sex with men. She claimed to have
bewitched one man who rejected her advances, and when he
died in the late 1890s she boasted about having killed him. The
man's son was so enraged by this that he threw her into the
Colorado River, where she drowned. In telling this story Devereux's Mohave informants were convinced that Sahaykwisa
claimed witchcraft intentionally so that someone would kill her.
They explained that she wanted to die and join the spirits of
those she had earlier loved.[19]

While this story does not have a happy ending, it does nevertheless point out that female-female relationships were recognized. Sahaykwisa was killed because it was believed that she
had killed another person by witchcraft, not because of her gender status or her sexual relations with women.

While the social role of the *hwame* was in some ways like that
of men, the story of Sahaykwisa does not support Blackwood's
view of gender *crossing*. The Mohaves did not in fact accept

Sahaykwisa as a full-fledged man, and the wife was teased on that regard. She was regarded as a *hwame,* having a distinct gender status that was different than men, women, or *alyha.* Mohaves thus had four genders in their society.

To what extent an amazon was accepted as a man is unclear. The variation that existed among Indians of the Far West typifies this matter. The Cocopa *warrhameh* cut her hair and had her nose pierced as men did, and did not get tattooed as women did.[20] Among the late nineteenth-century Klamath a woman named Co'pak "lived like a man. . . . She tried to talk like a man and invariably referred to herself as one." Co'pak had a wife, with whom she lived for many years, and when the wife died Co'pak "observed the usual mourning, wearing a bark belt as a man does at this time." Nevertheless, this mourning may have been the standard for a "husband" rather than for a "man," and we do not know if Klamath custom made a distinction between the two categories. Co'pak also retained woman's dress, which certainly implies a less than total crossover. Other Klamaths continued to see her as a manlike woman rather than as a man.[21]

A survey of California Indian groups that recognized amazon status revealed that in half of the groups amazons performed both men's and women's work, while in the other half they did only men's work.[22] No doubt this variation of roles is typical of cultural diversity in aboriginal America generally.

Unlike Western culture, which tries to place all humans into strict conformist definitions of masculinity and femininity, some Native American cultures have a more flexible recognition of gender variance. They are able to incorporate such fluidity into their worldview by recognizing a special place for berdaches and another one for amazons. "Manlike Woman" is how Indians described the Kutenai female, and that phrase recurs in anthropological literature when direct translations are given. By paying more attention to words used by Indians themselves, we can make more precise definitions. Gender theory is now beginning to make such distinctions. Terms like gender crossing imply that there are only two genders, and one must "cross" from one to the other. As with the male berdache, most recent theorists argue, the amazon is either a distinct gender role, or is a gender-mixing status, rather than a complete changeover to an opposite sex role.[23]

WARRIOR WOMEN IN THE GREAT PLAINS

When we turn to the nomadic Plains cultures, the picture becomes even more complex. Here, an accepted amazon status was generally lacking. Female divergence into male activity was not recognized as a distinct gender comparable to the institutionalized berdache role. Women could participate in male occupations on the hunt or in warfare, but this did not imply an alternative gender role. Precisely because they had various activities open to them on a casual and sporadic basis, there was not as much need to recognize a specific role for females behaving in a masculine way. For example, they could become "Warrior Women." Such a woman might join a war party for a specific occasion, like a retribution raid for the death of a relative. She might even accumulate war honors, called *coup*. But since it did not affect her status as a woman, she should not be confused with an amazon. Male warriors simply accepted female fighters as acting within the parameters of womanhood, without considering them a threat to their masculinity.[24]

Warrior women were not the same as amazons partly because their menstruation continued to define them as women. Among Plains peoples, as among many other American Indians, blood was seen as an important and powerful spiritual essence. An individual who bled would not be able to control the power of this bleeding, so if a person bled it might disrupt any important activity that depended on spiritual help, like a hunt or a raid. Consequently, if a woman began her period, the raid would have to be delayed while the spirits were placated. As a result of this belief, the "manly hearted women" who sometimes participated in warfare were almost always postmenopausal.[25]

This belief was not just a restriction on women; a male who bled from an accident or a wound had to go through the same efforts to placate the spirits. The matter was more a question of power than of restriction. Menstruation "was not something unclean or to be ashamed of," according to the Lakota shaman Lame Deer, but was sacred. A girl's first period was cause for great celebration. Still, Lame Deer concluded, "menstruation had a strange power that could bring harm under some circumstances."[26] Paula Gunn Allen explains: "Women are perceived to be possessed of a singular power, most vital during menstruation. . . . Indians do not perceive signs of womanness as contamination; rather they view them as so powerful that other 'medicines' may be cancelled by the very presence of that power." American Indians thought of power not so much in terms of political or economic power, but as supernatural power. Being a matter of spirituality, woman's power comes partly by her close association with the magical properties of blood.[27]

Another possible factor inhibiting the development of amazon status among Plains women had to do with the economic need for their labor and procreation. Women were responsible for the preparation of buffalo meat. Since a successful hunter could kill more bison than one woman could dress and preserve for food or trade, every available woman was needed to do this work. This economic system limited women's choice of occupation and put more pressure on them to marry than in other North American cultures. Furthermore, with the loss of men from warfare, there was the expectation that every woman would marry and have children.[28]

There was such a strong need for female labor that Plains men began taking multiple wives. A typical pattern was for an overworked wife to encourage her husband to take a second wife. The first wife now had higher status, as a senior wife who directed younger women, and the family as a whole benefited from the extra output of the additional wife. Quite often it would be the younger sisters of the first wife who were later brought in as co-wives. This pattern gave advantages to women. It kept female siblings together, giving them support and strength throughout their lives. In contrast to Western culture, which keeps women separated by promoting competition among them for men, Plains polygyny meant that wives were added to the family rather than replaced by divorce and serial monogamy.[29]

Despite these pressures on women to marry and procreate, even in the Plains culture there were exceptions. An amazon role was followed by a few females, with the most famous example being Woman Chief of the Crows. She was originally a Gros Ventre Indian who had been captured by Crow raiders when she was ten years old. She was adopted by a Crow warrior, who observed her inclination for masculine pursuits. He allowed her to follow her proclivities, and in time she became a fearless horseback rider and skilled rifle shooter. Edward Denig, a white frontiersman who lived with the Crows in the early nineteenth century, knew Woman Chief for twelve years. He wrote that when she was still a young woman she "was equal if not superior to any of the men in hunting both on horseback and foot. . . . [She] would spend most of her time in killing deer and bighorn, which she butchered and carried home on her back when hunting on foot. At other times she joined in the surround on horse, could kill four or five buffalo at a race, cut up the animals without assistance, and bring the meat and hides ·home."[30]

After the death of the widowed man who adopted her, she assumed control of his lodge, "performing the double duty of father and mother to his children." She continued to dress like other women, but Denig, writing in 1855, remembered her as "taller and stronger than most women—her pursuits no doubt tending to develop strength of nerve and muscle." She became famous for standing off an attack from Blackfoot Indians, in which she killed three warriors while remaining unharmed herself: "This daring act stamped her character as a brave. It was sung by the rest of the camp, and in time was made known to the whole nation."[31]

A year later she organized her first raid and easily attracted a group of warriors to follow her. She stole seventy horses from a Blackfoot camp, and in the ensuing skirmish killed and scalped two enemies. For these acts of bravery she was awarded *coups,* and by her subsequent successful raids she built up a large herd of horses. As a successful hunter, she shared her meat freely with others. But it was as a warrior, Denig concluded, that her fame was most notable. In every engagement with enemy tribes, including raids on enemy camps, she distinguished herself by her bravery. Crows began to believe she had "a charmed life which, with her daring feats, elevated her to a point of honor and respect not often reached by male warriors." The Crows were proud of her, composing special songs to commemorate her gallantry. When the tribal council was held and all the chiefs assembled, she took her place among them, as the third-highest-ranked person in the tribe.[32]

Woman Chief's position shows the Crows' ability to judge

individuals by their accomplishments rather than by their sex. Their accepting attitude also included Woman Chief's taking a wife. She went through the usual procedure of giving horses to the parents of her intended spouse. A few years later, she took three more wives. This plurality of women added also to her prestige as a chief. Denig concluded, "Strange country this, where [berdache] males assume the dress and perform the duties of females, while women turn men and mate with their own sex!"[33]

Denig's amazement did not denote any condemnation on his part, for individual traders on the frontier often accepted Indian ways of doing things. Rather, he respected his friend as a "singular and resolute woman. . . . She had fame, standing, honor, riches, and as much influence over the band as anyone except two or three leading chiefs. . . . For 20 years she conducted herself well in all things." In 1854 Woman Chief led a Crow peacekeeping mission to her native Gros Ventre tribe. Resentful because of her previous raids against them, some Gros Ventres trapped her and killed her. Denig concluded sadly, "This closed the earthly career of this singular woman." Her death so enraged the Crows that they refused to make peace with the Gros Ventres for many years.[34] Woman Chief's exceptionally high status was rather unique on the Plains; stories that were passed down made her a hero in the classic Plains mode. Even her death, at enemy hands, was typical of the pattern for the honored male warrior.

WIVES OF AMAZONS

What about the wives of the amazon? Woman Chief, like the other amazons, evidently had no difficulty finding women to marry. Yet, these women did not identify as lesbian in the Western sense of the word. American Indian women were not divided into separate categories of persons as is the case with Anglo-American homosexual and heterosexual women. The white lesbian often sees herself as a member of a minority group, distinct from and alienated from general society. She is seen as "abnormal," the opposite of "normal" women, and often suffers great anguish about these supposed differences. Paula Gunn Allen writes, "We are not in the position of our American Indian fore-sister who could find safety and security in her bond with another woman because it was perceived to be destined and nurtured by non-human entities, and was therefore acceptable and respectable."[35]

With the exception of the amazon, women involved in a relationship with another female did not see themselves as a separate minority or a special category of person, or indeed as different in any important way from other women. Yet, they were involved in loving and sexual relationships with their female mates. If their marriage to an amazon ended, then they could easily marry heterosexually without carrying with them any stigma as having been "homosexual." The important consideration in the Indian view is that they were still fulfilling the standard role of "mother and wife" within their culture. The traditional gender role for women did not restrict their choice of sexual partners. Gender identity (woman or amazon) was important, but sexual identity (heterosexual or homosexual) was not.[36]

WOMEN-IDENTIFIED WOMEN

Socially recognized marriages between an amazon and her wife only tell part of the story. Relationships between two women-identified women were probably more common. American Indians, while not looking down on sex as evil or dirty, generally see it as something private. Consequently, it is not something that is talked about to outsiders, and there is not much information on sexual practices. It is most important for a woman to have children, but in many tribes a woman's sexual exclusiveness to the child's father is not crucial. Thus, a woman might be sexually active with others without worrying that she or her children would be looked down on. In many Native American societies, a woman has the right to control her own body, rather than it being the exclusive property of her husband. As long as she produces children at some point in her life, what she does in terms of sexual behavior is her own private business.[37]

Individual inclinations, after all, are usually seen as due to a direction from the spirits. This spiritual justification means that another person's interference might be seen as a dangerous intrusion into the supernatural. "In this context," writes Paula Gunn Allen, "it is quite possible that Lesbianism was practiced rather commonly, as long as the individuals cooperated with the larger social customs." Allen wrote a poem to native "Beloved Women" which expresses this attitude of noninterference:

> It is not known if those
> who warred and hunted on the plains . . .
> were Lesbians
> It is never known
> if any woman was a lesbian
> so who can say. . . .
> And perhaps the portents are better
> left written only in the stars. . . .
> Perhaps
> all they signify is best left
> unsaid.[38]

It is precisely this attitude, that sexual relations were not anyone else's business, that has made Indian women's casual homosexuality so invisible to outsiders. Except for some female anthropologists, most white observers of native societies have been males. These observers knew few women, other than exceptional females who acted as guides or go-betweens for whites and Indians. Most writers expressed little interest in the usual female lifestyle. Yet even if they did, their access to accurate information would be limited to bits that they could learn from Indian males. Given the segregation of the sexes in native society, women would not open up to a male outsider about their personal lives. Even Indian men would not be told much about what went on among the women.[39]

Given these circumstances, it is all the more necessary for women researchers to pursue this topic. Openly lesbian ethnographers would have a distinct advantage. In contrast to institutionalized male homosexuality, female sexual variance seems more likely to express itself informally. Again, enough cross-cultural fieldwork has not been done to come to definite conclusions. However, Blackwood suggests that female-female erotic relationships may be most commonly expressed as informal pairings within the kin group or between close friends.[40]

GENDER AND SEXUAL VARIANCE AMONG CONTEMPORARY INDIAN WOMEN

In what ways do these patterns continue today? An idea of the type of data that might be gathered by contemporary field-workers is contained in a report by Beverly Chiñas, who has been conducting research among the Isthmus Zapotecs of southern Mexico since 1966. While she details an accepted ber-dache status for males, among females the picture is somewhat different. In two decades of fieldwork she has observed several instances of women with children leaving their husbands to live with female lovers. She sees these relationships as lesbian: "People talk about this for a few weeks but get used to it. There is no ostracism. In the case of the lesbians, they continued to appear at fiestas, now as a couple rather than as wives in hetero-sexual marriages." At religious festivals, she points out, such female couples do not stand out, since every woman pairs up with another woman to dance together as a couple. There is virtually no male-female couple activity in religious contexts. The sexes are always separated in ceremonies, with different roles and duties.[41]

The only negative reaction that Chiñas reports concerned an unmarried daughter of a close friend and informant who "left her mother's home and went to another barrio to live with her lesbian lover. The daughter was only 25 years old, not beyond the expected age of heterosexual marriage. The mother was very upset and relations between mother-daughter broke off for a time but were patched up a year later although the daughter continued to live with her lesbian partner."[42]

The Zapotec mother's anger at her daughter was due to the latter's evident decision not to have children. By refusing to take a husband at least temporarily, the daughter violated the cultural dictate that females should be mothers. It was thus not lesbian-ism per se that caused the mother-daughter conflict. It would be interesting to know if the mother was reconciled by the daughter's promise that she would get pregnant later. If so, it would fit into the traditional pattern for American Indian women. The importance of offspring in small-scale societies cannot be ignored; female homosexual behavior has to accommodate to society's need to reproduce the population.

Chiñas explains that in such *marimacha* couples, "one will be the *macho* or masculine partner in the eyes of the community, i.e., the 'dominant' one, but they still dress as women and do women's work. Most of the lesbian couples I have known have been married heterosexually and raised families. In 1982 there were rumors of a suspected lesbian relationship developing between neighbor women, one of whom was married with husband and small child present, the other having been abandoned by her husband and left with children several years previously."[43]

These data offer an example of the kind of valuable findings that direct fieldwork experience can uncover. The fact that one of the women was looked on as the macho one, even though she did not cross-dress, points up the relative *un*importance of cross-dressing in a same-sex relationship. An uninformed outsider might have no idea that these roles and relationships exist, and might assume that the practice had died out among the modern Zapotecs.

Since the field research that could answer these questions has not yet been done with enough Native American societies, I am reluctant to agree with Evelyn Blackwood's statement that by the end of the nineteenth century "the last cross-gender females seem to have disappeared."[44] Such a statement does not take into account the less formalized expressions of gender and sexual variance. If I had trusted such statements about the supposed disappearance of the male berdache tradition, I never would have carried out the fieldwork to disprove such a claim.

As also occurs with the berdaches, contemporary Indians perceive similarities with a Western gay identity. A Micmac berdache, whose niece recently came out publicly as gay, reports that the whole community accepts her: "The family members felt that if she is that way, then that's her own business. A lot of married Indian women approach her for sex. A male friend of mine knows that she has sex with his wife, and he jokes about it. There is no animosity. There might be some talking about her, a little joking, but it is no big deal as far as people on the reserve are concerned. There is never any condemnation or threats about it. When she brought a French woman to the community as her lover, everyone welcomed her. They accept her as she is."[45]

Despite the value of such reports, it is clear that a male cannot get very complete information on women's sexuality. I hope that the data presented here will inspire women ethnographers to pursue this topic in the future.

Paula Gunn Allen, who is familiar with Native American women from many reservations, states that there is cultural continuity. She wrote me that "There are amazon women, recognized as such, *today* in a number of tribes—young, alive, and kicking!"[46] They may now identify as gay or lesbian, but past amazon identities, claims Beth Brant (Mohawk), "have everything to do with who we are now. As gay Indians, we feel that connection with our ancestors." Erna Pahe (Navajo), cochair of Gay American Indians, adds that this connection gives advantages: "In our culture [and] in our gay world, anybody can do anything. We can sympathize, we can really feel how the other sex feels. [We are] the one group of people that can really understand both cultures. We are special." Paula Gunn Allen also emphasizes this specialness, which she sees as applying to non-Indian gay people as well. "It all has to do with spirit, with restoring an awareness of our spirituality as gay people."[47] As with the berdache tradition for males, modern Indian women's roles retain a connection with past traditions of gender and sexual variance. There is strong evidence of cultural revitalization and persistence among contemporary American Indians.

12 Social Constructions / Essential Characters: A Cross-Cultural Viewpoint

While comparative study of female gender variance is not the central topic of this book,[1] it is important to point out that American Indian cultures are not unique in recognizing a special status and respected role for individuals like berdaches and amazons. Many societies, in various areas of the world, have a special gender category which seems to be generally comparable to the berdache role. This chapter is a survey of some of these institutions, concluding with a statement about the implications of this cross-cultural research for a theory of gender variance and sexual variance among humans.

SIBERIA

Probably the closest institution to berdachism outside the Americas is among the reindeer-herding peoples of Siberia. The ancestors of Native Americans migrated from this area between 30,000 and 15,000 years ago. The presence of a tradition similar to berdachism among the peoples of Siberia suggests that this role has existed among at least some American Indians from their earliest arrival in the New World.

A major source for Siberian ethnography is Waldemar Bogoras, a Russian anthropologist who lived among the Chukchi in eastern Siberia from 1890 to 1901. He devoted a section of his book to "Sexual Perversion and Transformed Shamans," noting the close connection between homosexual behavior, gender variance, and spiritual power. The Chukchi refer to such a person as a "soft man (yirka-la ul) meaning a man transformed into a being of a softer sex." The transformation takes place gradually when the boy is between ages eight and fifteen, the critical years when shamanistic inspiration usually manifests itself. The Chukchi feel that this transformation is due to powerful spirits. Though people sometimes make jokes about the peculiar ways of soft men, the Chukchi respect them highly for their healing abilities and fear their spiritual or psychic powers.[2]

The soft man keeps his masculine name, but otherwise "leaves off all pursuits and manners of his sex, and takes up those of a woman. . . . He learns the use of these quickly, because the spirits are helping him." Bogoras knew several soft men, but considered Tilu Wgi to be the most remarkable. He described this thirty-five-year-old Chukchi as physically "wholly masculine and well developed besides." Nevertheless, with his hair arranged in the manner of Chukchi women, his face "looked very different from masculine faces. . . . All the ways of this strange creature were decidedly feminine. . . . I heard him gossip with the female neighbors in a most feminine way, and even saw him hug small children with evident envy for the joys of motherhood."[3]

While homosexual behavior was not limited to soft men, and there was even a case of one soft man who had a female wife before taking a male husband, in general Chukchi same-sexuality focused on the soft men. Bogoras wrote that a soft man "seeks to win the good graces of men, and succeeds easily with the aid of the spirits. Thus he has all the young men he could wish for striving to obtain his favor." One young soft man even created something of a problem in the 1890s because all of the eligible bachelors "beset him with their courtship to the great detriment and offense of the lawful [female] beauties." When a soft man chose a husband, Bogoras wrote,

The marriage is performed with the usual rites, and I must say that it forms a quite solid union, which often lasts till the death of one of the parties. The couple live much in the same way as do other people. The man tends his herd and goes hunting and fishing, while the "wife" takes care of the house, performing all domestic pursuits and work. They cohabit in a perverse way, *modo Socratis,* in which the transformed wife always plays the passive role.[4]

Soft men excelled in shamanism because of their close association with the spirit world, which made them "dreaded even by the untransformed shamans." A soft man would never have to worry about being treated badly because his supernatural protector would retaliate for any slight. Though having a soft man as a spouse marked high status for a man, the role of the husband could be difficult. The soft man's personal spirit was "said to play the part of a supernatural husband. . . . This husband is supposed to be the real head of the family, and to communicate his orders by means of his transformed wife. The human husband, of course, has to execute these orders faithfully under fear of prompt punishment. Thus in a household like that, the voice of the wife is decidedly preponderant." In the case of Tilu Wgi's husband, who was, Bogoras noted, "altogether a normal well-balanced person," he followed his spouse's wishes in most serious matters. Once, when he attempted to chastize Tilu Wgi, the transformed one "gave him so powerful a kick that it sent him foremost from their common sleeping room. This proves that the femininity of Tilu Wgi was more apparent than real."[5]

Not only the Chukchi, but other peoples of eastern Siberia recognized soft men. Koryak, Kamchadal, and Asiatic Eskimo men commonly had a soft man as a concubine in addition to their female wives. "The women were not displeased, but associated with their male rivals in quite friendly fashion." However, by 1900 the practice had declined greatly due to the meddling interference and complaints of Russian government officials.[6]

This practice was also evident throughout much of northeast Asia. The main authority on the ancient folk religion of Korea suggests that it was closely connected to that of Siberia. Androgynous males who served as shamans were known for their curing abilities, and also their ability to predict the future. They would often be concubines to men.[7]

Related peoples of the Bering Sea area of Alaska also had male concubines. Numerous Russian explorers noted, usually in condemnatory terms, the practice as being most common among the Aleuts and the Kodiak Island Eskimos. For example, the explorer Davydov reported in amazement in 1812 that androgynous Kodiak males, called *schopans* or *achnuceks,* did female work and had one or sometimes even two husbands: "These individuals are not only not looked down upon, but instead they are obeyed in a settlement and are not seldom wizards."[8] As noted earlier, Kodiak parents raised a boy androgynously, and then married him to a wealthy man before his fifteenth birthday. Having such a person in a family provided social prestige for both the parents and the husband. The boy-wife was treated with great respect.[9]

POLYNESIA

Polynesian societies also institutionalized male gender variance in the *mahu* role. *Mahus* are defined on the basis of doing women's work, but they also act as the passive partner in sexual acts with men. Masculine men might have sex with each other, and a *mahu* might abdicate the status and marry a woman, but if he remains in the *mahu* role he will not have sex with women. *Mahus* were often attached to chief's households, and were considered prestigious persons. An English captain in Tahiti in 1789 reported one of his sailors being "very much smitten with a dancing girl . . . but what was his surprise when the performance was ended, and after he had been endeavoring to persuade her to go with him on board our ship, which she assented to, to find this supposed dancer, when stripped of her theatrical paraphernalia, [was] a smart dapper lad." James Wilson, a missionary in Tahiti during the 1790s, described *mahus* as dressing in women's clothing, and seeking "the courtship of men the same as women do, nay, are more jealous of the men who cohabit with them, and always refuse to sleep with women. We are obliged here to draw a veil over practices too horrible to mention. . . . Women do not despise those fellows, but form friendships with them."[10]

Another Englishman at the same time, a sailor named Morrison from the *HMS Bounty,* remarked that *mahus* "are in some respects like the Eunuchs of India but are not castrated. They never cohabit with women but live as they do. They pick their beards out and dress as women, dance and sing with them and are as effeminate in their voice. They are generally excellent hands at making and painting of cloth, making mats and every other woman's employment. They are esteemed valuable friends in that way." The infamous Captain William Bligh of the *Bounty* also reported meeting "a man [who] had great marks of effeminacy about him . . . and of a class of people common in Otaheite called Mahoo, that the men had frequent connections with him and that he lived, observed the same ceremonies, and ate as the women did. . . . The women treat him as one of their sex, and he observed every restriction that they do, and is equally respected and esteemed."[11]

Holding the *mahu* role is a prized position, since only one person is allowed to claim the status in each village. Families gently encourage certain boys to prepare for the roles, so that if a *mahu* dies or resigns the most suitable one would be ready to take over the position. Likewise, in the Marquesas Islands, *mahus* are merely categorized as males who prefer a woman's life and desire men. Men who have sexual relations with a *mahu* consider it no different from having sex with a female, and see no impact on their own identity other than to reinforce their male identity.[12]

Ethnographer Robert Levy interviewed some men in Tahiti in the early 1960s, who detailed their sexual involvement with a *mahu* without embarrassment. An informant told him that *mahus* "really believe that [semen] is first class food for them. Because of that mahu are strong and powerful. The seminal fluid goes throughout his body. It's like the doctors say about vitamins. I have seen many mahu and I've seen that they are very strong." On the sexual experience this man said, "It's just like doing it with a woman, but his way of doing it is better than with a woman, as you just take it easy while he does it to you."

Another informant stated, "When you go to the mahu it's more satisfactory. The sexual pleasure is very great." Asked if he had any embarrassment about doing this, he replied, "No, you're not ashamed. You don't put any value on it. It's like feed-

ing the mahu with the penis. . . . You don't take it seriously."[13]
A man from the United States who lived for three months in
Tahiti in 1984 reported to me that *mahus* are still quite prevalent
in Tahiti. Tourists look down on them, but the native Tahitians
are indifferent. The Tahitian attitude is that "They're just other
people. They're really men, but they are good workers and do
good service for others, so who cares."[14] Tahitians consider *mahus* to be that way "naturally," and there is no discussion of the
origins of *mahu* tendencies because things that are natural are
not subject to moral evaluation. Sometimes it is said that a *mahu*
is born that way, and that a tendency to be *mahu* runs in certain
families. Tahitians say simply that God creates the *mahu* and that
is the way it is.[15]

Nevertheless, other Tahitians say that adults encourage children to take the *mahu* role. Levy observed this kind of socialization by a woman, who referred constantly to her friend's
three-year-old son as *mahu* when she was talking to him.
Though the boy did not seem effeminate, the boy's mother accepted this encouragement with amusement. Levy reports that
he had the feeling that the woman was trying to coach the boy
into being a *mahu*.[16] Similar customs exist in Hawaii, in Samoa,
where the role is called *fafafini* ("like a lady"), and also among
the Maori of New Zealand.[17] The widespread acceptance of this
kind of gender variance by cultures spread throughout the Pacific may also indicate its ancientness.

As a means of exploring the cross-cultural similarities of gender variance, in 1984 I made a brief fieldtrip to Hawaii to interview traditional Hawaiian *mahus*. The ones I met impressed me
as being very similar to berdaches. They are androgynous in
character, do women's work as well as men's, may dress in unisex clothing or a mixture of women's and men's clothing, are
sexually active with men, and have certain special roles in traditional Hawaiian religion.

The *mahu* is the one who usually cares for parents in their old
age, and retains the greatest closeness to both parents as the
other children move away to form their own families. *Mahu* is
integral to the way the family works as an institution. The social
utility of having a child as a *mahu* is clear. *Mahu* informants

explain that they are not considered either women or men, but are "kind of a third entity." One traditionalist says, "His relations with the parents would be stronger than the other members of the family. Because of this, the *mahu* would be more highly respected."[18]

Though the status of the *mahu* has declined considerably among westernized Hawaiians today, in the traditional religion a *mahu* could gain additional status as a *tahiku* dancer. This ancient form of the hula, a religious ceremony done with chanting, was dominated by *mahus*. According to an informant, "The chanter usually is *mahu* because he has no outside distractions in marriage. They remained separated from all women so that they could concentrate on what was necessary for the hula. . . . Traditional hula dancers, and especially *mahu* dancers even today are cherished by the traditional people. They are practically worshiped. All would like to dance as the *mahus* dance."

To be sure, homosexual behavior is not always associated with gender variance; there are masculine men who will have sex with a *mahu* or with each other. But it is expected that the *mahu* will be sexual with men. As with the berdache, however, *mahu* status involves more than sex. When I asked the difference between a *mahu* and a gay identity, a traditionalist *mahu* told me, "*Mahus* hold on to the traditional Hawaiian spirituality and value our feminine ways. . . . *Mahu* is part of the culture, it's natural. I guess for the *haoles* [whites] who find out they're gay—it's harder for them. You don't get that kind of isolation with Hawaiians, because we've always existed here. . . . On the mainland the [Judeo-Christian] religion doesn't allow a culture of acceptance. Gays have liberated themselves only sexually, but they have not yet learned their place in a spiritual sense."[19] As with the berdaches I talked with, the *mahu* saw the difference from a gay identity not in terms of the different character of the individual, but of the spiritual role taken by the *mahu*.

INDIA

In large-scale societies, cultural diversity makes for a more complicated picture, but we still see institutionalized forms of gender variance. In India, for example, with its wide range of religious sects and ideas of acceptable behavior, the role of sexual expression ranges from celibacy to anal- and phallic-worshiping promiscuity. The celebration of oral and anal heterosexual practices has created a climate for acceptance of similar practices between individuals of the same sex. Even before the impact of sex-negative European Christianity, however, social attitudes were ambiguous because of differing opinions about non-masculine males. South Asian mythology is full of examples of gods who were hermaphroditic, and there was a widespread belief in a third sex. Certain persons were considered as neither male nor female, or were seen as having changed from one sex to another. Androgynous males, usually incorrectly labeled by English writers as eunuchs, were often associated with same-sex desire. Ancient Indian sex manuals discussed at length the different ways that these individuals used their mouths to produce orgasm for their male partners.[20]

In modern India, the most notable example of gender variance is a cult of males who dress and live as an alternative gender and are known as *hijras*. They perform as mediums for female goddesses, which gives them a special role at weddings and after births. In addition, many of them take the passive role as prostitutes for men. Anthropologists disagree about the extent to which they are involved in sexual behavior with men, partly because Indians are so close-mouthed about even accepted forms of sexuality. But *hijras* are "an example par excellence of the cultural construction of gender, being both 'neither man nor woman' and 'man and woman.'"[21] One anthropologist reported on his 1978 fieldwork in North Gujarat:

Almost none of the hijras I saw were effeminate in physical appearance, although many adopted caricatured feminine traits. One . . . showed a very strong chest and arms. He appeared to have recently shaved and had a strikingly handsome—and very masculine—face. He also wore a sari, the traditional dress of Indian women, and had a long, carefully combed braid that hung to the middle of his back. The androgyny—suggesting the characteristics of both sexes rather than suggesting neither—was extraordinary. . . . The hijra are neither male nor female. They have an intermediate or additional sexual identity, but they are not "unnatural" because of it. Male and female are poles on a continuum rather than two types with a fixed boundary between them.[22]

OTHER AREAS OF ASIA AND AFRICA

The fluidity of gender roles is well represented in an analysis of gender variance in several areas. It is not the purpose of this book to provide a survey of such institutionalized roles around the world, but mention of a few instances will provide references for future research. In Southeast Asia, the Vietnamese *dô'ng bo'ng* shaman fills an alternative gender role and dresses like a man sometimes and like a halfman–halfwoman at other times. This shamanistic role represents a holdover from pre-Buddhist folk religions.[23] On the Indonesian island of Celebes, similar shamans are part of the court of an important person, serving rather as a male version of a geisha.[24] Urbanized areas of Indonesia have institutionalized an entertainment role for nonmasculine males in the ancient *ludruk* theater. They are referred to as *alus,* which denotes a quality of aristocracy and idealism, and are known to be able to arouse men erotically. Though they are referred to by anthropologists as transvestites, such singers "often accentuate the fact that they combine male and female elements." And their songs have been compared to "a prayer, voiced by a priest . . . reminiscent of certain Javanese rites."[25] When I was in the Philippines in 1983, I observed similar entertainment roles by markedly androgynous males who were also known as homosexual.

Horrified European travelers, missionaries, and anthropologists in other areas have observed the connection in many traditional cultures between gender variance and same-sex relations. Several sources note the occurrence of "transvestite shamans" in various areas of Africa, for example among the Zulus and in Zanzibar.[26] Males in an alternative gender role are active as prostitutes for men in Oman, and in other areas.[27]

EUROPEAN CASTRATI

While there likely existed earlier forms of androgyny in European folk traditions, practically the only practice that is comparable to institutionalized gender variance in Christian Europe originated with church music. The high soprano voices of young boys were highly valued in early modern Europe, and the Church would pay lower-class parents for boys with good voices. The main problem with investing in the training of a boy singer was that at puberty he would lose this valued talent when his voice changed. To preserve the high voice of their best students, choir directors began the practice of cutting off the boys' testicles.

When opera emerged as a popular form of musical theater in seventeenth-century Italy, it seemed natural for castrati to become the singers of female roles. In European theater women did not appear on the stage, and female parts were played by young men. Castrati became the highest-paid opera singers, the prima donnas of the high culture of their time. Cross-dressing for the opera, and often in their daily life as well, the castrati were renowned for their free sexuality as well as for their feminine dress and demeanor. Though their masculinity was questionable, their high status was not.[28]

It is perhaps not farfetched to suggest that the high prestige of the castrati in European high culture led to the establishment of a new tradition of gender mixing in the West. Though the popularity of the castrati declined, it merged with a folk tradition of androgynous males known in England as Mollies, which led in the nineteenth century to entertainment by female impersonators known as drag queens.[29]

HOMOSEXUALITY AND MASCULINITY

Melanesia

On the one hand, cross-cultural data in widely separated cultures reveals that there is a strong relationship between a socially defined androgynous character among males and a proclivity for same-sex eroticism. On the other hand, the existence of homosexual behavior between masculine men, in an equally varied group of cultures, shows that homosexual behavior is not limited to nonmasculine males. This is especially notable in cultures that take the opposite approach of those in which gender variance is institutionalized. Instead of associating male-male sex with androgyny, as hetero-gender, these other cultures associate it with hypermasculinity. It is often assumed that male-male sexual relations are necessary for the absorption of masculinity. It is intra-gender.

This notion is most emphasized in various parts of Melanesia. In many areas of southern lowlands New Guinea and nearby islands, there is a strong cultural belief that there are two body fluids that bring about human life and growth: breast milk and semen. Infants need woman's milk to grow, but in the Melanesian view boys cannot grow to become men without ingesting semen from adult males. Melanesian societies that have this belief institutionalize male homosexual behavior as obligatory for all boys, as part of their socialization into manhood. Though there is variation of specific beliefs and practices, the typical pattern is that boys between the ages of about seven and thirteen are taken from the maternal household and placed in a boys' house set away from the village. For a period of several months to several years, depending on the culture, boys avoid all contact with females as they are prepared in elaborate initiations for manhood.[30]

Sperm, the essence of manhood, is not seen as something that forms spontaneously. These Melanesians believe that it is a scarce resource that must be planted in the boy by a mature male. In some societies this is done by the boy performing oral sex on the man, in others by receiving anal intercourse, and in others by having the sperm rubbed on his body. The homosexual behavior is thus a duty of men (women are also seen as strengthened by absorbing sperm), and it is ritualized as part of male initiation ceremonies. While casual homosexual acts may take place, they must always be with the boy receiving the older male's semen. To reverse roles would be considered damaging to the boy's growth.

The most important homosexual relationship for a boy is with his mentor, who is assigned by his father and is ideally his mother's brother. This mentor is responsible for educating the boy and seeing that he is raised into proper manhood. They sleep together and work together until the boy is mature. In the Melanesian view, years of ingesting semen has an effect, as evidenced by the fact that the boy grew to adulthood. Thus, in a cultural pattern almost directly opposite to Western stereotypes about "corrupting innocent children," masculinity and proper growth is absorbed through homosexual acts and male nurturance. Instead of fearing sex and keeping boys ignorant of it, Melanesians see sex as a key to the growth of spirit in heart and mind as well as physical growth.

This overlay of ritual and male duty makes Melanesian notions of homoeroticism seem quite different from the berdache tradition. Yet, both are ways for a society to construct sexual behavior between males, allowing close erotic bonding between individuals. Melanesian males are closely united in an egalitarian warriorhood. Just as heterosexual intercourse cements marriage, in Melanesia homosexual acts cement warriorhood. Both heterosexual marriage and homosexual relationships are integral to social harmony, in that they widen the network of individuals to whom one is tied by close emotional bonds.

Because a boy is expected to engage in these sexual acts with older males does not mean that he will become a lifelong exclusive homosexual. Just as every boy is expected to be repeatedly sexually penetrated by older males, followed by a stage when he in turn supplies semen to younger boys, so at a later time he is expected to get married to a woman. In some groups he is even expected to give up sex with boys altogether after his first or second child is born. He does not have a "gay" lifelong pairing with a man of similar age. We cannot even properly call him a lifelong bisexual, because he is homosexual at one stage of his life, followed by a period when he is bisexual, and then (in some societies) ends up as heterosexual in his later years.

All of this shows the extreme plasticity of human behavior, with cultural norms shaping people in widely divergent ways. It destroys the Western notion that homosexual behavior is somehow "unnatural," "deviant," or "abnormal." Homosexual behavior in many of these Melanesian societies, at least before Christian missionaries and colonial governments suppressed it, was the norm; it was normal in that context.

All males in these societies in New Guinea are expected to participate in homosexual acts, but we cannot tell much about gender variance because the intensive masculine initiation rites admit no gender nonconformity. Moreover, the universality of bisexual behavior renders the concept of sexual variance inapplicable for those societies. Rather than divide society into heterosexuals and homosexuals, these people keep unity among men by making every male follow the same mixture of eroticism toward both men and women.[31]

Azande Boy-Wives

Though other societies did not institutionalize man-boy sex to the same degree as in New Guinea, there was (and still is, in some cases) a strong man-boy sexual tradition in many cultures. Among some Australian aboriginals it was not unusual for an unmarried man to take a prepubescent boy as a "wife," with the boy fulfilling this social and sexual role until after reaching puberty. Likewise, among the Azande of East Africa a young adult warrior was expected to take a boy as a "temporary wife" before later marrying a woman. He even went through the formality of paying a bride-price to the boy's family, while the boy did domestic duties for the warrior. After reaching age twenty the boy-wife would himself take a younger boy as a sexual and affectional partner, and he would fulfill the warrior role himself. Such a practice was the major means by which boys were socialized to their later warrior role. It likely also insured a smoother heterosexual marriage later on, after the male had played both sides in the husband-wife routine.[32]

Even for the married Azande men, boys were sometimes brought into the family as pages, to be available sexually, especially during those times (such as preparing to consult oracles) when heterosexual activity was forbidden. Though the culture set the rule of boys as only auxiliary partners for married men, a variation of individual preferences has been noted by an anthropologist who recognized that some men paid more attention to their boy partner than to their female wife.[33]

Medieval Japan

Japan, especially during the Tokugawa period, before 1865, also celebrated relationships between men and boys. Japanese mythology suggests that the great cultural hero Kobo Daishi, founder of the Shingon sect of Buddhism, first popularized homosexuality around the year 800. As with the all-male warriorhoods, groups of male Buddhist monks were known for housing boys in the Zen temples, and the passion aroused by these boys is the subject of many love poems written during the medieval times. Religious laws forbade monks to have sexual relations with women, but did not proscribe other kinds of sexuality. As a consequence, the Portuguese Jesuit missionary Alassandro Valiquano reported from Japan in the late 1500s that homosexual behavior was "regarded so lightly that both the boys and the men who consort with them brag and talk about it openly without trying to cover the matter up." The monks, he wrote, not only considered their loves to be unsinful, but "even something quite natural and virtuous." Though the missionaries severely condemned homosexuality during the fifteenth and sixteenth centuries, their tirades seemed to have little effect on the Japanese.[34]

In the military samurai class there also developed a tradition of passionate and heroic devotion between male lovers. The usual model was for the adult samurai warrior to court a boy, and if the boy accepted, they would establish a patron-vassal tie. The boy's parents would prepare their son for sexual relations by having him relax with a special smooth wooden implement gently inserted in his rectum. The boy would serve his samurai lover as an aide in battle, and as personal secretary in times of peace. The man, in turn, educated the boy to assume the high samurai role upon maturity.

Similarly, in traditional China same-sex relations commonly occurred on an age-gradient basis between master and servant or between teacher and student. In Chinese history the most notable incidents concerned the loving relationships some of the emperors had with their male court favorites. Idealized love is presented in the famed incident in which an emperor cut the sleeve of his robe rather than disturb the sleep of his boy lover who lay next to him.[35] There was no universal stage every male would have to go through, as in New Guinea, but males with a preference for male love were encouraged to take a boy as a consort.

Middle East

In general, many precolonial Arabic cultures also accepted male homosexual behavior, mostly in the form of relations between men and boys. Poetry and song celebrated the special erotic attractions of boys. Anthropologists have probed the nature of these formalized man-boy marriages, which existed among the Berbers of the North African Siwah oasis area, for example, and also more casual homosexual behavior in other Muslim areas.[36]

One of the most notable forms of the institutionalization of masculinity through male bonding was the Mamluk system of government. Sultans would buy young boys as slaves, mostly from nomadic tribes of eastern Turkey and the Caucasus, and then raise them to be their loyal palace guards. In Egypt, and also in various areas of Mesopotamia, these palace guards actually ran the government. In some cases they overthrew the sultan and became the established power in name as well as in fact. Having been raised in an all-male group, Mamluks did not marry women. When a Mamluk reached adulthood his master freed him, and he in turn would buy his own boy slave. This boy became the servant, confidant, lover, and eventually heir to the master who would free him upon his maturity. Mamluks kept their power and influence over the generations by passing down this heirship from man to boy. They are one of the world's most notable examples of an all-male society, which continued without heterosexual families, and they governed large areas of the Middle East for centuries.[37]

Partly due to knowledge of the Mamluks, European travelers long associated man-boy sex with the Middle East and the Turkish empire. They even noted the spread of "boy brides" to Christian Albania under Muslim rule. It was from the Middle East, after all, that the word *bardaj* originated. There, however, it meant a boy who was a man's lover rather than the alternative gender role the word *berdache* later came to signify among American Indians. In 1850 the French writer Flaubert wrote to a friend from the Turkish empire: "Since we are speaking of bardaches, this is what I know of the matter. Here it is well regarded. One owns up to sodomy and talks about it at luncheon."[38]

Greece

The acceptance of masculinizing intergenerational male-male eroticism in Middle Eastern culture was partly a heritage of the ancient Greeks. Greece is the most famous example of the association between masculinity and homoeroticism. Unfortunately, when Greek homosexuality is discussed, it is usually presented as being a unique and strange aberration. Considering the foregoing examples from other societies around the world, however, what one realizes about the Greeks is how common their sexual patterns were. As in the other cultures mentioned above, it would not have been proper to continue a lover relationship after a youth matured. A pair might remain friends for life, but each turned to new adolescents as erotic partners. In this type of relationship, as is obvious in the many examples of Greek homoerotic painting that celebrate the beauty of the male body, it is the youth who chose to accept or reject the courting of the man. Since this erotic relationship frequently provided the basis for the boy's education, vocational training, and socialization into adulthood it made for a system in which youth had much more say in their own situation than pre-adults usually have.[39]

This strong association between homoeroticism and education, between sexuality and male training for adulthood, is a common factor in cultures that emphasize man-boy relationships. Whether in association with New Guinea initiation rites, Azande and Japanese warrior training, or Greek education, this male nurturance was distinct from female child rearing. Perhaps these cultures might recognize that some individuals would be more or less homosexually inclined, but they would have regarded the monosexual exclusive homosexuals and exclusive heterosexuals as odd. Same-sex relations were not only accepted, but celebrated. On the other hand, a man who did not eventually marry a woman would be seen as neglecting his social duty. The male role, in both same-sex and other-sex relations, was cast in terms of the ideal of manhood. Homosexual behavior did not threaten men's masculinity; it ensured it.

This brief survey shows that cultures can shape human variation in extremely diverse ways. In examining American Indian berdachism, and comparing it to other gender-variant institutions around the world, we can see many similarities. Yet we also see sharp contrasts to the masculinizing male bonding cultures. Why do some societies institutionalize an alternative gender as the socially acceptable form of homosexual expression, while others institutionalize such a different man-boy hypermasculine pattern?

Perhaps there is still not enough factual data to suggest anything more than a hypothesis, but a crucial factor seems to be a culture's attitude toward women. While American Indian and Melanesian societies, for example, are both gender-differentiated and sex-segregated, American Indian men generally respect women while Melanesian men generally distrust women. If men fear women, and see femininity as pollution, then they will likewise fear feminine character traits in males. They will work to suppress androgyny, and to insure male unity in opposition to women, by forcing all males to be masculine. Homoeroticism is just one among many means for strengthening these masculine bonds between the generations. In contrast, if men value women then it is not considered bad if a male displays some character traits more like those of a woman. Androgyny is not suppressed, as it is in the hypermasculine societies, but valued.

Yet despite their differences, alternative gender and hypermasculine societies end up with the same result: the unity of men as a group. Unlike Western culture, which categorizes individuals into opposite dichotomies as heterosexuals and homosexuals, and in which males of each group often feel antagonistic toward the other, these other cultures avoid such divisions.

Melanesians avoid separate homosexual and heterosexual identities by pushing every male toward sexual involvement with both males and females. While still perhaps allowing for individual preference within those ideal boundaries, they discourage monosexual extremes. In contrast, societies with an alternative gender emphasize the difference of the berdache or his equivalent to such an extent that he is no longer considered a man. They focus on the high-status social role of the nonmasculine male, rather than on sexual behavior, but they encourage him to be sexual with men. A masculine person, whether he has sex with a berdache or not, is still considered a man. There is no separation of males into opposite groups of homosexuals and heterosexuals; men's unity is preserved because same-sex behavior is not a matter of great concern. Because the androgynous male has a unique status outside masculinity, everyone's position in the society is secured, without stigma and without deviance.

WESTERN HISTORY AND GENDER VARIANCE

Being aware of the cross-cultural context may help us better understand the changes in gender variance and sexual variance in Western culture. In European and Euro-American history, we can see three types of sexual variance, with two sharp changes due to major repressive campaigns against sexuality in the thirteenth and the twentieth centuries. European culture had inherited its first pattern from the ancient Greek type of man-boy bonding. Despite the influence of Christianity, such ancient traditions of intergenerational male love survived into the medieval era. But after about 1250, such traditions were ruthlessly suppressed. "Sodomy," by which accusers of the time often meant boy-love (since that was the most common form at the time), was associated with the Islamic enemy and with heresy.[40]

This suppression practically wiped out a cultural tradition, leaving Europe without culturally acceptable forms of male-male sexual behavior. While same-sex behavior no doubt continued to occur in private, or outside the bounds of established society (as among the pirates), it was not to emerge in an institutionalized form until popularized by gender-bending entertainment figures like the castrati and the drag queen. The castrati emerged in new forms of popular culture, during a creative period that was developing new styles of music and theater. Vastly different from the man-boy pattern that had become so tainted with heresy and so associated with the alien Muslims, the castrati had emerged from two of the central institutions of Europe: the church and the theater. What form of same-sex be-

havior could be less threatening? Though more research is necessary before definite conclusions can be reached, it is likely that
these roles helped to make an association of sexual variance and
gender variance in the mind of modern Europe and the Americas.[41]

With such an association, eventually another era of suppression occurred in the twentieth century that was in many ways
quite like the Inquisition. In Europe, both the German Nazis
and the Russian Stalinists campaigned to eliminate everything
considered weak and effeminate among males. They destroyed
a flourishing homosexual rights movement and placed unnum-
bered thousands of homosexuals in concentration camps.[42] In
the United States, "sexual perversion" replaced anti-Semitism
and ethnic prejudice as a favored political scapegoat, especially
in the McCarthy witchhunts and the Eisenhower purges of the
1950s. Thousands lost their jobs, were jailed, or experienced
severe harassment from police and the Federal Bureau of Investigation.

The two derogatory images of homosexuality with which
American males have been bombarded in this century are "the
child molester" and "the sissy." It is not surprising that males
who are attracted to other males would react against these images. Prompted by this reaction, a third pattern of same-sex
relations emerged. Perhaps drawing some inspiration from the
male marriages on the frontier and the "buddy system" pairings
in the armed forces, this pattern became much more popular
during World War II. This new masculine erotic bonding was
different from the man-boy pattern and the gender-mixing pattern which had earlier existed. The new image that emerged out
of World War II was the army buddy pair, masculine to the core,
and above age eighteen.

These adult homosexual relationships formed the basis for a
"gay" subculture, that largely rejected its cultural roots. Drag
queens, pedophiles, and youths below eighteen were shunted
aside both politically and socially as a masculine gay community
emerged in a number of American cities. With a focus on bars
where masculine adult men mixed among themselves, the older
forms of gender variance became distinctly second rate. In reaction against the stereotypes, the witchhunts, and the purges,

and also as a means of trying to make themselves respectable to society at large, homophile organizations in the 1950s and 1960s became politically active and began to call for an end to discrimination on the basis of sexual orientation.

For a brief time in the late 1960s and the early 1970s, it seemed that a gender-mixing aspect might reemerge in the new militancy of Gay Liberation. In 1969, the drag queens began a massive riot against police harassment, at the Stonewall bar in New York's Greenwich Village. The radicalized era, in which social standards (and especially gender standards) were being questioned by numerous groups of young women and men, presented an opportunity in which nonconformists could challenge several conventions. But such radicalism was not to last. By the late 1970s the mood was more conservative. Even as the gay community grew stronger, it shifted its focus from Gay Liberation (revolutionizing society) to Gay Rights (getting the same rights as the majority). A new mood of masculinity took hold among gay men, represented by the "clone" look: work clothes and boots, short hair, and mustaches. There was little room for nonconformists.[43]

THEORETICAL PERSPECTIVES

The outline of modern gay history is beginning to be understood, and we have come to realize that a gay subculture is of fairly recent origin in Western history. Historians may be able to trace a recognizable gay community, at least in London, to the seventeenth century, but in North America such a sense of community did not emerge until the nineteenth century.[44] This community is a product of urbanization and a reaction against stigmatization. Gay identity is just one form of social construction, one direction in which same-sex relations may be shaped. With such wide variation of both homosexual and heterosexual desire among many people, the Western view, that every person is either a homosexual or a heterosexual, does not hold up under cross-cultural analysis. Neither category makes much sense in societies like Melanesia, where we cannot properly speak in terms of gay and straight. Such societies demonstrate that there is quite a bit of difference between male-male sexual behavior and a homosexual identity. The many variations in sexuality worldwide are exploding our notion that humans are neatly categorized as homosexuals or heterosexuals. Institutions like the berdache are leading us also to question the categories of men and women.

Taking inspiration from the writings of Michel Foucault, a group of historians and sociologists has emphasized that it is inadequate to see sexuality as a biological constant. They rightly point out that sexual identity is not set by nature as an essential part of each individual, but that sexual desires, like other aspects of human behavior, are largely influenced by the culture in which a person happens to be born.[45] Yet, having said all that, it is not improper to suggest that the current interpretation, known as social constructionism, has gone too far.

Social constructionists postulate that culture is in total control, that individuals are basically blank slates upon which culture writes. While this degenerates to the old debate of nurture versus nature, which biologists have largely abandoned, it ignores the many biological, hormonal, environmental, cultural, sociological, and psychological influences that combine in very complex ways to shape human behavior. By looking only at the discussion of the social establishment, social constructionists examine history from the top down rather than from the bottom up. If we are going to see a larger reality, we must also recognize that individual character has a role in shaping culture, in a person's accepting or rejecting certain options that the culture offers. If behavior is socially constructed, of what is it constructed? What is the substructure on which a culture inscribes its variations?

Human behavior observed around the world does not exhibit limitless variety; there are patterns and similarities that repeat themselves beyond anything that can be explained by diffusion from one society to another. Social scientists have been struggling to understand these similarities for decades, and there are no simple answers.

Because of the complexity of cross-cultural comparisons, the certitude of social constructionists in proclaiming that no other people before "the modern homosexual" had a similar identity seems foolhardy.[46] Such a view ignores folk traditions about certain types of persons, called "fairies," "queers," and a myriad other terms, in Europe and elsewhere. And in emphasizing the discontinuities of a modern homosexual identity, social constructionists discount the implications from cross-cultural research. Their view is quite ethnocentric, and in its focus on the modern West blithely dismisses anything we might learn about sexual variance and gender variance in other cultures. Sociologist Kenneth Plummer stated the constructionist view in its most extreme form: "Why should one even begin to contemplate the notion that the berdache has anything at all to do with homosexuality in our terms?" And Jeffrey Weeks suggests that there is no "separate homosexual role" among American Indians because in those societies "There's no place for the homosexual; it's actually a place for someone who just happens to be a biological man who lives the life of a woman and becomes a woman. . . . There are only men and women, quite straightforward."[47]

As I established earlier, seeing the berdache as a woman is inaccurate. Indian societies constructed an alternative gender, and put their emphasis on the berdache's character and social role rather than only on sexual behavior. This is certainly a social construction, and by that construction the men who had sex with the berdache do not have a distinct identity from men who didn't. Yet, the berdache does have an identity, which seems much more a reflection of the individual's innate character. And judging from the evolution of that identity from berdache to gay, and contemporary Indian people's comparison of the two roles, such folk definitions show a berdache identity to be much more similar to a queen identity among nonmasculine gay men than it is to an identity as a woman.

Social constructionists argue that a gay identity is unique in history, that there was no such separate category of person before modern Europe. They suggest that a person who engaged in the "sin of sodomy" had no identity as being different. Yet, evidence suggests that a distinct identity did exist, and had words that described it. Did a man who had a strong preference for sex with another male not have an identity as a "sodomite"? While the reference to Sodom, with its sense of doom, would hardly seem able to inspire anyone to a positive identity, the meaning of that word to the participants in same-sex acts is still unclear. Perhaps "sodomite" is not as different from "homosexual" as we have been led to believe. Both terms were imposed from external, professional elites, as stigmatizing terms.

By focusing on a derogatory word imposed by an antagonistic establishment, we may be getting a distorted image of the actual life identity of a person from the past. When we look instead at terms used within the stigmatized group itself, we find much more emphasis on character: a person in the subculture today is more likely to call themselves gay or even queen than homosexual, and for the good reason that one's identity is a product of more than sex alone. There are words in other cultures which denote a different identity, with the Indian words for berdache being examples.

When seventeenth-century Europeans used the word *berdache,* or applied it to American Indians, they had a clear meaning in mind. Such a meaning denoted both androgyny and sexual involvement with other males. Since gender mixing was a major component of same-sex behavior at the time, we can hardly find fault with observers for associating the two. The berdache certainly thought of themselves as different, and their society agreed. This difference was at least partly associated with sexual involvement with men. If we are going to consider only the Western "modern homosexual" as a completely unique identity and therefore the only proper object of focus, as social constructionists have done, then such a definition will blind us to a diversity of same-sex behaviors and identities.

How we see other cultures in the past has much to do with our attitudes toward the future. If we study only the "modern homosexual," what about those growing numbers of people who dislike fitting their sexuality into either/or boxes of gay or straight? Homosexual identity will surely change in the future. The modern Western gay role has not been, or will be, the only role which sees individuals as distinctly different on the basis of same-sex attraction and androgynous character.

Today, in a world where peoples are interacting more intensively, knowledge of this diversity—and recognition that the "modern homosexual" and the "modern heterosexual" are not the pinnacle of evolution—is necessary both politically and socially. The next frontier of research on both sexual and gender variance is to understand the many varieties of identities and roles. How they are different and alike is the question that will enrich our understanding much more than the simple answers that they are all the same or all different. They are both. The interaction of continuity and change is at the base of the human story, and any theory that ignores one of those elements is faulty. The interaction of these aspects, and of the social with the personal, is what is important. Their opposition is a false dichotomy.

We can look to institutions like the berdache for new ways of thinking about sexual variance, love between persons of the same sex, and flexibility in gender roles. We can see from the berdache that friendship is just as important a value as family, and that such emotions and tendencies erotically expressed are not unnatural. We can question whether a separated gay subculture, a minority lifestyle built around sexual preferences, is more preferable to integration of gender variance and same-sex eroticism into the general family structure and the mainstream society. We can use the American Indian concept of spirituality to break out of the deviancy model, to reunite families, and to offer special benefits to society as a whole. At the least, our awareness of alternative attitudes and roles can allow us to appreciate the diversity of the human population, and the similarities that we share across the boundaries of culture.

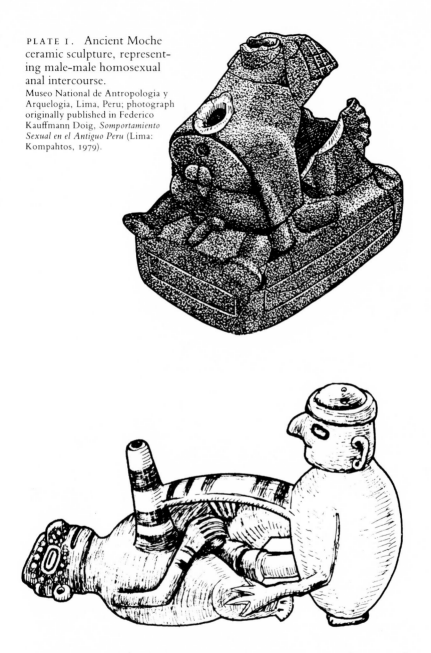

PLATE 1. Ancient Moche ceramic sculpture, representing male-male homosexual anal intercourse.
Museo National de Antropologia y Arquelogia, Lima, Peru; photograph originally published in Federico Kauffmann Doig, *Somportamiento Sexual en el Antiguo Peru* (Lima: Kompahtos, 1979).

PLATE 2. Ancient Vicus ceramic sculpture, showing one male having anal intercourse while the other holds his penis in his hand.
Private collection; photograph originally published in Federico Kauffmann Doig, *Somportamiento Sexual en el Antiguo Peru* (Lime: Kompahtos, 1979).

PLATE 5. Spanish explorer Balboa orders Indians accused of sodomy to be eaten alive by dogs.
Theodor de Bry engraving (1594), based on an account by Girolamo Benzoni in the 1540s; New York Public Library, Rare Book Room, De Bry Collection.

PLATE 6. "Dance to the Berdache," a sketch drawn by George Catlin in the 1830s while among the Sac and Fox Indians.
Printed in George Catlin, *North American Indians*; original sketch in National Museum of American Art, Smithsonian Institution, Washington, D.C.

PLATE 7. Barebreasted Plains Indian woman hunting a buffalo.
Painted by Alfred Jacob Miller, 1837; Walters Art Gallery, Baltimore, Maryland.

PLATE 8. Shoshone woman roping a horse.
Painted by Alfred Jacob Miller, 1837; Walters Art Gallery, Baltimore, Maryland.

PLATE 9. We-wha, Zuni berdache, ca. 1885.
National Anthropological Archives, Smithsonian Institution, Washington, D.C.

PLATE 10. A group of Zuni Indians, females on the left, males on the right, and the berdache We-wha in the middle, signifying the position of the berdache between women and men.
Southwest Museum, Los Angeles, California.

PLATE 11. Zuni berdache
We-wha, who was known as a
skillful weaver, ca. 1885.
National Anthropological Archives,
Smithsonian Institution, Washington,
D.C.

PLATE 12 (*right*). A Crow
berdache, probably *Osh-Tisch*
(Finds-Them-and-Kills-Them), ca.
1900.
Museum of the American Indian, Heye
Foundation, New York City.

PLATE 13 (*left*). Tolowa berdache
shaman, also headman of his
village in northern California,
wearing insignia of his wealth, ca.
1910.
National Anthropological Archives,
Smithsonian Institution, Washington, D.C.

PLATE 14. An Alaska Yupik berdache, singing and drumming traditional songs, at a social event sponsored by Gay American Indians, San Francisco, May 16, 1985.
Courtesy Gay American Indians.

PLATE 15. A member of Gay American Indians looks to the future.
Courtesy Gay American Indians.

PLATE 16. Randy Burns, co-founder of Gay American Indians.
Photograph by Stephen Stewart.

Notes

INTRODUCTION

1. Mary Douglas, *Purity and Danger* (Baltimore: Penguin, 1966), p. 52. I am grateful to Theda Perdue for convincing me that Douglas's ideas apply to berdachism. For an application of Douglas's thesis to berdaches, see James Thayer, "The Berdache of the Northern Plains: A Socioreligious Perspective," *Journal of Anthropological Research* 36 (1980): 292–93.

2. Charles Callender and Lee Kochems, "The North American Berdache," *Current Anthropology* 24 (1983): 444–46.

3. Manuscript by C. C. Trowbridge in the archives of George Mason University, Washington, D.C. I am grateful to Raymond Fogelson for this reference, in a personal communication, 17 October 1980.

4. Harald Broch, "A Note on Berdache Among the Hare Indians of Northwestern Canada," *Western Canadian Journal of Anthropology* 7 (1977): 95–101.

5. A. L. Kroeber, "Psychosis or Social Sanction," *Character and Personality* 8 (1940): 204–15.

6. Henry Angelino and Charles Shedd, "A Note on Berdache," *American Anthropologist* 57 (1955): 121–25.

7. Sue-Ellen Jacobs, "Berdache: A Brief Review of the Literature," *Colorado Anthropologist* 1 (1968): 25–40.

8. Jonathan Katz, *Gay American History* (New York: Thomas Crowell, 1976).

9. The best recent writings published on berdachism include: Evelyn Blackwood, "Sexuality and Gender in Certain Native American Tribes: The Case of Cross-Gender Females," *Signs* 10 (1984): 27–42; Callender and Kochems, "North American Berdache"; Jay Miller, "People, Berdaches, and Left-Handed Bears: Human Variation in Native America," *Journal of Anthropological Research* 38 (Fall 1982): 274–87; Thayer, "Berdache of the Northern Plains," pp. 287–93; Harriet Whitehead, "The Bow and the Burden Strap: A New Look at Institutionalized Homosexuality in Native North America," in *Sexual Meanings,* ed. Sherry Ortner and Harriet Whitehead (Cambridge: Cambridge University Press, 1981), pp. 80–115; Donald Forgey, "The Insti-

tution of Berdache among the North American Plains Indians," *Journal of Sex Research* 11 (1975): 1–15.

10. There is a tradition in the Amazon Basin, very different from berdachism, which needs fieldwork. It is similar in some ways to the male rituals of initiation in Melanesia.

11. Edith McLeod, "White Cindy, Mystery Figure," *Siskiyou Pioneer and Siskiyou County Historical Society Yearbook* 2 (Spring 1953): 33.

12. Quoted and translated in Claude Courouve, "The Word 'Bardache,'" *Gay Books Bulletin* 8 (Fall–Winter 1982): 18–19. See also Angelino and Shedd, "Note on Berdache," p. 121.

13. Translated in Courouve, "Word," p. 18. Courouve's research is typical of the type of excellent analysis that is possible for scholars of various fields who wish to pursue cross-cultural studies in homosexuality.

14. Joseph François Lafitau, *Moeurs des sauvages americquains* (Paris: Saugrain, 1724), vol. 1, p. 52; translated by Warren Johansson in Katz, *Gay American History*, p. 289.

15. Kenneth E. Read, "The *Nama* Cult Recalled," in *Ritualized Homosexuality in Melanesia*, ed. Gilbert Herdt (Berkeley: University of California Press, 1984), pp. 215–17.

16. Ibid.

17. Thomas Fitzgerald, "A Critique of Anthropological Research on Homosexuality," *Journal of Homosexuality* 2 (1977): 285–397.

18. Luke Standing Elk, Cheyenne informant 5, August 1982. Despite his statement, he later told me some interesting information on *hemaneh* or *a-he-e ma' ne'*. It was always surprising to me how much Indian people would reveal to me, since I made it clear to everyone I interviewed that this was for publication.

CHAPTER ONE

1. Joseph François Lafitau, *Moeurs des sauvages americquains* (Paris: Saugrain, 1724), vol. 1, p. 52; translated by Warren Johansson in Jonathan Katz, *Gay American History* (New York: Thomas Crowell, 1976), pp. 288–89.

2. Jaques Marquette, "Of the First Voyage Made . . . ," in *The Jesuit Relations*, ed. Reuben Gold Thwaites (Cleveland: Burrows, 1896–1901), vol. 59, p. 129; reprinted in Katz, *Gay American History*, p. 287.

3. E. W. Gifford, "The Kamia of Imperial Valley," *Bureau of American Ethnology Bulletin* 97 (1931): 12.

4. By using present tense verbs in this text, I am not implying that such activities are necessarily continuing today. I sometimes use the present tense in the "ethnographic present," unless I use the past tense when I am referring to something that has not continued. Past tense implies that all such practices have disappeared. In the absence of fieldwork to prove such disappearance, I am not prepared to make that assumption, for reasons discussed in Part II on the historic changes in the berdache tradition.

5. Elsie Clews Parsons, "The Zuni La' Mana," *American Anthropologist* 18 (1916): 521; Matilda Coxe Stevenson, "Zuni Indians," *Bureau of American Eth-*

nology Annual Report 23 (1903): 37; Franklin Cushing, "Zuni Creation Myths," *Bureau of American Ethnology Annual Report* 13 (1894): 401–3. Will Roscoe clarified this origin story for me.

6. W. W. Hill, "Note on the Pima Berdache," *American Anthropologist* 40 (1938): 339.

7. Aileen O'Bryan, "The Dine': Origin Myths of the Navaho Indians," *Bureau of American Ethnology Bulletin* 163 (1956): 5; W. W. Hill, "The Status of the Hermaphrodite and Transvestite in Navaho Culture," *American Anthropologist* 37 (1935): 273.

8. Martha S. Link, *The Pollen Path: A Collection of Navajo Myths* (Stanford: Stanford University Press, 1956).

9. O'Bryan, "Dine'," pp. 5, 7, 9–10.

10. Ibid.

11. Lakota informants, July 1982. See also William Powers, *Oglala Religion* (Lincoln: University of Nebraska Press, 1977).

12. For this admittedly generalized overview of American Indian religious values, I am indebted to traditionalist informants of many tribes, but especially those of the Lakotas. For a discussion of native religions see Dennis Tedlock, *Finding the Center* (New York: Dial Press, 1972); Ruth Underhill, *Red Man's Religion* (Chicago: University of Chicago Press, 1965); and Elsie Clews Parsons, *Pueblo Indian Religion* (Chicago: University of Chicago Press, 1939).

13. Alfred Kroeber, "The Arapaho," *Bulletin of the American Museum of Natural History* 18 (1902–7): 19.

14. Parsons, "Zuni La' Mana," p. 525.

15. Alexander Maximilian, *Travels in the Interior of North America, 1832–1834*, vol. 22 of *Early Western Travels*, ed. Reuben Gold Thwaites, 32 vols. (Cleveland: A. H. Clark, 1906), pp. 283–84, 354. Maximilian was quoted in German in the early homosexual rights book by Ferdinand Karsch-Haack, *Das Gleichgeschlechtliche Leben der Naturvölker* (The same-sex life of nature peoples) (Munich: Verlag von Ernst Reinhardt, 1911; reprinted New York: Arno Press, 1975), pp. 314, 564.

16. Oscar Koch, *Der Indianishe Eros* (Berlin: Verlag Continent, 1925), p. 61.

17. George Devereux, "Institutionalized Homosexuality of the Mohave Indians," *Human Biology* 9 (1937): 509.

18. Ibid., p. 501.

19. Ibid.

20. Ibid., pp. 508–9.

21. C. Daryll Forde, "Ethnography of the Yuma Indians," *University of California Publications in American Archaeology and Ethnology* 28 (1931): 157.

22. Ruth Underhill, *Social Organization of the Papago Indians* (New York: Columbia University Press, 1938), p. 186. This story is also mentioned in Ruth Underhill, ed., *The Autobiography of a Papago Woman* (Menasha, Wisc.: American Anthropological Association, 1936), p. 39.

23. John Fire and Richard Erdoes, *Lame Deer, Seeker of Visions* (New York: Simon and Schuster, 1972), pp. 117, 149.

24. Theodore Stern, *The Klamath Tribe: A People and Their Reservation* (Seattle: University of Washington Press, 1965), pp. 20, 24. Theodore Stern, "Some Sources of Variability in Klamath Mythology," *Journal of American Folklore* 69 (1956): 242ff. Leslie Spier, *Klamath Ethnography* (Berkeley: University of California Press, 1930), p. 52.

25. Alice Joseph, et al., *The Desert People* (Chicago: University of Chicago Press, 1949), p. 227.

26. Quoted in Forde, "Ethnography of the Yuma," p. 157. Although he distorted the data on berdache, see also Leslie Spier, *Yuman Tribes of the Gila River* (Chicago: University of Chicago Press, 1933), pp. 6, 242–43.

27. Joseph Quiñones, Yaqui informant 1, January 1985.

28. Stephen Powers, *Tribes of California*, ed. Robert Heizer (originally published 1877; reprint Berkeley: University of California Press, 1976).

29. Alfred Kroeber, *Handbook of the Indians of California* (Berkeley: University of California Press, 1953), p. 497.

30. Erminie Voegelin, *Culture Element Distribution: Northeast California* (Berkeley: University of California Press, 1942), vol. 20, pp. 134–35, 228-B note. Ralph Beals, "Ethnology of the Nisenan," *University of California Publications in American Archaeology and Ethnology* 31 (1933), p. 376.

31. Clark Wissler, "Societies and Ceremonial Associations in the Oglala Division of the Teton Dakota," *Anthropological Papers of the American Museum of Natural History* 11, pt. 1 (1916): 92; Powers, *Oglala Religion*, pp. 57–59.

32. Ronnie Loud Hawk, Lakota informant 4, July 1982.

33. Terry Calling Eagle, Lakota informant 5, July 1982.

34. James O. Dorsey, "A Study of the Siouan Cults," *Bureau of American Ethnology Annual Report* 11 (1889–90): 378. It is unclear from the sources what would happen if a boy tried to get the man's tools and was successful, since the instances cited always have the boy getting the women's tools. If he got the bow and arrow, presumably he would not become a berdache, but would retain the power to seduce men.

35. Nancy Lurie, "Winnebago Berdache," *American Anthropologist* 55 (1953): 708; Alice Fletcher, "The Elk Mystery or Festival: Ogallala Sioux," *Reports of the Peabody Museum of American Archaeology and Ethnology* 3 (1887): 281; Erik Erikson, "Childhood and Tradition in Two American Indian Tribes," *Psychoanalytic Study of the Child* 1 (1945): 329, based on Erikson's visit to Sioux reservations in the 1930s with anthropologist H. Scudder Mekeel; Robert H. Lowie, "The Assiniboine," *Anthropological Papers of the American Museum of Natural History* 4 (1909): 42; George Dorsey and James Murie, *Notes on Skidi Pawnee Society* (Chicago: Field Museum of Natural History, 1940), p. 108; Alfred Bowers, *Mandan Social and Ceremonial Organization* (Chicago: University of Chicago Press, 1950), p. 298; George Will and Herbert Spinden, *The Mandans* (Cambridge: Harvard University Press, 1906), p. 128.

36. James S. Thayer, "The Berdache of the Northern Plains: A Socioreligious Perspective," *Journal of Anthropological Research* 36 (1980): 289.

37. Alfred Bowers, "Hidatsa Social and Ceremonial Organization," *Bureau of American Ethnology Bulletin* 194 (1965): 326.

38. Fletcher, "Elk Mystery," p. 281.

39. Alice Fletcher and Francis La Flesche, "The Omaha Tribe," *Bureau of American Ethnology Annual Report* 27 (1905–6): 132.

40. Harriet Whitehead offers a valuable discussion of this element of the vision quest in "The Bow and the Burden Strap: A New Look at Institutionalized Homosexuality in Native North America," in *Sexual Meanings,* ed. Sherry Ortner and Harriet Whitehead (Cambridge: Cambridge University Press, 1981), pp. 99–102. See also Erikson, "Childhood," p. 329.

CHAPTER TWO

1. Peter Grant, "The Sauteux Indians about 1804," in *Les Bourgeois de la Compagnie du Nord-Ouest,* ed. L. R. Masson (Quebec: Imprimarie, 1890), vol. 2, p. 357. See also Vernon Kinietz, *Chippewa Village* (Bloomfield, Mich.: Cranbrook Press, 1947), p. 155.

2. Cieza de León, *Historia del Peru* (1553), quoted in Francisco Guerra, *The Pre-Columbian Mind* (London: Seminar Press, 1971), p. 91.

3. Clark Wissler, "Societies and Ceremonial Associations in the Oglala Division of the Teton Dakota," *Anthropological Papers of the American Museum of Natural History* 11, pt. 1 (1916): 92.

4. Alfred Bowers, "Hidatsa Social and Ceremonial Organization," *Bureau of American Ethnology Bulletin* 194 (1965): 167–68.

5. Wes Fortney, Cheyenne informant 2, August 1982.

6. Matilda Coxe Stevenson, "The Zuni Indians," *Bureau of American Ethnology Annual Report* 23 (1901–2): 37–38.

7. Ibid., pp. 37–38, 310. Similarly, the Navajo berdaches had a reputation for excelling in ritual performance; see W. W. Hill, "The Status of the Hermaphrodite and Transvestite in Navaho Culture," *American Anthropologist* 37 (1935): 275.

8. Richard Green and John Money, "Stage-Acting, Role-Taking, and Effeminate Impersonation during Boyhood," *Archives of General Psychiatry* 15 (1966): 535–38. James D. Weinrich, "Human Reproductive Strategy" (Ph.D. diss., Harvard University, 1976), pp. 175–76. Michael Ruse, "Are There Gay Genes? Sociobiology and Homosexuality," *Journal of Homosexuality* 6 (1981): 23–24. Joseph Harry, *Gay Children Grown Up* (New York: Praeger, 1982), chap. 1.

9. On the various aspects of shamanism, see William Thomas Corlett, M.D., *The Medicine Man of the American Indian and His Cultural Background* (Baltimore: Charles C. Thomas, 1935); Andreas Lommel, *Shamanism: The Beginnings of Art* (New York: McGraw Hill, 1967); John Lee Maddox, *The Medicine Man* (New York: MacMillan, 1923); Joe Medicine Crow, "From M.M. to M.D.: Medicine Man to Doctor of Medicine," *Occasional Papers of the Museum of the Rockies* (Bozeman: Montana State University, 1979); Dale Valory, "Yurok Doctors and Devils: A Study in Identity, Anxiety and Deviance" (Ph.D. diss., University of California, Berkeley, 1970); and Virgil Vogel, *American Indian Medicine* (Norman: University of Oklahoma Press, 1970).

10. See Luis Kemnitzer, "Structure, Content, and Cultural Meaning

of *Yuwipi:* A Modern Lakota Healing Ritual," *American Ethnologist* 3 (1976): 261–80.

11. W. W. Hill, "The Status of the Hermaphrodite and Transvestite in Navahjo Culture," *American Anthropologist* 37 (1935): 275; Gladys Reichard, *Social Life of the Navajo Indians* (New York: Columbia University Press, 1928), p. 150.

12. John One Grass, Lakota informant 3, July 1982.

13. Vincent White Cloud, Lakota informant 2, July 1982; William Powers, *Oglala Religion* (Lincoln: University of Nebraska Press, 1977), pp. 57–58; John Fire and Richard Erdoes, *Lame Deer, Seeker of Visions* (New York: Simon and Schuster, 1972), p. 150.

14. George Grinnell, *The Cheyenne Indians* (New Haven: Yale University Press, 1923), vol. 2, p. 40; E. Adamson Hoebel, *The Cheyennes* (New York: Holt, Rinehart and Winston, 1978), p. 83.

15. Luke Standing Elk, Cheyenne informant 5, August 1982.

16. George Devereux, "Institutionalized Homosexuality of the Mohave Indians," *Human Biology* 9 (1937): 516. Robert Heizer, ed., *Handbook of North American Indians: California* (Washington, D.C.: Smithsonian Institution, 1978), vol. 8, pp. 131, 134, 502, 512. Erminie Voegelin, *Culture Element Distribution: Northeast California* (Berkeley: University of California Press, 1942) vol. 20, pp. 134–35. For the story of a Klamath berdache shaman who was both greatly respected and feared, see Edith McLeod, "White Cindy, Mystery Figure," *Siskiyou Pioneer and Siskiyou County Historical Society Yearbook* 2 (1953): 32–34.

17. Alfred Kroeber, *Handbook of the Indians of California* (Berkeley: University of California Press, 1953), pp. 46, 497. Voegelin, *Culture Element,* pp. 134–35.

18. Twila Giegle Dillon, Lakota informant 6, July 1982.

19. Terry Calling Eagle, Lakota informant 5, July 1982.

20. Hill, "Status," p. 275.

21. Terry Calling Eagle, Lakota informant 5, July 1982.

22. Robert Lowie, *The Crow Indians* (New York: Farrar and Rinehart, 1935), p. 48. S. C. Sims, "Crow Indian Hermaphrodites," *American Anthropologist* 5 (1903): 580–81.

23. Ruth Landes, *The Prairie Potawatomi* (Madison: University of Wisconsin Press, 1970), pp. 36–37.

24. Royal B. Hassrick, *The Sioux* (Norman: University of Oklahoma Press, 1964), pp. 134–35, 313. Powers, *Oglala Religion,* pp. 57–58.

25. Terry Calling Eagle, Lakota informant 5, July 1982.

26. Fire and Erdoes, *Lame Deer,* pp. 117, 150.

27. Hassrick, *Sioux,* p. 134.

28. Bowers, "Hidatsa Organization," p. 256.

29. Ruth Landes, *The Mystic Lake Sioux: Sociology of the Mdewakantonwan Santee* (Madison: University of Wisconsin Press, 1968), pp. 37–38; Harold Driver, *Indians of North America* (Chicago: University of Chicago Press, 1969), pp. 383–84; E. Adamson Hoebel, *The Cheyenne: Indians of the Great Plains* (New York: Holt, Rinehart and Winston, 1978), pp. 34–35; David Greenberg,

"Why Was the Berdache Ridiculed?" *Journal of Homosexuality* 11 (1985): 179–189.

30. Greenberg, "Why Was the Berdache Ridiculed?" p. 183–85.

31. Ibid.

32. Charles Allen, Omaha informant 3, June 1982.

33. Victor Robinson, Omaha informant 1, June 1982.

34. Terry Calling Eagle, Lakota informant 5, July 1982. This statement was repeated to me almost word for word in a separate interview with Michael One Feather, Lakota informant 14, April 1985.

35. Edith McLeod, "White Cindy, Mystery Figure," *Siskiyou Pioneer and Yearbook* 11 (Spring 1953): 32–34.

36. Bowers, "Hidatsa Organization," pp. 167–68.

37. John One Grass, Lakota informant 3, July 1982. The shaman Lame Deer typifies this ambivalence, with his juxtaposition of the following positive and negative statements about *winkte:* "We accept him for what he wants to be. That's up to him. Still, fathers did not like to see their boys hanging around a *winkte*'s place and told them to stay away. There are good men among the *winktes* and they have been given certain powers" (Fire and Erdoes, *Lame Deer,* p. 149). See also Hassrick, *Sioux,* pp. 133–35. However, William Powers suggests that these viewpoints are not traditional Lakota attitudes, since *winktes* are *wakan;* William Powers, "Comment," *Current Anthropology* 24 (1983): 461–62.

38. For the concept of the variants having a different window, I am grateful to Harry Hay, who originated his ideas from a study of the medieval court jester. This "fool" was often the only one who could speak the truth, since he was outside the norm and not considered a threat. Hay's philosophical writings are currently being edited for publication by Bradley D. Rose.

39. Jerry Baldy, Hupa informant 1, 18 September 1985.

40. Michael One Feather, Lakota informant 14, April 1985.

41. Nancy Lurie, "Winnebago Berdache," *American Anthropologist* 55 (1953): 708, 710.

42. Michael One Feather, Lakota informant 14, April 1985.

43. Fire and Erdoes, *Lame Deer,* pp. 149–50.

CHAPTER THREE

1. Louis Armand de Lom d'Arce de Lahontan, *New Voyages to North America,* ed. Reuben Gold Thwaites (Chicago: McClurg, 1905), vol. 2, p. 462.

2. Calvin Jumping Bull, Lakota informant 1, July 1982.

3. Alfred Bowers, *Mandan Social and Ceremonial Organization* (Chicago: University of Chicago Press, 1950), p. 168; Alfred Bowers, "Hidatsa Social and Ceremonial Organization," *Bureau of American Ethnology Bulletin* 194 (1965): 502; William Whitman, "The Oto," *Columbia University Contributions to Anthropology* 28 (1969): 50; Frederica de Laguna, "Tlingit Ideas about the Indian," *Southwestern Journal of Anthropology* 10 (1954): 178.

4. Lakota ethnographer Luis Kemnitzer, personal communication, 3 June 1982.

5. Michael One Feather, Lakota informant 14, April 1985.

6. Richard White, Omaha informant 2, June 1982.

7. Quoted in Ales Hrdlicka, *The Anthropology of Kodiak Island* (New York: AMS Press, 1975), p. 79.

8. Georg Langsdorff, *Voyages and Travels in Various Parts of the World during the Years 1803–1807* (Carlisle, Pa.: George Philips, 1817), pp. 345, 64; Martin Sauer, *An Account of a Geographical and Astronomical Expedition to the Northern Parts of Russia . . . 1785–1794* (London, 1802), pp. 160, 176; Hubert Bancroft, "The Koniagas," in *The Native Races of the Pacific States of North America* (New York: Appleton, 1875), vol. 1, p. 82; Havelock Ellis, *Studies in the Psychology of Sex* (New York: Random House, 1910, 1936), vol. 2, pt. 2, pp. 16–17.

9. Fernandez de Piedrahita, quoted in Antonio Requena, "Noticias y Consideraciones Sobre las Anormalidades Sexuales de los Aborígenes Americanos: Sodomía," *Acta Venezolana* 1 (July–September 1945): 16. An English translation of this article, titled "Sodomy among Native American Peoples," appears in *Gay Sunshine* nos. 38–39 (Winter 1979): 37–39.

10. Father Gerónimo Boscana, "Indians at the Missionary Establishment of St. Juan Capistrano, Alta California" (c. 1826), trans. in Jonathan Katz, *Gay American History* (New York: Crowell, 1976), p. 614. See another translation in Gerónimo Boscana, *Chinigchinich* (Banning, Calif.: Malki Museum Press, 1978), p. 54.

11. Harry Hay, personal communication, 1 September 1985.

12. Edmund White, *States of Desire: Travels in Gay America* (New York: E. P. Dutton, 1980), pp. 99–101.

13. Calvin Jumping Bull, Lakota informant 1, July 1982.

14. Royal Hassrick, *The Sioux: Life and Customs of a Warrior Society* (Norman: University of Oklahoma Press, 1964), pp. 133–34, 144–45.

15. George Devereux, "Institutionalized Homosexuality of the Mohave Indians," *Human Biology* 9 (1937): 517.

16. Charles Callender and Lee Kochems, "The North American Berdache," *Current Anthropology* 24 (1983): 443–70.

17. Donald Forgey, "The Institution of Berdache among the North American Plains Indians," *Journal of Sex Research* 11 (1975): 12. This interpretation is also put forth by Hassrick, *Sioux*, pp. 133–34.

18. Alan Bell, Martin Weinberg, and Sue Hammersmith, *Sexual Preference: Its Development in Men and Women* (Bloomington: Indiana University Press, 1981).

19. Jennie Joe, Navajo informant 1, November 1984.

20. Beverly Chiñas, "Isthmus Zapotec 'Berdaches,'" *Newsletter of the Anthropological Research Group on Homosexuality* 7, pt. 2 (May 1985): 1–4.

21. Ronnie Loud Hawk, Lakota informant 4, July 1982.

22. Harry Hay, personal communication, 1 September 1985.

23. Jerry Baldy, Hupa informant 1, September 1985.

24. Margaret Mead, *Sex and Temperament in Three Primitive Societies* (New York: Morrow Quill, 1935, 1963), p. 294.

25. Elsie Clews Parsons, "The Zuni La' Mana," *American Anthropologist* 18 (1916): 521–22.

26. Edward Thompson Denig, *Five Indian Tribes of the Upper Missouri,* ed. John Ewers (Norman: University of Oklahoma Press, 1961), pp. 187–88.

27. S. C. Simms, "Crow Indian Hermaphrodites," *American Anthropologist* 5 (1903): 580–81.

28. Pierre Liette, "Memoir of Pierre Liette on the Illinois Country," in *The Western Country in the Seventeenth Century,* ed. Milo Quaife (New York: Citadel, 1962), pp. 112–13; quoted in Katz, *Gay American History,* p. 228.

29. Ruth Underhill, *Social Organization of the Papago Indians* (New York: Columbia University Press, 1938), p. 186. It is improper to assume, as some theorists on berdachism have, that a ceremonial or visionary origin of berdachism is in opposition to childhood character. Both are reflections of the child's spirit.

30. Robert Stoller, "Two Feminized Male American Indians," *Archives of Sexual Behavior* 5 (1976): 530.

31. Michael One Feather, Lakota informant, 14, April 1985. What is interesting in this description is the similarity of this life history to that of gay North American men. Weinberg, Bell, and Hammersmith (*Sexual Preference*) found this same pattern of gender variance in childhood to be about the only factor with which they could find a correlation to adult homosexuality. What is notable is that the focus of Western research is usually on sexual preference, while the emphasis of many Indians is clearly on the character of the person.

32. Jerry Baldy, Hupa informant 1, September 1985.

33. Joseph Quiñones, Yaqui informant 1, January 1985.

34. Richard E. Grant, fieldnotes, May 1978 and June 1985, personal communication, 14 July 1985.

35. Ibid.

36. Elsie Clews Parsons, "The Zuni La' Mana," *American Anthropologist* 18 (1916): 521–28.

37. W. Matthews, quoted in Ferdinand Karsch-Haack, *Das Gleichgeschlechtliche Leben der Naturvölker* (The same-sex life of nature peoples) (Munich: Verlag von Ernst Reinhardt, 1911; reprinted New York: Arno Press, 1975), p. 321.

38. Jerry Baldy, Hupa informant 1, September 1985.

39. Snowbird Community Singing, Robbinsville, North Carolina, 1973. Perhaps there is a cross-cultural pattern of association between music and flamboyant nonmasculine males which warrants further investigation.

40. Ellie Rides a Horse, Crow informant 3, August 1982.

41. Jerry Running Elk, Lakota informant 9, July 1982.

42. Terry Calling Eagle, Lakota informant 5, July 1982.

43. Jerry Baldy, Hupa informant 1, September 1985.

44. Jennie Joe, Navajo informant 1, October 1982.

45. Clellan Ford, *Smoke From Their Fires: The Life of a Kwakiutl Chief* (New Haven: Yale University Press, 1941), p. 130.

46. Stephen Powers, *Tribes of California,* ed. Robert Heizer (originally published 1877; reprint Berkeley: University of California Press, 1976), p. 132.

47. Ruth Landes, *The Prairie Potawatomi* (Madison: University of Wisconsin Press, 1970), p. 197.

48. Irving Hallowell, "American Indians White and Black: The Phenomenon of Transculturation," *Current Anthropology* 4 (1963): 519–31.

49. Bowers, "Hidatsa Organization," p. 167.

50. Lakota informant 5, July 1982.

51. I am grateful to Maurice Kenny, Mohawk poet, for this insight. Personal communication, 22 November 1982.

52. Joe Medicine Crow, Crow informant 2, August 1982.

53. Alfred Kroeber, "Handbook of the Indians of California," *Bureau of American Ethnology Bulletin* 78 (1925): 46.

54. Leslie Spier, *Yuman Tribes of the Gila River* (Chicago: University of Chicago Press, 1933), p. 242.

55. Matilda Coxe Stevenson, "The Zuni Indians," *Bureau of American Ethnology Annual Report* 23 (1901–2): 37–38, 310–13.

56. Nancy Lurie, "Winnebago Berdache," *American Anthropologist* 55 (1953): 708.

57. On the Hopi see Martin Duberman, ed., "1965 Native American Transvestism," *New York Native,* 21 June 1982, p. 46. For the Lakotas see Erik H. Erikson, "Childhood and Tradition in Two American Indian Tribes," *Psychoanalytic Study of the Child* 1 (1945): 329–30; John One Grass, Lakota informant 3, July 1982; John Fire and Richard Erdoes, *Lame Deer, Seeker of Visions* (New York: Simon and Schuster, 1972), p. 149. Stoller, "Two Feminized [Mohaves]," p. 531; Robert Lowie, "The Assiniboine," *Anthropological Papers of the American Museum of Natural History* 4 (1909): 42; Joe Medicine Crow, Crow informant 2, August 1982; Robert Lowie, *The Crow Indians* (New York: Farrar and Rinehart, 1935), p. 48.

58. Vincent White Cloud, Lakota informant 2, July 1982.

59. Simms, "Crow Hermaphrodites," p. 580.

60. Marie Watson-Franke, "A Woman's Profession in Guajiro Culture: Weaving," *Antropológica* (Caracas) 37 (1974): 24–40.

61. Ruth Underhill, ed., *The Autobiography of a Papago Woman* (Menasha, Wisc.: American Anthropological Association, 1936), pp. 39, 44.

62. Underhill, *Papago Indians,* p. 186.

63. Chiñas, "Isthmus Berdaches," p. 2.

64. Callender and Kochems, "North American Berdache." In a survey of California Indian cultures, there were always noted a few exceptions about the shamanism or the homosexuality of berdaches, but no exceptions regarding women's work. Erminie Voegelin, *Culture Element Distribution: Northeast California* (Berkeley: University of California Press, 1942), vol. 20, pp. 134–35.

65. Chiñas, "Isthmus Berdaches," p. 2.

66. See Jeannette Mirsky, "The Dakota," in *Cooperation and Competition among Primitive Peoples,* ed. Margaret Mead (New York: McGraw Hill, 1937), pp. 416–17; and Landes, *Prairie Potawatomi,* pp. 36, 41.

67. Ralph Linton, *The Study of Man* (New York: Appleton Century Crofts, 1936), p. 480.

68. Lakota informant 4, July 1982.

69. These points have been well developed by Donald Forgey, "Institution of Berdache," p. 10; and by Harriet Whitehead, "The Bow and the Burden Strap: A New Look at Institutionalized Homosexuality in Native North America," in *Sexual Meanings,* ed. Sherry Ortner and Harriet Whitehead (Cambridge: Cambridge University Press, 1981), p. 107.

70. Robert Heizer, ed., *Handbook of North American Indians. Volume 8: California* (Washington, D.C.: Smithsonian Institution, 1978), pp. 131, 134; Alfred Kroeber, *Handbook of the Indians of California* (Berkeley: University of California Press, 1953), p. 497.

71. W. W. Hill, "The Status of the Hermaphrodite and Transvestite in Navaho Culture," *American Anthropologist* 37 (1935): 275–76.

72. Ibid., p. 278.

73. Harriet Whitehead overemphasizes the importance of work roles and material prosperity as a reason for boys to assume berdache status, but she does make a valid point that desire for material prosperity and prestige is not arbitrarily opposed to a psychosexual explanation of berdachism. See Whitehead, "Bow and Burden Strap," p. 107.

74. Vincent White Cloud, Lakota informant 2, July 1982.

75. Landes, *Prairie Potawatomi,* pp. 196, 316.

76. Stevenson, "Zuni Indians," pp. 37–38, 310–13.

77. Hill, "Status," p. 274.

78. Ibid.

CHAPTER FOUR

1. Jacques Marquette, "Of the First Voyage Made . . . ," in *The Jesuit Relations,* ed. Reuben Gold Thwaites (Cleveland: Burrows, 1896–1901), vol. 59, p. 129; reprinted in Jonathan Katz, *Gay American History* (New York: Thomas Crowell, 1976), p. 287.

2. Joseph François Lafitau, *Moeurs des sauvages americquains* (Paris: Saugrain, 1724), vol. 1, p. 52; translated by Warren Johansson in Katz, *Gay American History,* p. 288.

3. An excellent short statement of women's high status in American Indian cultures, written by an Indian woman, is Paula Gunn Allen, "Lesbians in American Indian Cultures," *Conditions* 7 (1981): 67–87. Other studies that make this point clear include Evelyn Blackwood, "Sexuality and Gender in Certain Native American Tribes: The Case of Cross-Gender Females," *Signs* 10 (1984): 28, 32–34; Beatrice Medicine, "Warrior Women—Sex Role Alternatives for Plains Indian Women," in *The Hidden Half: Studies of Plains Indian Women,* ed. Patricia Albers and Beatrice Medicine (Washington, D.C.: University Press of America, 1983), pp. 267–80; and Beverly Chiñas, *The Isthmus Zapotecs: Women's Roles in Cultural Context* (New York: Holt, Rinehart and Winston, 1973). For further elaboration on female gender variance, see Chap-

ter 11. For a worldwide context for understanding egalitarian societies, see Charlotte O'Kelly, *Women and Men in Society* (New York: Van Nostrand, 1980), chap. 3; and M. Kay Martin and Barbara Voorhies, *Female of the Species* (New York: Columbia University Press, 1975), chap. 7. See also Peggy Sanday, *Female Power and and Male Dominance: On the Origins of Sexual Inequality* (Cambridge: Cambridge University Press, 1981); Eleanor Leacock, *Myths of Male Dominance: Collected Articles on Women Cross-Culturally* (New York: Monthly Review Press, 1981); Mona Etienne and Eleanor Leacock, ed., *Women and Colonization: Anthropological Perspectives* (New York: Bergin, 1980); Mina Davis Caulfield, "Equality, Sex and Mode of Production," in *Social Inequality: Comparative and Developmental Approaches,* ed. Gerald Berreman (New York: Academic Press, 1981), pp. 201–19.

4. Jay Miller, "People, Berdaches, and Left-Handed Bears: Human Variation in Native America," *Journal of Anthropological Research* 38 (Fall 1982): 280.

5. It is in this aspect where anthropologist Harriet Whitehead makes a mistake in assuming an antagonistic relation between the sexes as a basis for the berdache to become "superior" to women; see Harriet Whitehead, "The Bow and the Burden Strap: A New Look at Institutionalized Homosexuality in Native North America," in *Sexual Meanings,* ed. Sherry Ortner and Harriet Whitehead (Cambridge: Cambridge University Press, 1981), p. 86. A critique of Whitehead, and a good summary of the position of women in Indian societies, is contained in Blackwood, "Sexuality and Gender." See also Allen, "Lesbians in American Indian Cultures," pp. 67–87.

6. Matilda Coxe Stevenson, "The Zuni Indians," *Bureau of American Ethnology Annual Report* 23 (1901–2): 310.

7. Robert Lowie, *The Crow Indians* (New York: Farrar and Rinehart, 1935), p. 48; S. C. Simms, "Crow Indian Hermaphrodites," *American Anthropologist* 5 (1903): 580–81; Ruth Landes, *The Prairie Potawatomi* (Madison: University of Wisconsin Press, 1970), p. 200.

8. Robert Stoller, "Two Feminized Male American Indians," *Archives of Sexual Behavior* 5 (1976): 531.

9. Quoted in Francisco Guerra, *The Pre-Columbian Mind* (New York: Seminar Press, 1971), p. 67. There are a number of reports, for different tribes at different time periods, which specify that berdaches are tall or big. Such statements are frequent enough to be noted, but they are not common enough to be seen as a general tendency. In my fieldwork and interviews with berdaches of many cultures, all of the ones I have met are of average size, so I feel such reports are not typical.

10. Quoted in Katz, *Gay American History,* pp. 285–86.

11. Joe Medicine Crow, Crow informant 2, August 1982; Lowie, *Crow,* p. 48.

12. Alice Fletcher and Francis La Flesche, "The Omaha Tribe," *Bureau of American Ethnology Annual Report* 27 (1905–6): 133.

13. Alexander Henry and David Thompson, *New Light on the Early History of the Greater Northwest,* ed. Elliott Coues (New York: Harper, 1897), vol. 1,

pp. 163–65. Evidently this person is the same as Ozaw-wen-dib, "Yellow Head," mentioned by John Tanner in his narrative of 1830.

14. Perrin du Lac, *Voyage dans les deux Louisianes* (Lyon: Bruyset, Aîné et Buyand, 1805), pp. 318, 352; quoted in Katz, *Gay American History,* pp. 612–13.

15. John One Grass, Lakota informant 3, July 1982.

16. George B. Grinnell, *The Cheyenne Indians* (New Haven: Yale University Press, 1923), vol. 2, p. 40.

17. E. Adamson Hoebel, *The Cheyennes* (New York: Holt, Rinehart and Winston, 1978), p. 83.

18. Grinnell, *Cheyenne,* pp. 39–41; Hoebel, *Cheyennes,* p. 83.

19. Ruth Underhill, *Social Organization of the Papago Indians* (New York: Columbia University Press, 1938), p. 186.

20. W. W. Hill, "The Status of the Hermaphrodite and Transvestite in Navaho Culture," *American Anthropologist* 37 (1935): 273–79.

21. Vincent White Cloud, Lakota informant 2, July 1982.

22. Charlotte Heth, personal communication, 4 May 1983; Donald Fixico, personal communication, 8 April 1983. Both of these Indian people remember seeing berdaches in these traditional turtle-shell rattle dances on Creek and Seminole lands in Oklahoma. Since I am not aware of any other references to berdachism in the documents on these southeastern groups, these references mark the need for further investigation. It also is an indication that we cannot trust the absence of documentation to mean that berdachism was absent in a group.

23. Beverly Chiñas, "Isthmus Zapotec 'Berdaches,'" *Newsletter of the Anthropological Research Group on Homosexuality* 7, pt. 2 (May 1985): 4.

24. Victor Robinson, Omaha informant, June 1982.

25. Elsie Clews Parsons, "The Zuni La' Mana," *American Anthropologist* 18 (1916): 521–28.

26. An excellent discussion of this use of a Go-Between to settle differences is in Vine Deloria and Clifford Lytle, *American Indians, American Justice* (Austin: University of Texas Press, 1983).

27. Hill, "Status," p. 275; Margaret Mead, *The Changing Culture of an Indian Tribe* (New York: Columbia University Press, 1932), p. 189.

28. Ibid.; William Powers, "Comment," *Current Anthropology* 24 (1983): 461–62.

29. Grinnell, *Cheyenne,* pp. 42, 39; Hoebel, *Cheyennes,* p. 83.

30. Nancy Lurie, "Winnebago Berdache," *American Anthropologist* 55 (1953): 710; Henry Angelino and Charles Shedd, "A Note on Berdache," *American Anthropologist* 57 (1955): 125; Charles Callender and Lee Kochems, "North American Berdache," *Current Anthropology* 24 (1983): 443.

31. Hill, "Status," p. 273.

32. Parsons, "Zuni La' Mana," pp. 521–22.

33. Margaret Mead, *Sex and Temperament in Three Primitive Societies* (New York: Morrow Quill, 1935, 1963), pp. 294–95.

34. Pierre Liette, "Memoir of Pierre Liette on the Illinois Country," in *The Western Country in the Seventeenth Century,* ed. Milo Quaife (New York: Citadel, 1962), pp. 112–13; quoted in Katz, *Gay American History,* p. 228.

35. Joe Medicine Crow, Crow informant 2, August 1982.

36. Parsons, "Zuni La' Mana," p. 523.

37. Stevenson, "Zuni Indians," plate XCIV, p. 417. There are several photographs of We'wha in the National Anthropological Archives, Smithsonian Institution, and in the Southwest Museum, Los Angeles.

38. Grinnell, *Cheyenne,* p. 39.

39. Anon. Omaha informant, June 1982.

40. Ronnie Loud Hawk, Lakota informant 4, July 1982.

41. Calvin Jumping Bull, Lakota informant 1, July 1982.

42. Vincent White Cloud, Lakota informant 2, July 1982.

43. Claude Schaeffer, "The Kutenai Female Berdache: Courier, Guide, Prophetess, and Warrior," *Ethnohistory* 12 (1965): 217–18; Victor Robinson, Omaha informant 1, June 1982.

44. Luis Kemnitzer, personal communication, June 1982.

45. To be fair, Hill was trying to distinguish berdaches from hermaphrodites, who "usually dress as women," but the use of the term *transvestite* leads to these problems. Hill, "Status," p. 275.

46. John Fire and Richard Erdoes, *Lame Deer, Seeker of Visions* (New York: Simon and Schuster, 1972), p. 149.

47. Chiñas, "Isthmus Berdaches," p. 2.

48. Edith McLeod, "White Cindy, Mystery Figure," *Siskiyou Pioneer and Yearbook* 2 (1953): 32–34.

49. Michael One Feather, Lakota informant 14, April 1985.

50. Clellan Ford, *Smoke From Their Fires: The Life of a Kwakiutl Chief* (New Haven: Yale University Press, 1941), pp. 130–31.

51. Lakota informant 4, July 1982.

52. Joe Little Coyote, Jim King, Luke Standing Elk, Cheyenne informants, August 1982.

53. Elva One Feather, Lakota informant 8, July 1982.

54. Stan White Dog, Lakota informant 7, June 1985.

55. Stephen Powers, *Tribes of California,* ed. Robert Heizer (originally published 1877; reprint Berkeley: University of California Press, 1976), p. 132; Stevenson, "Zuni Indians," pp. 37–38; Thomas Yellowtail, Crow informant 4, August 1982.

56. See Callender and Kochems, "North American Berdache."

57. John Money and Anke Ehrhardt, *Man & Woman, Boy & Girl* (Baltimore: Johns Hopkins University Press, 1972), p. 5.

58. Hill, "Status," p. 273.

59. John Money, personal communication, July 1985.

60. See Chapter 11 for an account of the usual situation, in which nonfeminine females have a distinct role from male berdaches.

61. Victor Robinson, Omaha informant 1, June 1982.

62. Angelino and Shedd, "Note on Berdache," p. 125.

63. Calvin Jumping Bull, Lakota informant 1, July 1982.

64. Lakota informant 1, July 1982.

65. Ronnie Loud Hawk, Lakota informant 4, July 1982.

66. Angelino and Shedd, "Note on Berdache," p. 125.

67. Alfred Kroeber, "Psychosis or Social Sanction," *Character and Personality* 8 (1940): 209–10.

68. Whitehead, "Bow and Burden Strap," pp. 93, 96.

69. James Dorsey, "A Study of the Siouan Cults," *Bureau of American Ethnology Annual Report* 11 (1889–90): 516.

70. While these ideas are my own, the literature on transsexualism is large. See Anne Bolin, "In Search of Eve: Transsexual Rites of Passage," (Ph.D. diss., University of Colorado, Boulder, 1983); Richard Green, *Sexual Identity Conflict in Children and Adults* (New York: Basic Books, 1974); Richard Green and John Money, *Transsexualism and Sex Reassignment* (Baltimore: Johns Hopkins University Press, 1969); John Money and Patricia Tucker, *Sexual Signatures: On Being a Man or a Woman* (Boston: Little, Brown, 1975); J. G. Raymond, *The Transsexual Empire: The Making of the She-Male* (Boston: Beacon Press, 1979); Robert Stoller, *Sex and Gender: On the Development of Masculinity and Femininity* (New York: Science House, 1968); and the classic by Harry Benjamin, *The Transsexual Phenomenon* (New York: Julian Press, 1966).

71. Gladys Reichard, *Social Life of the Navajo Indians* (New York: Columbia University Press, 1928), p. 150.

72. Hill, "Status," p. 279.

73. Bill Little Bull, Lakota informant 10, July 1982.

74. Robert Lowie, "The Assiniboine," *Anthropological Papers of the American Museum of Natural History* 4 (1909): 42.

75. Thomas Yellowtail, Crow informant 4, August 1982. Among the Lakotas, *winktes* also used to call each other "sister." Fire and Erdoes, *Lame Deer,* p. 150.

76. A. B. Holder, "The Bote: Description of a Peculiar Sexual Perversion Found among the North American Indians," *New York Medical Journal* 50 (December 7, 1889): 623–25; quoted in Katz, *Gay American History,* pp. 312–13.

77. Chiñas, "Isthmus Berdaches," pp. 1–2. This notion of a third, or intermediate, sex appeared in English writings by the late nineteenth century (see Chapter 10).

78. Harry Hay, personal communication, 1 September 1985.

79. Callender and Kochems, "North American Berdache," p. 443.

80. Sue-Ellen Jacobs, "Comment," *Current Anthropology* 24 (1983): 459–60. She and I have been corresponding about this matter since 1980, and our ideas have evolved similarly.

81. Callender and Kochems, "North American Berdache," p. 443.

82. Charles Callender and Lee Kochems, "Men and Not-Men: Male Gender-Mixing Statuses and Homosexuality," *Journal of Homosexuality* 11 (1985): 165–78. Each of us has been influenced by the work of the other; Lee Kochems heard a paper I delivered in Chicago in 1981, from a "third gender" perspec-

tive. I then modified my views, as they have theirs from the "institutionalized woman" perspective, to end up with a gender-mixing perspective. Harriet Whitehead also is now using "gender-mixing" as her approach, as evidenced by her commentary in the "Gender Crossing" session at the Annual Meeting of the American Anthropological Association, Denver, November 1984. Only Evelyn Blackwood continues to argue for the term "gender crossing," as applied to females, but even she agrees that the male berdache status may be more properly seen as a mixture or alternative role. See Blackwood, "Sexuality and Gender."

83. Ferdinand Karsch-Haack, *Das Gleichgeschlechtliche Leben der Naturvölker* (The same-sex life of nature peoples) (Munich: Verlag von Ernst Reinhardt, 1911; reprinted New York: Arno Press, 1975), p. 327.

84. Henry and Thompson, *New Light,* vol. 1, p. 163.

85. Stevenson, "Zuni Indians," p. 313; Parsons, "Zuni La' Mana," p. 528.

86. D. B. Mandelbaum, "The Plains Cree," *Anthropological Papers of the American Museum of Natural History* 37 (1940): 256.

87. Fire and Erdoes, *Lame Deer,* p. 150.

88. James Thayer, "The Berdache of the Northern Plains: A Socioreligious Perspective," *Journal of Anthropological Research* 36 (1980): 292–93.

89. Grinnell, *Cheyenne,* pp. 39–41.

90. Lakota informant 2, July 1982.

91. Lakota informant 4, July 1982.

92. Lakota informant 5, July 1982.

93. Calvin Jumping Bull, Lakota informant 1, July 1982.

CHAPTER FIVE

1. Fernandez de Oviedo, quoted in Francisco Guerra, *The Pre-Columbian Mind* (London: Seminar Press, 1971), p. 55.

2. Fernandez de Piedrahita, quoted in Antonia Requena, "Noticias y Consideraciones Sobre las Anormalidades Sexuales de los Aborígenes Americanos: Sodomía," *Acta Venezolana* 1 (July–September 1945): 16. An English translation of this article, titled "Sodomy among Native American Peoples," appears in *Gay Sunshine* nos. 38–39 (Winter 1979): 37–39.

3. Pedro Faxes, "Supplemento Noticia del Misiones de Monterey y California por Pedro Faxes" (1775), papers of Pedro Fages, second military governor of California, Library of the California Historical Society.

4. Louis Armand de Lom d'Arce de Lahontan, *New Voyages to North America,* ed. Reuben Gold Thwaites (Chicago: McClurg, 1905), vol. 2, p. 462; quoted in Jonathan Katz, *Gay American History* (New York: Thomas Crowell, 1976), p. 611, n. 7.

5. Henri de Tonti, "An Account of Monsieur de La Salle's Last Expedition . . . ," *Collections of the New-York Historical Society,* series 1, vol. 2 (1814): 237–38; quoted in Katz, *Gay American History,* p. 611, n. 7.

6. Zenobius Membré, *Discovery and Exploration of the Mississippi Valley . . . ,* trans. John Shea (Albany, N.Y.: McDonough, 1903), p. 155; quoted in Katz, *Gay American History,* p. 611, n. 7.

7. Pierre Liette, "Memoir of Pierre Liette on the Illinois Country," in *The*

Western Country in the Seventeenth Century, ed. Milo Quaife (New York: Citadel, 1962), pp. 112–13; quoted in Katz, *Gay American History,* p. 228.

8. Pierre François Xavier de Charlevoix, *Journal of a Voyage to North America* (London: Dodsley, 1761), vol. 2, p. 80; quoted in Katz, *Gay American History,* p. 290.

9. Ruth Underhill, *Social Organization of the Papago Indians* (New York: Columbia University Press, 1938), p. 117.

10. Mohave informants, February 1984. NOTE: Because I do not wish to violate the privacy of my informants, when I am speaking of their sexual behavior I do not quote individuals by name, or footnote them, except in some instances when, at their request, I have been using an alias throughout the book.

11. George Devereux, *Mohave Ethnopsychiatry* (Washington, D.C.: Smithsonian Institution, 1969), pp. viii–ix. Originally published as *Bureau of American Ethnology Bulletin 175.*

12. George Devereux, "Institutionalized Homosexuality of the Mohave Indians," *Human Biology* 9 (1937): 518, 498–99.

13. Devereux, *Mohave Ethnopsychiatry,* pp. xii–xiii.

14. Fred Voget, "American Indians," in *The Encyclopedia of Sexual Behavior,* ed. Albert Ellis and Albert Abarbanel (New York: Hawthorn Books, 1961), vol. 1, pp. 99–100.

15. Richard Grant, personal communication, 14 July 1985.

16. Quoted in Guerra, *Pre-Columbian Mind,* pp. 172–3.

17. Beverly Chiñas, "Isthmus Zapotec 'Berdaches,'" *Newsletter of the Anthropological Research Group on Homosexuality* 7 (May 1985): 1–4.

18. Ibid.

19. Navajo informant, January 1985.

20. H. Clay Trumbull, *Friendship the Master Passion* (Philadelphia: Wattles, 1894), pp. 71–72, 165–66.

21. Francis Parkman, *The Oregon Trail* (Madison: University of Wisconsin Press, 1969), pp. 280–83.

22. C. Daryll Forde, "Ethnography of the Yuma Indians," *University of California Publications in American Archaeology and Ethnology* 28 (1931): 157.

23. Devereux, "Institutionalized Homosexuality," pp. 507–8.

24. Victor Tixier, *Tixier's Travels on the Osage Prairies,* ed. John McDermott (Norman: University of Oklahoma Press, 1940), p. 182.

25. Omer Stewart, personal communication, 17 November 1984.

26. John Honigmann, *The Kaska Indians: An Ethnographic Reconstruction,* Yale University Publications in Anthropology 51 (New Haven: Yale University Press, 1954), p. 130; Cornelius Osgood, *Ingalik Social Culture,* Yale University Publications in Anthropology 53 (New Haven: Yale University Press, 1958), pp. 222–23.

27. James Dorsey, "A Study of the Siouan Cults," *Bureau of American Ethnology Annual Report* 11 (1889–90): 467.

28. Edmund White, *States of Desire: Travels in Gay America* (New York: E. P. Dutton, 1980), p. 100.

29. Ruth Landes, *The Mystic Lake Sioux: Sociology of the Mdewakantonwan*

Santee (Madison: University of Wisconsin Press, 1968), pp. 32, 112, 128. David Greenberg develops this line of reasoning in an important essay, "Why Was the Berdache Ridiculed?" *Journal of Homosexuality* 11 (1985): 165–78.

30. Jennie Joe, Navajo informant 1, August 1985.

31. Greenberg, "Why Was the Berdache Ridiculed?"

32. Alice Fletcher, "The Elk Mystery or Festival: Ogallala Sioux," *Reports of the Peabody Museum of American Archaeology and Ethnology* 3 (1887): 281.

33. A. B. Holder, "The Bote: Description of a Peculiar Sexual Perversion Found among North American Indians," *New York Medical Journal* 50 (December 7, 1889): 623–25; quoted in Katz, *Gay American History*, pp. 312–13.

34. Devereux, "Institutionalized Homosexuality," pp. 514–15.

35. Alfred Kroeber, "The Arapaho," *Bulletin of the American Museum of Natural History* 18 (1902–7): 19–20. Krober switched from English to Latin for this description: "Viro connexum petente, consensum praebuit; dorso recumbens et penem ventri deponens, permisit accessum in anum."

36. Devereux, "Institutionalized Homosexuality," pp. 510–11. See also pp. 499 and 514–15 for references to the popularity of anal intercourse.

37. Ibid., p. 511.

38. Clellan Ford, *Smoke From Their Fires: The Life of a Kwakiutl Chief* (New Haven: Yale University Press, 1941), pp. 129–30.

39. Robert Stoller, "Two Feminized Male American Indians," *Archives of Sexual Behavior* 5 (1976): 530–31.

40. Robert Lowie, "Notes on Shoshonean Ethnography," *Anthropological Papers of the American Museum of Natural History* 20 (1924): 282–83.

41. Omer Stewart, "Homosexuality among the American Indians and Other Native Peoples of the World," *Mattachine Review* 6 (February 1960): 13.

42. White, *States of Desire*, pp. 99–100.

43. Ford, *Smoke From Their Fires*, p. 130.

44. Richard Grant, personal communication, 14 July 1985.

45. W. W. Hill, "The Status of the Hermaphrodite and Transvestite in Navaho Culture," *American Anthropologist* 37 (1935): 276, 278.

46. Harald Broch, "A Note on Berdache among the Hare Indians of Northwestern Canada," *Western Canadian Journal of Anthropology* 7 (1977): 97.

47. Ibid., pp. 97–98.

48. Ibid., p. 98.

49. Ibid., p. 99.

50. Ibid., p. 99.

51. Ibid., p. 98.

52. Bob Waltrip, "Elmer Gage: American Indian," *ONE Magazine* 13 (March 1965): 6–10.

53. Erik Erikson, "Childhood and Tradition in Two American Indian Tribes," *Psychoanalytic Study of the Child* 1 (1945): 329–30. Erikson did fieldwork on Lakota reservations with anthropologist H. Scudder Mekeel in the 1930s.

54. Underhill, *Papago Indians*, p. 186.

55. Ibid., p. 117.

56. My thanks to Paul Voorhis and Raymond DeMallie for analyzing this passage. Their conclusions are that the text is neither Sauk and Fox nor Dakota.

57. George Catlin, *Illustrations of the Manners, Customs, and Conditions of the North American Indians, with Letters and Notes,* 10th ed. (London: Henry Bohn, 1866), vol. 2, pp. 214–15; quoted in Katz, *Gay American History,* p. 302.

CHAPTER SIX

1. Cabeza de Vaca quoted in Francisco Guerra, *The Pre-Columbian Mind* (London: Seminar Press, 1971), p. 67.

2. Alanson Skinner, *Notes on the Eastern Cree and Northern Saulteaux* (New York: American Museum of Natural History, 1912), pp. 151–52; Nancy Lurie, "Winnebago Berdache," *American Anthropologist* 55 (1953): 708, 710; Clark Wissler, "Societies and Ceremonial Associations in the Oglala Division of the Teton Dakota," *Anthropological Papers of the American Museum of Natural History* 11, pt. 1 (1916): 92; Lakota informants, July 1982; Leslie Spier, *Yuman Tribes of the Gila River* (Chicago: University of Chicago Press, 1933), p. 242.

3. Ronald Olson, *The Quinault Indians* (Seattle: University of Washington Press, 1936), p. 99.

4. Erminie Voegelin, *Culture Element Distribution: Northeast California* (Berkeley: University of California Press, 1942), vol. 20, pp. 134–35. This was also the pattern among the Pomo; see Edward Gifford and Alfred Kroeber, *Culture Element Distribution: Pomo* (Berkeley: University of California Press, 1937), vol. 4, p. 153.

5. James Dorsey, "A Study of the Siouan Cults," *Bureau of American Ethnology Annual Report* 11 (1889–90): 378–79.

6. Paul-Louis Faye, "Notes on the Southern Maidu," *Publications in American Archaeology and Ethnology* 20 (1923): 45.

7. W. W. Hill, "The Status of the Hermaphrodite and Transvestite in Navaho Culture," *American Anthropologist* 37 (1935): 273–79.

8. Lakota informant 4, July 1982.

9. Edmund White, *States of Desire: Travels in Gay America* (New York: E. P. Dutton, 1980), p. 100.

10. Ralph Linton, *The Study of Man* (New York: Appleton-Century, 1936), p. 480.

11. George Devereux, "Institutionalized Homosexuality of the Mohave Indians," *Human Biology* 9 (1937): 518.

12. Alfred Bowers, "Hidatsa Social and Ceremonial Organization," *Bureau of American Ethnology Bulletin* 194 (1965): 167.

13. Gerónimo Boscana, "Indians at the Missionary Establishment of St. Juan Capistrano, Alta California" (1814–26), in *Chinigchinich . . . Boscana's Historical Account* (Santa Ana, Calif.: Fine Arts, 1933), pp. 54, 170–71; quoted in Jonathan Katz, *Gay American History* (New York: Thomas Crowell, 1976), p. 614.

14. Matilda Coxe Stevenson, "The Zuni Indians," *Bureau of American Ethnology Annual Report* 23 (1901–2): 38.

15. George Devereux, *Mohave Ethnopsychiatry* (Washington, D.C.: Smithsonian Institution, 1969), pp. 84, 101.

16. Devereux, "Institutionalized Homosexuality," p. 513.

17. Ibid., pp. 514, 518.

18. Ralph Beals, "Ethnology of the Nisenan," *University of California Publications in American Archaeology and Ethnology* 31 (1933): 376.

19. This is true for other tribes, but see as examples, for the Mohave, Devereux, "Institutionalized Homosexuality," pp. 500–501; and C. Daryll Forde, "Ethnography of the Yuma Indians," *University of California Publications in American Archaeology and Ethnology* 28 (1931): 157.

20. Leslie Spier, *Klamath Ethnography* (Berkeley: University of California Press, 1930), p. 52.

21. Devereux, "Institutionalized Homosexuality," pp. 514, 521.

22. Ibid., p. 514.

23. Bowers, "Hidatsa Organization," p. 167.

24. Beverly Chiñas, "Isthmus Zapotec 'Berdaches,'" *Newsletter of the Anthropological Research Group on Homosexuality* 7 (May 1985): 2–3.

25. Ibid.

26. Ibid.

27. Charles Callender and Lee Kochems, "The North American Berdache," *Current Anthropology* 24 (1983): 443–56.

28. Clellan Ford, *Smoke From Their Fires: The Life of a Kwakiutl Chief* (New Haven: Yale University Press, 1941), p. 132.

29. Jennie Joe, Navajo informant 1, January 1985.

30. Martha Austin, Najavo informant 3, February 1985.

31. Ruth Underhill, ed., *The Autobiography of a Papago Woman* (Menasha, Wisc.: American Anthropological Association, 1936), p. 43. Underhill repeats this story in her book *Social Organization of the Papago Indians* (New York: Columbia University Press, 1938), p. 187.

32. Ford, *Smoke From Their Fires*, p. 130.

33. Henry Angelino and Charles Shedd, "A Note on Berdache," *American Anthropologist* 57 (1955): 125.

34. James Thayer, "The Berdache of the Northern Plains: A Socioreligious Perspective," *Journal of Anthropological Research* 36 (1980): 288.

35. Harriet Whitehead, "The Bow and the Burden Strap: A New Look at Institutionalized Homosexuality in Native North America," in *Sexual Meanings*, ed. Sherry Ortner and Harriet Whitehead (Cambridge: Cambridge University Press, 1981), pp. 80–115; Callender and Kochems, "North American Berdache." A weakness of the latter essay is that the authors make statements based on both male and female "berdaches," which confuse two traditions that Indians see as separate and distinct.

36. Forde, "Ethnography of the Yuma," p. 157.

CHAPTER SEVEN

1. John Boswell, *Christianity, Social Tolerance, and Homosexuality: Gay People in Western Europe from the Beginning of the Christian Era to the Fourteenth Century* (Chicago: University of Chicago Press, 1980).

2. Francisco Guerra, *The Pre-Columbian Mind* (London: Seminar Press, 1971), p. 221. This book is the best starting point for future research on ber-dachelike traditions in Latin America. The Latin influence has relevance for North America because of the significant Spanish impact on the Indians of California and the Southwest.

3. Guerra, p. 226.

4. Dennis Werner, "A Cross-Cultural Perspective on Theory and Research on Male Homosexuality," *Journal of Homosexuality* 4 (Summer 1979): 358–59.

5. Americo Castro, *The Structure of Spanish History* (Princeton, N.J.: Princeton University Press, 1952), pp. 82–83.

6. Guerra, *Pre-Columbian Mind*, p. 222. This brief suggestion of this thesis on Spanish homphobia deserves much more research, which I hope that historians will undertake.

7. Quoted in Antonio Requena, "Noticias y Consideraciones Sobre las Anormalidades Sexuales de los Aborígenes Americanos: Sodomía," *Acta Venezolana* 1 (July–September 1945): 32. An English translation of this article, titled "Sodomy among Native American Peoples" appears in *Gay Sunshine* nos. 38–39 (Winter 1979): 37–39.

8. Quoted in Requena, "Anormalidades Sexuales," pp. 1–3. A similar statement is quoted from Francisco López de Gomara about the natives of the Mexican port of San Anon.

9. Quoted in Guerra, *Pre-Columbian Mind*, p. 56.

10. Federico Kauffmann Doig, *Sexual Behaviour in Ancient Peru* (Lima: Kompahtos, 1979), pp. 46–51. For examples of surviving homoerotic art, see Guerra, *Pre-Columbian Mind*, plate I.

11. Guerra, *Pre-Columbian Mind*, pp. 123–24.

12. Quoted in Requena, "Anormalidades Sexuales," p. 7.

13. Cieza de León, *Historia del Peru* (1553), quoted in Guerra, *Pre-Columbian Mind*, p. 91.

14. Bernal Díaz del Castillo, *Historia Verdadera de la Nueva España*, vol. 1, p. 202; quoted in Requena, "Anormalidades Sexuales," p. 8.

15. Quoted in Richard Burton, *The Book of the Thousand Nights and a Night* (1886; reprint New York: Heritage Press, 1934), vol. 1, p. 211.

16. Quoted in Guerra, *Pre-Columbian Mind*, p. 190. Even the French complimented this action; see Joseph François Lafitau, *Moeurs des sauvages americquains* (Paris: Saugrain, 1724), vol. 1, p. 52; trans. in Jonathan Katz, *Gay American History* (New York: Thomas Crowell, 1976), pp. 288–89.

17. Quoted in Guerra, *Pre-Columbian Mind*, pp. 59, 61. On the impact of disease, see Alfred Crosby, *The Columbian Exchange: Biological and Cultural Consequences of 1492* (Westport, Conn.: Greenwood Press, 1972), pp. 35–63.

18. Fernandez de Oviedo, Historia Natural de las Indias (1926), vol. 1, pp. 532, 193; quoted in Guerra, *Pre-Columbian Mind*, pp. 55–56.

19. Ibid., pp. 59, 61.

20. Quoted in Lewis Hanke, *The Spanish Struggle for Justice in the Conquest of America* (Boston: Little, Brown, 1965), p. 47. No reader in the 1980s could fail to notice the parallel today, as fundamentalist Christians cite the current Acquired Immune Deficiency Syndrome (AIDS) epidemic as an indication of

God's attack on gay men (they do not explain why lesbians are exempt). The irony of the Spanish attack on Indian sinfulness is that the diseases turned out to have been due to the Spanish themselves.

21. Jerald Milanich and William Sturtevant, eds., *Francisco Pareja's 1613 Confesionario: A Documentary Source for Timucuan Ethnography,* trans. Emilio Moran (Tallahassee: Florida Division of Archives, 1972), pp. 43, 48, 75, 76; quoted in Katz, *Gay American History,* pp. 286–87.

22. Pedro Font, *Font's Complete Diary of the Second Anza Expedition,* trans. Herbert Bolton (Berkeley: University of California Press, 1930), vol. 4, p. 105; quoted in Katz, *Gay American History,* p. 291.

23. Francisco Palou, *Relación histόria de la vida y apostόlicas tareas del venerable Padre Fray Junípero Serra* (Mexico City: Zuñiga y Ontiveros, 1787), p. 222; trans. in Katz, *Gay American History,* p. 292.

24. Gerónimo Boscana, "Indians at the Missionary Establishment of St. Juan Capistrano, Alta California" (1814–26), in *Chinigchinich . . . Boscana's Historical Account* (Santa Ana, Calif.: Fine Arts, 1933); quoted in Katz, *Gay American History,* p. 614.

25. Pedro Cieza de León, quoted in Guerra, *Pre-Columbian Mind,* p. 89.

26. Francisco López de Gomora, quoted in Guerra, *Pre-Columbian Mind,* pp. 85–87.

27. Clark Taylor, "Mexican Gaylife in Historical Perspective," *Gay Sunshine* nos. 26–27 (Winter 1975–76): 1–3.

28. Alfred Metraux, "Boys' Initiation Rites: Religion and Shamanism," vol. 5 of *Handbook of South American Indians, Bureau of American Ethnology Bulletin* 143 (1949): 588–89. See also Alfred Metraux, "Le Samanisme Araucan," *Revista del Instituto de Antropología* 2 (1942): 309–62; and Louis Faron, *Hawks of the Sun: Mapuche Morality and Its Ritual Attributes* (Pittsburgh: University of Pittsburgh Press, 1964).

29. Beverly Chiñas, "Isthmus Zapotec 'Berdaches,'" *Newsletter of the Anthropological Research Group on Homosexuality* 7 (May 1985): 1–4. Other ethnographers among the Zapotecs who have gathered considerable information on *ira' muxe,* but who have not yet published it, are professors Anya Peterson Royce and Della Collins Cook, both of Indiana University.

30. Steve Greene, personal communication, 13 October 1982.

31. See Guerra, *Pre-Columbian Mind,* pp. 76, 172–73.

32. Nancy Farriss, *Maya Society Under Colonial Rule* (Princeton, N.J.: Princeton University Press, 1984), is a valuable ethnohistory of the centuries since the Spanish conquest. Farriss points out that while the conquest transformed the upper echelons of Maya society from a complex social hierarchy to a peasant society, it was less destructive to the folk traditions of the common people than it was in central Mexico.

33. For this and my other interviews in Yucatán during the month of January 1983, I express my appreciation to Raymundo Concha, who served as my traveling companion and interpreter during my fieldwork. His efforts helped to ensure the accuracy of my interviewing.

34. Erskine Lane, "Guatemalan Diary," *Gay Sunshine* nos. 26–27 (Winter 1975–76): 13–15.

35. Ibid.

36. Paul Kutsche, "Situational Homosexuality in Costa Rica," *Anthropological Research Group on Homosexuality Newsletter* 4 (Fall 1983): 8–13.

37. Ibid.

38. Lane, "Guatemalan Diary," p. 13.

39. Ibid. Thorough research on male homosexuality in present-day Mexico has been done by Clark Taylor, "El Ambiente: Mexican Male Homosexual Social Life" (Ph.D. diss., University of California, Berkeley, 1978); David Lennox, "Homosexuality in Mexico: Repression or Liberation?" (unpublished typescript in the International Gay and Lesbian Archives, Hollywood, California, 1976); and Joseph Carrier, "Urban Mexican Male Homosexual Encounters: An Analysis of Participants and Coping Strategies" (Ph.D. diss., University of California, Irvine, 1971). Carrier's most valuable publications on the topic include "Cultural Factors Affecting Urban Mexican Male Homosexual Behavior," *Archives of Sexual Behavior* 5 (1976): 103–24; "Sex-Role Preference as an Explanatory Variable in Homosexual Behavior," *Archives of Sexual Behavior* 6 (1977): 53–65; and "Homosexual Behavior in Cross Cultural Perspective," in *Homosexual Behavior: A Modern Reappraisal,* ed. Judd Marmor (New York: Basic Books, 1980), pp. 109–20.

CHAPTER EIGHT

1. The following discussion on buccaneers depends heavily on ideas developed in B. R. Burg, *Sodomy and the Perception of Evil: English Sea Rovers in the Seventeenth Century Caribbean* (New York: New York University Press, 1983).

2. Ibid., chap. 2; for treatment by the law of same-sex behavior, see B. R. Burg, "Ho Hum, Another Work of the Devil: Buggery and Sodomy in Early Stuart England," *Journal of Homosexuality* 6 (1980): 69–78.

3. Burg, *Sodomy,* chap. 4.

4. Ibid., chap. 2.

5. Ibid., chap. 4. The lack of much specific evidence on the sexual behavior of the pirates is the greatest weakness of Burg's book. However, his piecing together of the typical background of a pirate, and his chain of reasoning showing the persistent lack of association with women in the life of the pirate is convincing. This is not to suggest that males of self-conscious homosexual inclinations as a group decided to go out and become pirates so they could establish a gay paradise. Far from it. It is just that those males with this type of background who were satisfied with it most likely participated in the type of sex that was available and that was familiar to them. Those with strong heterosexual feelings would not have remained in an all-male society.

6. Burg, *Sodomy,* chap. 3.

7. Arthur Gilbert, "Buggery and the British Navy, 1700–1861," *Journal of Social History* 10 (1976): 72–98.

8. Ibid., p. 73.

9. Douglas McMurtie, "Notes on the Psychology of Sex," *American Journal of Urology* 10 (1914): 436. My thanks to James Foshee for referring me to this essay.

10. Josiah Flynt, "Homosexuality Among Tramps," in *Studies in the Psychology of Sex: Sexual Inversion,* ed. Havelock Ellis (New York: F. A. Davis Co., 1902), pp. 220–24; Nels Anderson, *The Hobo* (Chicago: University of Chicago Press, 1923), p. 148.

11. Burg, *Sodomy,* chap. 4. Remarkably similar is a practice in the Chinese province of Fukien, where there is a particular reputation for homosexual behavior among sailors. As with the pirates, they believed women on board their ships to be unlucky. A mature sailor, called a *ch'i hsung,* would establish a relationship with a youth *ch'i ti.* The family of the youth treated the man as if he were a bridegroom. The sexual nature of their relationship is referred to in the word used to describe sexual acts between males, *ch'i.* See Vern Bullough, *Sexual Variance in Society and History* (Chicago: University of Chicago Press, 1976), p. 304.

12. Burg, *Sodomy,* chap. 4.

13. Ibid., chap. 4.

14. April 15, 1871; quoted in Clifford Westermeier, "Cowboy Sexuality: A Historical No-No?" *Red River Valley Historical Review* 2 (1974): 94.

15. Bruce Siberts quoted in Walker Wyman, *Nothing But Prairie and Sky* (Norman: University of Oklahoma Press, 1954), pp. 100–101.

16. Badger Clark, *Sun and Saddle Leather* (Boston: Richard Badger, Gorham Press, 1915, 1919), pp. 67–69.

17. Westermeier, "Cowboy Sexuality," p. 101.

18. Manuel Boyfrank to Roger Austin, 16 December 1974, Manuel Boyfrank Papers, International Gay and Lesbian Archives, Los Angeles.

19. Anon. quoted in Winston Leyland, ed., *Flesh: True Homosexual Experiences* (San Francisco: Gay Sunshine Press, 1982), p. 14.

20. Alfred Kinsey, Wardell Pomeroy, and Clyde Martin, *Sexual Behavior in the Human Male* (Philadelphia: Saunders, 1948), pp. 455–57.

21. Ibid., pp. 630–31.

22. Dorothy Crew, frontier informant, Interior, South Dakota, June 1982.

23. Martin Duberman, "Writhing Bedfellows . . ." *Journal of Homosexuality* 6 (1980): 93.

24. For an argument for evaluating women's relationships, which can also be applied to men, see Blanche Wiesen Cook, "The Historical Denial of Lesbianism," *Radical History Review* 20 (1979): 60–65.

25. Jonathan Katz, *Gay/Lesbian Almanac: A New Documentary* (New York: Harper, 1983), pp. 68–70; Jonathan Katz, *Gay American History* (New York: Thomas Crowell, 1976), pp. 16–19.

26. Katz, *Gay/Lesbian Almanac,* p. 75.

27. *Gay American History,* p. 39.

28. Katz, *Gay/Lesbian Almanac,* p. 237.

29. Frederik Hammerich letters, quoted in ibid., pp. 237–39.

30. Reuben Gold Thwaites, ed., *Original Journals of the Lewis and Clark*

Expeditions (New York: Dodd & Mead, 1904–5), vol. 1, p. 239. Donald Jackson, ed., *Letters of the Lewis and Clark Expedition* (Urbana: University of Illinois Press, 1962), p. 531; quoted in Katz, *Gay American History*, p. 293.

31. Henri de Tonti, "An Account of Monsieur de La Salle's Last Expedition . . . ," *Collections of the New-York Historical Society*, series 1, vol. 2 (1814): 237–38; quoted in Katz, *Gay American History*, p. 611, n. 7.

32. Edwin James, *Account of an Expedition from Pittsburgh to the Rocky Mountains* (Philadelphia: H. C. Carey, 1822–23), vol. 1, pp. 129, 267; quoted in Katz, *Gay American History*, p. 299.

33. Thomas McKenny, *Sketches of a Tour to Lakes, of the Character and Customs of the Chippeway Indians* (Baltimore: Fielding Lucas, 1827), pp. 315–16; quoted in Katz, *Gay American History*, p. 300.

34. Alexander Maximilian, *Travels in the Interior of North America*, ed. Reuben Gold Thwaites (Cleveland: A. H. Clark, 1906), vol. 22, pp. 283–84, 354; quoted in Katz, *Gay American History*, p. 615.

35. George Catlin, *Illustrations of the Manners, Customs, and Conditions of the North American Indians, with Letters and Notes*, 10th ed. (London: Henry Bohn, 1866), vol. 2, pp. 214–15; quoted in Katz, *Gay American History*, p. 302.

36. Anon. [William George Drummond Stewart], *Altowan, or Incidents of Life and Adventure in the Rocky Mountains*, ed. J. Watson Webb (New York: Harper, 1846), vol. 1, pp. 53–55. My thanks to James Foshee for locating this reference.

37. Henry Schoolcraft, *Information Respecting the History, Conditions and Prospects of the Indian Tribes of the United States* (Philadelphia: Lippincott, 1852).

38. Dr. William Hammond, "The Disease of the Scythians (Morbus Feminarum) and Certain Analogous Conditions," *American Journal of Neurology and Psychiatry* 1 (1882): 339–55; quoted in Katz, *Gay American History*, pp. 181–82.

39. Stephen Powers, *Tribes of California*, ed. Robert Heizer (originally published 1877; reprint Berkeley: University of California Press, 1976), p. 132.

40. Peter Grant, "The Sauteux Indians about 1804," in *Les Bourgeois de la Compagnie du Nord-Ouest*, ed. L. R. Masson (Quebec: Imprimarie, 1890), vol. 2, p. 357.

41. John Tanner, *A Narrative of the Captivity and Adventures of John Tanner*, ed. Edwin James (New York: Carvill, 1830), pp. 105–6; quoted in Katz, *Gay American History*, p. 301.

42. Victor Tixier, *Tixier's Travels on the Osage Prairies*, ed. John McDermott (Norman: University of Oklahoma Press, 1940), p. 182.

43. For the development of this idea that U.S. literature has as a major theme the sanctification of male love as the ultimate emotional experience, see Leslie Fiedler's essay "Come Back to the Raft Ag'in Huck Honey," in his *An End to Innocence* (Boston: Beacon Press, 1955), pp. 143–48. That these male marriages were often on the frontier or the sea is a reflection of the all-male fringe societies that existed among sailors and frontiersmen.

44. Certainly we can see these push-pull factors operating in twentieth-century U.S. migration. There is in some respects a re-creation of an all-male fringe community (and a parallel all-female fringe community) in major urban

areas. This type of fringe society, however, has been transformed into a very different thing, due not only to the urban revolution but also to the creation of the new idea of personal identities based on sexual orientation. The sexualization of the United States in the twentieth century has put great pressure on people to decide on an identity as "a heterosexual" or "a homosexual." This is a new social construction, one that violated the earlier taboo on talking about sex, which ironically allowed male-male (and female-female) relationships to exist in a restricted but sheltered manner. The role of these same-sex urban communities in attracting people who desire a certain amount of isolation from general society, and a greater chance for same-sex relationships, should not be ignored. Perhaps there is a relationship between the fact that large urban homosexual communities in the United States emerged only after the end of the frontier era.

45. The process of Indians taking in non-Indians began in the east and moved west as the frontier did. Some of the initial absorbing groups, like the Lumbees of North Carolina, absorbed so many escaping whites and blacks that they became essentially a triracial society. See Adolph Dial and David Eliades, *The Only Land I Know: A History of the Lumbee Indians* (San Francisco: Indian Historian Press, 1975); Walter L. Williams, ed., *Southeastern Indians Since the Removal Era* (Athens: University of Georgia Press, 1979); Irving Hallowell, "American Indians White and Black: Transculturation," *Current Anthropology* 4 (1963): 519–31.

46. Hallowell, "American Indians."

47. Omer Stewart, "Homosexuality among the American Indians and Other Native Peoples of the World," *Mattachine Review* 6 (February 1960): 14. Stewart got this information from anthropologist Frank Essene, who interviewed Pomo Indians for the 1930s Culture Element Survey carried out by the University of California Anthropology Department.

48. Gonzalo Solis de Meras, *Pedro Menendez de Aviles* (1567), trans. Jeannette Conner (Deland, Fla.: Florida State Historical Society, 1923), pp. 180–81; quoted in Katz, *Gay American History,* pp. 15–16.

49. James Adair, *History of the American Indians,* pp. 156–57; quoted in John Swanton, "Social Organization and Social Usages of Indians of the Creek Confederacy," *Bureau of American Ethnology Annual Report* 42 (1928): 364.

50. Andy Adams, *Log of a Cowboy* (1903; reprint Boston: Houghton Mifflin Co., 1955), pp. 312–14. My thanks for this reference go to James Foshee.

51. Charles Warren Stoddard, "A South Sea Idyl," *Overland Monthly* 3 (September 1869): 258–64; quoted in Katz, *Gay American History,* p. 501.

52. Charles Warren Stoddard to Walt Whitman, 2 April 1870, in *The Whitman Correspondence,* ed. Edwin H. Miller (New York: New York University Press, 1961), vol. 2, p. 445; quoted in Katz, *Gay American History,* p. 507.

CHAPTER NINE

1. Walter L. Williams, "From Independence to Wardship: The Legal Process of Erosion of American Indian Sovereignty, 1810–1903," *American Indian Culture and Research Journal* 7 (1984): 5–32.

2. Walter L. Williams, "United States Indian Policy and the Debate over Philippine Annexation: Implications for the Origins of American Imperialism," *Journal of American History* 66 (1980): 810–31.

3. George Grinnell, "The Indian on the Reservation," *Atlantic Monthly* 83 (February 1899): 256–60.

4. Martin Duberman, ed., "Documents in Hopi Indian Sexuality," *Radical History Review* 20 (Spring 1979): 105, 124.

5. Theodore Stern, *The Klamath Tribe: A People and Their Reservation* (Seattle: University of Washington Press, 1965), p. 114.

6. Alfred Bowers, "Hidatsa Social and Ceremonial Organization," *Bureau of American Ethnology Bulletin* 194 (1965): 315.

7. A. B. Holder, "The Bote: Description of a Peculiar Sexual Perversion Found among North American Indians," *New York Medical Journal* 50 (December 7, 1889): 623–25; quoted in Katz, *Gay American History*, pp. 312–13.

8. S. C. Simms, "Crow Indian Hermaphrodites," *American Anthropologist* 5 (1903): 581.

9. Robert Lowie, *The Crow Indians* (New York: Farrar and Rinehart, 1935), p. 48.

10. Joe Medicine Crow, Crow informant 2, August 1982.

11. For background on the Crows at this time see Frederick Hoxie, "Building a Future on the Past: Crow Indian Leadership in an Era of Division and Reunion," in *Indian Leadership*, ed. Walter L. Williams (Manhattan, Kans.: Sunflower University Press, 1984), pp. 76–84.

12. Phyllis Rogers, Navajo informant 2, May 1983.

13. Robert Stoller, "Two Feminized Male American Indians," *Archives of Sexual Behavior* 5 (1976): 530; Michael One Feather, Lakota informant 14, April 1985.

14. Clellan Ford, ed., *Smoke From Their Fires: The Life of a Kwakiutl Chief* (New Haven: Yale University Press, 1941), p. 130.

15. Oscar Kock, *Der Indianishe Eros* (Berlin: Verlag Continent, 1925), p. 64.

16. Hubert H. Bancroft, *The Native Races of the Pacific States of North America* (New York: Appleton, 1875), vol. 1, p. 82.

17. Carl Lumholtz, *New Trails in Mexico* (New York: Charles Scribner's Sons, 1912), pp. 252–53.

18. Robert Berkhofer, *Salvation and the Savage: An Analysis of Protestant Missions and American Indian Response, 1787–1862* (Lexington: University of Kentucky Press, 1965); Oliver Elsbree, *The Rise of the Missionary Spirit in America* (Williamsport, Pa.: Williamsport Printing Co., 1928), pp. 150–52; G. G. Brown, "Missionaries and Cultural Diffusion," *American Journal of Sociology* 50 (1944): 214.

19. Joseph François Lafitau, *Moeurs des sauvages americquains* (Paris: Saugrain, 1724), vol. 1, pp. 603–4, 608; trans. in Katz, *Gay American History*, p. 288.

20. Isaac McCoy, *History of Baptist Indian Missions* (Washington, D.C.: William Morrison, 1840), pp. 360–61.

21. John One Grass, Lakota informant 3, July 1982.

22. Calvin Jumping Bull, Lakota informant 1, July 1982.

23. Thomas Yellowtail, Crow informant 4, August 1982.

24. W. W. Hill, "The Status of the Hermaphrodite and Transvestite in Navaho Culture," *American Anthropologist* 37 (1935): 274, 279.

25. Willard W. Hill, *Navaho Humor* (Menasha, Wisc.: Banta, 1943), pp. 12–13.

26. Dorothea Leighton and Clyde Kluckholm, *Children of the People* (Cambridge: Harvard University Press, 1947), p. 78. Harry Hay remembers that Kluckholm knew *nadle* while doing fieldwork in the 1940s (Harry Hay, personal communication, 25 February 1980). It would be interesting for a biographer of Kluckholm to check to see if there are any revealing fieldnotes in the National Anthropological Archives.

27. Hill, "Status," pp. 276–78.

28. Leslie Spier, *Klamath Ethnography* (Berkeley: University of California Press, 1930), pp. 51–52. For a view contradicting Spier, see Edith R. McLeod, "White Cindy: Mystery Figure," *Siskiyou Pioneer and Yearbook* 2 (Spring 1953): 32.

29. Ibid. Omer Stewart also questions this tendency of some anthropologists to accept disapproving statements about berdaches without recognizing the historical influence of Western homophobia. Omer Stewart, "Homosexuality among the American Indians and Other Native Peoples of the World," *Mattachine Review* 6 (February 1960): 14–15.

30. Leslie Spier, *Yuman Tribes of the Gila River* (Chicago: University of Chicago Press, 1933), p. 242.

31. For a particularly biased viewpoint that distorts the ethnographic evidence, see Marvin Opler, "Anthropological and Cross-Cultural Aspects of Homosexuality," in *Sexual Inversion,* ed. Judd Marmor (New York: Basic Books, 1965), pp. 108–23. See especially p. 114, where he assumes that because homosexuality is a "deviation" it is thereby necessarily condemned by a society.

32. George Devereux, "Institutionalized Homosexuality of the Mohave Indians," *Human Biology* 9 (1937): 526–27; Lowie, *Crow,* p. 48; Thomas Fitzgerald, "A Critique of Anthropological Research on Homosexuality," *Journal of Homosexuality* 2 (1977): 389. See also Martin Duberman's response, in *Radical History Review* 21 (1980).

33. Matilda Coxe Stevenson, "The Zuni Indians," *Bureau of American Ethnology Annual Report* 23 (1901–2): 38.

34. Elsie Clews Parsons, "The Zuni La' Mana," *American Anthropologist* 18 (October–December 1916): 526.

35. The Acoma man who acted as Hammond's escort, and whom the doctor had treated for illness, did develop enough of a sense of trust with the doctor that he did confide "with perfect equanimity, that he himself, in his younger days, had made use of the *mujerado* of his pueblo in the manner referred to." What is remarkable is that Hammond, even as early as 1851, was able to get no other Indians to talk more specifically about the *mujerado.* See William Hammond, "The Disease of the Scythians (Morbus Feminarum) and Certain Analogous Conditions," *American Journal of Neurology and Psychiatry*

1 (1882): 330-55; quoted in Katz, *Gay American History,* pp. 181-82.

36. Anna Gayton, *Yokuts and Western Mono Ethnography* (Berkeley: University of California Press, 1948), p. 106. Nancy Lurie, "Winnebago Berdache," *American Anthropologist* 55 (1953): 708-9.

37. Richard Grant, personal communication, 14 July 1985.

38. A. L. Kroeber, "Psychosis or Social Sanction," *Character and Personality.* 8 (1940): 209-10; Paula Gunn Allen, "Lesbians in American Indian Cultures," *Conditions* 7 (1981): 84.

39. Duberman, "Documents in Hopi," pp. 109, 112, 113.

40. Mischa Titiev, *Old Oraibi: A Study of the Hopi Indians of Third Mesa* (1944; reprint New York: Kraus, 1971), p. 205-B; Richard Grant, personal communication, 14 July 1985.

41. Peggy Reeves Sanday, *Female Power and Male Dominance: On the Origins of Sexual Inequality* (Cambridge: Cambridge University Press, 1981).

42. Bowers ("Hidatsa Organization," p. 168) concludes that the disappearance of the berdache tradition resulted primarily from the collapse of the aboriginal ceremonial system, which followed the end of warfare. While it is certainly true that the ancient religion declined, this explanation ignores the primary role of acculturation forced on Indians by whites.

43. Lurie, "Winnebago Berdache," pp. 708, 709.

44. Harry Hay, personal communication, 25 February 1980; James Roland, Cheyenne informant 1, August 1982; Scott Dewey, Arapaho informant 1, August 1982.

45. Lakota Studies Department, "Hanta Yo: Authentic Farce" (Rosebud, S.D.: Sinte Gleska College, 1980), pp. 6, 8. My criticism of the homophobia of this pamphlet is not to be interpreted as a defense of the historical novel *Hanta Yo,* which rightly deserves condemnation for its basic misunderstanding of Lakota culture. However, one of my informants, a Lakota berdache, claims that in the main the novel's portrayal of homosexual behavior was fairly accurate; see Ruth Beebe Hill, *Hanta Yo: An American Saga* (Garden City, N.Y.: Doubleday, 1979), p. 313.

46. This controversy was reported in Harry Hay and John Burnside, "Gay Awareness and the First Americans," *RFD* no. 20 (Summer 1979): 18-19.

47. Maurice Kenny, "Tinselled Bucks: An Historical Study in Indian Homosexuality," *Gay Sunshine* nos. 26-27 (Winter 1975-76): 17.

48. William T. Hagan, *Indian Police and Judges* (New Haven: Yale University Press, 1966), p. 123.

49. William T. Hagan, personal communication, 11 February 1980.

50. Hagan, *Indian Police,* p. 115.

51. Theodore Stern, *The Klamath Tribe: A People and Their Reservation* (Seattle: University of Washington Press, 1965), p. 114; and Hiroto Zakoji, "Klamath Culture Change," (M.A. thesis, University of Oregon, 1953).

52. Terry Calling Eagle, Lakota informant 5, July 1982.

53. These reports are quoted in Havelock Ellis, *Studies in the Psychology of Sex* (New York: Random House, 1910, 1936), vol. 2, pt. 2, pp. 16-17.

54. Stevenson, "Zuni Indians," pp. 310, 380; Triloki Pandey, "Anthropologists at Zuni," *Proceedings of the American Philosophical Society* 116 (1972): 327.

55. Triloki Pandey, personal communication, 1 June 1983.

56. Wes Fortney, Cheyenne informant 2, August 1982.

57. Terry Calling Eagle, Lakota informant 5, July 1982.

58. Berard Haile, "Navaho Games of Chance and Taboo," *Primitive Man* 6 (1933): 39; Gladys Reichard, *Navaho Religion* (New York: Bollingen Foundation, 1950), pp. 140–41.

59. Harry Hay, personal communication, 25 February 1980.

60. Gene Weltfish, *The Lost Universe* (New York: Basic Books, 1965), p. 29.

61. Ronnie Loud Hawk, Lakota informant 4, July 1982.

62. Harriet Duncan Munnick, *Catholic Church Records of the Pacific Northwest: Vancouver and Stellamaris Mission,* trans. Mikell Warner (St. Paul, Ore.: French Prairie Press, 1972), pp. 83–84. I would like to thank Indiana Matters of the British Columbia Provincial Archives for this source.

63. Harry Hay, personal communication, 13 February 1980.

64. Interview with a Pueblo Indian, in Edmund White, *States of Desire: Travels in Gay America* (New York: E. P. Dutton, 1980), pp. 99–101.

65. Crow informant 3, August 1982.

66. Elsie Clews Parsons, "The Zuni La' Mana," *American Anthropologist* 18 (1916): 523.

67. John Fire and Richard Erdoes, *Lame Deer, Seeker of Visions* (New York: Simon and Schuster, 1972), p. 149.

68. Donald Forgey, "The Institution of Berdache among the North American Plains Indians," *Journal of Sex Research* 11 (February 1975): 6–7.

69. Elva One Feather, Lakota informant 8, July 1982.

70. Ruth Underhill, *Social Organization of the Papago Indians* (New York: Columbia University Press, 1938), p. 186.

71. Walter Williams, ed., *Southeastern Indians Since the Removal Era* (Athens: University of Georgia Press, 1979).

72. Gladys Reichard, *Social Life of the Navajo Indians* (New York: Columbia University Press, 1928), p. 150.

73. Interview by Maurice Kenny, "Tinselled Bucks: An Historical Study in Indian Homosexuality," *Gay Sunshine* nos. 26–27 (Winter 1975–76): 17.

74. Harry Hay, personal communication, 25 February 1980.

75. Jennie Joe, Navajo informant 1, October 1982.

CHAPTER TEN

1. Edward Westermarck, *The Origin and Development of Moral Ideas* (London: Macmillian, 1908, 1926); see also Westermarck's *Memories of My Life* (New York: Macaulay Co., 1929). There is an oral tradition within anthropology that Westermarck was actively homosexual, and enjoyed relationships with his male informants in North Africa where he did fieldwork; Omer Stewart, personal communication, 17 November 1984.

2. Ferdinand Karsch-Haack, *Das Gleichgeschlechtliche Leben der Naturvolker* (Munich: Reinhardt, 1911; reprinted New York: Arno Press, 1975).

3. James Steakley, *The Homosexual Emancipation Movement in Germany*

(New York: Arno Press, 1975); Magnus Hirschfeld, *Die Homosexualität des Mannes und des Weibes* (Berlin: Louis Marcus, 1914); Magnus Hirschfeld, ed., *Jahrbuch fur sexuelle Zwischenstufen* (1900–1934).

4. Edward Carpenter, *Intermediate Types among Primitive Folk: A Study in Social Evolution* (London: Allen and Unwin, 1914; reprinted New York: Arno Press, 1975). Several of Karl Ulrichs's most important essays have been translated and analyzed by Michael Lombardi, "Karl Heinrich Ulrichs" (Ph.D. diss., ONE Institute of Homophile Studies, Los Angeles, 1984). The best book on the English pioneers is Jeffrey Weeks, *Coming Out: Homosexual Politics in Britain, from the Nineteenth Century to the Present* (London: Quartet Books, 1977).

5. Harry Hay, personal communication, 25 February 1980.

6. Jonathan Katz, *Gay American History* (New York: Thomas Crowell, 1976), pp. 413, 419–20.

7. John D'Emilio, *Sexual Politics, Sexual Communities: The Making of a Homosexual Minority in the United States, 1940–1970* (Chicago: University of Chicago Press, 1982).

8. Jim Kepner, personal communication, 9 May 1983.

9. W. Dorr Legg, "The Berdache and Theories of Sexual Inversion," *One Institute Quarterly of Homophile Studies* 5 (Spring 1959): 59–63.

10. Dorr Legg, personal communication, 12 September 1985; see Katz, *Gay American History*, p. 326, for an assessment of the impact of Clellan Ford and Frank Beach, *Patterns of Sexual Behavior* (New York: Harper, 1951).

11. Donald Cory, ed., *Homosexuality, A Cross-Cultural Approach* (New York: Julian Press, 1956); Dorr Legg, personal communication, 9 May 1983 and 12 September 1985.

12. Stewart's speech was later published as "Homosexuality among the American Indians and Other Native Peoples of the World," *Mattachine Review* 6 (January 1960): 9–15, and (February 1960): 13–19; Henry Hay, "The Hammond Report," *One Institute Quarterly of Homophile Studies* 6 (Winter-Spring 1963): 1–21, 65–67; Bob Waltrip, "Elmer Gage: American Indian," *ONE Magazine* no. 13 (March 1965): 6–10.

13. Harry Hay, personal communication, 12 September 1985; Sue-Ellen Jacobs, personal communication, 1 June 1984.

14. Katz, *Gay American History*, p. 284.

15. Maurice Kenny, "Tinselled Bucks: An Historical Study in Indian Homosexuality," *Gay Sunshine* nos. 26–27 (Winter 1975–76): 16–17; Dean Gengle, "Reclaiming the Old New World: Gay Was Good with Native Americans," *The Advocate*, 28 January 1976, pp. 40–41; Arthur Evans, *Witchcraft and the Gay Counterculture* (Boston: Fag Rag Books, 1978); Mitch Walker, *Visionary Love* (San Francisco: Treeroots Press, 1980).

16. Charles Allegre, "Le Berdache, est-il un modele pour nous?" *Le Berdache* 1 (June 1979): 21–24; J. Michael Clark, "The Native American Berdache: A Resource for Gay Spirituality," *RFD* no. 40 (Fall 1984): 22, 28.

17. Judy Grahn, personal communication, 15 May 1983; Judy Grahn, *Another Mother Tongue: Gay Words, Gay Worlds* (Boston: Beacon Press, 1984).

18. Will Roscoe, *Making History: The Challenge of Gay Studies* (San Francisco, 1984), p. 48.

19. Will Roscoe, "Gay American Indians: Creating an Identity from Past Traditions," *The Advocate* 29 October 1985, p. 48.

20. Kevin Prather, personal communication, 1 September 1985.

21. Paula Gunn Allen, personal communication, 3 June 1983.

22. Harry Hay, personal communication, 25 February 1980.

23. Harry Hay, personal communication, 13 February 1980.

24. Ronnie Loud Hawk, Lakota informant 4, July 1982.

25. Gengle, "Reclaiming."

26. Ibid.; Randy Burns, personal communication, 24 October 1980; Roscoe, "Gay American Indians," p. 46.

27. Randy Burns, personal communication, 24 October 1980. A photograph of Burns, and another of Erna Pahe, current president of GAI, appear in Stephen Stewart, *Positive Image: A Portrait of Gay America* (New York: William Morrow, 1985), pp. 143, 150–51.

28. Randy Burns, personal communication, 24 October 1980; Roscoe, "Gay American Indians," p. 45; Will Roscoe, ed., *A Bibliography and Index of Berdache and Gay Roles among North American Indians* (San Francisco: Gay American Indians, 1985). The current GAI address is 1347 Divisadero Street, no. 312, San Francisco Calif. 94115.

29. Michael One Feather, Lakota informant 14, April 1985.

30. Lakota informant 2, July 1982.

31. Gaston, "Lettre ouverte au Berdache," *Le Berdache* 1 (June 1979): 20.

32. Vincent White Cloud, Lakota informant 2, July 1982.

33. Calvin Jumping Bull, Lakota informant 1, July 1982.

34. Twila Giegle Dillon, Lakota informant 6, July 1982.

35. Terry Calling Eagle, Lakota informant 5, July 1982.

36. Ibid.

37. Though Oklahoma Kiowas have a publicly expressed negative attitude toward homosexuality, gay identity is fairly common among the Kiowas and their families tend to feel positively toward them. Tony Brown, Oklahoma Creek-Cherokee informant, May 1983.

38. Hupa informant, September 1985.

39. Ruth Landes, *The Prairie Potawatomi* (Madison: University of Wisconsin Press, 1970), pp. 196–97, 316.

40. Ibid., pp. 26, 190–91, 195–97.

41. Ibid., pp. 196, 198–99, 201.

42. Martin Duberman, "1965 Native American Transvestism," *New York Native,* 21 June–4 July 1982, p. 46.

43. Robert Stoller, "Two Feminized Male American Indians," *Archives of Sexual Behavior* 5 (1976): 531–32, 536.

44. Jerry Running Elk, Lakota informant 9, July 1982.

45. Margaret Mead, "Cultural Determinants of Sexual Behavior," in *Sex and Internal Secretions,* ed. William Young (Baltimore: Williams and Wilkins,

3rd ed., 1961), p. 1452. My thanks to James Weinrich for reminding me of this quote.

46. Anon. Hupa informant, September 1985.

47. Calvin Fast Wolf, Lakota informant 13, June 1982.

48. Jim Young, Lakota informant 15, February 1980.

49. Joe Little Coyote, Cheyenne informant 3, August 1985.

50. Robert Black, Omaha informant 4, June 1982.

51. Calvin Fast Wolf, Lakota informant 13, June 1982.

52. Joe Medicine Crow, Crow informant 2, August 1982.

53. Gary Johnson and Thomas Yellowtail, Crow informants 1 and 4, August 1982.

54. "Penthouse Interview: Russell Means," *Penthouse Magazine,* April 1981, p. 138.

55. Gary Johnson, Crow informant 1, August 1982.

56. Ronnie Loud Hawk, Lakota informant 4, July 1982.

57. Phyllis Rogers, Navajo informant 2, May 1983.

58. Cliff Powell, Choctaw informant 1, May 1983.

59. Michael One Feather, Lakota informant 14, April 1985.

60. Roscoe, "Gay," pp. 45, 48.

61. Micmac informant, September 1985.

62. Quoted in Roscoe, "Gay," p. 48.

63. Paula Gunn Allen, personal communication, 3 June 1983.

64. "Winkte," in Maurice Kenny, *Only As Far As Brooklyn* (Boston: Good Gay Poets, 1979), pp. 10–11.

65. Quoted in Rosa von Praunheim, *Army of Lovers* (London: Gay Men's Press, 1980), p. 148.

66. Waltrip, "Elmer Gage," p. 10; quoted in Katz, *Gay American History,* p. 332.

CHAPTER ELEVEN

1. Pedro de Magalhães de Gandavo, "History of the Province of Santa Cruz," ed. John Stetson, *Documents and Narratives Concerning the Discovery and Conquest of Latin America: The Histories of Brazil* 2 (1922): 89.

2. Evelyn Blackwood, "Sexuality and Gender in Certain Native American Tribes: The Case of Cross-Gender Females," *Signs: Journal of Women in Culture and Society* 10 (1984): 27–42. These tribes are listed on p. 29: California (Achomawi, Atsugewi, Klamath, Shasta, Wintu, Wiyot, Yokuts, Yuki), Southwest (Apache, Cocopa, Maricopa, Mohave, Navajo, Papago, Pima, Yuma), Northwest (Bella Coola, Haisla, Kutenai, Lillooet, Nootka, Okanagon, Queets, Quinault), Great Basin (Shoshoni, Ute, Southern Ute, Southern and Northern Paiute), Subarctic (Ingalik, Kaska), and northern Plains (Blackfoot, Crow).

3. Alice Joseph, et al., *The Desert People* (Chicago: University of Chicago Press, 1949), p. 227.

4. C. Daryll Forde, "Ethnography of the Yuma Indians," *University of*

California Publications in American Archeology and Ethnology 28 (1931): 157; Leslie Spier, *Yuman Tribes of the Gila River* (Chicago: University of Chicago Press, 1933), p. 243.

5. Forde, "Ethnography of the Yuma," p. 157. E. W. Gifford, "The Cocopa," *University of California Publications in American Archeology and Ethnology* 31 (1933): 294.

6. John J. Honigmann, *The Kaska Indians: An Ethnographic Reconstruction* (New Haven: Yale University Press, 1964), pp. 129–30.

7. Cornelius Osgood, *Ingalik Social Culture* (New Haven: Yale University Press, 1958); commented on in Blackwood, "Sexuality and Gender," p. 32.

8. K. J. Crowe, *A History of the Original Peoples of Northern Canada* (Montreal: McGill-Queen's University Press, 1974), pp. 77–78, 90.

9. Honigmann, *Kaska*, pp. 129–30.

10. Claude Schaeffer, "The Kutenai Female Berdache: Courier, Guide, Prophetess, and Warrior," *Ethnohistory* 12 (1965): 195–216.

11. Quoted in ibid.

12. Alexander Ross, *Adventures of the First Settlers on the Oregon or Columbia River* (London: Smith and Elder, 1849), pp. 85, 144–49; quoted in Schaeffer, "Kutenai Female."

13. John Franklin, *Narrative of a Journey to the Shores of the Polar Seas* (London: J. Murray, 1823), p. 152; quoted in Schaeffer, "Kutenai Female."

14. T. C. Elliott, ed. "John Work's Journal," *Washington Historical Quarterly* 5 (1914): 190; quoted in Schaeffer, "Kutenai Female."

15. Quoted in Schaeffer, "Kutenai Female," pp. 215–16.

16. George Devereux, "Institutionalized Homosexuality of the Mohave Indians," *Human Biology* 9 (1937): 503. George Devereux, *Mohave Ethnopsychiatry* (Washington, D.C.: Smithsonian Institution, 1969), p. 262.

17. Devereux, *Mohave Ethnopsychiatry*, pp. 416–17.

18. Ibid., p. 262.

19. Ibid., pp. 416–420.

20. E. W. Gifford, "The Cocopa," *University of California Publications in American Archeology and Ethnology* 31 (1933): 257–94.

21. Leslie Spier, *Klamath Ethnography* (Berkeley: University of California Press, 1930), p. 53.

22. Erminie Voegelin, *Culture Element Distribution: Northeast California* (Berkeley: University of California Press, 1942), vol. 20, pp. 134–35.

23. Charles Callender and Lee Kochems, "Men and Not-Men: Male Gender-Mixing Statuses and Homosexuality," *Journal of Homosexuality* 11 (1985); and by the same authors, "The North American Berdache," *Current Anthropology* 24 (1983): 443–56. See also Harriet Whitehead, "The Bow and the Burden Strap: A New Look at Institutionalized Homosexuality in Native North America" in *Sexual Meanings,* ed. Sherry Ortner and Harriet Whitehead (Cambridge: Cambridge University Press, 1981), pp. 80–115. The beginnings of a sophisticated approach, recognizing cultural variation in the number and statuses of genders, are suggested in M. Kay Martin and Barbara Voorhies, *Female of the Species* (New York: Columbia University Press, 1975), chap. 4.

24. Beatrice Medicine, "'Warrior Women'—Sex Role Alternatives for Plains Indian Women," in *The Hidden Half: Studies of Plains Indian Women,* ed. Patricia Albers and Beatrice Medicine (Washington, D.C.: University Press of America, 1983), p. 269. Though Medicine criticizes Sue-Ellen Jacobs for suggesting that Plains Warrior Women were parallel to berdachism, Jacobs has clarified that "they should not be confused with transsexuals, third gender people, homosexuals or others." Sue-Ellen Jacobs, personal communication, 17 May 1983. See also Whitehead, "Bow and Burden Strap," pp. 86, 90–93; Donald Forgey, "The Institution of Berdache among the North American Plains Indians," *Journal of Sex Research* 11 (1975): 1; and Ruth Landes, *The Mystic Lake Sioux* (Madison: University of Wisconsin Press, 1968).

25. Ibid., pp. 92–93; Oscar Lewis, "The Manly-Hearted Women among the Northern Piegan," *American Anthropologist* 43 (1941): 173–87.

26. John Fire and Richard Erdoes, *Lame Deer, Seeker of Visions* (New York: Simon and Schuster, 1972), pp. 148–49.

27. Paula Gunn Allen, "Lesbians in American Indian Cultures," *Conditions* 7 (1981): 76.

28. Blackwood, "Sexuality and Gender," p. 39; Jeannette Mirsky, "The Dakota," in *Cooperation and Competition among Primitive Peoples,* ed. Margaret Mead (Boston: Beacon Press, 1961), p. 417.

29. The best recent works on the position of Plains women are the essays in Albers and Medicine, *Hidden Half.*

30. Edwin Thompson Denig, *Five Indian Tribes of the Upper Missouri,* ed. John Ewers (Norman: University of Oklahoma Press, 1961), pp. 195–200.

31. Ibid.

32. Ibid.

33. Ibid.

34. Ibid.

35. Allen, "Lesbians," pp. 68, 78–79.

36. Blackwood, "Sexuality and Gender," pp. 35–36.

37. Allen, "Lesbians," pp. 65–66, 73.

38. Ibid.

39. Blackwood, "Sexuality and Gender," p. 38; Allen, "Lesbians," pp. 79–80; Albers and Medicine, *Hidden Half,* pp. 53–73.

40. Evelyn Blackwood, "Some Comments on the Study of Homosexuality Cross-Culturally," *Anthropological Research Group on Homosexuality Newsletter* 3 (Fall 1981): 8–9. Important source material on female homosexual behavior is in the classic study by Ferdinand Karsch-Haack, *Das Gleichgeschlechtliche Leben der Naturvölker* (The same-sex life of nature peoples) (Munich: Verlag von Ernst Reinhardt, 1911). It and Judy Grahn, *Another Mother Tongue: Gay Words, Gay Worlds* (Boston: Beacon Press, 1984), are the starting points for future cross-cultural research on lesbianism. Just two examples of female-female relationships which bear further investigation include groups of women silk weavers, "spinsters," in China—see Agnes Smedley, *Portraits of Chinese Women in Revolution* (Old Westbury, N.Y.: Feminist Press, 1976)—and female marriages in Africa—see Denise O'Brian, "Female Husbands in

Southern Bantu Societies," in *Sexual Stratification,* ed. Alice Schlegel (New York: Columbia University Press, 1977).

41. Beverly Chiñas, "Isthmus Zapotec 'Berdaches,'" *Newsletter of the Anthropological Research Group on Homosexuality* 7 (May 1985): 3–4.

42. Ibid.

43. Ibid.

44. Blackwood, "Sexuality and Gender," p. 38.

45. Joseph Sandpiper, Micmac informant 1, September 1985.

46. Paula Gunn Allen, personal communication, 6 September 1985.

47. Quoted in Will Roscoe, "Gay American Indians: Creating an Identity from Past Traditions," *The Advocate,* 29 October 1985, pp. 45–48.

CHAPTER TWELVE

1. Evelyn Blackwood has done an excellent survey of the ethnographic literature for women in her thesis "Lesbian Behavior in Cross-Cultural Perspective" (M.A. thesis, San Francisco State University, 1984.). Theoretical perspectives are contained in Suzanne Kessler and Wendy McKenna, *Gender: An Ethnomethodological Approach* (New York: Wiley, 1978), pp. 23–31; and in Evelyn Blackwood, ed., "Anthropology and Homosexual Behavior: Special Issue," *Journal of Homosexuality* 11 (Summer 1985). For males see Dennis Werner, "A Cross-Cultural Perspective on Theory and Research on Male Homosexuality," *Journal of Homosexuality* 4 (Summer 1979): 345–47, 360; J. M. Carrier, "Homosexual Behavior in Cross Cultural Perspective," In *Homosexual Behavior: A Modern Reappraisal,* ed. Judd Marmor (New York: Basic Books, 1978), p. 120; Wainwright Churchill, *Homosexual Behavior Among Males: A Cross-Cultural and Cross-Species Investigation* (New York: Hawthorn Books, 1967); John Kirsch and James Rodman, "The Natural History of Homosexuality," *Yale Scientific* 51 (Winter 1977): 7–13; James Weinrich, "Human Reproductive Strategy," (Ph.D. diss., Harvard University, 1976); Randolph Trumbach, "London's Sodomites," *Journal of Social History* 11 (Fall 1977): 3–5; Vern Bullough, *Sexual Variance in Society and History* (New York: Wiley, 1976); Alfred Kinsey et al., *Sexual Behavior in the Human Male* (Philadelphia: W. B. Saunders Co., 1948), pp. 638–39, 650–51; Robert Padgug, "Sexual Matters: On Conceptualizing Sexuality in History," *Radical History Review* 20 (1979): 10–15.

2. Waldemar Bogoras, *The Chuckchee,* Memoirs of the American Museum of Natural History, vol. 11, pt. 2 (New York, 1907), pp. 449–51.

3. Ibid., pp. 450–51, 453.

4. Ibid., pp. 455, 451.

5. Ibid., pp. 453, 452, 454.

6. Ibid., pp. 456, 457; Iwan Bloch, *Anthropological Studies in the Strange Sexual Practices of All Races,* 1902 trans. (New York: Anthropological Press, 1933), p. 51.

7. Charles Allen Clark, *Religions of Old Korea* (Seoul: Christian Literature Society of Korea, 1961), pp. 182–86. David Eyde gave me a photograph that he took of a Korean male shaman dressed in feminine clothing. Laurel Kendall

of the American Museum of Natural History has done fieldwork with these shamans.

8. Quoted in Ales Hrdlicka, *The Anthropology of Kodiak Island* (New York: AMS Press, 1975), p. 79. See Chapter 3 Note 7 for the continuation of this quote.

9. Georg Langsdorff, *Voyages and Travels in Various Parts of the World during the Years 1803–1807* (Carlisle, Pa.: George Philips, 1817), pp. 345, 64; Martin Sauer, *An Account of a Geographical and Astronomical Expedition to the Northern Parts of Russia . . . 1785–1794* (London, 1802), pp. 160, 176; Hubert Bancroft, "The Koniagas," in *The Native Races of the Pacific States of North America* (New York: Appleton, 1875), vol. 1, p. 82.

10. George Mortimer, *Observations and Remarks Made During a Voyage* (London, 1791), p. 47; James Wilson, *A Missionary Voyage to the Southern Pacific Ocean, 1796–8* (London, 1799), p. 200; both as quoted in Bengt Danielsson, *Love in the South Seas,* (New York: Reynal, 1956), pp. 148–52.

11. Quoted in Robert Levy, *Tahitians: Mind and Experience in the Society Islands* (Chicago: University of Chicago Press, 1973), pp. 130–31.

12. Danielsson, *Love,* pp. 147–53; Craighill Handy, *The Native Culture of the Marquesas* (Honolulu: University of Hawaii, 1923), p. 103; Levy, *Tahitians,* pp. 130–40; Trumbach, "London's Sodomites," pp. 6–7. Extensive early references to homosexuality in Polynesia, especially Tahiti and the Marquesas Islands, regarding both *mahus* and masculine men, as well as women, are contained in Ferdinand Karsch-Haack, *Das Gleichgeschlechtliche Leben der Naturvolker* (Munich: Verlag von Ernst Reinhardt, 1911; reprint New York: Arno Press, 1975). See also Charles Warren Stoddard's experiences in Hawaii, as reported in the last part of Chapter 8. My experience in the Philippines, in November 1983, with males who openly desired sexual relations but who had no identity as "homosexual" or even "bisexual," reinforces the prevalence of this attitude.

13. Levy, *Tahitians,* pp. 134–35.

14. Brad Hammer, personal communication, 15 April 1985.

15. Levy, *Tahitians,* pp. 139, 239.

16. Ibid., p. 139.

17. The acceptance of *mahu* was observed particularly on the Hawaiian island of Molokai, where the traditional attitudes have continued more strongly, by ethnographers Maria Lepowsky, John Acevedo, and Wayne Wooden; personal communications 1985. Alison Laurie, "Homosexuality among the Maori of New Zealand," paper presented at the Sex and the State Conference, Toronto, July 1985.

18. A brief report of an interview in Hawaii is in Walter Williams, "Sex and Shamanism: The Making of a Hawaiian Mahu," *The Advocate,* 2 April 1985, pp. 48–49.

19. Ibid.

20. Bullough, *Sexual Variance,* pp. 248, 257–58, 261–63; Leonard Zwilling (University of Wisconsin), "Homosexuality as Seen in Indian Buddhist Texts," paper presented at the Gay Academic Union Conference, Northwestern University, Evanston, Ill., October 10, 1983.

21. Serena Nanda, "The Hijras of India: A Transvestite/Transsexual Community," *Anthropological Research Group on Homosexuality* 4 (Fall 1983): 6–8; interview with Triloki Pandey (University of California, Santa Cruz), 2 June 1983.

22. Richard Herrell (University of Chicago), "Notes on the Hijras of India," unpublished typescript to Walter Williams, 25 August 1982. If my own experience with American Indian berdache is any guide, the only way to accurately discover the sexual feelings of these individuals is to have openly gay researchers live among them. The reluctance of Indians to talk about same-sex desire has too often provided the excuse for nongay researchers to claim that such homosexual aspects should be deemphasized. Serena Nanda has done important field research based on observation and interviews with *hijras* of Bangalore and Bombay. See Serena Nanda, "The Hijras of India: Cultural and Individual Dimensions of an Institutionalized Third Gender Role," *Journal of Homosexuality* 11 (1985): 35–54.

23. Jimmy Pham, personal communication, 26 July 1985; Elliott Heiman and Cao Van Le, "Transsexualism in Vietnam," *Archives of Sexual Behavior* 4 (1975): 89–95.

24. Janet Hoskins, personal communication, 15 September 1985.

25. James Peacock, *Rites of Modernization: Symbolic and Social Aspects of Indonesian Proletarian Drama* (Chicago: University of Chicago Press, 1968), pp. 168, 198, 204–9. See also Peacock's paper in Barbara Babcock, ed., *Reversible World* (Ithaca, N.Y.: Cornell University Press, 1978).

26. An excellent bibliography on these practices is Wayne Dynes, "Homosexuality in Sub-Saharan Africa," *Gay Books Bulletin* 9 (Spring–Summer 1983): 20–21.

27. Unni Wikan, "Man Becomes Woman: Transsexuals in Oman as a Key to Gender Roles," *Man* 13 (1977): 665–67; with several comments on the piece in following issues. See also Unni Wikan, *Behind the Veil in Arabia* (Baltimore: Johns Hopkins University Press, 1982); Edward Westermarck, *The Origin and Development of Moral Ideas* (London: Macmillan, 1908), and Westermarck's autobiography, *Memories of My Life* (New York: Macaulay Co., 1929). Vern Bullough, *Sexual Variance in Society and History*, gathers together a remarkable amount of data for the Middle East, India, and China.

28. Although it is fictional in form, the historical research done by Anne Rice for her book *Cry to Heaven* (New York: Knopf, 1982) is impressive. This is another topic in which future research needs to be done.

29. Trumbach, "London's Sodomites," pp. 1–2; Alan Bray, *Homosexuality in Renaissance England* (London: Gay Men's Press, 1982).

30. Gilbert Herdt, ed., *Ritualized Homosexuality in Melanesia* (Berkeley: University of California Press, 1984); Ray Kelly, *Etero Social Structure* (Ann Arbor: University of Michigan Press, 1977); Ray Kelly, "Etero Social Structure: A Study in Structural Contradiction" (Ph.D. diss., University of Michigan, 1974); Werner, "Cross-Cultural Perspective," p. 358; Carrier, "Homosexual Behavior," pp. 112–114; Gilbert Herdt, *Guardians of the Flutes* (New York: McGraw-Hill, 1981); F. E. Williams, *Papuans of the Trans-Fly* (Oxford:

Oxford University Press, 1936); J. van Raal, *Dema* (The Hague: Martinus Nijhoff, 1966); John Layard, *Stone Men of Malekula* (London: Chatto and Windus, 1942); Gunnar Landtman, *The Kiwai Papuans of British New Guinea* (London: Macmillan, 1927); Trumbach, "London's Sodomites," p. 5; William Davenport, "Sexual Patterns and Their Regulation in a Society of the Southwest Pacific," in *Sex and Behavior,* ed. Frank Beach (New York: John Wiley, 1965).

31. See the works listed in n. 30.

32. Trumbach, "London's Sodomites," pp. 5-7; John Layard, "Homoeroticism in Primitive Society as a Function of the Self," *Journal of Analytical Psychology* 4 (1959): 106; A. G. R. Ravenscroft, "Some Habits and Customs of the Chingalee Tribe, Northern Territory, S. A." *Transactions of the Royal Society of South Australia* 15 (1892): 121-22; Edward Hardman, "Notes on Some Habits and Customs of the Nations of Kimberly District, Western Australia," *Proceedings of the Royal Irish Academy* 7 (1889-1891): 73-74; E. E. Evans-Pritchard, "Sexual Inversion among the Azande," *American Anthropologist* 72 (1970): 1428-34.

33. Evans-Pritchard, "Sexual Inversion," pp. 1428-34; Carrier, "Homosexual Behavior," pp. 102, 116-17; A. E. Ashworth and W. M. Walker, "Social Structure and Homosexuality," *British Journal of Sociology* 23 (June 1972): 155-56.

34. Maggie Childs, "Japan's Homosexual Heritage," *Gai Saber* 1 (Spring 1977): 41-45.

35. Ibid.; Bullough, *Sexual Variance,* pp. 300-06; Trumbach, "London's Sodomites," pp. 5-6. In Japan in particular, it is easy to see the relationship between a culture's tolerance for homosexuality and its attitudes toward population growth. The pre-1865 Tokugawa period was a time of stable population, in which the limits of comfortable physical subsistence and ecological balance had been reached. Overpopulation had to be kept down by abortion and infanticide. In such an ecological state, it is not surprising that homosexuality would be tolerated. Taboos against nonreproductive forms of sex seem to be stronger in societies that try to maximize their population growth (for example, the ancient Hebrews, America before 1960, or Stalinist Russia). With this in mind it is not surprising that Japanese society responded to Western pressures for condemning homosexuality and abortion only after the 1860s, when new economic opportunities produced a need for increased population growth. Werner ("Cross Cultural Perspective," pp. 358-59) uses a survey of societies in the Human Relations Area Files to note the close relationship between pro–population growth and antihomosexual attitudes. He notes as an example the dramatic turnabout of government policy in the Soviet Union. In 1917 the Bolsheviks, who were not concerned about population growth, abolished both antiabortion laws and antisodomy laws. But by the 1930s Joseph Stalin's regime emphasized population growth, and reinstated antiabortion laws at the same time as it carried out mass arrests of homosexuals. Such a hypothesis would explain why America, from the colonial period to the twentieth century, with its strong emphasis on population increase, would also be antihomosexual. When birth control, abortion, and

nonreproductive sex became more accepted after 1960, this was accompanied by a greater toleration for gay people.

36. Bullough, *Sexual Variance,* pp. 205, 221–44; Trumbach, "London's Sodomites," pp. 6, 9; Westermarck, *Origin and Development,* chap. 43; Westermarck, *Memories;* Walter Cline, *Notes on the People of Siwah* (Menasha, Wisc.: American Anthropological Association, 1936), pp. 17–19.

37. Donald Little, *An Introduction to Mamluk Historiography* (Montreal: McGill-Queen's University Press, 1970); Allen Edwardes, *The Jewel in the Locus: A Historical Survey of the Sexual Culture of the East* (New York: Julian Press, 1959), pp. 200–215; Paul Hardman, "Homoaffectionalism: The Civilizing Factor" (Ph.D. diss., ONE Institute, Los Angeles, 1986), chap. 8.

38. Gustave Flaubert to Louis Bouilhet, 15 January 1850, translated in Claude Courouve, "The Word 'Bardache,'" *Gay Books Bulletin* 8 (Fall–Winter 1982): 18–19.

39. K. J. Dover, *Greek Homosexuality* (Cambridge: Harvard University Press, 1978); Bullough, *Sexual Variance,* p. 99. Sergent, *Homosexuality in Greek Myth* (Boston: Beacon Press, 1986), covers the parallels with Melanesia.

40. John Boswell, *Christianity, Social Tolerance, and Homosexuality* (Chicago: University of Chicago Press, 1980); Bullough, *Sexual Variance.*

41. Stephen Murray, *Social Theory, Homosexual Realities* (New York: Gay Academic Union, 1984), pp. 51–53. This is an important theoretical work which, while brief, suggests many new directions for research.

42. James Steakley, *The Homosexual Emancipation Movement in Germany* (New York: Arno Press, 1975).

43. The outline of recent gay history is traced in John D'Emilio, *Sexual Politics, Sexual Communities: The Making of a Homosexual Minority in the United States, 1940–1970* (Chicago: University of Chicago Press, 1982).

44. Trumbach, "London's Sodomites"; Bray, *Homosexuality in Renaissance England;* Jonathan Katz, *Gay American History* (New York: Thomas Crowell, 1976).

45. Michel Foucault, *The History of Sexuality* (London: Allen Lane, 1979); Weeks, *Coming Out;* Jonathan Katz, *Gay/Lesbian Almanac* (New York: Harper and Row, 1983).

46. My ideas in this section have been shaped by discussions with Larry Gross, Wayne Dynes, Gert Hekma, Rick Bébout, Gregory Sprague, George Chauncey, and Martin Duberman, among others. They are part of a growing number of scholars who see the need to move beyond the essentialist–social constructionist debate. For an attempt to answer his critics, and to move toward a middle ground, see John Boswell, "Towards the Long View: Revolutions, Universals and Sexual Categories," *Salmagundi* No. 58–59 (Fall 1982–Winter 1983): 89–113.

47. Jeffrey Weeks and Kenneth Plummer interview Mary McIntosh, "'The Homosexual Role' Revisited," in *The Making of the Modern Homosexual,* ed. Kenneth Plummer (Totowa, N.J.: Barnes & Noble, 1981), pp. 47–49.

Bibliography

ABBREVIATIONS

BAE   Bureau of American Ethnology (Annual Reports and Bulletins, published by the Smithsonian Institution in Washington, D.C.).

GAH   *Gay American History* (documentary reprint collection; see citation under Jonathan Katz). For the convenience of the reader, rare publications are listed if reprinted.

Ackroyd, Peter. *Dressing Up: Transvestism and Drag: The History of an Obsession.* New York: Simon and Schuster, 1979.

Albers, Patricia, and Beatrice Medicine, editors. *The Hidden Half: Studies of Plains Indian Women.* Washington, D.C.: University Press of America, 1983.

Allegre, Charles. "Le Berdache, est-il un modele pour nous?" *Le Berdache* 1 (June 1979): 21–24.

Allen, Paula Gunn. "Lesbians in American Indian Cultures." *Conditions* 7 (1981): 67–87.

Anderson, Nels. *The Hobo.* Chicago: University of Chicago Press, 1923.

Angelino, Henry, and Charles Shedd. "A Note on Berdache." *American Anthropologist* 57 (1955):121–26.

Ashworth, A. E., and W. M. Walker. "Social Structure and Homosexuality." *British Journal of Sociology* 23 (June 1972): 155–56.

Bancroft, Hubert. *The Native Races of the Pacific States of North America.* New York: Appleton, 1875.

Beals, Ralph. "Ethnology of the Nisenan." *University of California Publications in American Archeology and Ethnology* 31 (1933): 335–76.

Bell, Alan, Martin Weinberg, and Sue Hammersmith. *Sexual Preference: Its Development in Men and Women.* Bloomington: Indiana University Press, 1981.

Benjamin, Harry. *The Transsexual Phenomenon.* New York: Julian Press, 1966.

Berkhofer, Robert. *Salvation and the Savage: An Analysis of Protestant Missions and American Indian Response, 1787–1862.* Lexington: University of Kentucky Press, 1965.

Blackwood, Evelyn. "Breaking the Mirror: The Construction of Lesbianism and the Anthropological Discourse on Homosexuality." *Journal of Homosexuality* 11 (1985): 1–18.

———. "Lesbian Behavior in Cross-Cultural Perspective." M.A. thesis. San Francisco State University, 1984.

———. "Sexuality and Gender in Certain Native American Tribes: The Case of Cross-Gender Females." *Signs: Journal of Women in Culture and Society* 10 (1984): 27–42.

Bleibtreu-Ehrenberg, Gisela. "Homosexualitat und Transvestition im Schamanismus." *Anthropos* 65 (1970): 189–228.

Bloch, Iwan, *Anthropological Studies in the Strange Sexual Practices of All Races.* 1902 translation. New York: Anthropological Press, 1933.

Bogoras, Waldemar. *The Chuckchee.* Memoirs of the American Museum of Natural History, vol. 11, pt. 2. New York, 1907. Pp. 449–51.

Bolin, Anne. "In Search of Eve: Transsexual Rites of Passage," Ph.D. dissertation. University of Colorado, Boulder, 1983.

Boscana, Gerónimo. "Indians at the Missionary Establishment of St. Juan Capistrano, Alta California" (1814–1826). In *Chinigchinich . . . Boscana's Historical Account.* Santa Ana, Calif.: Fine Arts, 1933. Reprinted in *GAH,* p. 614.

Bossu, Jean-Bernard. *Jean-Bernard Bossu's Travels in the Interior of North America, 1751–1762.* Edited by John Feiler. Norman: University of Oklahoma Press, 1962.

Boswell, John. *Christianity, Social Tolerance, and Homosexuality: Gay People in Western Europe from the Beginning of the Christian Era to the Fourteenth Century.* Chicago: University of Chicago Press, 1980.

———. "Towards the Long View: Revolutions, Universals and Sexual Categories." *Salmagundi* nos. 58–59 (Fall 1982–Winter 1983): 89–113.

Bowers, Alfred. "Hidatsa Social and Ceremonial Organization," *BAE Bulletin* 194 (1965): 167–326.

———. *Mandan Social and Ceremonial Organization.* Chicago: University of Chicago Press, 1950.

Bray, Alan. *Homosexuality in Renaissance England.* London: Gay Men's Press, 1982.

Broch, Harald. "A Note on Berdache among the Hare Indians of Northwestern Canada." *Western Canadian Journal of Anthropology* 7 (1977): 95–101.

Brown, G. G. "Missionaries and Cultural Diffusion." *American Journal of Sociology* 50 (1944): 214.

Brown, Judith. "A Note on the Division of Labor by Sex." *American Anthropologist* 72 (1970): 1073–78.

Bullough, Vern. *Sexual Variance in Society and History.* Chicago: University of Chicago Press, 1976.

Burg, B. R. "Ho Hum, Another Work of the Devil: Buggery and Sodomy in Early Stuart England." *Journal of Homosexuality* 6 (1980): 69–78.

———. *Sodomy and the Perception of Evil: English Sea Rovers in the Seventeenth Century Caribbean.* New York: New York University Press, 1983.

Burton, Richard. "Terminal Essay." In *The Book of the Thousand Nights and a Night*. London: The Burton Club, 1886, vol. 10.

Callender, Charles, and Lee Kochems. "Men and Not-Men: Male Gender-Mixing Statuses and Homosexuality." *Journal of Homosexuality* 11 (1986): 165–178.

———. "The North American Berdache." *Current Anthropology* 24 (1983): 443–56. See also comments and reply following, pp. 456–70.

Carpenter, Edward. *Intermediate Types among Primitive Folk: A Study in Social Evolution*. London: Allen and Unwin, 1914. Reprinted New York: Arno Press, 1975.

Carrier, Joseph. "Cultural Factors Affecting Urban Mexican Male Homosexual Behavior." *Archives of Sexual Behavior* 5 (1976): 103–24.

———. "Homosexual Behavior in Cross Cultural Perspective." In *Homosexual Behavior: A Modern Reappraisal*. Edited by Judd Marmor. New York: Basic Books, 1980.

———. "Sex-Role Preference as an Explanatory Variable in Homosexual Behavior." *Archives of Sexual Behavior* 6 (1977): 53–65.

———. "Urban Mexican Male Homosexual Encounters: An Analysis of Participants and Coping Strategies." Ph.D. dissertation, University of California, Irvine, 1971.

Castro, Americo. *The Structure of Spanish History*. Princeton, N.J.: Princeton University Press, 1952.

Catlin, George. *Illustrations of the Manners, Customs, and Conditions of the North American Indians, with Letters and Notes*. Tenth edition. London: Henry Bohn, 1866. Vol. 2. Reprinted in *GAH*, p. 302.

Caulfield, Mina Davis. "Equality, Sex and Mode of Production." In *Social Inequality: Comparative and Developmental Approaches*. Edited by Gerald Berreman. New York: Academic Press, 1981. Pp. 201–19.

Charlevoix, Pierre Francois Xavier de. *Journal of a Voyage to North America*. London: Dodsley, 1761. Reprinted in *GAH*, p. 290.

Childs, Maggie. "Japan's Homosexual Heritage." *Gai Saber* 1 (Spring 1977): 41–45.

Chiñas, Beverly, "Isthmus Zapotec 'Berdaches.'" *Newsletter of the Anthropological Research Group on Homosexuality* 7 (May 1985): 1–4.

———. *The Isthmus Zapotecs: Women's Roles in Cultural Context*. New York: Holt, Rinehart and Winston, 1973.

Churchill, Wainwright. *Homosexual Behavior Among Males: A Cross-Cultural and Cross-Species Investigation*. New York: Hawthorn Books, 1967.

Clark, Charles Allen. *Religions of Old Korea*. Seoul: Christian Literature Society of Korea, 1961.

Clark, J. Michael. "The Native American Berdache: A Resource for Gay Spirituality." *RFD* no. 40 (Fall 1984): 22–30.

Cline, Walter. *Notes on the People of Siwah*. Menasha, Wisc.: American Anthropological Association, 1936.

Cook, Blanche Wiesen. "The Historical Denial of Lesbianism." *Radical History Review* 20 (1979): 60–65.

Corlett, William Thomas, M.D. *The Medicine Man of the American Indian and His Cultural Background.* Baltimore: Charles C. Thomas, 1935.

Cory, Donald W. *Homosexuality in a Cross-Cultural Perspective.* New York: Julian, 1956.

Courouve, Claude. "The Word 'Bardache.'" *Gay Books Bulletin* 8 (Fall–Winter 1982): 18–19.

Crosby, Alfred. *The Columbian Exchange: Biological and Cultural Consequences of 1492.* Westport, Conn.: Greenwood Press, 1972.

Cushing, Frank. "Outlines of Zuni Creation Myths." *BAE Annual Report* 13 (1894): 401–13.

Danielsson, Bengt. *Love in the South Seas.* New York: Reynal, 1956.

Davenport, William. "Sexual Patterns and Their Regulation in a Society of the Southwest Pacific." *Sex and Behavior.* Edited by Frank Beach. New York: John Wiley, 1965.

DeCecco, John. "Definition and Meaning of Sexual Orientation." In *Nature and Causes of Homosexuality: A Philosophical and Scientific Inquiry.* Edited by Noretta Koertge. New York: Haworth Press, 1981.

D'Emilio, John. *Sexual Politics, Sexual Communities: The Making of a Homosexual Minority in the United States, 1940–1970.* Chicago: University of Chicago Press, 1982.

Denig, Edwin Thompson. *Five Indian Tribes of the Upper Missouri.* Edited by John Ewers. Norman: University of Oklahoma Press, 1961.

Devereux, George. "Institutionalized Homosexuality of the Mohave Indians." *Human Biology* 9 (1937): 498–527.

———. *Mohave Ethnopsychiatry.* Washington, D.C.: Smithsonian Institution, 1969.

Dial, Adolph, and David Eliades. *The Only Land I Know: A History of the Lumbee Indians.* San Francisco: Indian Historian Press, 1975.

Doig, Federico Kauffmann. *Sexual Behaviour in Ancient Peru.* Lima: Kompah-tos, 1979.

Dorsey, George, and James Murie. *Notes on Skidi Pawnee Society.* Chicago: Field Museum of Natural History, 1940.

Dorsey, James O. "A Study of the Siouan Cults." *BAE Annual Report* 11 (1889–90): 378–467.

Douglas, Mary. *Purity and Danger.* Baltimore: Penguin, 1966.

Dover, K. J. *Greek Homosexuality.* Cambridge: Harvard University Press, 1978.

Driver, Harold. *Indians of North America.* Chicago: University of Chicago Press, 1969.

———. "Culture Element Distributions: Southern Sierra Nevada." *University of California Anthropological Records* 1, pt. 2 (1937): 90–109.

———. "Culture Element Distributions 10: Northwest California." *University of California Anthropological Records* 1, pt. 6 (1939): 347.

Drucker, Philip. "Culture Element Distributions 5: Southern California." *University of California Anthropological Records* 1, pt. 1 (1937): 27–49.

————. "Culture Element Distributions 17: Yuman-Piman." *University of California Anthropological Records* 6, pt. 3 (1941): 90–163.

Duberman, Martin. "Documents in Hopi Indian Sexuality." *Radical History Review* 20 (1979): 99–130.

————. "Hopi Indians Redux." *Radical History Review* 21 (1980): 177–87.

————. "1965 Native American Transvestism." *New York Native*. 21 June 1982, pp. 12, 46.

————. "Writhing Bedfellows . . ." *Journal of Homosexuality* 6 (1980): 85–101.

Dynes, Wayne. "Homosexuality in Sub-Saharan Africa." *Gay Books Bulletin* 9 (Spring–Summer 1983): 20–21.

Edwardes, Allen. *The Jewel in the Locus: A Historical Survey of the Sexual Culture of the East*. New York: Julian Press, 1959.

Eliade, Mircea. *Mephistopheles and the Androgyne: Studies in Religious Myth and Symbol*. Translated by J. J. Cohen. New York: Sheed and Ward, 1965.

Ellis, Havelock. *Studies in the Psychology of Sex*. New York: Random House, 1910, 1936.

Elsbree, Oliver. *The Rise of the Missionary Spirit in America*. Williamsport, Pa.: Williamsport Printing Co., 1928.

Erikson, Erik. "Childhood and Tradition in Two American Indian Tribes." *Psychoanalytic Study of the Child* 1 (1945): 319–50.

Essene, Frank. "Culture Element Distributions 21: Round Valley." *University of California Anthropological Records* 8, pt. 1 (1942): 90–163.

Etienne, Mona, and Eleanor Leacock, editors. *Women and Colonization: Anthropological Perspectives*. New York: Bergin, 1980.

Evans, Arthur. *Witchcraft and the Gay Counterculture*. Boston: Fag Rag Books, 1978.

Evans-Pritchard, E. E. "Sexual Inversion among the Azande." *American Anthropologist* 72 (1970): 1428–34.

Farb, Peter. *Humankind*. Boston: Houghton Mifflin Co., 1978.

Faron, Louis. *Hawks of the Sun: Mapuche Morality and Its Ritual Attributes*. Pittsburgh: University of Pittsburgh Press, 1964.

Faye, Paul-Louis. "Notes on the Southern Maidu." *Publications in American Archaeology and Ethnology* 20 (1923): 45.

Fire, John, and Richard Erdoes. *Lame Deer, Seeker of Visions*. New York: Simon and Schuster, 1972.

Fitzgerald, Thomas. "A Critique of Anthropological Research on Homosexuality." *Journal of Homosexuality* 2 (1977): 285–397.

Fletcher, Alice. "The Elk Mystery or Festival: Ogallala Sioux." *Reports of the Peabody Museum of American Archaeology and Ethnology* 3 (1887): 276–88.

Fletcher, Alice, and Francis La Flesche. "The Omaha Tribe." *BAE Annual Report* 27 (1905–6).

Flynt, Josiah. "Homosexuality Among Tramps." In *Studies in the Psychology of Sex: Sexual Inversion*. Havelock Ellis. New York: Random House, 1910, 1936.

Font, Pedro. *Font's Complete Diary of the Second Anza Expedition*. Translated by Herbert Bolton. Berkeley: University of California Press, 1930. Reprinted in *GAH*, p. 291.

Ford, Clellan. *Smoke From Their Fires: The Life of a Kwakiutl Chief.* New Haven: Yale University Press, 1941.

Ford, Clellan, and Frank Beach. *Patterns of Sexual Behavior.* New York: Harper, 1951.

Forde, C. Daryll. "Ethnography of the Yuma Indians." *University of California Publications in American Archeology and Ethnology* 28 (1931): 83–278.

Forgey, Donald. "The Institution of Berdache among the North American Plains Indians." *Journal of Sex Research* 11 (1975): 1–15.

Foucault, Michel. *The History of Sexuality.* London: Allen Lane, 1979.

Gandavo, Pedro de Magalhães de. "History of the Province of Santa Cruz." Edited by John Stetson. *Documents and Narratives Concerning the Discovery and Conquest of Latin America: The Histories of Brazil* 2 (1922): 89–232.

Gayton, Anna. *Yokuts and Western Mono Ethnography.* Berkeley: University of California Press, 1948.

Gengle, Dean. "Reclaiming the Old New World: Gay Was Good with Native Americans." *The Advocate,* 28 January 1976, pp. 40–41.

Gifford, E. W. "The Cocopa." *University of California Publications in American Archeology and Ethnology* 31 (1933): 257–95.

———. "The Kamia of Imperial Valley," *BAE Bulletin* 97 (1931): 12–81.

———. "Northeastern and Western Yavapai." *University of California Publications in American Archeology and Ethnology* 34 (1936): 296–99.

Gifford, Edward, and Kroeber, Alfred. *Culture Element Distribution, Volume 4: Pomo.* Berkeley: University of California Press, 1937.

Gilbert, Arthur. "Buggery and the British Navy, 1700–1861." *Journal of Social History* 10 (1976): 72–98.

Gould, Richard. "Tolowa." In *Handbook of North American Indians.* Volume 8, *California.* Edited by Robert Heizer. Washington, D.C.: Smithsonian Institution, 1978.

Grahn, Judy. *Another Mother Tongue: Gay Words, Gay Worlds.* Boston: Beacon Press, 1984.

Grant, Peter. "The Sauteux Indians about 1804." In *Les Bourgeois de la Compagnie du Nord-Ouest.* Edited by L. R. Masson. Quebec: Imprimarie, 1890. Vol. 2, pp. 303–366.

Green, Richard. *Sexual Identity Conflict in Children and Adults.* New York: Basic Books, 1974.

———. "Mythological, Historical and Cross-Cultural Aspects of Transsexualism." In *Transsexualism and Sex Reassignment.* Edited by Richard Green and John Money. Baltimore: Johns Hopkins University Press, 1969.

Greenberg, David. "Why Was the Berdache Ridiculed?" *Journal of Homosexuality* 11 (1985): 179–190.

Grinnell, George. *The Cheyenne Indians.* New Haven: Yale University Press, 1923.

———. "The Indian on the Reservation." *Atlantic Monthly* 83 (February 1899): 256–60.

Guerra, Francisco. *The Pre-Columbian Mind*. London: Seminar Press, 1971.

Hagan, William T. *Indian Police and Judges*. New Haven: Yale University Press, 1966.

Haile, Berard. "Navaho Games of Chance and Taboo." *Primitive Man* 6 (1933): 39–45.

———. *Women versus Men: A Conflict of Navajo Emergence*. Lincoln: University of Nebraska Press, 1981.

Hallowell, Irving. "American Indians White and Black: The Phenomenon of Transculturation." *Current Anthropology* 4 (1963): 519–31.

Handy, Craighill. *The Native Culture of the Marquesas*. Honolulu: University of Hawaii, 1923.

Hanke, Lewis. *The Spanish Struggle for Justice in the Conquest of America*. Boston: Little, Brown, 1965.

Hansen, Bert. "Historical Construction of Homosexuality." *Radical History Review* 20 (1979): 66–73.

Hardman, Edward. "Notes on Some Habits and Customs of the Nations of Kimberly District, Western Australia." *Proceedings of the Royal Irish Academy* 7 (1889–91): 73–74.

Hardman, Paul. "Homoaffectionalism: The Civilizing Factor." Ph.D. dissertation. ONE Institute, Los Angeles, 1986.

Harry, Joseph. *Gay Children Grown Up*. New York: Praeger, 1982.

——— and Man Singh Das. *Homosexuality in International Perspective*. New Delhi, Vikas, 1980.

Hart, Donn. "Homosexuality and Transvestism in the Philippines." *Behavioral Science Notes* 3 (1968): 211–48.

Hassrick, Royal B. *The Sioux: Life and Customs of a Warrior Society*. Norman: University of Oklahoma Press, 1964.

Hay, Harry, and John Burnside. "Gay Awareness and the First Americans." *RFD* no. 20 (Summer 1979): 18–19.

Hay, Henry. "The Hammond Report." *ONE Institute Quarterly of Homophile Studies* 6 (1963): 1–21.

Heiman, Elliott, and Cao Van Le. "Transsexualism in Vietnam." *Archives of Sexual Behavior* 4 (1975): 89–95.

Heizer, Robert, ed. *Handbook of North American Indians: California*. Washington, D.C.: Smithsonian Institution, 1978. Volume 8.

Henry, Alexander, and David Thompson. *New Light on the Early History of the Greater Northwest*. Edited by Elliott Coues. New York: Harper, 1897.

Herdt, Gilbert. *Guardians of the Flutes: Idioms of Masculinity*. New York: McGraw-Hill, 1981.

———, editor. *Ritualized Homosexuality in Melanesia*. Berkeley: University of California Press, 1984.

Herrell, Richard. "Notes on the Hijras of India." Unpublished typescript, 25 August 1982.

Hill, Ruth Beebe. *Hanta Yo: An American Saga*. Garden City, N.Y.: Doubleday, 1979.

Hill, Willard W. *Navaho Humor*. Menasha, Wisc.: Banta, 1943.

———. "Note on the Pima Berdache." *American Anthropologist* 40 (1938): 338–40.

———. "The Status of the Hermaphrodite and Transvestite in Navaho Culture." *American Anthropologist* 37 (1935): 273–79.

Hirschfeld, Magnus. *Die Homosexualität des Mannes und des Weibes*. Berlin: Louis Marcus, 1914.

———, editor. *Jahrbuch für sexuelle Zwischenstufen* (1900–1932).

Hoebel, E. Adamson. *The Cheyennes: Indians of the Great Plains*. New York: Holt, Rinehart and Winston, 1978.

Hoffman, W. J. "The Mide'wiwim or Grand Medicine Society of the Ojibwa." *BAE Annual Report* (1891): 153.

Holder, A. B. "The Bote: Description of a Peculiar Sexual Perversion Found among the North American Indians." *New York Medical Journal* 50 (7 December 1889): 623–25. Partly reprinted in *GAH*, pp. 312–13.

Honigmann, John. *The Kaska Indians: An Ethnographic Reconstruction*. Yale University Publications in Anthropology 51. New Haven: Yale University Press, 1954.

Hoxie, Frederick. "Building a Future on the Past: Crow Indian Leadership in an Era of Division and Reunion." In *Indian Leadership*. Edited by Walter L. Williams. Manhattan, Kans.: Sunflower University Press, 1984.

Hrdlicka, Ales. *The Anthropology of Kodiak Island*. New York: AMS Press, 1975.

Ihara, Saikaku. *Comrade Loves of the Samurai*. Tokyo: Tuttle, 1972. Reprint of 1682 edition.

Jackson, Donald, editor. *Letters of the Lewis and Clark Expedition*. Urbana: University of Illinois Press, 1962.

Jacobs, Sue-Ellen, "Berdache: A Brief Review of the Literature." *Colorado Anthropologist* 1 (1968): 25–40.

———. "Comment on 'The North American Berdache.'" *Current Anthropology* 24 (1983): 459–60.

James, Edwin. *Account of an Expedition from Pittsburgh to the Rocky Mountains*. Philadelphia: H. C. Carey, 1822–23. Reprinted in *GAH*, p. 299.

Jones, William. "Fox Texts." *Publications of the American Ethnological Society* 1 (1907): 314–55.

Joseph, Alice, et al. *The Desert People*. Chicago: University of Chicago Press, 1949.

Karlen, Arno. *Sexuality and Homosexuality*. London: MacDonald, 1971.

Karsch-Haack, Ferdinand. *Das Gleichgeschlechtliche Leben der Naturvölker* (The same-sex life of nature peoples). Munich: Verlag von Ernst Reinhardt, 1911. Reprinted New York: Arno Press, 1975.

Katz, Jonathan. *Gay American History*. New York: Thomas Crowell, 1976.

———. *Gay/Lesbian Almanac: A New Documentary*. New York: Harper, 1983.

Kelly, Ray. *Etero Social Structure*. Ann Arbor: University of Michigan Press, 1977.

Kenny, Maurice. *Only As Far As Brooklyn*. Boston: Good Gay Poets, 1979.

———. "Tinselled Bucks: An Historical Study in Indian Homosexuality." *Gay Sunshine* nos. 26–27 (Winter 1975–76): 17.

Kessler, Suzanne, and Wendy McKenna. *Gender: An Ethnomethodological Approach*. New York: Wiley, 1978.

Kinietz, Vernon. *Chippewa Village*. Bloomfield, Mich.: Cranbrook Press, 1947.

Kinsey, Alfred, Wardell Pomeroy, and Clyde Martin. *Sexual Behavior in the Human Male*. Philadelphia: Saunders, 1948.

Kirk, Kris, and Ed Heath. *Men in Frocks*. London: Gay Men's Press, 1985.

Kirsch, John, and James Rodman. "The Natural History of Homosexuality." *Yale Scientific* 51 (Winter 1977): 7–13.

Koch, Oscar. *Der Indianishe Eros*. Berlin: Verlag Continent, 1925.

Kroeber, Alfred. "The Arapaho." *Bulletin of the American Museum of Natural History* 18 (1902–7): 19–20.

———. *Handbook of the Indians of California*. Berkeley: University of California Press, 1953. Originally published as *BAE Bulletin* 78 (1925).

———. "Psychosis or Social Sanction." *Character and Personality* 8 (1940): 204–15.

Kutsche, Paul. "Situational Homosexuality in Costa Rica." *Anthropological Research Group on Homosexuality Newsletter* 4 (Fall 1983): 8–13.

Lac, Perrin du. *Voyage dans les deux Louisianes*. Lyon: Bruyset Aîné et Buyand, 1805. Reprinted in *GAH*, pp. 612–13.

Lacey, E. A. "Latin America." *Gay Sunshine* no. 40 (1979): 22–31.

Lafitau, Joseph François. *Moeurs des sauvages americquains*. Paris: Saugrain, 1724. Vol. 1, p. 52. Translated by Warren Johansson in *GAH*, p. 288.

Lahontan, Louis Armand de Lom d'Arce de. *New Voyages to North America*. Vol. 2. Edited by Reuben Gold Thwaites. Chicago: McClurg, 1905. Reprinted in *GAH*, p. 611, n. 7.

Lakota Studies Department, *Hanta Yo: Authentic Farce*. Rosebud, S.D.: Sinte Gleska College, 1980.

Landes, Ruth. "The Abnormal among the Ojibwa Indians." *Journal of Abnormal and Social Psychology* 33 (1953): 14–33.

———. "A Cult Matriarchate and Male Homosexuality." *Journal of Abnormal and Social Psychology* 35 (1940): 386–97.

———. *The Mystic Lake Sioux: Sociology of the Mdewakantonwan Santee*. Madison: University of Wisconsin Press, 1968.

———. *The Prairie Potawatomi*. Madison: University of Wisconsin Press, 1970.

Landtman, Gunnar. *The Kiwai Papuans of British New Guinea*. London: Macmillan, 1927.

Lane, Erskine. "Guatemalan Diary." *Gay Sunshine* nos. 26–27 (Winter 1975–76): 13–15.

Langsdorff, Georg. *Voyages and Travels in Various Parts of the World during the Years 1803–1807*. Carlisle, Pa.: George Philips, 1817.

Layard, John. "Homoeroticism in Primitive Society as a Function of the Self." *Journal of Analytical Psychology* 4 (1959): 106.

———. *Stone Men of Malekula*. London: Chatto and Windus, 1942.

Leacock, Eleanor. *Myths of Male Dominance: Collected Articles on Women Cross-Culturally*. New York: Monthly Review Press, 1981.

Legg, W. Dorr. "The Berdache and Theories of Sexual Inversion." *One Institute Quarterly of Homophile Studies* 5 (Spring 1959): 59–63.

Leighton, Dorothea, and Clyde Kluckholm. *Children of the People*. Cambridge: Harvard University Press, 1947.

Lennox, David. "Homosexuality in Mexico: Repression or Liberation?" Unpublished typescript in the International Gay and Lesbian Archives, Hollywood, California, 1976.

Levy, Robert. "The Community Function of Tahitian Male Transvestism: A Hypothesis." *Anthropological Quarterly* 44 (1971): 12–21.

———. *Tahitians: Mind and Experience in the Society Islands*. Chicago: University of Chicago Press, 1973.

Lewis, Oscar. "The Manly-Hearted Women among the Northern Piegan." *American Anthropologist* 43 (1941): 173–87.

Lewis, Thomas. "Oglala Sioux Concepts of Homosexuality and the Determinants of Sexual Identification." *Journal of the American Medical Association* 225 (16 July 1973): 312–13.

Liberty, Margot. "Hell Came with Horses: The Changing Role of Plains Indian Women Through Time." *Montana: The Magazine of Western History* 32 (1982): 10–19.

Liette, Pierre. "Memoir of Pierre Liette on the Illinois Country." In *The Western Country in the Seventeenth Century*. Edited by Milo Quaife. New York: Citadel, 1962. Reprinted in *GAH*, p. 228.

Linton, Ralph. *The Study of Man*. New York: Appleton-Century, 1936.

Link, Martha Schevill. *The Pollen Path: A Collection of Navajo Myths*. Stanford: Stanford University Press, 1956.

Little, Donald. *An Introduction to Mamluk Historiography*. Montreal: McGill-Queen's University Press, 1970.

Lommel, Andreas. *Shamanism: The Beginnings of Art*. New York: McGraw Hill, 1967.

Lowie, Robert H. "The Assiniboine." *Anthropological Papers of the American Museum of Natural History* 4 (1909): 42.

———. *The Crow Indians*. New York: Farrar and Rinehart, 1935.

———. "Notes on Shoshonean Ethnography." *Anthropological Papers of the American Museum of Natural History* 20 (1924): 183–324.

———. *Primitive Religion*. New York: Liveright, 1924.

Lumholtz, Carl. *New Trails in Mexico*. New York: Charles Scribner's Sons, 1912.

Lurie, Nancy. *Mountain Wolf Woman*. Ann Arbor: University of Michigan Press, 1961.

———. "Winnebago Berdache." *American Anthropologist* 55 (1953): 708–12.

McCoy, Isaac. *History of Baptist Indian Missions*. Washington, D.C.: William Morrison, 1840.

McIntoch, Mary. "The Homosexual Role." *Social Problems* 16 (1968): 182–92.

McKenny, Thomas. *Sketches of a Tour to Lakes, of the Character and Customs of the Chippeway Indians*. Baltimore: Fielding Lucas, 1827. Reprinted in *GAH*, p. 300.

McLeod, Edith. "White Cindy, Mystery Figure." *Siskiyou Pioneer and Yearbook* 11 (Spring 1953): 32–34.

Maddox, John Lee. *The Medicine Man.* New York: MacMillan, 1923.

Mandelbaum, D. B. "The Plains Cree." *Anthropological Papers of the American Museum of Natural History* 37 (1940): 256.

Margolin, Malcolm. *The Ohlone Way.* Berkeley, Calif.: Heyday Books, 1978.

Marmor, Judd, editor. *Homosexual Behavior: A Modern Reappraisal.* New York: Basic Books, 1978.

Marquette, Jacques. "Of the First Voyage Made . . ." *Jesuit Relations.* Edited by Reuben Gold Thwaites. Cleveland: Burrows, 1896–1901. Vol. 59, p. 129. Reprinted in *GAH*, p. 287.

Martin, M. Kay, and Barbara Voorhies. *Female of the Species.* New York: Columbia University Press, 1975.

Maximilian, Alexander. *Travels in the Interior of North America, 1832–1834.* Vol. 22 of *Early Western Travels.* Edited by Reuben Gold Thwaites. 32 volumes. Cleveland: A. H. Clark, 1906. Volumes 22–23.

Mead, Margaret. *The Changing Culture of an Indian Tribe.* New York: Columbia University Press, 1932.

———. "Cultural Determinants of Sexual Behavior." In *Sex and Internal Secretions.* Edited by W. C. Young. Baltimore: Williams and Wilkins, third edition, 1961.

———. *Male and Female: A Study of the Sexes in a Changing World.* New York: William Morrow, 1949.

———. *Sex and Temperament in Three Primitive Societies.* New York: Morrow Quill, 1935, 1963.

Means, Russell. "Penthouse Interview: Russell Means." *Penthouse Magazine,* April 1981, p. 137–39.

Medicine, Beatrice. "'Warrior Women'—Sex Role Alternatives for Plains Indian Women." In *The Hidden Half: Studies of Plains Indian Women.* Edited by Patricia Albers and Beatrice Medicine. Washington, D.C.: University Press of America, 1983. Pp. 267–80.

Medicine Crow, Joe. "From M.M. to M.D.: Medicine Man to Doctor of Medicine." *Occasional Papers of the Museum of the Rockies.* Bozeman: Montana State University, 1979.

Membré, Zenobius. *Discovery and Exploration of the Mississippi Valley. . . .* Translated by John Shea. Albany, N.Y.: McDonough, 1903. Reprinted in *GAH,* p. 611, n. 7.

Meras, Gonzalo Solis de. *Pedro Menendez de Aviles* (1567). Translated by Jeannette Conner. Deland, Fla.: Florida State Historical Society, 1923. Reprinted in *GAH,* pp. 15–16.

Metraux, Alfred. "Boys' Initiation Rites: Religion and Shamanism." In "Handbook of South American Indians." *BAE Bulletin* 143 (1949) pt. 5.

———. "Le Samanisme Araucan." *Revista del Instituto de Antropología* 2 (1942): 309–62.

Milanich, Jerald, and William Sturtevant, editors. *Francisco Pareja's 1613 Confesionario: A Documentary Source for Timucuan Ethnography.* Translated by

Emilio Moran. Tallahassee: Florida Division of Archives, 1972. Reprinted in *GAH,* pp. 286–87.

Miller, Jay. "People, Berdaches, and Left-Handed Bears: Human Variation in Native America." *Journal of Anthropological Research* 38 (1982): 274–87.

Mirsky, Jeannette. "The Dakota." In *Cooperation and Competition among Primitive Peoples.* Edited by Margaret Mead. Boston: Beacon Press, 1961.

Money, John. "Gender: History, Theory and Usage of the Term in Sexology and Its Relationship to Nature/Nurture," *Journal of Sex and Marital Therapy* 11 (1985): 71–79.

—— and Anke Ehrhardt. *Man & Woman, Boy & Girl.* Baltimore: Johns Hopkins Press, 1972.

—— and Margaret Lamacz. "Gynemimesis and Gynemimetophilia: Individual and Cross-Cultural Manifestations of a Gender-Coping Strategy Hitherto Unnamed," *Comprehensive Psychiatry* 25 (1984): 392–403.

——, Mark Schwartz and Viola Lewis. "Adult Erotosexual Status and Fetal Hormonal Masculinization and Demasculinization: 46,XX Congenital Virilizing Adrenal Hyperplasia and 46,XY Androgen-Insensitivity Syndrome Compared." *Psychoneuroendocrinology* 9 (1984): 405–15.

—— and Patricia Tucker. *Sexual Signatures: On Being a Man or a Woman.* Boston: Little, Brown, 1975.

Mortimer, George. *Observations and Remarks Made During a Voyage.* London, 1791.

Munnick, Harriet Duncan, editor. *Catholic Church Records of the Pacific Northwest: Vancouver and Stellamaris Mission.* Translated by Mikell Warner. St. Paul, Ore.: French Prairie Press, 1972.

Munroe, Robert. "Male Transvestism and the Couvade: A Psycho-Cultural Analysis." *Ethos* 8 (1980): 49–59.

——, and Ruth Munroe. "Male Transvestism and Subsistence Economy." *Journal of Social Psychology* 103 (1977): 307–8.

——, John Whiting, and David Hally. "Institutionalized Male Transvestism and Sex Distinctions." *American Anthropologist* 71 (1969): 87–91.

Murphy, Robert. "Social Structure and Sexual Antagonism." *Southwestern Journal of Anthropology* 15 (1959): 189–98.

Murray, Stephen. *Social Theory, Homosexual Realities.* New York: Gay Academic Union, 1984.

Nanda, Serena. "The Hijras of India: A Transvestite/Transsexual Community." *Anthropological Research Group on Homosexuality Newsletter* 4 (Fall 1983): 6–8.

——. "The Hijras of India: Cultural and Individual Dimensions of an Institutionalized Third Gender Role." *Journal of Homosexuality* 11 (1986): 35–54.

Newcomb, W. W. *The Indians of Texas from Prehistoric to Modern Times.* Austin: University of Texas Press, 1961.

Newton, Esther. *Mother Camp: Female Impersonators in America.* Englewood Cliffs, N.J.: Prentice Hall, 1972.

O'Brian, Denise. "Female Husbands in Southern Bantu Societies." In *Sexual*

Stratification. Edited by Alice Schlegel. New York: Columbia University Press, 1977.

O'Bryan, Aileen. "The Dine': Origin Myths of the Navaho Indians." *BAE Bulletin* 163 (1956).

O'Kelly, Charlotte. *Women and Men in Society*. New York: Van Nostrand, 1980.

Olson, Ronald. *The Quinault Indians*. Seattle: University of Washington Press, 1936.

———. "Social Organization of the Haida of British Columbia." *University of California Anthropological Records* 2, pt. 5 (1940): 199–200.

Opler, Marvin. "Anthropological and Cross-Cultural Aspects of Homosexuality." In *Sexual Inversion*. Edited by Judd Marmor. New York: Basic Books, 1965.

Ortner, Sherry, and Harriet Whitehead, editors. *Sexual Meanings*. Cambridge: Cambridge University Press, 1981.

Osgood, Cornelius. *Ingalik Social Culture*. Yale University Publications in Anthropology 53. New Haven: Yale University Press, 1958.

Padgug, Robert. "Sexual Matters: On Conceptualizing Sexuality in History." *Radical History Review* 20 (1979): 10–15.

Palou, Francisco. *Relación historia de la vida y apostólicas tareas del venerable Padre Fray Junípero Serra*. Mexico City: Zuñiga y Ontiveros, 1787. Translated in *GAH*, p. 292.

Pandey, Triloki. "Anthropologists at Zuni." *Proceedings of the American Philosophical Society* 116 (1972): 321–37.

Parkman, Francis. *The Oregon Trail*. Madison: University of Wisconsin Press, 1969.

Parsons, Elsie Clews. "Isleta, New Mexico." *BAE Annual Report* 47 (1932): 245–47.

———. "The Last Zuni Transvestite." *American Anthropologist* 41 (1939): 338–40.

———. *Pueblo Indian Religion*. Chicago: University of Chicago Press, 1939.

———. "The Zuni La' Mana." *American Anthropologist* 18 (1916): 521–28.

Peacock, James. *Rites of Modernization: Symbolic and Social Aspects of Indonesian Proletarian Drama*. Chicago: University of Chicago Press, 1968.

Plummer, Kenneth, editor. *The Making of the Modern Homosexual*. Totowa, N.J.: Barnes & Noble, 1981.

Powers, Stephen. *Tribes of California*. Edited by Robert Heizer. Berkeley: University of California Press, 1976. Reprint of 1877 edition.

Powers, William. "Comment on The North American Berdache." *Current Anthropology* 24 (1983): 461–62.

———. *Oglala Religion*. Lincoln: University of Nebraska Press, 1977.

Praunheim, Rosa von. *Army of Lovers*. London: Gay Men's Press, 1980. See interview of Tri-Base Collective.

Ravenscroft, A. G. R. "Some Habits and Customs of the Chingalee Tribe, Northern Territory, S.A." *Transactions of the Royal Society of South Australia* 15 (1892): 121–22.

Raudot, Antoine Denis. *Indians of the Western Great Lakes.* Ann Arbor: University of Michigan Press, 1965.

Rawson, Philip, editor. *Primitive Erotic Art.* New York: G. P. Putnam's Sons, 1973.

Raymond, J. G. *The Transsexual Empire: The Making of the She-Male.* Boston: Beacon Press, 1979.

Reichard, Gladys. *Navaho Religion.* New York: Bollingen Foundation, 1950.

———. *Social Life of the Navajo Indians.* New York: Columbia University Press, 1928.

Requena, Antonio. "Noticias y Consideraciones Sobre las Anormalidades Sexuales de los Aborígenes Americanos: Sodomía." *Acta Venezolana* 1 (July–September 1945): 16. An English translation of this article, titled "Sodomy among Native American Peoples," appears in *Gay Sunshine* nos. 38–39 (Winter 1979): 37–39.

Romans, Bernard. *A Concise Natural History of East and West Florida.* New Orleans: Pelican Publication Co., 1961. Reprint of 1775 edition.

Roscoe, Will. "Gay American Indians: Creating an Identity from Past Traditions." *The Advocate,* 29 October 1985, pp. 45–49.

———. *Making History: The Challenge of Gay Studies.* San Francisco, 1984.

Ruse, Michael. "Are There Gay Genes? Sociobiology and Homosexuality." *Journal of Homosexuality* 6 (1981): 5–34.

Sanday, Peggy Reeves. *Female Power and Male Dominance: On the Origins of Sexual Inequality.* Cambridge: Cambridge University Press, 1981.

Sapir, Edward, and Leslie Spier. "Notes on the Culture of the Yana." *University of California Anthropological Records* 3, pt. 3 (1943): 275.

Sauer, Martin. *An Account of a Geographical and Astronomical Expedition to the Northern Parts of Russia . . . 1785–1794.* London, 1802.

Schaeffer, Claude. "The Kutenai Female Berdache: Courier, Guide, Prophetess, and Warrior." *Ethnohistory* 12 (1965): 195–216.

Schoolcraft, Henry. *Information Respecting the History, Conditions and Prospects of the Indian Tribes of the United States.* Philadelphia: Lippincott, 1852.

Signorini, Italo. "Transvestism and Institutionalized Homosexuality in North America." *Atti del XL Congresso Internazionale degli Americanisti.* Genova: Tilgher, 1972. Volume 2.

Simms, S. C. "Crow Indian Hermaphrodites." *American Anthropologist* 5 (1903): 580–81.

Skinner, Alanson. *Notes on the Eastern Cree and Northern Saulteaux.* New York: American Museum of Natural History, 1912.

———. "Social Life and Ceremonial Bundles of the Menomini Indians." *Anthropological Papers of the American Museum of Natural History* 13 (1913): 34.

Smedley, Agnes. *Portraits of Chinese Women in Revolution.* Old Westbury, N.Y.: Feminist Press, 1976.

Spier, Leslie. *Klamath Ethnography.* Berkeley: University of California Press, 1930.

———. *Yuman Tribes of the Gila River.* Chicago: University of Chicago Press, 1933.

Starr, J. P. "Boys, Men and Love." Unpublished typescript, 1925. Baker Memorial Library, ONE Institute, Los Angeles.

Steakley, James. *The Homosexual Emancipation Movement in Germany.* New York: Arno Press, 1975.

Stern, Theodore. *The Klamath Tribe: A People and Their Reservation.* Seattle: University of Washington Press, 1965.

———. "Some Sources of Variability in Klamath Mythology." *Journal of American Folklore* 69 (1956): 242ff.

Stevenson, Matilda Coxe. "The Zuni Indians." *BAE Annual Report* 23 (1901–2): 1–634.

Stewart, Omer. "Culture Element Distributions 1: Northern Paiute." *University of California Anthropological Records* 4, pt. 3 (1941): 362–440.

———. "Culture Element Distributions 28: Ute-Southern Paiute." *University of California Anthropological Records* 6, pt. 4 (1944): 298–332.

———. "Homosexuality among the American Indians and Other Native Peoples of the World." *Mattachine Review* 6 (January 1960): 9–15, and (February 1960): 13–19.

Stoddard, Charles Warren. "A South Sea Idyl." *Overland Monthly* 3 (September 1869): 258–64.

Stoller, Robert. *Sex and Gender: On the Development of Masculinity and Femininity.* New York: Science House, 1968.

———. *Sex and Gender, Volume 2: The Transsexual Experiment.* New York: Jason Aronson, 1975.

———. "Two Feminized Male American Indians." *Archives of Sexual Behavior* 5 (1976): 529–38.

Swanton, John. "Social Organization and Social Usages of Indians of the Creek Confederacy." *BAE Annual Report* 42 (1928): 364.

Tanner, John. *A Narrative of the Captivity and Adventures of John Tanner.* Edited by Edwin James. New York: Carvill, 1830. Reprinted in *GAH,* p. 301.

Taylor, Clark. "El Ambiente: Mexican Male Homosexual Social Life." Ph.D. dissertation. University of California, Berkeley, 1978.

———. "Mexican Gaylife in Historical Perspective." *Gay Sunshine* nos. 26–27 (Winter 1975–76): 1–3.

Tedlock, Dennis. *Finding the Center.* New York: Dial Press, 1972.

Thayer, James S. "The Berdache of the Northern Plains: A Socioreligious Perspective." *Journal of Anthropological Research* 36 (1980): 287–93.

Thwaites, Reuben Gold, editor. *The Jesuit Relations.* Cleveland: Burrows, 1896–1901.

———, editor. *Original Journals of the Lewis and Clark Expeditions.* New York: Dodd & Mead, 1904–5.

Titiev, Mischa. *Old Oraibi: A Study of the Hopi Indians of Third Mesa.* New York: Kraus, 1971. Reprint of 1944 edition.

Tixier, Victor. *Tixier's Travels on the Osage Prairies.* Edited by John McDermott. Norman: University of Oklahoma Press, 1940.

Tonti, Henri de. "An Account of Monsieur de La Salle's Last Expedition . . ."

Collections of the New York Historical Society. Series 1, vol. 2 (1814): 237–38. Reprinted in *GAH*, p. 611, n. 7.

Trumbach, Randolph. "London's Sodomites." *Journal of Social History* 11 (Fall 1977): 3–5.

Underhill, Ruth, editor. *The Autobiography of a Papago Woman.* Menasha, Wisc.: American Anthropological Association, 1936.

————. *Red Man's Religion.* Chicago: University of Chicago Press, 1965.

————. *Social Organization of the Papago Indians.* New York: Columbia University Press, 1938.

Valory, Dale. "Yurok Doctors and Devils: A Study in Identity, Anxiety and Deviance." Ph.D. dissertation. University of California, Berkeley, 1970.

Van Baal, J. *Dema.* The Hague: Martinus Nijhoff, 1966.

Voegelin, Erminie. *Culture Element Distribution 20: Northeast California.* Berkeley: University of California Press, 1942.

————. "Tubatulabal Ethnography." *University of California Anthropological Records* 2, pt. 1 (1938): 47.

Vogel, Virgil. *American Indian Medicine.* Norman: University of Oklahoma Press, 1970

Voget, Fred. "American Indians." In *The Encyclopedia of Sexual Behavior.* Edited by Albert Ellis and Albert Abarbanel. New York: Hawthorn Books, 1961. Vol. 1, pp. 90–109.

Walker, Mitch, *Visionary Love.* San Francisco: Treeroots Press, 1980.

Waltrip, Bob. "Elmer Gage: American Indian." *One Magazine* no. 13 (March 1965): 6–10. Reprinted in *GAH*, p. 332.

Weeks, Jeffrey. *Coming Out: Homosexual Politics in Britain, from the Nineteenth Century to the Present.* London: Quartet Books, 1977.

————. *Sex, Politics and Society.* London: Longman, 1981.

Weinrich, James D. "Human Reproductive Strategy." Ph.D. dissertation. Harvard University, 1976.

Weltfish, Gene. *The Lost Universe.* New York: Basic Books, 1965.

Werner, Dennis. "A Cross-Cultural Perspective on Theory and Research on Male Homosexuality." *Journal of Homosexuality* 4 (1979): 345–62.

Westermarck, Edward. *Memories of My Life.* New York: Macaulay Co., 1929.

————. *The Origin and Development of Moral Ideas.* London: Macmillan, 1908, 1926.

Westermeier, Clifford. "Cowboy Sexuality: A Historical No-No?" *Red River Valley Historical Review* 2 (1974): 92–113.

White, Edmund. *States of Desire: Travels in Gay America.* New York: E. P. Dutton, 1980.

White, Leslie. "Luiseno Social Organization." *University of California Publications in American Archeology and Ethnology* 8 (1963): 146–87.

————. "New material from Acoma." *BAE Bulletin* 136 (1943): 301–59.

Whitehead, Harriet. "The Bow and the Burden Strap: A New Look at Institutionalized Homosexuality in Native North America." In *Sexual Meanings.* Edited by Sherry Ortner and Harriet Whitehead. Cambridge: Cambridge University Press, 1981.

Whitam, Frederick. "Childhood Indicators of Male Homosexuality." *Archives of Sexual Behavior* 6 (1977): 89–96.

———. "The Pre-Homosexual Male Child in Three Societies: The United States, Guatemala, Brazil." *Archives of Sexual Behavior* 9 (1980): 87–99.

———. "A Reply to Goode on 'The Homosexual Role.'" *Journal of Sex Research* 17 (1981): 66–72.

Whitam, Frederick, and M. J. Dizon. "Occupational Choice and Sexual Orientation in Crosscultural Perspective." *International Review of Modern Sociology* 9 (1979): 137–49.

Whitman, Walt. *The Correspondence*. Edited by Edwin H. Miller. New York: New York University Press, 1961.

Wikan, Unni. *Behind the Veil in Arabia*. Baltimore: Johns Hopkins University Press, 1982.

———. "Man Becomes Woman: Transsexuals in Oman as a Key to Gender Roles." *Man* 13 (1977): 665–67.

Will, George, and Herbert Spinden. *The Mandans*. Cambridge: Harvard University Press, 1906.

Williams, F. E. *Papuans of the Trans-Fly*. Oxford: Oxford University Press, 1936.

Williams, Walter L. "From Independence to Wardship: The Legal Process of Erosion of American Indian Sovereignty, 1810–1903." *American Indian Culture and Research Journal* 7 (1984): 5–32.

———. "Sex and Shamanism: The Making of a Hawaiian Mahu." *The Advocate*, 2 April 1985, pp. 48–49.

———. "United States Indian Policy and the Debate over Philippine Annexation: Implications for the Origins of American Imperialism." *Journal of American History* 66 (1980): 810–31.

———, editor. *Indian Leadership*. Manhattan, Kans.: Sunflower University Press, 1984.

———, editor. *Southeastern Indians Since the Removal Era*. Athens: University of Georgia Press, 1979.

Wilson, James. *A Missionary Voyage to the Southern Pacific Ocean, 1796–8*. London: Smith, 1799.

Wissler, Clark. "Societies and Ceremonial Associations in the Oglala Division of the Teton Dakota." *Anthropological Papers of the American Museum of Natural History* 11, pt. 1 (1916).

Zwilling, Leonard. "Homosexuality as Seen in Indian Buddhist Texts." Paper presented at the Gay Academic Union Conference, Northwestern University, Evanston, 10 October 1983.

Index

NOTE: The name for berdache in a particular native language, when known, appears in italics in parentheses following the tribe's name. An Indian person's tribe is inserted in parentheses following her or his name.

Go-Between (negotiator), 70–71,
84, 227–28
Government. *See* Canadian govern-
ment; United States government
Grant, Peter, 31, 167–68
Grant, Richard, 52, 90, 187n.37
Greece, 9, 267
Greenberg, David, 40, 95
Grinnell, George B., 69, 177
Gros Ventres, 81, 244, 246
Guajiro, 58

Hairstyle, 74, 75, 100, 221
Haliwa-Saponi, 97
Hammond, William, 166–67, 185–
86
Hare Indians, 102–5
Hawaiians, 173–74, 222–23, 257. *See
also* Polynesia
Hay, Harry, 6, 199n.74, 202–5, 209,
283n.38
Healing. *See* Medical curing; Sha-
mans
Hebrews, 315n.35
Heredity; berdachism and, 45, 257
Hermaphrodite, 10, 21–22, 63, 77,
166–67, 202, 259, 290n.45
Heterosexual behavior of berdaches,
120–23, 208. *See also* Bisexual
flexibility; Homosexual behavior;
Sexuality
Hidatsa (*miati*), 29–30, 32, 38, 41,
79, 114, 119, 164, 178
Hijra. See India
Hill, Williard W., 61, 63–64, 75, 81,
102, 124, 183–84
Hirschfeld, Magnus, 201–2
Historians, critique of, 8
Hoboes, 155–56
Holder, Dr. A. B., 81, 178–79
Homesteaders, 161. *See also* Frontier
Homoerotic art, 135–36
Homophobia: among contemporary
Indians, 14, 40, 187–92, 228,
304n.29; among Europeans, 131–
34, 204, 270, 315n.35; among
Latin American *mestizos,* 147–51;
among scholars, 8, 12, 124, 184,
186, 304n.31; among white
North Americans, 162–63, 166,

178–84, 189, 315n.35; avoided by
Indians, 106–7, 225; reasons for,
133, 315n.35; as a reason for homosexuals to go to the frontier,
166–69. *See also* Christianity; English; French; Russians; Spanish
Homosexual behavior: boys raised
for 45–47; as casual and humorous, 40, 89–93, 113; in Europe,
9–10, 132; on the frontier, 152–
75; in men's traveling work
group, 69, 102–6; spirituality
and, 31, 37, 88, 90. *See also* Berdache; Christianity; Marriage;
Sodomy
Homosexual partnerships: between a
berdache and a man, 93–120,
121–26, 144–45, 256; between a
berdache and a white man, 169–
72; between a berdache and a
boy, 100; between two berdaches,
93–94, 97; between boys, 90–91,
99, 143–44; between two men,
91–93, 154, 156; reversal of sex
roles between a man and a berdache, 96–97, 144–45; between
women (*See* Amazon; Woman-
Woman marriage, Women, sexuality of); between a man and a
boy (*See* Intergenerational relationships)
Homosexual techniques: anal intercourse, 93, 97–99, 115, 159, 253,
262; documentation of, 162; masturbation, 89, 159; oral-genital,
93, 96, 115, 159, 191, 256, 259,
262
Hopi, 52, 58, 90, 101, 177–78, 186–
87, 188, 221
Hudson's Bay Company, 68–69, 83
Huichol, 141
Human Relations Area Files, 12
Humiliation; berdache power to in-
flict, 108
Humor, sex as. *See* Joking
Hunting: berdaches' avoidance of,
57, 60; berdaches' participation
in, 69
Hupa, 42, 50, 51, 53, 97, 219, 222–
23

Walter L. Williams is professor of ethnohistory in the Program for the Study of Women and Men in Society at the University of Southern California. The recipient of research fellowships from the American Council of Learned Societies and the Woodrow Wilson Foundation, Williams has written numerous essays on interethnic relations and is the author of three books: *Southeastern Indians Since the Removal Era*, *Black Americans and the Evangelization of Africa*, and *Indian Leadership*.